Japan's Long Stagnation, Deflation, and Abenomics

Kenji Aramaki

Japan's Long Stagnation, Deflation, and Abenomics

Mechanisms and Lessons

palgrave
macmillan

Kenji Aramaki
Tokyo Woman's Christian University
Tokyo, Japan

University of Tokyo
Tokyo, Japan

ISBN 978-981-13-2175-7 ISBN 978-981-13-2176-4 (eBook)
https://doi.org/10.1007/978-981-13-2176-4

Library of Congress Control Number: 2018953058

Cover Image: © 2nix / Getty Images
Cover Design by Tjaša Krivec

This Palgrave Macmillan imprint is published by the registered company Springer Nature Singapore Pte Ltd.
The registered company address is: 152 Beach Road, #21-01/04 Gateway East, Singapore 189721, Singapore

Preface

The objective of this book, which covers the Japanese economy since the 1980s, is to identify the mechanism of formation and collapse of a huge bubble and the subsequent long economic stagnation and deflation and to discover challenges that the current Japanese economy faces.

I worked mainly in the field of international finance in the Ministry of Finance of Japan for about 30 years and then moved to Tokyo University, where I taught international economics for more than 10 years. The reason why I have written a book on the Japanese economy, which is not strictly my specialty, is that I have had a strong desire to find out an answer to my long-held questions, that is, "Why did the Japanese economy fall to its current situation?" and "Was it inevitable?"

It was 1976, when I started to work, more than 40 years ago. The Japanese economy at that time was dynamic and filled with increasingly strengthened confidence. At the height of the euphoria of the bubble of the late 1980s, I was working as economist at the International Monetary Fund. Personally, I did not like what was going on with the Japanese economy at that time, but my confidence in the strength of the Japanese economy did not change. Even after the collapse of the bubble in the 1990s, I felt that the Japanese economy would be able to return at any moment to the previous conditions, which had been filled with vitality. However, the reality did not turn out that way. The Japanese economy experienced a serious financial crisis in the late 1990s, and deflation set in. Even after entering the 2000s, low growth continued, and the Japanese economy lagged behind the growth of the global economy for decades. Japan held a share that was higher than 9% in the world exports of goods and services in the first half of the 1990s, but at present it is less than half that, at about 4%. China's nominal GDP, which was 18% of Japan's nominal GDP in 1996, is 2.3 times larger than that of Japan, as of 2017.[1] No one at that time expected to see the economy as it is in 2017, and I have thought that it is the responsibility of our generation to answer "why?"

However, the work to find out an answers presented many difficulties, as there were limited opportunities to exchange views outside the field of my expertise, which is international finance. I chose, for the first time, to examine the issues of the Japanese economy as a topic in a seminar class that I taught at the Faculty of Arts and Sciences of Tokyo University in the summer term of 2011, and I started to read extensively the relevant articles and materials. In 2014, I was awarded the opportunity to conduct research as a visiting professor at the School of Oriental and African Studies (SOAS) of London University. There, I gave lectures on the Japanese economy as a guest lecturer, while conducting research on international financial crises. Preparatory work for these guest lectures motivated me to further analyze the Japanese economy. Since the summer of 2015, when I left SOAS, I have given presentations on the Japanese economy in London, Berlin, and Zurich at the conferences of the Japan Economy Network (JEN), which is an international network of researchers on the Japanese economy that my colleagues at the SOAS, including Dr. Ulrich Voltz, Prof. Machiko Nissanke, and Dr. Sotoshi Miyamura, and myself organized in 2015 at a conference, together with the economists in attendance. The book gradually came into a concrete shape, and it has taken more than seven years to complete.

The central argument of the book is that, at the center of the anomalies and difficulties of the Japanese economy over an extended period of time including formation and collapse of the bubble, the financial crisis, and deflation, were corporate behaviors that have changed while showing substantial fluctuations. For example, the biggest negative legacy that the bubble left with Japan was excess assets (those assets for which sufficient demand is not expected and, therefore, are necessarily unprofitable) of the corporate sector. The reason why the economy did not show a strong growth for a long time after the collapse of the bubble is that, as sales by companies stopped growing and economic growth decelerated following

[1] IMF *World Economic Outlook*, April 2018. Nominal GDP in terms of home currency of each country is converted to the dollar using market exchange rate.

the burst of the bubble, the excess assets (unprofitable assets) expanded. Companies could not swiftly dispose of such excess assets, and investment was depressed for an extended period of time. Furthermore, despite sales not increasing, wages continued to increase in the early years after the collapse of the bubble, and profits of companies were further depressed by this factor. Companies' responses at that time to the problems brought about by the collapse of the bubble were "passive," and this passivity led to a lengthening of the economic stagnation. When the financial crisis broke out in the late 1990s, under the deteriorating business conditions and with a sharp aggravation of funding environments, which were described as not only "new loan curbing" but also as "outstanding loan withdrawing," company response shifted at a stroke to a "crisis response." Companies forcefully proceeded with wage reduction, replacement of regular workers with non-regular workers, further restraint of investment, and strengthening of their net asset position. Around this period, deflation started with the declining wage level. The Japanese economy slowed further, and fundamental changes occurred with the financial crisis.[2]

Due to such responses by companies, excess assets together with excess debts and excess employment were removed by the mid-2000s, and the economy returned to the normal. However, a defensive attitude of companies that emerged after the financial crisis was maintained, such that restraint on investment and wages continued ("continued defensiveness" emerged). The biggest characteristics of the stagnation of the Japanese economy are, first, that it took as long as 15 years from the collapse of the bubble in the early 1990s to the elimination of the excesses and, second, that a defensive attitude on the part of companies continued (it has not been eliminated even now), even after the problems with the balance sheets of companies, which lay at the heart of the difficulties, had been rectified.

This book argues that behind the defensive attitude of companies is the low-growth expectations held by companies. Low-growth expectations became firmly rooted and settled under the reality of low growth that

[2] Companies changed their behavior significantly after the financial crisis. Many Japanese companies, which once placed a high priority on employment, forcefully pressed ahead with labor cost reduction through wage cuts and replacement of regular workers by non-regular workers, while protecting the employment of existing workers (Wakita [2014] described this as "fortified Japanese companies"). Under such developments, there has emerged serious social costs, such as very low marriage rates of young non-regular workers (see Chap. 7). Defensive behaviors of companies are producing negative externalities.

extended over a long period of time, from the 1990s (the average growth rate in 22 years from 1991 to 2012 was 1.0%). The total amount of (nominal) sales of all the profit-making companies in Japan increased by merely 1.9% from fiscal 1990, when the collapse of the bubble started, to fiscal 2016.[3] Japanese companies have been living in a world where growth does not exist for more than a quarter of a century.

Regarding the low-growth expectations formed under such reality, one view argues that, as the problems with the balance sheets of companies were resolved, the low-growth expectation has become not so much a reflection of economic reality, but rather a result of a habitualized way of thinking (i.e., a mindset), and therefore, it will change if the mindsets of companies are changed. In contrast, there is another view that argues that the low-growth expectations have a rational, most likely structural basis. A representative point of the latter view stresses the expected shrinkage of domestic markets due to population decline.

As I explain in the book, I do not think the latter view (one that contends that long-term and structural factors brought about the defensive attitudes of companies or low-growth performance) applies to the major part of the two-decade stagnation from the collapse of the bubble to the beginning of the 2010s (this is the period which we call "the long stagnation period" in the book). More specifically, I do not think that the view can explain the mechanism of stagnation during the period up to the mid-2000s, when the corporate sector finally eliminated the aftereffects of the collapse of the bubble. In particular, although it is highly possible that expectation of population decline will restrict corporate behaviors in the future, it is only since the second half of 2000s that the population decline has become a reality,[4] and it was not so long ago, probably only after the beginning of the 2010s, when the population decline was widely recognized as an important problem by the general public. In this book, it is argued that the fundamental mechanisms for the major part of the long stagnation was, one, the lengthening of the process of disposition of excess assets and, two, the strengthened defensiveness of companies after the financial crisis. Furthermore, while it is difficult to clearly distinguish the degree of their influence, factors arising from the defensive mindset (the

[3] Ministry of Finance of Japan "Financial Statements Statistics of Corporations by Industry."

[4] Statistics Bureau, Ministry of Internal Affairs and Communications, "Population Estimates."

part of defensiveness that does not seem to have a rational basis) still remain in the mechanism of low-growth expectations by companies and low-growth performances since the mid-2000s to the present.[5] Therefore, attempts to change such mindsets (e.g., governance reform that encourages companies to employ outside directors in their management, promotion of wage increases, and facilitating realization of higher growth than before through alteration of foreign demand to domestic demand by promoting such activities as tourism and inward foreign investment) are thought to be effective. However, the mindset of companies cannot explain the whole process and, particularly for the future, there is no denying that substantive issues still exist.

The comprehensive policy package that has been implemented by the Abe administration, known as Abenomics, aims at both encouraging changes in the mindset and addressing the substantive issues for the future. The package has brought about some positive outcomes. However, corporate behaviors have not significantly changed in a positive direction, and the process is only half accomplished. At the same time, concerns are rising about by-products, including the declining growth contribution of consumption, accumulation of potential risk in the financial system, and continued significant deterioration of the fiscal position. This describes the present condition of the Japanese economy.[6]

In writing this book, many people have extended their help to me. I would like to thank the undergraduate students who passionately participated in my seminar class in the summer of 2011, in which I first started to examine the Japanese economy intensively, and the undergraduates, graduates, and alumni of my seminar who participated in "the workshop on the Japanese economy," which I held in the Faculty of Arts and Sciences of Tokyo University. I am also very grateful to Dr. Takashi Omori (ex-director of the division in charge of writing the "Economic White Paper" in the Economic Planning Agency of Japan) who read the manuscript and gave very many fundamental as well as technical comments; Dr. Teru

[5] See Supplement to Chap. 6, in which the mechanism of stagnation is shown, with a focus on company behaviors, by flowcharts, respectively, for three periods: "Period of passive response" immediately after the collapse of the bubble; "Period of crisis response" after the financial crisis in the latter half of the 1990s; and "Period of continued defensiveness" from the mid-2000s.

[6] While the objective of the book is to identify the mechanism of anomalies and difficulties of the Japanese economy over the past 30 years from the bubble formation to present, it briefly touches on measures to deal with current challenges in the Chap. 7.

Nishikawa (Associate Professor, Yokohama National University) who offered many beneficial comments; Mr. Masaru Homma (The European Bank for Reconstruction and Development (EBRD)), Dr. Kunio Mikuriya (The World Customs Organization (WCO)); and Mr. Takao Tashiro (Japan Weather News) who gave useful comments on part of the book, Mr. Mahito Sugaya (Certified Accountant) who gave very insightful comments based on real-world experience; and Dr. Hiroshi Shibuya (Emeritus Professor, Tokyo University) who commented on the basic theme of the book. I am also very thankful to Professors Martin Fransman and Matthias Zachmann of The University of Edinburgh, who first encouraged me to write a book, after I gave a seminar in Edinburgh in 2015, on the issue of long stagnation.

I would like to extend my thanks to my colleagues and the administrative staff of the Department of Advanced Social and International Studies, School of Arts and Sciences, University of Tokyo, to which I belonged until March 2017. They kindly allowed and supported my sabbatical leave. As stated before, guest lectures that I gave during the sabbatical leave were a drive for the analysis in this book. I would like to express my gratitude to Dr. Machiko Nissanke, Professor Emeritus of SOAS, who accepted me as a visiting professor at SOAS; to SOAS Senior Lecturer Dr. Ulrich Voltz, who supported my research on the Japanese economy through formation and management of JEN that I noted before, and to SOAS Senior Lecturer Dr. Satoshi Miyamura, who gave advice on the lectures on the Japanese economy at SOAS. In particular, I am very grateful to Professor Emeritus Machiko Nissanke, who provided me with a comfortable research environment at SOAS and took time to usher a manuscript of the earlier version of the book, first drafted based on lecture notes, into publication. I am also thankful to the Tokyo Woman's Christian University for the current working environment, which they have provided for my research.

I am also very grateful to Ms. Patricia K. Mason, who thoroughly reviewed the manuscript and offered very insightful and superb editorial comments that greatly improved the manuscript. While I have worked for the Ministry of Finance of Japan for about 30 years, I did not become directly engaged in the issues that were most relevant to the themes of this book. I would like to make it clear that the entire contents of the book are based on public information and incorporate my personal thoughts. They do not represent views of any institution that I belonged to in the past. Data and their interpretations are mine, and if there are any misunderstandings or insufficiency, they are solely my responsibility.

Last but not least, I would like to thank Professor Frank Rövekamp of the Ludwigschafen University of Applied Sciences for his detailed and positive review of the book's outline, and to Palgrave Macmillan for publishing the book.

I will be very happy if this book could make some contribution to reconstruction of the Japanese society and economy and also could offer any useful lessons to other countries.

Tokyo, Japan Kenji Aramaki

Contents

List of Figures

List of Tables

CHAPTER 1

Introduction: Objectives and Main Arguments of the Book

1 Objectives and Main Arguments of the Book

This book examines the experience of the Japanese economy over last 30 years, from the 1980s, a time filled with a series of difficulties not observed in advanced countries in recent years, including the formation and collapse of a huge bubble, a two-decade-long economic stagnation, and chronic deflation, with an aim of identifying the mechanisms and drawing lessons for future economic policy management.

The Japanese economy grew to be the second largest economy next to the United States through the period of rapid growth from the 1950s to the early 1970s, and its per capita income rose to among the highest levels in the world. Even after the end of the era of rapid growth, the Japanese economy overcame shocks arising from the collapse of the Bretton Woods fixed exchange rate system and the shift to the floating exchange rate, as well as two oil crises in the 1970s, and continued to be an object of envy with its very low unemployment rate and solid economic growth. Its financial presence grew larger still under continued high economic performance, and it even began to be regarded as an economic threat to other countries in the 1980s. However, the Japanese economy formed a huge bubble in the latter half of the 1980s, and after the bubble's collapse at the beginning of the 1990s, it suffered from a long period of economic stagnation and deflation. Japan's nominal GDP, after hitting a peak of 534.1 trillion yen in 1997, stopped growing altogether and was 545.1 trillion

K. Aramaki, *Japan's Long Stagnation, Deflation, and Abenomics*,
https://doi.org/10.1007/978-981-13-2176-4_1

yen in 2017, only greater by mere 11.0 trillion yen (2.1%) 20 years later, after its peak in 1997.[1]

Why did such a long stagnation, which nobody could have imagined, occur? Although there have been extensive arguments, there is no definite consensus on the mechanism of the stagnation, and therefore, views still diverge on the lessons to be drawn. As briefly described later in this chapter, while the US economy recovered relatively speedily from the Global Financial Crisis (GFC) that struck in 2008, the European economies continued to show weaknesses in their recovery, and worries about a fall into deflation were not entirely dismissed until rather recently. Furthermore, the Chinese economy, which had been growing rapidly for several decades, started to decelerate and while the situation has stabilized, concerns over the future course of its economy have not been eliminated entirely. Did these economies face the risk of falling into long stagnation and deflation (or low inflation) that the Japanese economy experienced? If there was such a risk, at least at certain point in time after the crisis, what was the mechanism of such a risk? Assuming that these economies have successfully emerged from such a risk, what worked? If the economies did not successfully avoid the risk, what are the remaining problems? In order to answer such questions, it helps to have an understanding of the mechanism of long stagnation and deflation experienced by the Japanese economy.

While attempting to explore the mechanism of the bubble, stagnation, and deflation in Japan from the 1980s throughout this book, we seek answers to the following concrete key questions:

- Why was the bubble formed? What could have been done to prevent it?
- How did the bubble collapse? What impacts did the collapse of the bubble have on the economy?
- Why did the financial crisis break out in the late 1990s, as much as seven years after the collapse of the bubble? Why were the non-performing loan (NPL) problems that underlay the crisis not resolved sooner?

[1] In real terms, the average real growth rate since the collapse of the bubble until today has been 1.2%, which is about half of the average growth rate of the advanced countries (2.2%) (or, just one-third of the average growth rate of the world economy [3.6%]) over the period. If the Japanese economy had grown at the average rate of growth of advanced countries (2.2%), then the real GDP would have been 1.3 times as big as the actual size (if it had grown at the world average rate, it would have been 2 times as large). (Calculated using the IMF "World Economic Outlook April 2108 database").

- What impacts did the financial crisis have on the economy?
- Why did the vulnerability of the Japanese economy remain, even after the negative legacy of the formation and collapse of the bubble[2] and the shock of the financial crisis had been overcome by the mid-2000s? What are the fundamental problems the Japanese economy currently has?
- Will Abenomics be able to solve the fundamental problems of the Japanese economy?

The ultimate objective is to understand the mechanism of long stagnation and deflation and draw lessons for the future in Japan and for other economies through exploration of the answers to these questions.

The major characteristics of this book include the following:

- First, to capture the real cause of the anomalies and difficulties of the Japanese economy, we have taken an approach, based mainly on a thorough examination of data and facts. Since the early 2010s when we started examining the long stagnation of the Japanese economy, we did not espouse any theory or views in advance, but aimed to first study and analyze extensive arguments, data, and facts. This book draws on such work and tries to present a view that can most coherently explain what the data and facts indicate. This book has tried to comprehensively describe and understand the three-decade-long period of anomalies and difficulties of the Japanese economy, thereby offering a new perspective on the problem and contributing to the economic literature.
- Second, we present a view that it is appropriate to analyze the Japanese economy over 30 years by dividing the whole period into subperiods. The basic divisions are three: the bubble period from the mid-1980s to the beginning of the 1990s; the long stagnation period of more than 20 years from the beginning of the 1990s to the early 2010s; and the period of Abenomics from 2013. However, what is unique to this study is that the analysis of the long stagnation period is conducted by further dividing this period of more than 20 years into four subperiods. This view arose from the observation that the changes in the Japanese economy emerged suddenly after the collapse of the bubble, and the changes developed into a long-term phenomenon. In other words, the mechanism of stagnation is thought to have changed from one of an

[2] The negative legacy, as is explained in the book, refers mainly to the hangover of excessive assets and debt in the corporate sector.

abrupt nature to the one with a perpetual or structural nature through the long process of stagnation. The mechanism of stagnation must have changed over time. As is explained in this book, the turning point occurred with the financial crisis in the late 1990s. Specifically, the periods of study are divided as: Period I, from the period when the bubble burst at the beginning of the 1990s to just before the financial crisis in the latter half of 1990s; Period II, from the financial crisis to the early 2000s when the longest economic expansion since the Second World War started; Period III, from the first half of the 2000s to just before the GFC erupted in 2008; and Period IV, from the GFC to just before the start of the Abenomics.

- Third, we place a significant focus on the analysis of company behaviors. This focus also emerged from the data-centered approach. The Japanese economy underwent very substantial changes with the collapse of the bubble and also with the financial crisis. These changes include, for example, substantial restraint of private investment after the collapse of the bubble and the decline of nominal wages and consumer prices after the financial crisis. Most of these changes are related to corporate behaviors, and therefore, the analysis of these behaviors has become a very important element of this book. We examine how corporate behaviors evolved over these respective subperiods, including in the bubble period, after the collapse of the bubble, and after the financial crisis, based not only on macroeconomic data but also on the combined balance sheet data of all the profit-making companies in Japan.

The analyses of company behaviors are mainly conducted in Chap. 6, and these analyses suggest that corporate behaviors greatly changed in the process of long stagnation. Corporate behaviors during Period I after the burst of the bubble and before the financial crisis may be described as a "passive response," in which expansion of excessive asset holding and assumption of excessive debt, as well as a surge in labor costs developed. In the period from the financial crisis to the first half of the 2000s (a period broadly corresponding to Period II), companies tried to rapidly remove excessive assets and debt and cut labor costs in response to the financial crisis. Corporate behavior in this period is thus described as "crisis response." The elimination of excessive assets, debt, and employment was completed by the mid-2000s, that is, 15 years after the collapse of the bubble. However, restraints on private investment and on wages by companies, which became conspicuous in the period of crisis response, remained unchanged, continuing into Period III (the long recovery) and Period IV (GFC and afterward), and even into the period of Abenomics. Such corporate behaviors since the mid-2000s may be described as "sustained defensiveness." Why such defensive attitudes by companies continue is examined in detail in Chap. 6.

There are many inferences that can be drawn from the examination of the Japanese economy in this book. The most important is the danger involved in excessive asset holdings by economic agents. "Excessive" means a situation in which the asset concerned does not have sufficient demand (or revenue) for the goods and services that it produces. Hangovers of such excessive assets (low-profitability assets) bring about continuous pressures for the curtailment of asset holdings and restraint on investment. Low-profitability assets also compress profits and produce a pressure to cut costs such as wages and procurements. These pressures tend to reduce domestic demand through restraint on investment and consumption (through wage restraint), and may lead to a prolonged stagnation, possibly placing downward pressures on prices. Furthermore, when such asset holdings are financed by debt, costs and risk arising from excessive assets and debt may be shifted to the financial sector, raising the risk of a financial crisis. If a crisis does break out, it will likely leave an extensive scar on the economy. Furthermore, when an extended period of time is taken to eliminate excesses and overcome a financial crisis, behavior of economic agents can be substantially altered and the economy as a whole may shift to a different equilibrium situation (e.g., from a high- to a low-growth equilibrium).

Figure 1.1 shows development not in assets but in debt, in terms of the total amount of credit (i.e., debt if viewed from the private nonfinancial sector side) to private nonfinancial sector (corporate and household sectors combined) (in GDP ratio) for Japan, the United States, the Euro area, and China. The ratio for Japan rose from a level of 160% in the mid-1980s to above 200% at the end 1980s and reached a peak of 219.5% at the end of 1993. Thereafter, the ratio stayed above 200% until 2000, when the ratio fell below 200%, and it was in the mid-2000s when the ratio returned to the pre-bubble level of around 160%. During this period, the Japanese economy experienced a continued weakness in its economic recovery and the financial crisis due to NPL problems. In the United States, the ratio started to rise from a level over 120% in the latter half of 1990s to nearly 170% in mid-2008 just before the collapse of

Fig. 1.1 Total credit to private nonfinancial sector (in percent of nominal GDP). Source: Bank for International Settlements (BIS)

Lehman Brothers. The US ratio declined after that and became stabilized at a level near 150% since about 2012. The ratio for the Euro area rose from a level over 120% in 1999, to over 160% in the latter half of 2008, and has stayed at this level, showing no sign of decline. The ratio for China had been around 120% after entering the 2000s before a rapid increase, starting at the end of 2008. It rose over 200% in mid-2015 and has become flat more recently. It was at an extremely high level of 210.2% at the end June 2017.

Figures 1.2 and 1.3 show a breakdown of the ratio into that for corporate and household sectors. A rapid increase in debt in Japan took place in the corporate sector while debts of the household sector did not show a big increase. The problem of excessive debts (and accompanying excessive assets) was a problem of the corporate sector in Japan. A sharp increase in debts emerged in the household sector in the United States. As was indicated by the fact that the subprime loan problem triggered the GFC, the original problem in the United States was not with the corporate sector but with the household sector, and the figure shows that reduction in the debt level of the household sector progressed speedily. The relatively quick recovery of the US economy seems to have been founded on progress made in adjustments of debt level. By contrast, the problem in the Euro area was with the corporate sector, and there has been no progress in the

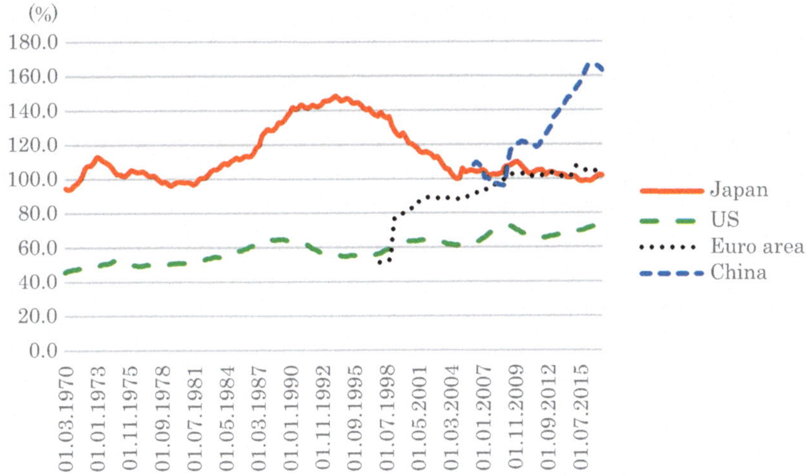

Fig. 1.2 Total credit to nonfinancial corporations (in percent of nominal GDP). Source: BIS

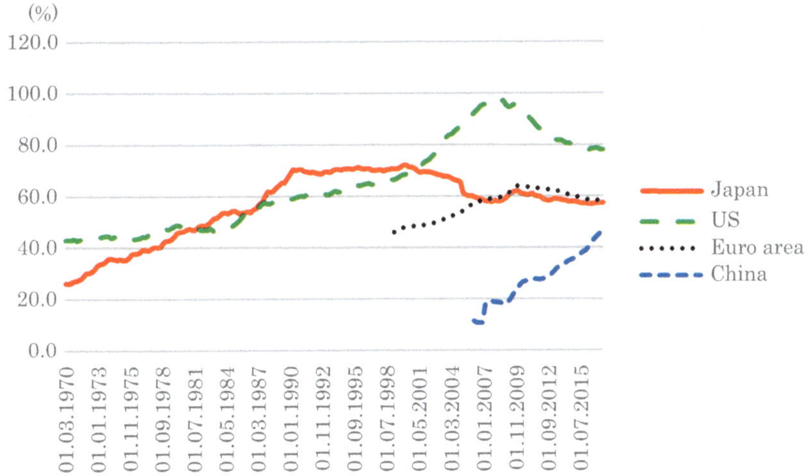

Fig. 1.3 Total credit to households (in percent of nominal GDP). Source: BIS

adjustments of debt level, which seems to be the reason behind the weak recovery in that region. In China, while the debt level of the household sector is increasing, the corporate sector seems to have a more serious problem. The rapid increase in debt level was triggered by the economic stimulus package amounting to 4 trillion RMB announced at the end of 2008. There should have been an expansion of assets behind the increasing debt. If these assets are not accompanied by sufficient demand, then it is possible that the excessive assets could become a burden similar to those excessive assets formed in the bubble era in Japan and could depress economic activities in the future for a long period of time in China. The corporate debt level hit a peak at the end of 2016 after the rapid increase and declined slightly in most recent period. However, it is still at a level of 160%, which is higher than the level in the bubble period in Japan, and is a matter of great concern.

Figure 1.4 shows total credit to the government sector. Together with Fig. 1.1 that shows total credit (in GDP ratio) to the private nonfinancial sector (corporate and household), these figures show that Japan's government debt increased by 121.8%, from 91.7% at the end of 1997 to 213.5% at the end of June 2017, while the private nonfinancial sector's debt

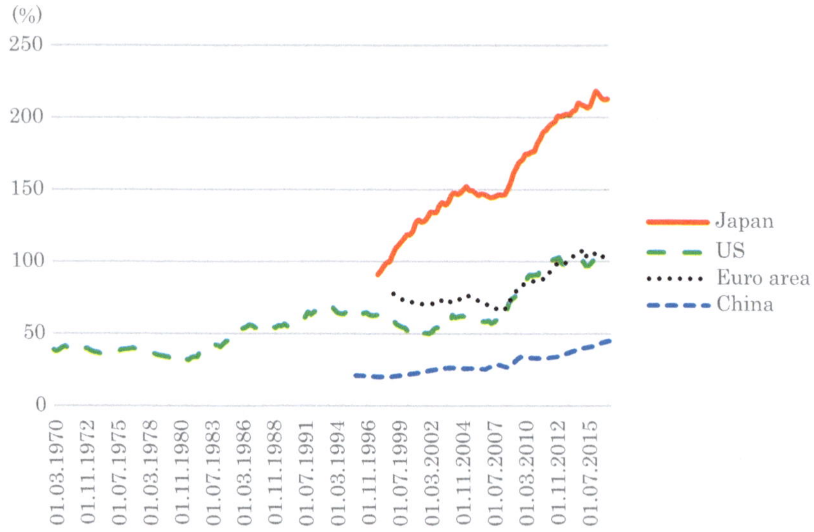

Fig. 1.4 Total credit to general government (in percent of GDP). Source: BIS

declined by just 50.3%, from 209.8% to 159.5% over the same period. Although the rise in government debt level was due mainly to growing social security expenditures arising from the aging of the population, falls in tax revenue due to stagnation, and repeated expenditure of fiscal stimuli, particularly in the 1990s, it may be said that the government bore much of the direct costs (such as the use of public funds to resolve NPL problems) and indirect costs (such as a rise in government expenditure in the form of unemployment allowances and economic stimulus, as well as revenue losses due to stagnation), which arose in the process of removing excessive debt (or excessive assets) from the economy. The US Government's debt increased by 30.0%, from 68.0% at the end of June 2008 (before the Lehman collapse) to 98.0% at the end of June 2017, while the private nonfinancial sector's debt declined by 16.9%, from 168.4% to 151.5% over the same period. The increase in government debt is about twice as big as the decline in the private nonfinancial sector's debt.

By contrast, while the Euro area's government debt increased by 22.2%, from 66.9% at the end of June 2008 to 89.1% at the end of June 2017, the private nonfinancial sector's debt also increased by 4.3% from 157.3% to 161.6% over the same period. Debt levels of both private and government sectors have been rising. As there is no progress in reducing the private sector's debt, we need to determine if it is at a sustainable level or if adjustments are needed. In the case of China, the government debt increased by 17.9%, from 27.8% at the end of June 2008 to 45.7% at the end of June 2017, while the private nonfinancial sector's debt increased by 94.9%, from 115.3% to 210.2% over the same period. We should expect that the government debt level will significantly rise if the private nonfinancial sector's excessive debts (and excessive assets) are to be reduced.[3]

The aforementioned is the most important inference, that is, the danger of holding excessive assets or assumption of excessive debt. Japan is a case

[3] The magnitude of increase in government debt depends on various factors including the pace and the magnitude of adjustments and whether the economy experiences a financial crisis or not. However, considering that even in the United States, where relatively quick adjustments were conducted, the increase in government debt is nearly twice as big as the decline in the private sector's debt, then the possible increase in government debts in China could be rather large, particularly if a financial crisis is experienced. If a reduction by 50% of the private sector's debt, say, to 160% (current level of Japan) (that is, a reduction by 50 percentage points) was conducted, it could be possible for government debt in China to go beyond 100% of GDP, which still seems to be a manageable level.

in which the risk involved was manifest in the worst possible way. It emerged through two channels. First was the extensive and deeply negative impacts on the economy, arising from the collapse of the bubble and the breakout of the financial crisis. As will be explained in the book, a financial crisis broke out in the latter half of the 1990s, that is, seven years after the collapse of the bubble, and the crisis greatly and deeply altered corporate behaviors. The biggest change was a drastic alteration of the employment policies of companies. Companies regarded the provision of employment as their social responsibility until the early 1990s, but they drastically changed their policies in the face of the crisis. Specifically, companies not only reduced the nominal wages but also cut down on regular employment and replaced their regular employees with non-regular employees such as fixed-term or part-time workers. Companies also started to rapidly remove excessive assets and debt, and the absolute size of physical assets started to decline. Under these circumstances, deflation emerged. The Japanese economy, having essentially returned to a normal position, does not seem to have fully rid itself of the aftereffects of the collapse of the bubble and shocks of the financial crisis. Overcoming this legacy continues to be an important challenge for Japan. A crisis can alter even basic behavioral principles of economic agents.

The second channel relates to expectation formation. If time necessary to remove excesses is lengthy after the collapse of a bubble, as well as to overcome impacts of a financial crisis, expectations held by companies and household may change, raising a risk of shifting the whole economy to a different equilibrium. Of particular importance is the effect of the lengthening of stagnation on the growth expectation of companies. A high-growth expectation may raise investment and accordingly, raise growth performance in a self-fulfilling way. By contrast, a low-growth expectation can discourage investment and tends to bring about low-growth performance. Therefore, in order to achieve high growth, it is important to maintain a high-growth expectation. However, if the actual growth performance continues to be low, then the growth expectation will be adjusted downward. As is discussed in this book, in Japan, elimination of excessive assets did not speedily progress after the collapse of the bubble; or rather, the total asset size increased until the mid-1990s, and it took around 15 years after the collapse of the bubble to eliminate excessive assets by the mid-2000s. Therefore, a significant restraint on investment continued for a long period of time, producing prolonged low growth. As a result, the growth expectation was adjusted downward, and the resultant low-growth expectation seems to have become firmly rooted. Once the growth expectation has been lowered, it is not easy to raise it. The difficulty in raising growth expectations is shown in the responses of companies (in their continuation of restraints on wages and investment) to the comprehensive economic policy package called "Abenomics," which includes large-scale monetary policy easing since 2013.

This book is structured as follows: Chap. 2 covers the formation of the bubble. Chapter 3 briefly describes the collapse of the bubble and subsequent economic developments, and proposes to divide some 20 years of stagnation from the collapse of the bubble to just preceding the Abenomics period into four subperiods. This chapter also examines Period I, which is the initial adjustment period after the collapse of the bubble until just before the financial crisis. Chapter 4 covers the financial crisis in the late 1990s and its impacts (Period II), the subsequent long recovery (Period III), and the turbulent era initiated by the GFC (Period IV). Chapter 5 examines the issue of deflation and monetary policy. Chapter 6 analyzes corporate behaviors in order to identify the real mechanism of stagnation and deflation. Chapter 7 covers Abenomics and challenges for the Japanese economy. The main points of each chapter are summarized below.

2 Chapter 2: Formation of a Bubble and Its Background

Chapter 2 analyzes causes of the huge bubble in the 1980s. The Japanese economy experienced a large-scale asset inflation (bubble) in the 1980s. Prices of both land and stocks increased nearly fivefold above the level in the first half of the 1980s, when a sharp price increase started, in some seven years to the peak at the end of the 1980s or the beginning of the 1990s. The real growth rate also rose from an average of over 3% during around ten years from the early 1970s when the high-speed growth ended until and including the first half of the 1980s to an average of higher than 5% in the second half of the 1980s. However, the bubble started to collapse at the beginning of the 1990s, which became a prelude to the subsequent long economic stagnation.

This chapter examines the process of asset inflation, particularly the land price surge, and shows that the price increase in commercial land in the very center of Tokyo in the first half of the 1980s, which was started probably by some real demand factor, changed into a bubble in the process of its spillovers to other areas and also to residential land prices.

Then, the chapter identifies two factors as causes of the bubble formation: one, problems with economic policy management in this period; and two, behaviors of financial institutions under financial liberalization. With respect to policy management, we note that the economic policies in this period were operating under two constraints, which altered policies and promoted the formation of the bubble. The first and biggest constraint on the economic policy management at that time was a fierce trade dispute with the United States. The market-oriented economic policies, including large-scale tax cuts adopted by the Reagan administration in the United States starting at the beginning of the 1980s ("Reaganomics") led to "twin deficits," that is, huge fiscal deficits and trade deficits in the United States. In contrast, against such factors as the surging dollar, Japan's current account surplus expanded, leading to fierce trade disputes with the United States. Solving the disputes became a serious challenge for Japan, which is dependent on the United States for its national security.

The second constraint on the policy management was a deterioration of the fiscal position, which proceeded rapidly due to economic stagnation after the two oil crises and the strengthening of social security since the first half of the 1970s. The administration at that time, which had abandoned the introduction of a consumption tax (the general consumption tax proposed under the Ohira administration), maintained a policy of fiscal consolidation without tax increase, that is, a policy of containing fiscal expansion during the major part of the 1980s. So, the principal policy agenda in the 1980s was focused on how to address the external friction without imposing a policy burden on the fiscal side.

Under these two constraints, the Nakasone administration, which started in the first half of the 1980s, pushed forward with deregulation, particularly urban redevelopment through deregulation on land use, as an important tool to expand domestic demand, but this policy provided a first drive for a rapid land price increase. As the external imbalances continued and protectionist movements mounted in the United States, Japan's administration took the position of accepting coordinated depreciation of the US dollar (or, yen appreciation), and moved forward with the United States to the adoption of the Plaza Accord by G-5 in 1985. However, once the appreciation of the yen gained a momentum in the market, it went far beyond the expectations of the related countries, doubling its value in about two years' time. Halting a further yen appreciation became an important policy agenda for the administration. Despite such yen appreciation, the external imbalances did not diminish soon and therefore, the United States did not soften its demand of Japan for domestic demand expansion. Under the circumstances, monetary easing was maintained for a prolonged period of time in order to solve the external disputes and also to prevent further appreciation of the yen. When the monetary policy stance switched to the tightening stance at the end of the 1980s, more than nine years had passed since any previous tightening. Furthermore, since about the mid-1980s, the administration started to emphasize the importance of transforming the Japanese economy into one that would not produce internationally incompatible external imbalances, by structurally reforming the economy (Maekawa Report 1986). In this way, the focus of the economic policies shifted from domestic economic objectives to external objectives to correct external imbalances. Deregulation, continued monetary policy easing, and the policy stance to give precedence to external objectives over domestic objectives all seem to have substantially contributed to the formation and expansion of the internal bubble, through implementation of such measures as enactment of laws promoting real estate-related development projects including resort facilities across Japan. These problems with economic policy management are the main factors that contributed to the formation of a bubble.

In addition to the problems with policy management, there was a second factor that worked toward the formation of the bubble—bank behaviors under financial liberalization. Financial liberalization started in the latter half of the 1970s. Due to such factors as reduced demand for funds after the end of the high-growth era and increased availability of diversified funding channels under the financial liberalization, large companies, which were once the important clients of financial institutions, reduced their dependence on borrowing from financial institutions. Against the background of such erosion of the traditional client base and declining profit margin under the financial liberalization, financial institutions expanded activities in new markets, particularly in real estate-related loans, substantially contributing to the formation of the bubble. It should be noted that financial liberalization was not accompanied by sufficient strengthening of regulation and supervision of risk management by financial institutions. In addition to these factors, active financial activities by companies, called "Zaiteku" (financing technology) and "Tochi Shinwa" (mythical trust in landholding) are also seen as causes of the bubble.

Due to the formation of the bubble, the private nonfinancial corporate sector, particularly the non-manufacturing sector, came to hold huge assets (typically, physical assets such as buildings and facilities) that were far greater than the size implied by the trend before the bubble period, and this imposed a very heavy burden on the Japanese economy in subsequent years.

3 Chapter 3: Collapse of the Bubble and the Start of the Long Stagnation

Chapter 3 first provides an overview of the collapse of the bubble and subsequent economic stagnation over two decades, then divides the whole stagnation period into four subperiods, and examines Period I, that is, the period of initial adjustment after the burst of the bubble and before the breakout of the financial crisis.

The bubble started to collapse at the beginning of the 1990s under the sharp tightening of monetary policy from the end of the 1980s and the introduction of the quantitative restrictions on real estate-related loans by banks. Behind these policies were concerns over widening social inequality between holders and non-holders of assets during the land price surge, and at that time little attention was paid for controlling the risk to the economy and financial system that would arise from the sharp asset price inflation and its collapse. Such policy orientation, in hindsight, resulted in inappropriate policymaking of crashing the bubble by aggressively countervailing policies.

Next, the chapter presents an overview of the economy in around 20 years after the collapse of the bubble, reiterating that the period is identified as a long stagnation period, with the average growth rate over the 20 years or so declining to a level less than one-fifth of the level during the bubble era and with a sharply rising unemployment rate. In terms of growth rate of per capita GDP, Japan's performance was also stagnant as compared with other advanced countries. Notably, there are three groups of arguments on the cause of the stagnation; the supply-side factor views, the demand-side factor views, and the financial sector-problem views. The supply-side factor views contend that such supply-side factors as the delay in enhancing production efficiency or demographic changes are behind the long stagnation. However, we note that the Japanese economy, particularly the nominal GDP, suddenly stopped growing at the beginning of the 1990s and that such a sudden change cannot be explained by structural factors, which usually change only gradually and, therefore, affect the economy in a gradual manner. Further, the Japanese economy generally had a deflationary gap, that is, supply capacity was in excess of demand during the long stagnation, and therefore, it is difficult to explain stagnation by limitations on supply capacity. Under the demand-side factor views, the handling of fiscal policy was criticized in that fiscal tightening in the late 1990s hindered economic recovery. Also, insufficient monetary policy easing was criticized for bringing about the long stagnation and deflation. As for fiscal policy, it is important to point out that fiscal policy substantially contributed to economic growth after the collapse of the bubble through a series of stimulus packages that were compiled almost yearly. Thus, it is argued, although there might have been a problem of timing in the adoption of fiscal tightening, the fundamental cause of the long stagnation from the beginning of the 1990s should be found in other factors. While monetary policy management is examined in detail in Chap. 5 (Deflation and monetary policy), it is suggested that the problem with the handling of monetary policy may have been more serious in crushing the bubble, through aggressive monetary tightening and quantitative restriction on real estate-related loans, rather than in the period after the collapse of the bubble. This point is exemplified by the fact that the rate of growth of money stock, which was over 10% per annum during the preceding years, collapsed into negative territory at the beginning of the 1990s. The financial sector-problem views contend, for example, that credit crunch, which reflected problems with financial sector soundness due to the NPLs, led to the stagnation. However, the lending attitudes of financial institutions were generally eased in the 1990s, excepting periods immediately after the collapse of the bubble and during the financial crisis in the latter half of 1990s. Therefore, credit tightening by financial institutions could not have been the cause of the stagnation, at least not during the early period of the stagnation after the collapse of the bubble and before the financial crisis (this initial period is considered to be the most critically important in the long stagnation).

After the overview, the chapter argues, as evidenced by the sudden halt of nominal GDP growth, the long stagnation was started by a discontinuous and abrupt factor (non-structural factor). At the same time, considering that the stagnation continued for more than 20 years, it seems that the changes that were started by an abrupt factor were structuralized in the process of stagnation, suggesting that the mechanism of the long stagnation seems to have changed in the process. Drawing on this argument and with a view to identifying the nature and change of the mechanism of stagnation (disease) from the examination of characteristics of the economy (symptoms), it is proposed that we adopt an approach of dividing these 20 years after the collapse of the bubble and until the start of the Abenomics, that is, from 1991 to 2012 inclusive, into four subperiods with different economic characteristics, so as to analyze the mechanism of stagnation in each subperiod. In light of developments in such factors as economic cycles, growth rate, private investment, and unemployment rate, these four subperiods have been determined to be as follows:

Period I (1991–1997): "Initial adjustment" period, starting from the collapse of the bubble to just before the start of the financial crisis
Period II (1998–2002): "Financial crisis and its impacts" period, covering those years from the breakout of the financial crisis to the beginning of the 2000s
Period III (2003–2007): "Long recovery" period, covering the long recovery started in the early 2000s to just before the GFC.
Period IV (2008–2012): "Global Financial Crisis and after" period that covers the period from the outbreak of the GFC to just before the start of the Abenomics.

Chapter 3 examines Period I (initial adjustment). The growth rate declined in Period I to a level lower than one-third of that in the bubble era, and the biggest drag came from the stagnation of investment. The investment stagnation is considered as to have arisen from stock adjustment, that is, downward adjustment of excessive capital stock brought about by excessive investment in the bubble era. Stock adjustment, in this period, became a prolonged process. The reason for such a lengthened process was due to the absolute size of the excessive assets but also to the fact that sales of companies suddenly stopped growing and even declined after the burst of the bubble. With the sales stagnation and the decline in actual growth rate, expected growth rate held by companies gradually declined, resulting in further lowering the level of required capital stock. So, throughout the initial adjustment period, the size of excessive capital stock did not decrease, instead increasing despite restraint on investment, thus placing more depressing pressures on investment for a prolonged period. In addition, the historic high value of the yen during the US–Japan trade disputes, which were intensified during the first term of the Clinton administration in the United States, hurt exports and placed additional negative impacts on investment. Furthermore, damages made to the balance sheet of companies and financial institutions due to the asset price deflation led to more cautious and contained investment. The declining growth rate lowered expected profitability of land and resulted in declines in land prices (land prices continued to decline for the next 14 years), producing additional damage to balance sheets.

What should be noted is the fact that the size of assets (and also liabilities) of the corporate sector continued to increase, even after the burst of the bubble and until the mid-1990s. This is particularly true with the non-manufacturing sector. This is probably because many of the excessive assets formed during the bubble era were the types of assets that needed substantial lead time before completion, such as real estate-related development projects. Due to such a time lag and because companies did not choose to quickly remove such low-profitability assets, stagnation of profits of companies continued for a long time, damaging their financial position and lowering their ability to repay their debts. This made the problems with the NPLs increasingly more serious and finally led to a crisis of the financial sector. An implication is that fiscal stimulus and monetary easing may have succeeded in buying time by creating additional demand (the government came to have huge debt as a result, though), but these macroeconomic policies did not (could not) contribute to the speedy disposition of the companies' excessive assets (or supply capacity) formed during the bubble era—a capacity that could not expect sustainable demand—and thus, were unable to prevent the crisis.

4 Chapter 4: The Financial Crisis and Its Impacts, Long Recovery, and Afterward

This chapter mainly examines the financial crisis and its impacts on the Japanese economy (i.e., Period II: 1998–2002), but also covers periods subsequent to the crisis until the Abenomics (i.e., Period III: 2003–2007 and Period IV: 2008–2012).

A financial crisis broke out in the autumn of 1997, seven years after the collapse of the bubble. Profits of companies declined significantly after the burst of the bubble, and NPLs increased year by year. With the decline in the value of collateralized real estate, failures of small- and medium-sized financial institutions started to surface in the first half of the 1990s. Traditionally, a troubled financial institution was acquired by a healthy financial institution, and all the business, such as deposits and loans, was assumed by the acquiring institution. However, as it gradually became difficult to find an assuming institution, an assuming bank was established, to which businesses of failed institutions were transferred and the Deposit Insurance Corporation (DIC) provided financial assistance (grants). Then, in the process of resolving housing loan companies that had large amounts of troubled real estate-related loans, tax money was used in order to maintain the financial soundness of creditor financial institutions. This use of tax money evoked very strong resentment among the public, and further use of tax money for the financial sector became almost taboo. However, in November 1997, after the failure of medium-sized securities companies led to a default in the interbank market for the first time since the Second World War, it became difficult for some financial institutions to obtain funding in the interbank market. Soon after, in the same month of November 1997, Hokkaido Takushoku Bank, one of the largest banks in Japan, and then Yamaichi Securities, one of the big four securities companies, failed one after the other. Long lines to withdraw funds formed in front of local banks, and the situation came close to a crisis. Against this background, a law that made possible capital injection into banks was enacted, and public money was used to strengthen the capital base of major banks in March 1998. While the situation was stabilized temporarily, troubles with the Long-Term Credit Bank of Japan (LTCB) surfaced in the summer of 1998, and new laws were enacted so as to introduce a strengthened capital injection scheme, tied with early correction measures based on the capital asset ratio and also to introduce a comprehensive resolution system for failed banks, including nationalization. Under the new laws, injection of capital four times as great as the funds injected in March 1998 was implemented in 15 banks in March 1999, and the LTCB and the Nippon Credit Bank, another LTCB, were nationalized in late 1998. Making use of this comprehensive safety net framework, the government strongly promoted disposition of NPLs. The goal of halving the NPL ratio, set by the government in 2002, was achieved in 2005, and the NPL problems (or, excess asset hangovers in the corporate sector) that had long been a burden on the Japanese economy were finally resolved.

Why were the NPL problems, which stayed with the economy for some 15 years, not resolved sooner? Companies did not promptly dispose of excessive assets that lay behind the NPL problems, and banks did not swiftly dispose of NPLs. Behind these developments, there were optimistic expectations for the future course of the economy in the initial stage: the magnitude of expected negative impacts that could result from prompt resolution of excessive assets or NPLs; managerial judgments to avoid realization of losses, increase in bankruptcies and unemployment, and aggravation of the economy; and the governance system that made such judgments possible. In the same vein, the government, charged with the responsibility of maintaining soundness of the economy and financial system, also took a long time to resolve the NPL problems. The reasons for this may include optimistic expectations for the future in the initial stage again, but also nonavailability of such a comprehensive safety net framework as had been introduced in 1997–1998 (in the absence of a comprehensive framework that included nationalization and capital injection, pushing a speedy resolution of NPL problems beyond the banks' capacity could create a situation beyond control).

Examination of what is said to be a successful case of coping with the collapse of the bubble and financial crisis in Scandinavian countries, reveals that existence of political will to use public money to save the financial system in the face of a financial crisis contributed to the early resolution of the crisis and a relatively prompt recovery of the economy. In Japan, the relevant authorities realized that the problems were more serious than expected in the early 1990s. If such information had been widely shared, it may have been possible to introduce a comprehensive framework that included capital injection and to solve the NPL problems much sooner. However, if such information had been extensively shared, it would have been highly likely that bank runs would have occurred, and a crisis would have emerged at the early stage of stagnation. Still, if the Japanese economy had a crisis at the beginning of 1990s, the subsequent developments might have been very different. The Japanese economy might have been able to go back, after the crisis, to a growth path similar to the one in the preceding periods. Although it is entirely with a hindsight, the very efforts to avoid a crisis in the early stage after the collapse of the bubble ultimately delayed the crisis and led to the alteration of the Japanese economy.

After the breakout of the crisis, significant and fundamental changes developed in the Japanese economy. In addition to the deterioration of the economy, first, the unemployment rate increased sharply from an average of 2.8% in Period I (1991–1997) to an average of 4.7% in Period II–IV (1998–2012). Second, the nominal wages started to fall, recording an accumulated fall of nearly 13% by 2012. Third, the number of regular employees peaked in 1997 and fell sharply after the crisis. Nearly 5 million regular employment positions (about 13% of the peak level) were lost by 2005, and the share of non-regular employment continued to increase. Fourth, the corporate sector changed from an excess investment to an excess savings sector. Fifth, the Consumer Price Index (CPI) (excluding fresh food) started to record a decline from mid-1998 and a mild deflation started. In this way, the corporate behaviors were greatly altered by the crisis, and the Japanese economy slowed further and entered the second stage of stagnation.

This chapter also briefly discusses Periods III and IV. The Japanese economy started the longest expansion beginning in the early 2000s, since following the Second World War. Although the two economic recoveries in the 1990s were both short-lived, the recovery in the 2000s continued for a long period of time extending longer than six years and was relatively strong in that investment made a positive contribution to growth. This was due to two factors: (1) The so-called three excesses, that is, excessive capital stock, excessive debt, and excessive employment, which the corporate sector assumed due to the formation and collapse of the bubble, had been eliminated and their levels returned to the pre-bubble levels by around mid-2000s. Thus, the negative legacy of the bubble was finally eliminated (this corresponds to the resolution of the NPL problems for the financial sector side). The second factor was favorable external environments of high growth with low inflation in the world economy, which was later termed "the great moderation." However, even during the long recovery, fundamental changes that had emerged in the Japanese economy (an elevated unemployment rate, the decline in nominal wages, the shift from regular to non-regular employment, companies' shift to net saver positions, and deflation) continued, and restraints on investment and on labor costs were maintained. In this period, in addition to these changes, other developments became more apparent, such as a decline in growth contribution of consumption under real wage reduction and increasing dependence on foreign trade, characteristics which are observed in the current Japanese economy.

Period IV (2008–2012) was a period when the Japanese economy experienced a series of external shocks, including the GFC, the European debt crisis, and the Great East Japan Earthquake. The Japanese economy recorded one of the deepest negative growth (annualized rates of 8.8% in Q4 2008 and 18.2% in Q1 2009) among the major advanced economies after the GFC, and its trade balance fell into deficit after the earthquake due to the increase in energy-related imports. Despite these developments, the yen-dollar exchange rate recorded a historic high. All these developments showed increasing external vulnerability of the Japanese economy.

Despite the economy having eliminated the negative legacy of the bubble and overcome shocks of the financial crisis in 15 years by the mid-2000s, the solid economic growth did not come back. The average growth rate over Periods III and IV (i.e., 2003–2012) was just 0.9%. Some factors may have been depressing the growth potential of the Japanese economy.

Viewed in this way, the Japanese economy seems have assumed two problems, even after having overcome the negative legacy of the bubble. The first is the lasting shortage of domestic demand and the growing dependence on foreign demand, coupled with the increased external vulnerability. The second is a possible decline in growth potential resulting from prolonged investment restraint. The key question is what has caused these problems. This point is examined further in Chaps. 5 and 6.

5 Chapter 5: Deflation and Monetary Policy

In Chaps. 2, 3, and 4, we examined what happened to the Japanese economy in the last 30 years, in a sequential manner, and also have attempted to understand the mechanism of the difficulties. However, our examination left us with an unanswered question: why did solid growth not return even after negative legacies of the bubble had been eliminated? In Chaps. 5 and 6, we try to address the issue of long stagnation and deflation, so as to capture the mechanism of the whole process including the problems with the current economy. To this end, this chapter focuses on the issues of deflation and monetary policy, and the next chapter examines corporate behaviors that, in the author's view, lie at the heart of the problem.

Chapter 5 first looks at evolution of deflation from the latter half of the 1990s, and presents an overview of the major arguments about its causes. Then, monetary policy management is assessed from the viewpoint of its effectiveness in the prevention of and for exiting from deflation.

The CPI (excluding fresh food) has been declining slightly for almost 15 years from mid-1998 to the first half of 2013, excepting brief periods of price increase. The average annual decline was −0.3% and the accumulated decline was −3.6%. Decline in the GDP deflator started in the first half of 1990s, earlier than the timing of the decline in CPI, and the degree of decline in the GDP deflator was greater than that of the CPI. As for the causes of deflation, there are three major arguments; (1) the supply-side argument identifies, as a cause of deflation, supply factors, such as penetration of cheap imports, technological progress including IT, and deregulation; (2) the demand factor argument regards weakness of the economy due to demand shortage as arising from such factors as insufficient monetary easing as a cause of deflation; and, (3) the financial sector-problem argument regards deficiency of the financial sector occurring due to NPLs as a cause of deflation. As for the supply-side argument, considering that the rate of import penetration became twofold in less than 20 years by the latter half of 2000, that price fall was greater for imported and import-competing goods than for other goods, and that the price of goods and services in the deregulated areas fell more than other goods, certainly supply-side factors contributed to the price decline. However, considering that such price declines that come from supply-side factors are generally beneficial and expected to contribute to an expansion of the economy, the arguments do not sufficiently explain the Japanese economy that had both stagnation and deflation at the same time. As for the demand factor argument, the existence of a deflationary gap (excess of supply over demand) that the Japanese economy has long suffered seems to support this view, and the arguments that criticize insufficiency of monetary policy have been mostly raised in this context. However, it is suggested here that the deflationary gap may be interpreted as showing that supply was in excess of a sustainable demand level rather than that actual demand is short of sustainable demand level, and thus, we must examine which interpretation is more relevant before conducting an assessment of monetary policy. As for the financial sector problem argument, as stated before, lending attitudes of financial institutions in the 1990s were eased, excepting periods just after the burst of the bubble and at the time of financial crisis, and, therefore, for Period I (initial adjustment period) the financial sector-problem view cannot explain stagnation and deflation (problems at the time of financial crisis are examined in Chap. 6 that analyzes company behaviors).

Then, the chapter examines the monetary policy. On monetary policy management before Governor Kuroda's easing under Abenomics (monetary policy under Abenomics is examined in Chap. 7), assessments were made separately for the period until the adoption of the zero interest rate policy (ZIRP) in 1999 (basically corresponding to the period before the Japanese economy started to have deflation and had been placed under the zero lower bound constraint on interest rate) and, then, for the period of subsequent quantitative easing in the 2000s (the period under deflation and with the zero lower bound constraint). As for the period up to the adoption of ZIRP, it is argued that monetary policy management could have been improved in three respects, as pointed out in an Federal Reserve Board (FRB) working paper (Ahearne et al. 2002). First, despite the Bank of Japan (BOJ) significantly easing monetary policy nine times from 1991 to 1995, and reducing the policy interest rate (official discount rate) to 0.5%, i.e., very close to zero, as the inflation rate decelerated more than expected, the real interest rate was kept high in the first half of the 1990s. Second, the BOJ interpreted price stability as zero inflation, admitting intermittent deflationary periods, which could be—and actually were—difficult to exit. Third, the BOJ sent messages to the markets that the increase in the interest rate was desirable by referring to the zero interest rate as an abnormal interest rate, and deterring decline in the long-term interest rate. Regarding the monetary policy management after entering the 2000s, that is, after the Japanese economy had fallen into deflation and had been placed under the zero lower bound constraint, the BOJ introduced the quantitative easing policy, targeting at the outstanding balance of the current accounts with the BOJ, which contributed to the fall in short- and medium-term interest rates. However, the rate of money stock increase did not change, bank loans continued to decline until mid-2000s, and deflation continued, showing a limitation of the policy effects.

We conclude that monetary policy, if managed differently, might have had greater stimulating effects on the economy in the period immediately after the collapse of the bubble. However, one can argue if the fundamental problem of the Japanese economy in that period was not demand shortage as is typically presumed, but rather excessive production capacity (excess assets), as previously suggested, then the most important action was not to stimulate demand but to reduce excessive capacity (excessive assets). For the latter (i.e., removal of excessive assets), what macroeconomic policies, including monetary policy, could do was limited.

6 Chapter 6: Deflation and the Mechanism of Corporate Behavior

In order to capture the fundamental mechanism of stagnation and deflation, we examine in Chap. 6 the behaviors of companies based on the combined statistics of financial statements of companies. The analysis is based on the Financial Statements Statistics of Corporations by Industry compiled by the Ministry of Finance, which covers all the profit-making corporations of 2.7 million that exist in Japan.

From the analysis of profit and loss, the following observations are made. The total amount of sales of companies, which had been increasing at an average rate of more than 6% in the 1980s, suddenly stopped growing soon after entering the 1990s and then started falling. The total amount of wages continued to increase for a while after entering the 1990s and became flat thereafter. The ratio of wages to sales, therefore, continued to increase, with a result that operating profits sharply declined after entering the 1990s and stagnated throughout the 1990s. By contrast, current profits started to recover in a rising trend in the 1990s due to improvements in the non-operational balance, which includes such items as interest payments, but unlike the 1980s, improvements in current profits did not lead to wage increases in and after the 1990s.

From the analysis of assets and liabilities, it is observed that both started to expand from the mid-1980s to a level greater than that implied by the then trend, continuing to grow, albeit at a slower pace in the first half of the 1990s. Subsequently, assets and liabilities started to shrink from the mid-1990s, returning to a level close to that implied by the pre-bubble trend by around mid-2000s. This means that it took about 15 years after the burst of the bubble for the corporate sector to complete its downward adjustments of the excessive assets and liabilities. A look at the composition of assets shows that physical assets, such as buildings and machineries (excluding land), started to decline from around the time of the financial crisis in the latter half of the 1990s. The total asset size started to expand again in the first half of 2000s, but physical assets (excluding land) continued to shrink until 2012. By contrast, securities held for investment purposes significantly increased.[4,5,6] The composition of assets has been altered. Parallel to the curtailment of domestic physical assets, the size of liabilities started to significantly decline after the mid-1990s, and then became flat as of the early 2000s.

[4]Most of the securities held for investment purpose are stocks, but their breakdown to domestic and foreign stocks is not available. If we convert the outstanding balance of Japan's foreign direct investment (FDI) vis-à-vis the rest of the world (year-end, denominated in US dollars) into yen using year-end exchange rates, we can see that the FDI balance accounts for 30–50% of the amount of securities held for investment purposes. In other words, half of the securities held for investment purposes may be stocks of domestic companies. They are canceled out in a consolidated basis and do not contribute to strengthening of the net asset position.

[5]Since the mid-2000s, outward FDI started to significantly increase and, particularly after the Lehman shock, the pace of outward FDI was accelerated.

[6]The combined amount of physical assets (excluding land) and the outstanding balance of FDI vis-à-vis the rest of the world (year-end, converted to yen) had been almost flat (or marginally decreased until 2012) after the financial crisis in the late 1990s, and only recently has started to show a rising trend. After the financial crisis, companies have proceeded with the reduction of domestic physical assets and the expansion of overseas production bases, gradually shifting production capacity from inside to outside the country.

A very significant change is observed with regard to net assets. While the rate of increase in net assets slowed down from the end of the 1980s, net assets started to increase sharply after the financial crisis, mainly through accumulated profits. Such development is more clearly observed in relation to the capital asset ratio. The capital asset ratio started to rise very sharply at the outbreak of the financial crisis and reached a historic high in recent years.

How should we interpret these developments in financial statements of companies? This chapter puts forward the following interpretation, drawing on the developments in financial statements and also on observations that have been made in the preceding chapters.

The problem started with the rapid expansion of asset size of the corporate sector (particularly the non-manufacturing sector) from the mid-1980s and the sudden stop and subsequent fall of sales growth after the burst of the bubble at the beginning of the 1990s. These developments indicate that the corporate sector came to have huge assets for which they could not expect sufficient sales, that is, excessive assets (low-profitability assets). This lay at the heart of the difficulties of the Japanese economy after the collapse of the bubble.

Under the circumstances, the corporate sector initially took the following responses. First, they restrained investment (investment stagnated) but did not swiftly remove excessive assets (the total assets hit a peak in the mid-1990s). Second, they basically maintained existing employment (regular employment showed a moderate increase until the second half of the 1990s). Third, they tried to restrain wage increases, but the combined amount of wages paid by the corporate sector continued to increase for some time. Fourth, as a result, operating profits stagnated, and companies tried to secure current profits by improving non-operational balances (through cutting down of interest payments, etc.). However, unlike the pattern seen until the 1980s, the improvements in current profits did not lead to increases in wages—that is, performance of companies and wage increases were delinked.

After the collapse of the bubble, the corporate sector initially pursued what may be called a traditional approach that placed importance on securing employment and took their time to dispose of excessive assets (this corresponds to the period preceding the financial crisis, and in Chap. 6, this period is called the "Passive response" period in light of the underlying corporate behavior). Under such response, costs and the risks of holding excessive (low-profitability) assets started to be shifted to the financial sector in the form of increasing NPLs, and then a financial crisis broke out in late 1990s. Faced with the crisis, the way the corporate sector addressed the problem of excessive assets dramatically changed, and with this change, the stagnation entered the second stage, as stated before. Specifically, with the breakout of the financial crisis, in addition to the deterioration of economic conditions, the lending attitude of financial institutions was suddenly tightened, including for small- and medium-sized borrowers for which the tightening, of lending attitudes after the burst of the bubble had been relatively moderate. In the face of such adverse changes in funding environments, the corporate sector seems to have started to forcefully strengthen its capital base. The net asset position and the capital asset ratio started to rise sharply. Strengthening of the net asset position was achieved mainly through the accumulation of profits. Under the prolonged sales stagnation, the only options open to companies to secure profits were reduction of labor costs, reduction of interest payments through repayment of debts, and sales of assets. Therefore, the companies embarked on full-fledged labor cost reduction through nominal wage reduction and curtailment of regular workers, replacing them with non-regular workers. They also started substantial repayments of debts and disposition of assets. Furthermore, companies strengthened their stance toward restraining investment, with a result that the size of physical assets, such as buildings and machineries, started to decline. Companies' responses in the second stage of stagnation suggest that the previous corporate behavioral pattern under which priority was given to securing employment and investment had been significantly altered. Companies now gave the first priority to strengthening their net asset position and placed importance on labor cost reduction, restraining investment, and accepting reduction in physical assets. In Chap. 6, in light of changes of company behaviors, the period from the financial crisis up to the first half of the 2000s is called "Crisis Response" period.

By the mid-2000s, shocks of the financial crisis were overcome, and removal of excessive assets and debt as well as excessive employment had been completed (it took about 15 years to remove excesses after the burst of the bubble). However, such defensive behaviors of companies to restrain labor costs and investment continued. Thus, in Chap. 6, the period from the mid-2000s to present is called the "Sustained Defensiveness" period. Such defensiveness of companies placed downward pressures on consumption (through wage restraint) and investment, bringing about structuralized demand shortage and depressed price levels. Restraint on wages also depressed price levels through production cost channels. In this way, what paved the way for the emergence of deflation is very likely to have been behavioral changes of companies triggered by the financial crisis.[7] This implies that deflation is not the cause of stagnation but the outcome of the fact that companies changed their behaviors after it became impossible to continue to hold excesses following the financial crisis. This interpretation does not deny a possibility that deflation itself may have added an extra burden on the economy, through its own mechanism to discourage employment and borrowings, and had made an exit from the low-growth cycle more difficult. However, still, the central problem of the Japanese economy is not deflation, but companies' defensive behaviors (structuralized defensiveness of companies) that had been drastically strengthened by the financial crisis, and it is important to overcome this mechanism.

The chapter, however, contends that we need to have a cautious look at whether defensiveness of companies, observed even today, should be regarded as wholly irrational. We need to understand why companies' defensiveness continued even after excesses had been eliminated by the mid-2000s.

As for restraint on domestic investment, we note that behind such behaviors are a depressed growth expectation for the domestic economy and relative high profitability of overseas operations, and restraint of domestic investment could have been the outcome of rational choice by companies.[8] The decline in expected growth rate proceeded year by year after the collapse of the bubble, hit bottom after the financial crisis, and became flat thereafter. In other words, the low-growth expectation became firmly rooted in the companies with the onset of the financial crisis. There are two types of interpretation on the long held low-growth expectation of companies. One interpretation attributes it to

[7] In addition to such behavioral changes of companies, however, it is possible that external factors such as international competition through cost reduction under the yen appreciation and a rapid catching-up of emerging market economies contributed to the nominal wage decline and the emergence of deflation. See Chap. 6 on this point.

[8] Under the continued restraint of investment, return on asset (ROA), which had been declining since the 1960s, hit a bottom in the latter half of 1990s and showed a slight increase in the 2000s.

the defensive mindset (a way of thinking that has become a common practice or a habit), and the other interpretation regards it as rational and founded on substantive factors, such as the shrinking and aging of the population.

As for wage restraint, if we compare developments of real income and labor productivity from the 1990s, we can see that the rise in real income exceeded that of labor productivity throughout the 1990s, and as a result, labor income share substantially increased in the 1990s. In the light of this development, the labor cost reduction that was started with the breakout of the financial crisis may be understood as an unavoidable process that aimed at correcting unsustainably high labor costs brought about by company response during a time of declining profits in the 1990s (i.e., the passive response to maintain employment and insufficiently restrain wages). In other words, the response can be considered rational. This interpretation does not explain whether the wage restraint, still present now, is rational. Chapter 6 argues that, under the long-held pricing behaviors of companies to maintain international competitiveness through restraint on export prices, labor cost reduction through the replacement of regular workers with non-regular workers backed by the existence of duality in the labor markets was effectively utilized as a tool to maintain competitiveness.

Although it is difficult to assess with certainty whether the current restraint on wages and investment is excessive or rational, it is clear that the negative consequences on the domestic economy caused by such restraint are surfacing. Growth contribution of consumption has declined. Prolonged investment restraint may have lowered export competitiveness and growth potential. Japan's share in world exports has been halved in the last two decades, and growth rate continues to be low.

To repeat, restraint on wages and investment by companies produced everlasting domestic demand shortages and vulnerable growth, and the long lasting investment restraint may have eroded export competitiveness and the growth potential of the Japanese economy. This is the problem that the current Japanese economy faces.

7 Chapter 7: Abenomics and Challenges for the Japanese Economy

Chapter 7 examines architecture and effects of "Abenomics," that is, a comprehensive package of economic policies that the Abe administration, starting in end-2012 has been implementing, and shows challenges for the Japanese economy.

Abenomics is composed of "three arrows": bold monetary policy to overcome deflation (first arrow), flexible fiscal policy to create demand and simulate dampened economy (second arrow), and growth strategy to restore confidence of corporations and households and to promote investment (third arrow).

The basic logic underlying Abenomics is that, as the Japanese economy is trapped in a vicious cycle of low growth and deflation, it is necessary to overcome deflation through monetary policy, to stimulate stagnant private economic activities through fiscal injection, and to realize the mid- and long-term growth led by the private sector through growth-oriented policies. In light of the interpretations discussed in Chap. 6, Abenomics is understood as a policy attempt to correct structuralized defensive behaviors of companies.

The first arrow, bold monetary easing, shot by Governor Kuroda, who succeeded Shirakawa in March 2013, took the form of the Quantitative and Qualitative Monetary Easing (QQE) announced in April 2013. QQE included the setting of the price stability target of a 2% CPI (excluding fresh food) annual increase to be achieved within about two years and the targeted increase in monetary base at an annual pace of about 60–70 trillion yen (raised to about 80 trillion yen in October 2014, and set as a benchmark not a target in September 2016) through purchase of assets, including long-term Japanese Government Bonds (JGBs). In February 2016, the BOJ introduced an additional measure of imposing a negative interest rate of −0.1% on part of the outstanding balance of currents accounts held by financial institutions at the BOJ (implemented from mid-February). Furthermore, in September 2016, the BOJ moved away from base money targeting, and instead adopted a policy focused on short-term and long-term interest rate control ("yield curve control"). As the second arrow, that is, on the fiscal policy front, economic stimulus packages were compiled four times—in January 2013, December 2013, December 2014, and August 2016. In April 2014, the consumption tax rate was increased for the first time in 17 years, from 5% to 8%. For the third arrow, that is, for the growth strategy, the administration adopted the "Japan Revitalization Strategy" in June 2013. The strategy set a goal of achieving around 3% nominal and 2% real GDP growth on average over the coming 10 years. The revised revitalization strategy, adopted in June 2014, included such items as reducing the effective rate of corporate tax to below 30% and deregulation in hard core areas, such as agriculture, health care, and energy (the revitalization strategy was further revised in June 2015, and June 2016).

The initial impacts of Abenomics, particularly those of the introduction of QQE, were dramatic. Stock price (Nikkei 225) rose by 88% in just over a one-year period to the end of 2013, and the yen depreciated against the US dollar until May 2013, by more than 20%, from the high of below 80 yen to over 100 yen to the dollar in a half year. However, subsequent developments are not as one-sided or dramatic as in the initial period, with positive movements and stagnation intermingled.

Chapter 7 assesses five years under the Abenomics as follows. First, the Abenomics, particularly in its initial phase, produced substantial depreciation of the yen and sharp rise of stock prices. This is most likely due to the change of expectation held by the foreign investors regarding Japanese economy, stock prices, and yen rate, which were triggered by bold monetary easing. Second, depreciation of the yen rate and the rise of stock prices have not changed the trend of real GDP growth by much so far. However, since Abenomics started, the interest rate has declined across the maturity from short term to long term, and bank lending has been maintaining the growth trend since the recovery period after the Lehman shock. The recovery momentum has been maintained. Third, a breakdown of the economic growth structure under Abenomics by demand components indicates, as compared with the period preceding Abenomics, the growth contribution of net exports has significantly increased, and the growth contribution of government expenditure has nearly doubled; in contrast, the contribution of consumption halved, and the growth contribution of private investment more or less remained unchanged. Fourth, price levels showed positive increase for more than two years from May 2013. This increase, however, is affected to a substantial degree by external developments, including yen depreciation (rather than improvements in domestic demand/supply conditions). Fifth, while company profits have been registering record highs, private investment, while increasing, has not shown significant increase; restraint on wages continues and cash and deposit holdings by companies have also been recording historic highs. Sixth, while the labor market shows the lowest unemployment rate since mid-1990s, tightening of demand and supply conditions is greater for non-regular workers compared to regular workers. The rate of wage increase is higher for non-regular workers. Companies have not changed their stance on restraining labor costs.

Therefore, under favorable policy environments where very coherent policies have been pursued with political stability, economic recovery has been continuing, and yet, companies have not perfectly exited from defensive behaviors of restraining investment and wages, and there has not been a significant change in growth trend. The structure of growth is problematic in that the growth contribution of consumption has been declining, and dependence of growth on government expenditure is increasing.

The biggest factor that has brought about the continuation of defensive behavior by companies seems to be the low-growth expectation of companies.[9]

It is difficult to assess whether the low growth expectation itself is due to the defensive way of thinking (mindset) that has been brought about by reality of low growth over a quarter of a century, or it is founded on rational factors such as population shrinkage. Judging from the accumulation of cash and deposit holdings by companies (implying an attitude of risk avoidance), the former factor seems to be working to a certain extent.

Furthermore, against the background of such factors as stagnation in wage increases and the increasing use of non-regular workers by companies, concern for the future is strong among households. After the anomaly and difficulties over more than 30 years, the Japanese economy has become an economy governed by low-growth expectation by companies and concerns for the future of Japanese households.

In order to exit from the current situation, companies need an expectation that their sales will grow, and households need an expectation that their

[9] The expected real growth rate of the Japanese growth rate held by companies (Cabinet Office, "Survey on Company Behavior") slightly rose after Abenomics started, but it then declined and has stayed at a level of just over 1% for the last few years.

incomes will steadily grow.[10] To realize such expectations, it is necessary to overcome negative influences of the defensive mindset, if any. But, at the same time, it is indispensable to tackle such substantive issues as population decline and measures to increase productivity.

Bibliography

English Reference

Kosai, Yutaka (1986) The Era of High-Speed Growth – Notes on the Postwar Japanese Economy. Tokyo: University of Tokyo Press.

[10] Kosai (1986) wrote, in the famous paragraph from the 1956 Economic White Paper, which announced the end of the postwar recovery, "there was … a concealed but profound fear that a slackening of the growth rate would accompany the end of postwar reconstruction" (Kosai 1986, 106). "Since high growth was not expected to continue beyond the recovery period, it was not generally thought that plant and equipment investment was undertaken in earnest on an all-out scale." "If growth were to continue beyond the recovery period, the capital stock would have to be expanded …. Firms that had begun to be confident that growth would continue set about as though with one accord to renovate their plant and equipment" (Kosai 1986, 108–9). This episode implies that the reality of high growth drove the companies toward investment, which led to the continuation of high growth.

CHAPTER 2

Formation of a Bubble and Its Background

Japan experienced a formation of a huge bubble in the 1980s, which turned out to be a prelude to the subsequent two-decade-long economic stagnation. In this chapter, we will look at what happened to the asset price (land and stocks) in Japan in the 1980s (Sect. 1), and why it happened and, what could (should) have been done to contain the bubble (Sect. 2). In examining causes of the bubble, we will look at two factors: economic policy management in the 1980s and bank behaviors under financial liberalization from the latter half of the 1970s.

1 Formation of a Bubble in the 1980s

Asset Price Inflation and Subsequent Fall

Figure 2.1 shows evolution of the urban land price index (commercial use, end March 2000 = 100) for the six largest cities in Japan from October 1954 to April 2012. Urban land price (commercial use) rose approximately 4.9 times in seven years from 107.8 in April 1983 to the peak of 525.4 in April 1990.[1]

[1] The rate of change in the urban commercial land price index (six largest cities) from six months before started to rise at a significantly higher pace than before, as early as in 1983, with the rate of increase nearly doubling from 3.1% in March 1983 (which was about the average rate of increase in the preceding two to three years) to 5.7% in October 1983, and it

K. Aramaki, *Japan's Long Stagnation, Deflation, and Abenomics*,
https://doi.org/10.1007/978-981-13-2176-4_2

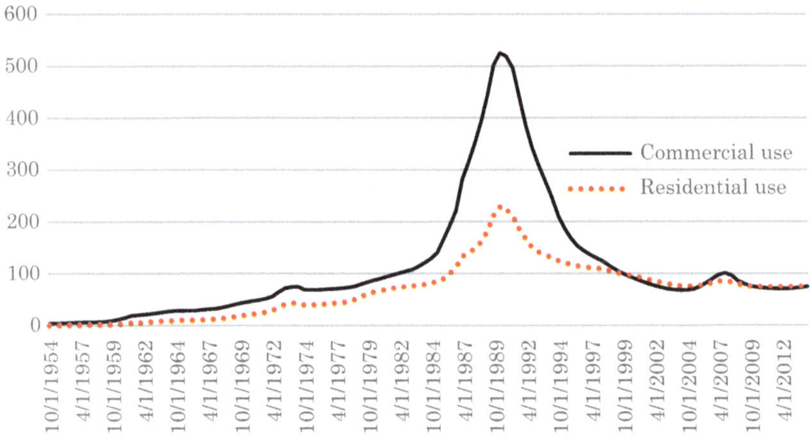

Fig. 2.1 Urban land price index: Six largest cities (end March 2000 = 100) October 1954–April 2012. Source: Japan Real Estate Institute

Urban land prices started to decline from October 1990 and continued to fall for 14 years to 67.2 in April 2004 (a decline of 87.0% from the peak in April 1990), which was the level in 1972–73, before it showed a minimal increase of 0.2% in October 2004.

For residential land, the urban land price index (residential use, end March 2000 = 100) for the six largest cities increased by about three times from 77.5 in April 1983 to the peak of 231.5 in April 1990. Then, it declined to 76.9 (the bottom at the time) in October 2004, losing 66.8% from the value at the peak.

Figure 2.2 shows that stock prices (Nikkei 225 [monthly average]) increased 5.4 times in a period slightly longer than seven years from 7,042 in August 1982 to 38,130 in December 1989.[2] The Nikkei 225

continued to rise to hit a peak of 27.2% in April 1987. Although it is not easy to determine the exact timing when the bubble started, it does not seem to be as late as the late 1980s (that is when the rate of increase started to fall) as sometimes argued (e.g., Okina et al. (2001) treats the four years from 1987 to 1990 "bubble period," partly due to difference in the definition of a bubble).

[2] From September 1982, the Nikkei monthly average almost continuously recorded positive growth from the previous month with occasional brief falls until December 1989, before it started to collapse in January 1990.

Fig. 2.2 Nikkei 225 (monthly average) June 1949–February 2013. Source: NIKKEI NEEDS

started to fall in January 1990, hit the bottom at 15,790 (−58.6% from the peak) in August 1992, that is, in less than three years, and then became fairly stabilized in the range of 16,000–21,000, before it resumed a fall in late 1997.

Transformation of the Asset Price Inflation to a Bubble

We saw a sharp rise and fall of asset prices from the 1980s. We now know what we were seeing was a bubble, but, as we see later, the asset price increase in the early stage of the process appears to have been based on real factors, that is, the increase may not have been a bubble initially. So, in this section, we will look at when and how the asset price increase turned into a bubble with reference to some existing research and reports.

Definition of an Asset Price Bubble

An asset price bubble may be defined as a phenomenon in which the price of asset rises beyond the level that is based on fundamentals. The price based on fundamentals (that is, the theoretical price) corresponds to the discounted present value of future returns to the asset and is expressed as follows, if the asset has no risk and if the return is fixed:[3]

$$P = R / i, \tag{2.1}$$

where R = return (office or housing rent, interest, etc.) to an asset, P = price of asset, i = long-term risk-free interest rate (typically, long-term government bond yield in the secondary market).

If the asset has a risk and the return to the asset grows each period at a fixed rate, g, the theoretical price will be written as:

$$P = R / \left(i + \alpha - g\right), \tag{2.2}$$

where α is the risk premium (an additional return on top of the return to a risk-free asset that is required for a risk asset to be held), and g is the growth rate of the return (R).

Theoretical and Actual Price of Land

Figure 2.3 shows the development in both the actual price and the theoretical price of land for commercial use in central Tokyo, as calculated by the Economic Planning Agency (EPA). Setting the level in 1983 as a base, the increase in the actual price started to exceed that of the theoretical price from around the mid-1980s and stayed above the theoretical price throughout the rest of 1980s.[4]

Figure 2.4 shows a different estimation. It shows that, from 1987 in Tokyo, the actual land price far exceeded the projected land price, which was calculated based on a regression analysis.

These two analyses suggest that there was a land price bubble at least in the latter half of the 1980s.

Spillovers of Land Price Increase

The foregoing suggests there was a land price bubble in Tokyo from around the mid-1980s. Let us see in more detail how the bubble was

[3] See the supplement to this chapter for the derivation of theoretical price (i.e., price based on fundamentals).

[4] In calculating the theoretical price, the prevailing levels of return and the interest rate were assumed to be unchanged for the future. See *Nenji Keizai Hokoku* (Annual Economic Report) *1991* (Economic Planning Agency).

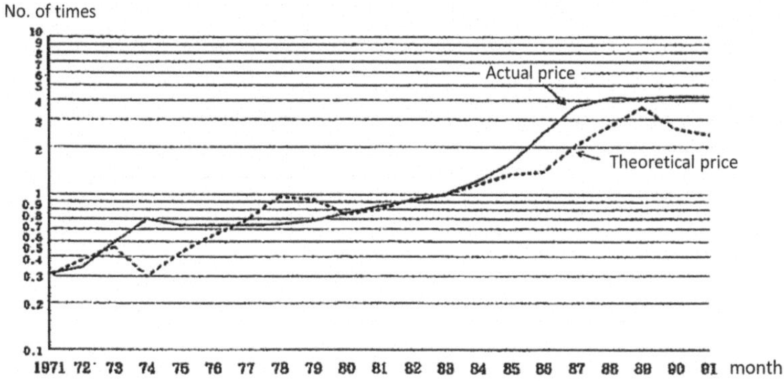

Fig. 2.3 Actual and theoretical land price (land for business use, Central Tokyo.1983 = 1) 1971–1991. Note: In calculating the theoretical price, the prevailing levels of return and the interest rate are assumed to be unchanged for the future. Source: Economic Planning Agency, *"Nenji Keizai Hokoku (Annual Economic Report) 1991"*

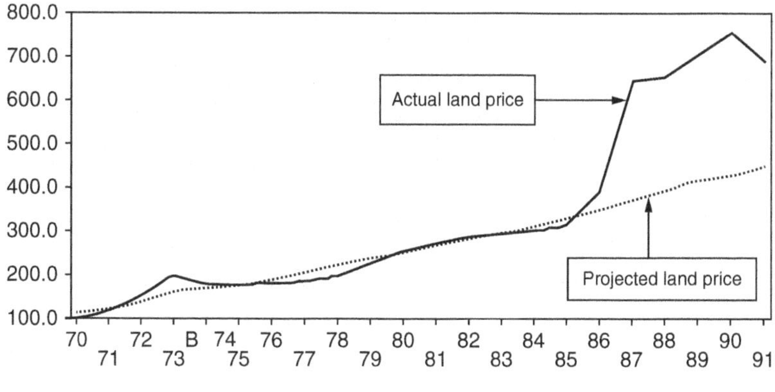

Fig. 2.4 Actual and projected land price (all uses) in Tokyo metropolitan area. Note: Land price is regressed on GDP of Tokyo and the long-term interest rate for 1970–1986. Source: Fiscal and Monetary Research Institute, Ministry of Finance, Japan, "Shisan kakaku hendo no mekanizumu to sono keizai koka" (The Mechanism of Asset Price Movements and its Economic Impacts), November 1993 *Finansharu Rebyu*

formed. Figure 2.5 shows land price developments by area and by type of use in Tokyo from the early 1980s to the beginning of the 1990s. We can see that the substantial land price increase started with commercial land in the center of Tokyo, as early as 1983, a few years earlier than the mid-1980s, which was suggested as the starting point of the bubble in the preceding analyses. Figure 2.5 also shows that there were spillovers of land price increases from the very center to the suburbs of Tokyo, and also, from commercial to residential use.

Figure 2.6 shows that spillovers of land price increases spread from Tokyo to two other metropolitan areas, namely, Osaka and Nagoya, and then to local areas.

Figures 2.5 and 2.6 indicate that the significant land price increase started in the very center of Tokyo for land for commercial use as early as in 1983,[5] and this development spread from land for commercial use to land for residential use and also, from the very center of Tokyo to other areas in Tokyo, then to other regions in Japan later in the 1980s. Next, we need to know why the commercial land price started to rise sharply in the center of Tokyo in the first place.

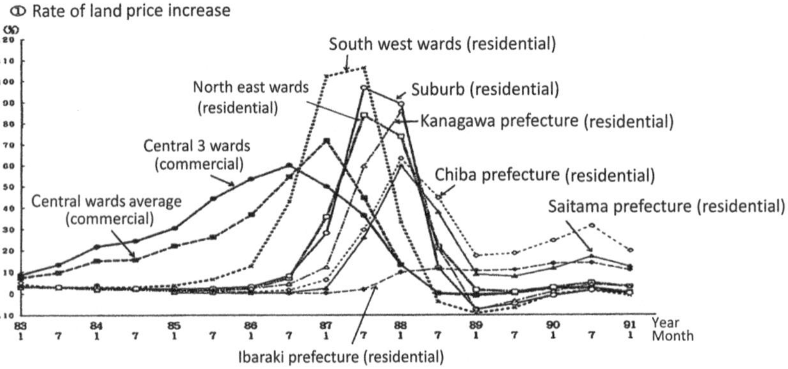

Fig. 2.5 Rate of land price increases by area and by type of use in the Tokyo metropolitan area, 1983–1991. Source: Economic Planning Agency, *Nenji Keizai Hokoku (Annual Economic Report) 1991*

[5] This is when the rate of commercial land price increase nearly doubled (see Endnote 1 in this chapter).

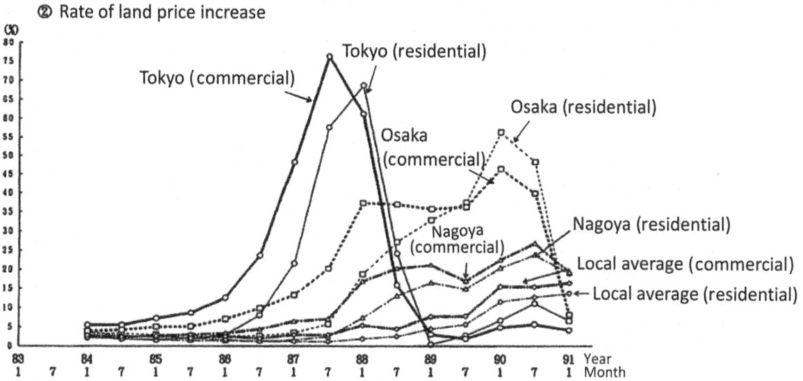

Fig. 2.6 Spillovers of land price increases from Tokyo to Osaka and Nagoya metropolitan areas and to local areas. Source: Economic Planning Agency, *Nenji Keizai Hokoku (Annual Economic Report) 1991*

There are factors that might have triggered the initial rise in commercial land prices in central Tokyo, such as increasing attention from abroad in financial markets in Tokyo and the expectation that a growing number of offices of foreign financial institutions would be established in Tokyo. Figure 2.7 shows that the vacancy rate of office space in Tokyo was rapidly falling and reached almost 0% in the mid-1980s. This implies that there was a real factor, that is, a tightening of demand/supply conditions for office space to explain the rise in the price of commercial land in Tokyo in the early 1980s. So, the significant rise in land prices may well have started by a fundamental factor at the beginning. Through the process of subsequent spillovers of price increase, however, to other land uses and to other areas, an element of bubble may have begun at that point, leading to a huge asset price bubble in extensive areas and sectors in Japan.

Theoretical and Actual Price of Stocks

Let us briefly look at the stock price increase. Here, a comparison between the theoretical and the actual stock prices also suggests that there might have been an element of a bubble in the latter half of 1980s. The interest rate-adjusted price/earning ratio (PER, i.e., stock price divided by profit per one unit of stock), that is, the interest rate multiplied by the PER, can

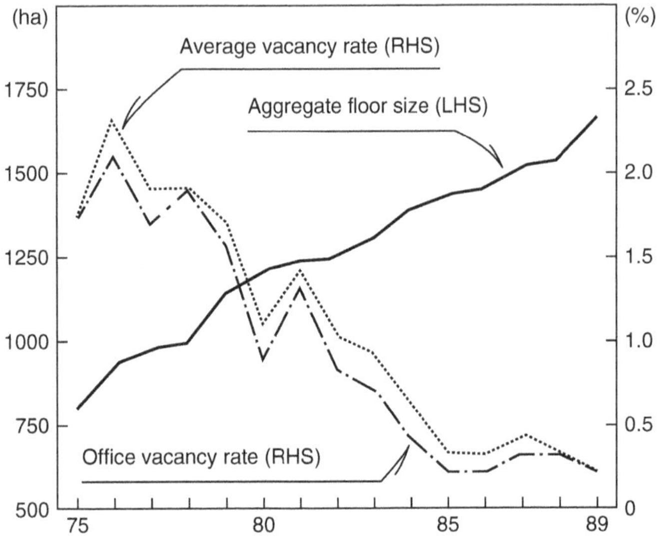

Fig. 2.7 Aggregate floor size of the buildings belonging to the Tokyo Building Association and average vacancy rate. Source: Bank of Japan, *"Chosa Geppo"* (Monthly Research Report) April 1990

be shown to correspond to the ratio of actual to theoretical stock prices.[6] Figure 2.8 shows that the interest rate-adjusted PER (= actual stock price/ theoretical price) grew more than fourfold in the late 1980s, exceeding previous peaks of 2.4 to 2.5 times at the end of 1970s and in the first half of 1980s. This development may be explained by either an increase in the expected growth rate of return or a decline in risk premium, or both.[7] Both factors symbolize strong confidence held by companies and individuals in the future course of the Japanese economy, which later turned out to be unrealistic.

Summary

From the foregoing, the following observations may be made:

[6] See 2.3 (Stock price) of Supplement to this chapter.

[7] The theoretical price rises if the risk premium (α) decreases, and/or the expected growth rate (g) of return increases in Eq. (2.2) on page 36.

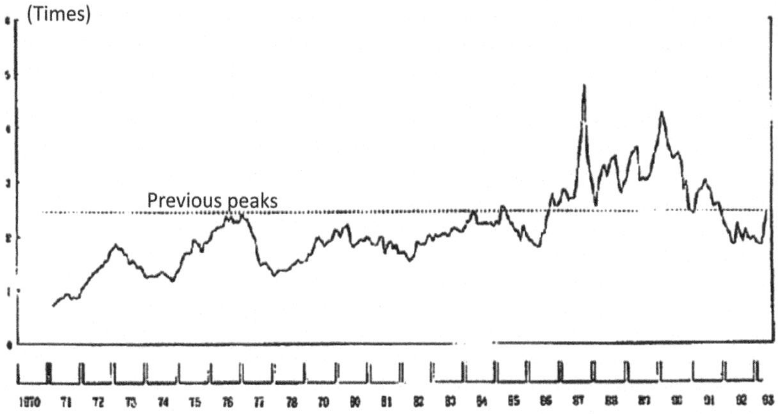

Fig. 2.8 Development in interest-rate-adjusted PER. Note: PER = price/earning ratio, i.e., stock price divided by profit per one unit of stock. Source: *Nenji Keizai Hokoku* (Annual Economic Report) *1993* (Economic Planning Agency)

First, the initial commercial land price rise in the central Tokyo may have been based on fundamental factors.

Second, the subsequent price surge in commercial land from around the mid-1980s in Tokyo, the spillovers to residential land prices in Tokyo and also to other areas in Japan, however, seem to have been a bubble.

Third, the stock price rise in the late 1980s may have reflected an increase in expected profit growth (GDP growth rate may have acted as its proxy) and a fall in risk premium under strong confidence in the economy (which seems to have led to positive risk taking by companies and individuals). However, both the high-growth expectation and low-risk premium were not realistic.

2 Why Did the Asset Price Bubble Develop? Could It Have Been Avoided?

So far, we have seen how the asset price bubble was formed. In this section, we look at why such a bubble emerged. Two major factors often mentioned as causes of the bubble are (1) economic policy management in the 1980s, particularly a large-scale monetary easing over an extended period of time; and (2) bank behaviors under financial liberalization initiated in the latter half of the 1970s. In what follows, we look at these factors one by one, and also examine what could (should) have been done to prevent the formation of a bubble.

Economic Policy Management

Chronology

A brief chronology of the important developments that happened in the two decades over the 1970s and 1980s is shown in Table 2.1.

We can see from this brief chronology that these two decades were full of many external turbulent incidents. The 1970s saw, first, the demise of the stable exchange rate regime (Nixon shock). The peg system was abandoned, and under the float system, the yen basically continuously appreciated for subsequent decades, bringing the Japanese economy from time to time to the state of "high yen driven stagnation." The 1970s also saw two oil crises, which drove the crude oil price (in terms of Arabian light) to nearly 20 times higher than its 2 US dollars per barrel in the early 1970s to around 40 US dollars per barrel in 1979,[8] and the world economy fell into a severe stagnation coupled with high inflation (stagflation). For Japan, both these developments (i.e., the collapse of the peg system and the yen appreciation, and the worldwide stagflation), together with the end of high-speed growth of the early 1970s, imposed a heavy burden on the fiscal policy management, bringing about a sharp aggrava-

Table 2.1 Major economic and political developments in the 1970s and 1980s

August 1971	Nixon shock
December 1971	Smithonian Accord
October 1973–	1st oil crisis
December 1978–	2nd oil crisis
January 1981–	1st Reagan administration
May 1984	Yen–Dollar Committee report
September 1985	Plaza Accord
April 1986	Maekawa report
February 1987	Louvre Accord
October 1987	Black Monday
June 1990	Final Report of Structural Impediments Initiative (SII)

[8] See Komine, Takao (2011a).

tion of the government fiscal position. Then, the 1980s saw a growing friction between Japan and the United States against the background of a worsening external trade balance of the United States during the first Reagan administration and expanding external surpluses of Japan.

These two factors, that is, deterioration of fiscal position and intensifying external disputes with the United States, provided the basic constraints on the Japan's economic policy management in this period. This is the first factor affecting the bubble formation. The deterioration of the fiscal position also acted as a push factor for financial liberalization to be explained later, which is the second factor affecting the bubble formation. We will first look at how Japan's economic policy management was conducted under these constraints, that is, trade disputes with the United States and deterioration of the fiscal position, and find out what such policy management has brought about.

Japan's Economic Policy Management in the 1980s Under the Two Major Constraints

Let us examine the economic policy management in the 1980s and its relationship with the bubble formation.

Fierce External Friction with US

Trade disputes with US presented a really difficult challenge for Japan's policy formulation. Figures 2.9 and 2.10 show developments in the external positions of US and Japan, respectively. The US current

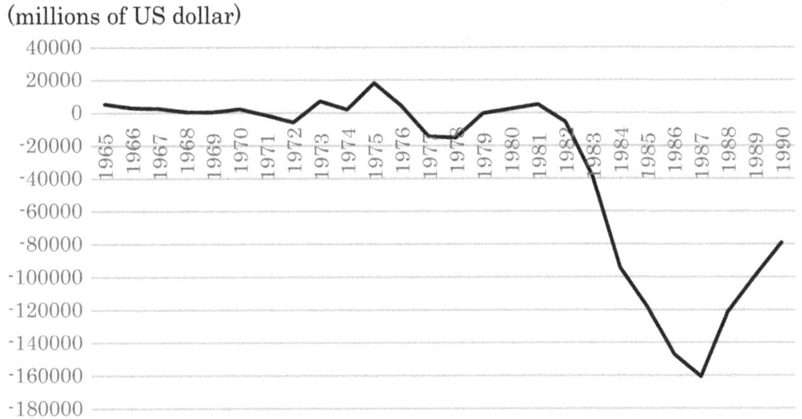

Fig. 2.9 Current account balance: US 1965–1990. Source: Bureau of Economic Analysis (BEA), US government

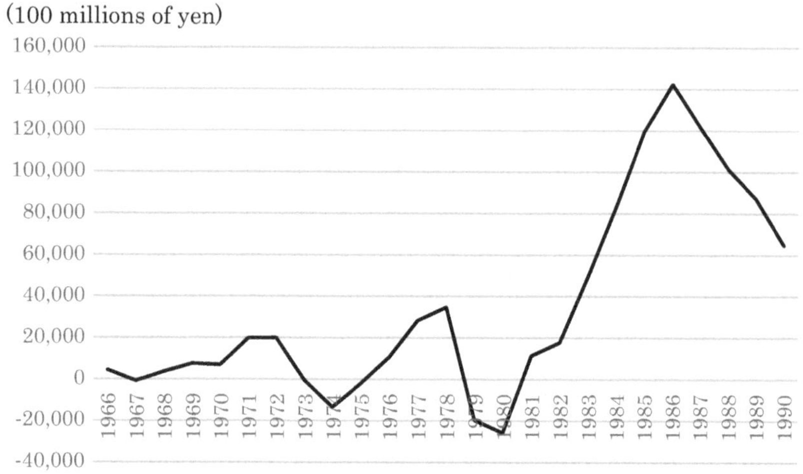

Fig. 2.10 Current account balance: Japan 1966–1990. Source: Cabinet Office, *"Choki Keizai Tokei Heisei 24"* (Long-term economic statistics FY 2012)

account balance deteriorated sharply in the first half of 1980s. By contrast, Japan's current account surplus significantly increased after entering the 1980s.

One of the backgrounds for these developments is found in the evolution of the Japanese economy at that time. In the stable growth era of 1974–1984, that is, an intermittent period between the high-speed growth era and the bubble period, the growth contribution of private investment in plant and equipment (Ip) sharply fell as compared with the preceding high-growth era, from 1.6% to 0.3% on average. By contrast, net exports (NE) became the major engine of growth, with the average growth contribution rising from −0.3% to 0.6% (Table 2.2 and Fig. 2.11). Although we will look at the factors behind these developments later, such growing dependence of the Japanese economy on exports, particularly exports to the United States, led to fierce trade disputes with the United States.

While Japan had trade disputes with the United States almost incessantly after the Second World War, as is indicated in the major cases of disputes listed in Table 2.3, the severity of disputes sharply increased as Japan's economy grew and its impacts became greater.

Table 2.2 Average growth contribution of private investment in plant and equipment and net exports: 1956–1973 (high-speed growth period), 1974–1984 (stable growth period), and 1985–1990 (bubble period) (%)

	1956–1973	*1974–1984*	*1985–1990*
Real GDP growth rate	9.3	3.3	4.6
Private investment in plant and equipment	1.6	0.3	1.7
Net exports	−0.3	0.6	−0.4

Source: Cabinet Office, GDP statistics

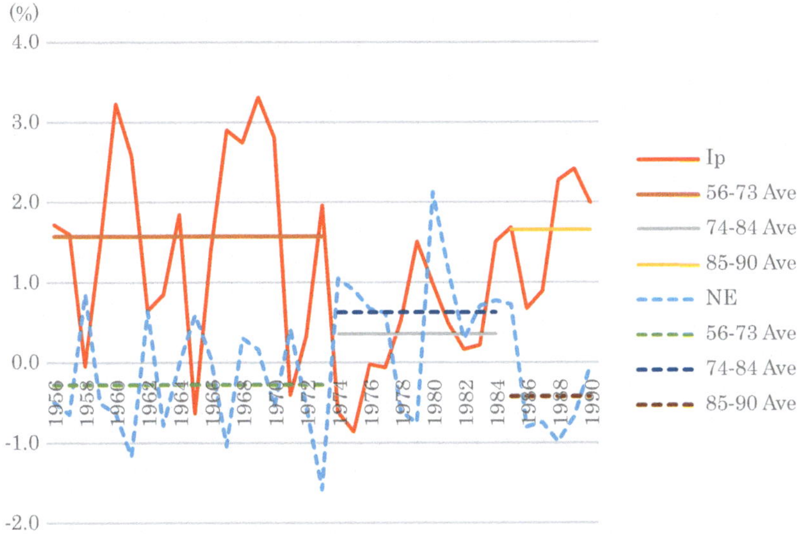

Fig. 2.11 Real GDP growth contribution by private investment in plant and equipment (Ip) and net exports (NE) in 1956–1973 (high-speed growth era), 1974–1984 (stable growth era), and 1985–1990 (bubble era). Source: Cabinet Office, GDP statistics

Table 2.3 Major trade disputes between Japan and US

1950s–	Textiles
1960s–	Steel, color TVs
1970s–	Beef and oranges, NTT (Nippon Telegraph and Telephone Corporation) procurement, automobiles
1980s–	Semi-conductors, mobile phones, etc.

Through the history of disputes, the focus of the negotiations shifted from export restraint (textiles, steel, color TVs, automobiles), to market access (NTT procurement, semi-conductors), and then to macro and structural factors (Structural Impediments Initiatives (SII) [1989–1990]), but the severity of disputes culminated with respect to automobiles, from the latter half of 1970s to 1980s. The share of imported cars significantly increased from over 10% at the end of 1950s to 18% in 1978, and then to 26% in 1980.[9] The Big Three automakers in the United States laid off workers, and one of the three, Chrysler came close to bankruptcy in 1980. Workers demonstrated by destroying a Japanese car with hammers.[10] In 1981, President Reagan publicized a rescue plan for the automobile industry and requested a voluntary export restraint from Japan. In 1981, voluntary export restraint was placed into operation by Japan, limiting exports to United States to 1.68 million units a year.

In March 1985, prior to the expiry of the voluntary export restraint, Reagan stated that he would not request an extension of the voluntary export restraint, based on the improvements in the performance of the US automobile industry, but Japan voluntarily extended export restraint. In response to the president's decision, dissatisfaction with Japan spread rapidly. As many as 400 bills aiming to protect US products were submitted to the US Congress a single year, 1985,[11] and the atmosphere in Washington, DC, was described by Japan's ex-Foreign Minister, Ōkita, as "the night before the war." In late March 1985, the US Senate passed a resolution, by 92 to 0, asking the president to retaliate against Japan, considered to be an unfair trade partner.

Under such circumstances, the policy agenda item in Japan with the highest priority became the alleviation of the growing tension with the United States. Before explaining policy responses by Japan, let us briefly look at the second constraint on Japan's policy management at that time (i.e., deterioration of the fiscal position).

Deterioration of the Fiscal Position

The second constraint came from the inside. With the economic growth rate significantly slowing down, Japan's fiscal balance, which had been basically in surplus until the early 1970s, dramatically changed, and the nation started to record a large deficit from mid-1970s (Fig. 2.12).

[9] See Komine (2011a).

[10] In 1982, a tragic incident happened in which a young Chinese man, who was mistaken for a Japanese man, was killed by laid-off automobile workers in Detroit.

[11] See Volcker and Gyoten (1992).

Fig. 2.12 General government fiscal balance (GDP ratio): Japan 1965–1990. Source: Cabinet Office

Causes of deficits can be found on both revenue and expenditure sides, and fiscal consolidation became a priority policy agenda in the 1980s. On the revenue side, due to the downward shift of the growth rate, the rate of revenue increase fell substantially. On the other hand, expenditures expanded, especially reflecting the reform of the social security system in 1973 (called "Social Security Year 1"). Also, due to the fiscal stimulus implemented as a result of the yen appreciation, oil crises, and international calls for domestic demand expansion ("Locomotive countries" arguments[12]), the dependence ratio of revenue on government bond financing sharply increased in the 1970s, reaching 39.6% in the initial budget for fiscal year 1979.

Prime Minister (PM) Ohira's administration, which started in 1978, declared that the fiscal year 1980 would be "the 1st year for fiscal consolidation" and that a general consumption tax would be introduced in fiscal year 1980. However, under strong opposition from members of his own ruling party, Ohira took back the proposal but still lost the absolute

[12] Ahead of the summit meeting in London in 1978, an argument gained a high profile that Japan, West Germany, and the United States, with their relatively good performance, should act as the locomotive countries to lead the recovery of the world economy.

majority in the lower (i.e., more powerful) house election in late 1979. After a hard fought internal battle within the ruling party (the "40 day battle"), Ohira was reelected as PM. The battle continued, however, and finally, a non-confidence resolution was adopted in the lower house in the absence from voting of a large number of ruling party members. Ohira dissolved the lower house, but in the midst of the campaign, he passed away. Although the ruling party won the election, the Suzuki administration, which succeeded Ohira's, committed itself to the pursuit of fiscal consolidation without tax increase, which constrained the scope of fiscal measures to cope with the policy agenda, including with the growing external frictions during most of the 1980s.

How Did the Government Respond?

We looked at how the government responded to these developments:

The basic observation was that, under mounting criticism from the United States for the external trade imbalance, highest priority in the economic policy formulation gradually shifted in the 1980s from domestic economic matters to the resolution of external economic conflict. With the government commitment to fiscal consolidation, maintained for the substantive part of 1980s, the policy choice roughly followed the following sequence from (a) to (c). In what follows, we will look at these responses.

(a) Export restraint and the expansion of domestic demand through deregulation, including urban redevelopment by "Minkatsu" (mobilization of private sector vitality)
(b) Coordinated exchange rate adjustments (Plaza Accord)
(c) Emphasis on the need to transform the Japanese economy into a domestic demand-driven one and on the expansion of domestic demand through monetary easing and, in the later stage, fiscal expansion (structural reform and expansionary macroeconomic policy).

Export Restraints and Deregulation

Export Restraints Could Not Solve the Disputes

Export restraints by Japan were frequently placed into force, as shown in Table 2.4. Although Japan first resorted to this measure to cope with the automobile dispute, as explained earlier, the problem was not resolved.

Table 2.4 Major cases of export restraint

Period	*Industry*	*Main outcomes*
Mid-1950s–early 1970s	Textiles	Voluntary export restraint (1955) and Japan–US cotton trade agreement (1957) Japan–US textile agreement (1972)
Mid-1960s–1970s	Steel	Japan–Europe–US agreement on voluntary export restraint (1969)
1960s–1970s	Color TVs	Japan–US orderly marketing agreement (1977)
1970s–1980s	Automobiles	Voluntary export restraint (1981)
Late 1970s–1980s	Semi-conductors	Japan–US semi-conductor agreement (1986)

Source: Kanagawa (1987, 1989) and Matsuzaki (1988)

Deregulation and Urban Redevelopment Attracted a Policy Focus

Under the circumstances, from the first half of the 1980s, deregulation and urban redevelopment started to be considered as an effective tool, compatible with fiscal consolidation to stimulate domestic demand.

PM Nakasone, who took office in 1982, focused on deregulation and mobilization of private sector vitality ("Minkatsu"), and particularly emphasized urban redevelopment ("Urban Renaissance"). In February 1983, PM Nakasone instructed the Ministry of Construction to ease land regulations, so as to make it possible for the private sector to build high rises in the center of metropolitan areas.[13] Also, in January 1983, the government decided to make use of government-owned land for urban redevelopment and housing supply, and subsequently sold a substantial amount of land in central Tokyo for rather high prices (which was later criticized as spurring the land prices hike and was suspended in 1987).[14]

Land-Related Projects Gained Attention Under the "Minkatsu" Policy

Under such policy developments, around 1983–1984, reporting began to describe a fierce race for land acquisition, financed by financial institutions and under way by small local real estate agents in the very center of Tokyo, with the aim of reselling them at a higher prices.[15]

[13] Komine (2011a, 112)
[14] Komine (2011a, 115–17)
[15] Komine (2011a, 123–4) quotes a writing by an ex-official of the Ministry of Construction,

In May 1985, the National Land Agency released "The Capital Remodeling Plan," which stated that demand for office space in central Tokyo in 2000 was estimated to be 8,700 ha, a 5,000 ha increase (equivalent to 250 high rises) over the 3,700 ha in 1985. This estimate was later criticized as inflaming the land price hike.[16]

Adjustment of the Exchange Rates

Despite these policies, the US current account deficit continued to expand, and Japan's policy efforts gradually shifted toward acceptance of exchange rate adjustments.

Behind this policy shift was a substantial appreciation of the US dollar in the first half of the 1980s. In the early years of the first term of the Reagan administration, the United States took a fundamentalist market (no intervention) approach to the surging dollar. In 1983, a report (referred to as the "Solomon Report," after the name of one of its authors), commissioned by the chairman of Caterpillar, Inc., was circulated in the United States; and the report argued for the need for financial liberalization in Japan and internationalization of the yen, with a view to correcting the yen–dollar exchange rates. In May 1984, the Yen–Dollar Committee, which was established by the Japanese Ministry of Finance and the US Treasury in the previous year, released a report filled with many financial deregulation commitments by Japan, as demanded by the Solomon Report. However, such measures did not have immediate impacts on the yen–dollar exchange rate, and therefore, did not contribute to a significant correction of the trade imbalance between the two countries.

The United States and Japan moved forward to the Plaza Accord

From around the end of 1984 to 1985, under rising protectionist pressure, the United States apparently sought a downward adjustment of the dollar (or upward adjustment of non-US dollar currencies), although its official stance was to regard the strong dollar as reflecting confidence in the US economy and bringing about benefits that included price stability.

In January 1985, the G5 released a public statement for the first time in which it considered the possibility of intervention in the foreign

who interviewed 20 local real estate agents that were actively buying land in the center of Tokyo. He wrote that out of 20 agents, only one mentioned the intended use of the land that it purchased, suggesting that they were buying land to resell at higher prices.

[16] However, in 2000, the size of office space in the central Tokyo turned out to be 8000 ha, not very far from the projection (Komine 2011a, 284).

exchange market to stabilize the exchange rate. In February 1985, coordinated intervention by Japan and the United States was conducted to contain further appreciation of the dollar.

In June 1985, in a meeting between Finance Minister Takeshita and US Treasury Secretary Baker, Takeshita proposed coordinated intervention in the foreign exchange markets, while Baker requested expansion of domestic demand. Also in June 1985, PM Nakasone met with Secretary Baker on the currency issue, and Nakasone is reported to have decided to accept the appreciation yen at that time.[17]

The Plaza Accord Achieved and the Yen Started to Have a Dramatic Appreciation

On September 22, 1985, at the G5 meeting, which took place in the Plaza Hotel in New York, released an agreement (the Plaza Accord), which stated, "some further orderly appreciation of the main non-dollar currencies against the dollar is desirable" in conjunction with policy commitments by each participating country. It has been reported that there was an agreement among the G5 to aim for 10–12%[18] depreciation of the dollar in the near future, written in a "non-paper" that was submitted to a preparatory meeting as a paper existing as non-existent.[19] Once coordinated intervention started, adjustment of exchange rates proceeded far beyond such a target, and the yen appreciated from 240 yen to the dollar on September 20, 1985, to 200 yen by the end of 1985, and further to below 180 yen in March 1986. The yen continued to appreciate to a record 159 yen in December 1986, and to 124 yen in December 1987, almost doubling its value against the US dollar in just a little more than two years (Fig. 2.13).

Structural Transformation of the Japanese Economy and Eased Macroeconomic Policy

Structural Reform of Japan's Economy—A Plan to Transform Japan's Economy to a Domestic Demand-led One Was Proposed and Restraint of Further Yen Appreciation Sought.

While the exchange rate adjustments were under way, another strand of thought was proposed that sought to transform the Japanese economy to

[17] Komine (2011a, 148)
[18] See Funabashi (1988) and Kondo (1999).
[19] See Funabashi (1988, 28–9). It has not been made publicly available yet.

Fig. 2.13 Yen–dollar exchange rate (monthly average) 1980–1989. Source: Bank of Japan

a domestic demand-led one. Also, the overshooting of the exchange rate adjustments motivated Japan's attempts to halt further yen appreciation, which, under the efforts by Finance Minister Miyazawa, led to the Louvre Accord for exchange rate stabilization.

As for the orientation toward transforming the economy to a domestic demand-led one, in October 1985, PM Nakasone convened a private study group headed by the previous Bank of Japan (BOJ) governor, Mr. Maekawa, to examine structural problems in the area of international economic relations and to formulate a medium- and long-term design of Japan's society and economy, which would be in harmony with international economies. This action was apparently prompted by the concern over the rising protectionist pressures in the United States.

In April 1986, the study group submitted a report ("Maekawa Report"), which included the following contentions:

- The large external imbalance has come to a critical phase, and we have set a national goal to reduce it to an internationally compatible level.

- The large current account deficit has its root in our economic structure, including its export orientation.
- In order to realize an internationally compatible economy, we have to realize a domestic demand-led economic growth and fundamentally change the structure of imports and exports and industries.

The essence of these contentions were included in subsequent reports of formal governmental advisory committees.

In Parallel with a Reform Proposal of the Japanese Economy, Attempts to Arrest Further Yen Appreciation Conducted

Finance Minister Miyazawa, who took over after Takeshita, who was involved in the Plaza Accord, was critical of the Accord and endeavored to establish an agreement for exchange rate stabilization among the G7, and an agreement was released on February 22, 1987 (Louvre Accord). The Accord stated as follows:

> "The Ministers and Governors agreed that the substantial exchange rate changes since the Plaza Agreement ... have now brought their currencies within ranges broadly consistent with underlying economic fundamentals .... In current circumstances, therefore, they agreed to cooperate closely to foster stability of exchange rates around current levels."

In the Accord, Japan promised to "follow monetary and fiscal policies which will help to expand domestic demand and thereby contribute to reducing the external surplus."

Influence of These Efforts on Macroeconomic Policy

These two factors, that is, the idea to transform the economy to a domestic demand-led economy and an attempt to halt further yen appreciation, set a framework for policy formulation in the late 1980s. This was particularly true in the area of monetary policy, as indicated by continuation of substantial monetary easing. Let us look at developments in monetary policy.

Interest Rate Reduced but Kept Relatively High in the First Half of the 1980s

Monetary policy was tightened from the beginning of 1979 to control inflationary pressure during the second oil crisis (discount rate was raised five times, by a total of 5.5%, to reach 9.0% in March 1980). As the economy started to slow down from around the spring of 1980, monetary policy was eased gradually from August 1980, and the discount rate came down to 5.5% in December 1981. The economy started to recover, led by export growth in the spring of 1983, and the monetary policy was broadly unchanged. Although reduced to 5.0% in October 1983, interest rates were kept high due to the high overseas interest rates (the US interest rate was exceptionally high at around 10–14% throughout the first half of 1980s), and concerns for the further yen depreciation.

Monetary Policy Significantly Eased Further in the Latter Half of the 1980s

With the slowing down of the economy due to the sharp yen appreciation after the Plaza Accord, an economic policy package for domestic-demand expansion through the maximum use of private sector vitality was adopted in October 1985. Furthermore, the discount rate was reduced five times from January 1986 to reach the historic low of 2.5% in February 1987, where it stayed until May 1989, when it was raised for the first time in the preceding nine years (Fig. 2.14). This most eased monetary environment was maintained during the peak of the bubble.

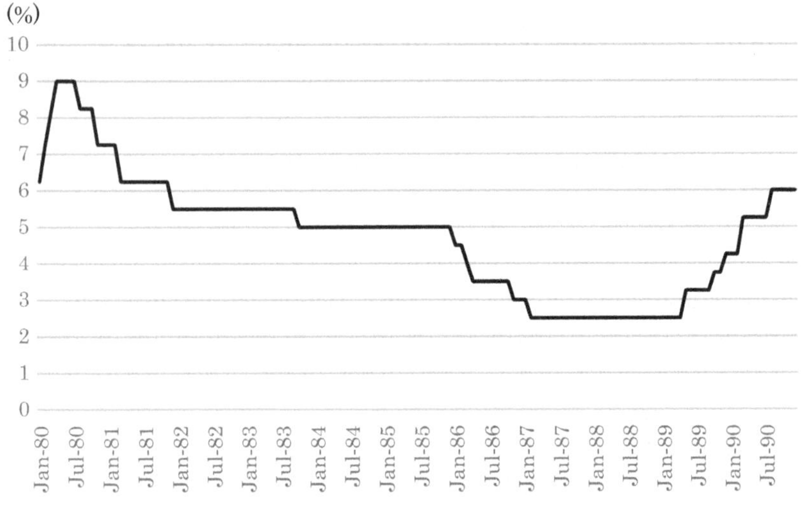

Fig. 2.14 Official discount rate: Japan 1980–1990. Source: Bank of Japan

Background for the Eased Monetary Policy over an Extended Period of Time

Why was the discount rate lowered to the historic low, and why did it stay there for more than two years in the latter half of 1980s? Table 2.5 shows how each instance of monetary easing was explained by the BOJ.

Distinct Characteristics Observed in BOJ's Explanations

There are some very distinctive characteristics that are observed in the explanations of the BOJ. First is that concerns over domestic economic conditions are stated, but they do not to play a major role in explaining BOJ's monetary policy decisions. Second is that the following three factors (all external) seem to be given crucial consideration instead:[20]

① Correction of external imbalances through expansion of domestic demand,
② Intention to halt further appreciation of the yen, and
③ Efforts for international coordination of macroeconomic policy.

Fiscal Measures Implemented in the Latter Half of the 1980s

On the fiscal policy side, stimulus packages were compiled, and fiscal consolidation efforts were finally halted in the late 1980s. In addition to the package in October 1985, mentioned before, in April and September 1986, packages of economic measures were compiled under the still growing current account surplus, which was due possibly to the J-curve effects and slowing down of the economy by yen appreciation (although it was later confirmed that the economy had hit bottom in November 1986). However, still in April 1987, President Reagan announced an imposition of a sanction tariff on certain imports from Japan in the face of growing criticism in the United States directed toward Japan, and in May 1987, a large economic measure with a project size amounting to 6 trillion yen was announced by Japan.

Other Policy Measures

Other policy measures implemented in this period during the aforementioned policy orientation shift toward a domestic demand-led economy included the enactment of laws to promote development of specific facilities or resorts, particularly in local areas.

In 1986, a law (the so-called Minkatsu law) was enacted to promote development of facilities and buildings, such as research centers, information facili-

[20] For such observations, see Okina, Shirakawa, and Shiratsuka (2002).

Table 2.5 BOJ's explanation of monetary policy changes in the late 1980s

Date of policy changes	*Contents of the change*	*Explanation by the BOJ*
January 30, 1986	5.0%→4.5%	The measure is expected to promote expansion of domestic demand and to contribute to correction of external imbalances through lowering the interest rate. The BOJ will continue to pay sufficient attention to the exchange rate developments. (Statement by the chairman of policy committee)
March 10, 1986	4.5%→4.0%	This reduction was decided particularly with the stabilization of exchange rate in mind (BOJ Governor Sumita (*Nihon Keizai Shinbun*, March 9, 1986)) (Note: This reduction was part of internationally coordinated reduction of the interest rate with US and West Germany, announced on the same day.)
April 21, 1986	4.0%→3.5%	BOJ hopes that this step will contribute to the further stabilization of the yen rate and the expansion of domestic demand and the correction of external imbalances (BOJ press release, April 19, 1986) (Note: The Federal Reserve Board (FRB) announced a reduction of discount rate on April 18.)
November 1, 1986	3.5%→3.0%	BOJ judged a further reduction in interest rate will be effective in stimulating domestic demand. It strongly hopes that the exchange rates will be stabilized (BOJ press release, October 31, 1986) (Note: Governor Sumita later acknowledged that he received a telephone call from Finance Minister Miyazawa, who was in US to meet with US Treasury Secretary Baker, and was informed of US' implicit request for a discount rate cut by BOJ. The joint statement by Miyazawa and Baker was released on the day of discount rate cut.)
February 23, 1987	3.0%→2.5%	A further appreciation of the yen may strengthen deflationary pressure on the economy and jeopardize achieving our country's fundamental policy of correcting external imbalances through domestic demand expansion and structural adjustment (BOJ press release, February 20, 1987) Governor Sumita said that this cut was determined by placing the most importance on the stabilization of the exchange rate (*Nihon Keizai Shinbun*, February 21, 1987) (Note: On the following day of the BOJ's release, G7 announced an agreement (Louvre Accord) to stabilize the exchange rates around the current levels.)

Source: Tabulated by the author, based on Komine (2011a, pp. 156–181)

ties, and international conference arenas by private sectors. One hundred eighty-seven projects were approved, about 80% of which were undertaken by entities funded by both private sector and local governments. Many of these entities later met with difficulties or faced with bankruptcy.

Furthermore, in 1987, a law (the so-called Resort Law) was enacted to promote development of resort facilities. Forty-two area projects submitted by 41 prefectures (i.e., regional governments) out of a total of 47 prefectures were approved, most of which planned to build facilities for skiing, golfing, and marine sports. Actual construction work for many of them began in 1991, when the economy started to stagnate, and in more than a few cases, projects were abandoned or went bankrupt.[21]

Rapid Expansion of Assets Held by Companies

Behaviors of economic agents significantly changed under these circumstances. This is particularly true with the corporate sector. Let us briefly see how the corporate sector changed, as evidenced in their financial statements compiled over the period.

Expansion of Physical Assets Held by Companies

Under such policy developments, there emerged a significant change in the corporate sector. Figures 2.15 and 2.16, respectively, show land and physical assets (excluding land) held by profit-making companies (excluding financial and insurance companies) that existed in Japan, with division into manufacturing and non-manufacturing industries. Both figures indicate that land and physical asset holdings were sharply expanded from the mid-1980s, and the expansion was far more significant in non-manufacturing industries than in manufacturing industries.

Figure 2.17 shows developments in the amount of physical assets (excluding land) held by four non-manufacturing industries (construction, transportation and postal services, wholesale and retail, and real estate), which were among major holders of such assets.[22] Physical assets include buildings, machinery, and equipment. From the figure, it is

[21] Komine (2011a, 118, 213, 232).

[22] The combined share in the total amount of physical assets of non-manufacturing industries held by these four industries accounted for 57% as of 1990, 6.1% for construction, 18.8% for transportation and postal services, 18.1% for wholesale and retail, and 14.1% for real estate. Major holders of physical assets, other than these four sectors as of 1990, are electricity (17.3%), entertainment (5.2%), and advertising (10.8%).

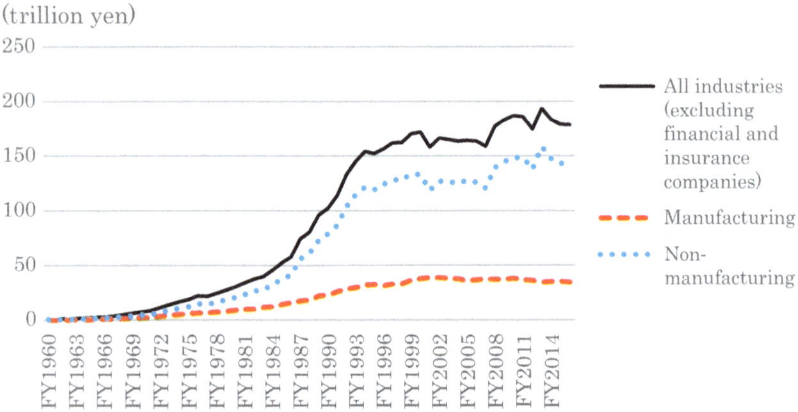

Fig. 2.15 Land holdings by all industries (excluding financial and insurance companies) and their breakdown between manufacturing and non-manufacturing sectors. Source: Ministry of Finance, "Financial Statements Statistics of Corporations by Industry"

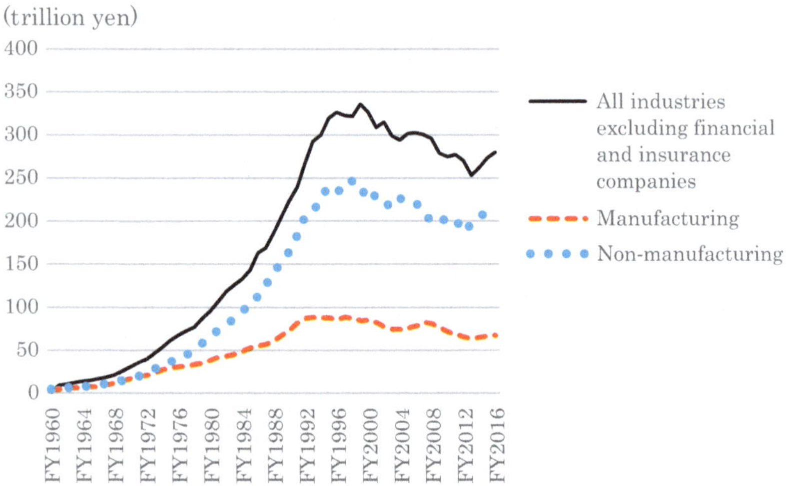

Fig. 2.16 Physical assets (excluding land) held by all industries (excluding financial and insurance companies) and their breakdown between manufacturing and non-manufacturing sectors. Source: Ministry of Finance "Financial Statements Statistics of Corporations by Industry"

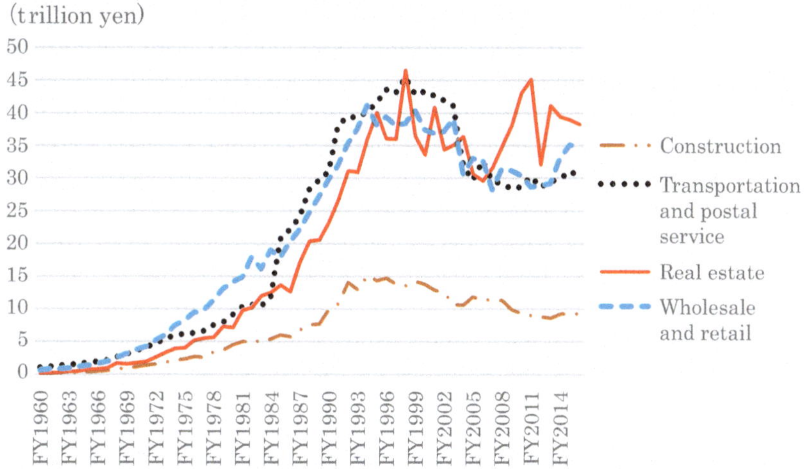

Fig. 2.17 Physical assets (excluding land) held by four major non-manufacturing industries. Source: Ministry of Finance, "Financial Statements Statistics of Corporations by Industry"

implied that real estate-related projects were actively undertaken by non-manufacturing industries from the mid-1980s. It should be noted that the expansion of physical assets continued until the first half of the 1990s, probably due to the time lag between planning and construction that was inherent in development projects.

What we have seen thus far indicates that companies in Japan, particularly those in the non-manufacturing sector, developed a gigantic stock of physical assets, including real estate-related ones. The level of these stocks turned out to be unsustainable and excessive, as was indicated by the fact that the levels continued to decline subsequently for the long period of time from the latter half of the 1990s. After the bubble period, the corporate sector was left with huge excessive assets.[23]

Economic Policy Management by the Government in the 1980s

The government's response to the two constraints in macroeconomic policy management may be summarized as follows.

[23] A detailed analysis of the balance sheets of the corporate sector is given in Chap. 6.

In the 1980s, policies were bound by two constraints, that is, external friction with the United States and fiscal deterioration, with the former playing the dominant role. In early years, efforts to cope with these two constraints through deregulation and "Minkatsu," particularly in the form of urban redevelopment promotion, apparently sowed a seed for subsequent land price hikes.

Under the extreme intensification of friction with the United States in the mid-1980s, Japan chose exchange rate adjustments, while the United States preferred domestic demand expansion. Furthermore, the then administration of Japan set as a medium- to long-term goal the transformation of Japan into an economy led by domestic demand to correct external imbalances, thus gradually shifting the focus of economic policy from domestic economic issues to solutions for external disputes. In the meantime, a serious domestic problem—the formation of a huge bubble—was in progress.

In parallel, Japan made efforts to halt further appreciation of the yen. Such efforts and the policy orientation toward a domestic demand-led economy apparently constrained macroeconomic policy management, which is responsible for the stabilization of the domestic economy, and led to a series of instances of monetary policy easing and then fiscal expansions, aggravating asset price inflation into the late 1980s. In this situation, the corporate sector acquired hugely excessive assets.

What Was Wrong with Economic Policy Handling in the 1980s?

From the foregoing examination, it is apparent that the economic policy management in the 1980s had unfavorable consequences, that is, contributing to the formation of a huge bubble. What was wrong then, and what should have been done?

In order to see what was wrong with economic policy handling in the 1980s, we need answers to the following questions:

Q1 What caused US external deficits?
Q2 What caused Japan's external surplus?

And after trying to answer these questions, we seek the answer to what should (could) have been done by Japan under the circumstances.

What Caused the Dramatic Expansion of US External Deficits in the 1980s?

With slogans such as "Strong America," and "Small Government," Reagan, who was elected in the previous year, assumed the presidency in 1981.

Reagan submitted his "Economic Recovery Plan," composed of (1) large-scale tax cuts to promote investment and to promote savings by medium- and high-income households that have high saving ratios; (2) expenditure cuts to avoid absorption by the government of increased savings by households; (3) deregulation; and (4) stable monetary policy. These policies were soon called Reaganomics.

The outcome of the Reaganomics was not quite what was initially expected or hoped for. Investment surged, but the household savings ratio followed a declining trend, due to falling inflation and unemployment rates and active stock markets, all stimulating consumption. Revenue fell short of projections due to lower than expected growth performance, and expenditure cuts were not achieved as planned due to the expansion of defense expenditure ("peace through strength") and continued expansion of social security expenditures, producing a deepening fiscal deficit.

An investment surge, coupled with a decreased savings ratio and deepening fiscal deficits, brought about an increasing excess of investment over savings (increased use of foreign savings to finance excess domestic investment), that is, expanding external deficits.[24]

At the same time, tight monetary policy from the end of 1970s to the beginning of 1980s brought about high interest rates that attracted capital inflows and a surging dollar.

These policies created huge external deficits on top of the fiscal deficit ("twin deficits").

[24] The IS balance approach to current account determination may be helpful in capturing this process.

We have a national account identity:

$$Y = Cp + Ip + Cg + Ig + X - M, \qquad (24.1)$$

Where Y = GDP, Cp = private consumption, Ip = private investment, Cg = government consumption, Ig = government investment, X=export, M = import

Using T for Tax and rearranging the identity, we have:

$$\{(Y - T - Cp) - Ip\} + (T - Cg) - Ig = X - M, \qquad (24.2)$$

i.e., (private savings – private investment) (= investment/savings balance of the private sector) + (government savings-government Investment) (= investment/savings balance of the government sector) = external balance. The combined savings/investment balance of private and government sectors moved to excess investment in the United States under Reaganomics, producing a huge external deficit.

Figure 2.18 shows developments in the savings/investment balance of the government sector and the current account balance. We can see that these two balances moved largely in a synchronized way during most of the 1980s, indicating that the expanding current account deficits were basically an internal US problem.

What Caused Japan's Expanding External Surplus in the 1980s?

Next, let us look at what brought about Japan's external surplus from the beginning of the 1980s. Three factors seem to have been relevant.

Dollar Appreciation

The US dollar appreciated substantially under a policy combination of stable monetary policy and expansionary fiscal policy. The nominal yen rate against the dollar was kept fairly low for the first half of the 1980s (see Fig. 2.13).

As the inflation rate was higher in the United States than in Japan in the 1980s (Fig. 2.19), the yen rate in real effective terms was fairly low, despite expanding external surpluses throughout the first half of 1980s, contributing to the continuation of current account imbalances (Fig. 2.20).

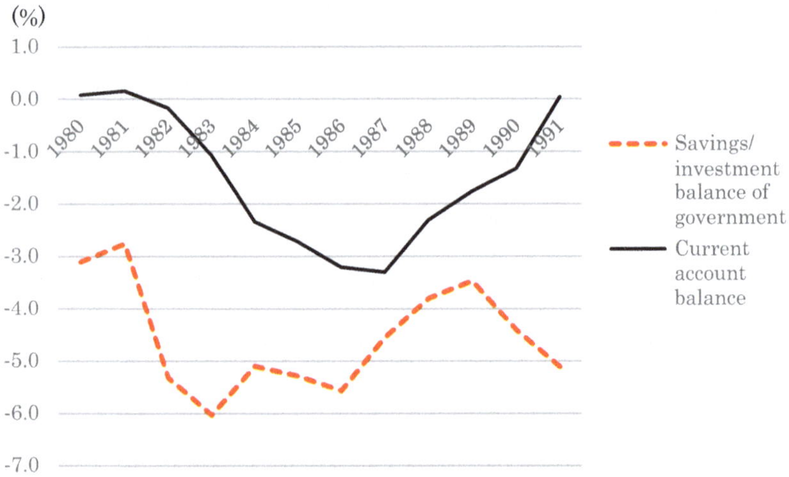

Fig. 2.18 Savings/investment balance of the government sector and current account balance (both in GDP ratio): US. Source: BEA; US government; IMF, "World Economic Outlook Database, October 2015"

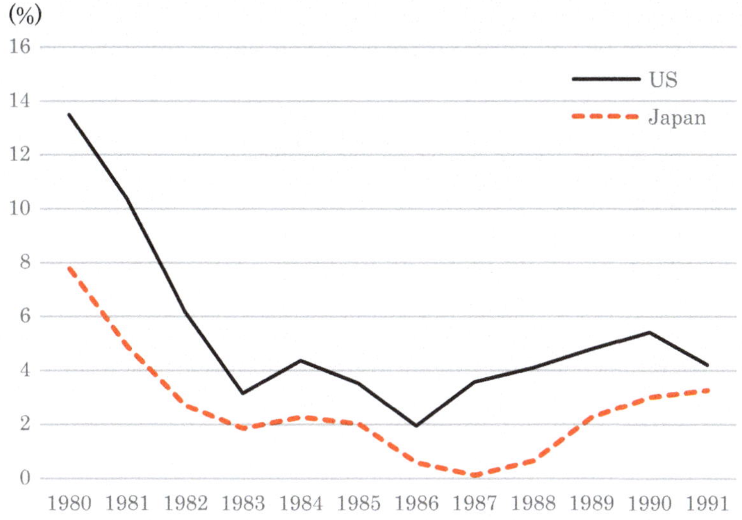

Fig. 2.19 Consumer Price Index (year-on-year change): US and Japan. Source: IMF, World Economic Outlook database October 2015

Fig. 2.20 Real effective exchange rate of the yen (2010 = 100), 1970–1990. Source: Bank of Japan

Difference in the Economic Cycles

Another factor behind Japan's current account surplus was a difference in the economic cycles of the two countries. The real GDP growth rate of the United States exceeded that of Japan in 1983 and 1984, as seen in Fig. 2.21, contributing to the expansion of Japan's exports.

Decline in Oil Prices

The third factor for Japan's current account surplus was the decline in oil prices. Oil prices started to fall at the beginning of the 1980s, significantly reducing Japan's import bills (Fig. 2.22).

The *Nenji Keizai Hokoku* (Annual Economic Report) FY 1984, prepared by the Economic Planning Agency, estimated that most of the increase in Japan's current account surplus of 15.1 billion US dollars from fiscal year 1982 to fiscal year 1983 could be explained by three factors: the fall in oil prices, the difference in the cyclical phase between Japan and the United States, and the exchange rate, as shown in Table 2.6.

If the deterioration in the US current account balance was basically a problem that had been created internally and if Japan's expanding current

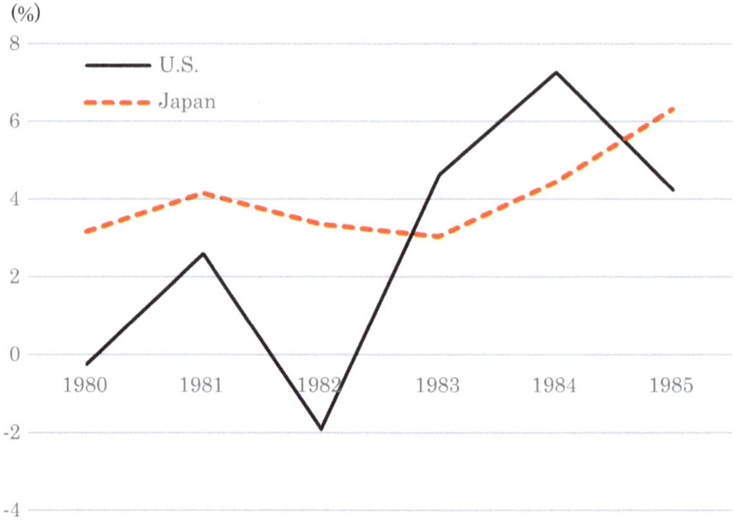

Fig. 2.21 Real GDP growth rate: US and Japan, 1980–1985. Source: IMF, World Economic Outlook database October 2015

Fig. 2.22 Crude oil prices (Dubai, in dollar per barrel), 1965–1999. Source: IMF, "International Financial Statistics" ("IFS")

Table 2.6 Factor analysis of Japan's current account surplus (estimate) (in 100 million US dollars)

	FY 1982	*FY 1983*	*Change*
Current account surplus (actual)	91	242	+151
Special factor (oil price)	37	64	+27
Cyclical factor	−72	45	+117
of which Domestic demand factor in Japan	40	55	+15
Domestic demand factor in US	−173	−135	+38
Exchange rate	61	125	+64
(Residual)	126	133	+7

Source: *Nenji Keizai Hokoku* FY1984 (Annual Economic Report), Economic Planning Agency

account surplus was mainly due to external factors (expansion of the US economy, appreciation of the US dollar, and the decline in oil prices), it follows that what should have been corrected was not Japan's policy but the US policy. Therefore, in terms of economics, Japan should not have responded to the US request to correct trade surplus.

Assuming that were the case, let us examine what Japan could have done to reduce its external imbalances if it was still considered appropriate (from a non-economic viewpoint) to respond to the US demand.

Table 2.7 GDP growth rate and private investment (year-on-year change, period average): 1956–1973, 1974–1984, 1985–1990 (%)

	1956–1973	*1974–1984*	*1985–1990*
Real GDP growth rate	9.3	3.3	4.6
Private investment in plants and equipment	17.3	3.0	10.4

Source: Cabinet Office

First, let us see if Japan could have increased private investment in plants and equipment (in this book, the words "private investment" and "private investment in plants and equipment" are used interchangeably). It is true that the rate of growth of private investment in plants and equipment slowed down markedly in the 1980s, as compared with the 1970s, as shown in Table 2.7.

Why did private investment in plants and equipment slow down? The answer may be found in the reduction in GDP growth rate from the time of the first oil crisis. If the GDP growth rate is expected to fall, then the level of private investment in plants and equipment relative to GDP may fall if companies invest in such a way as to maintain more or less a constant capital/output ratio, thereby depressing investment growth.[25]

[25] Assume that companies invest in plants and equipment so as to keep the capital–output ratio (K/Y) constant (a) under the expected GDP growth rate (ge) and also assume for the sake of simplicity there is no disposition of assets, then we have:

$$\mathrm{K} / \mathrm{Y} = \Delta K / \Delta Y = \mathrm{I} / \Delta Y = \mathrm{a}, \tag{25-1}$$

where K = capital stock, Y = GDP, I = private investment in plants and equipment

$$\Delta Y / \mathrm{Y} = \mathrm{ge} \tag{25-2}$$

From Eqs. (25.1) and (25.2):

$$\mathrm{I} / \Delta Y = \mathrm{I} / \left(\mathrm{Y} \times \mathrm{ge}\right) = \mathrm{a} \tag{25-3}$$

So, we have:

$$\mathrm{I} / \mathrm{Y} = \mathrm{a} \times \mathrm{ge} \tag{25-4}$$

The decline of the share of private investment in plants and equipment in GDP appears to reflect the reduction in expected growth rate, which may well follow actual growth performance, after the end of high economic growth, as shown in Fig. 2.23. If this is true, then Japan could not realistically expect the growth rate of private investment in plants and equipment to rise under the declining GDP growth rate.

Then, could we have increased government expenditure? In reality, the substantial expansion of government expenditure offset the decline in private investment from the latter half of the 1970s to the first half of the 1980s (Fig. 2.24). This action alone, however, could not have eliminated the growing external imbalances, and instead brought about another problem, that is, deterioration of the fiscal position.

Could we have increased consumption? In reality, as the economic growth slowed down, the share of consumption in real GDP, which was once over 60% in the mid-1970s, consistently declined on average to 59.7% in the second half of the 1970s, to 58.5% in the first half of the 1980s, and to 57.8% in the second half of the 1980s. If a shift to a domestic demand-led economy, as was proposed by the Maekawa Report, was to be materialized, increase in consumption level was needed. However, in reality, consumption seems to have been a passive component of the economy in Japan, and it is not clear if it can be an engine of economic growth.[26]

That is, the share of private investment in plants and equipment in GDP has positive correlation with the expected GDP growth rate, i.e., if the expected GDP growth rate falls, then the share of private investment in GDP also falls.

Relaxing the unrealistic assumption of zero disposal of assets, let us assume that the amount of disposed assets (D) is a fraction (b) of capital stock ($D = bK$). Then, $\Delta K = I - bK$, and therefore, Eq. (25.4) changes into

$$I / Y = a(ge + b) \tag{25-5}$$

So, basically, the same argument applies even under this formulation.

[26] As an argument for a need to enhance consumption in Japan, see Katz (1999). Whether we can raise growth contribution of consumption in a sustainable manner is an unanswered question even now, 30 years after the bubble period (see Chap. 7 for this point).

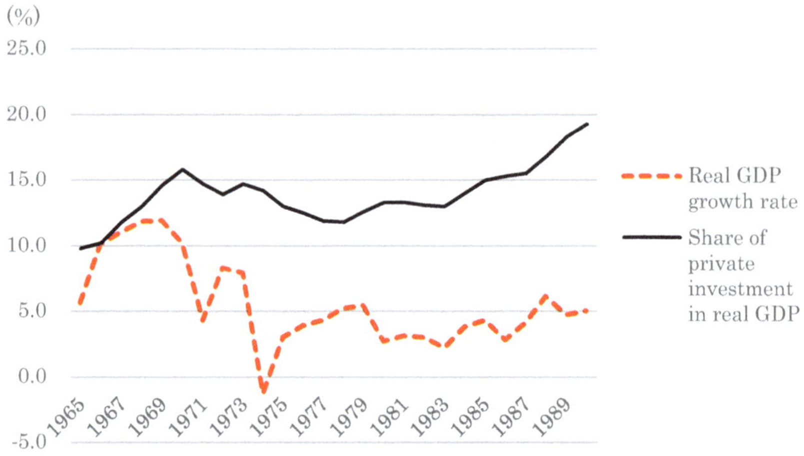

Fig. 2.23 Real GDP growth rate and share of private investment in plants and equipment in real GDP. Source: Cabinet Office

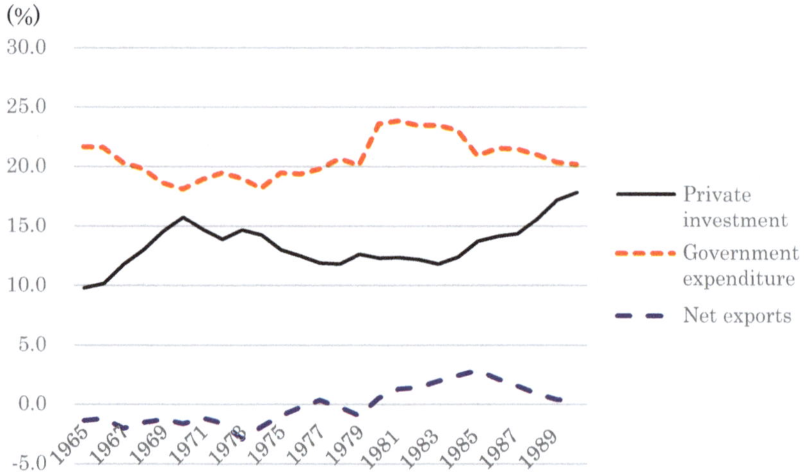

Fig. 2.24 Share in real GDP of private investment in plants and equipment, government expenditure, and net exports: Japan 1965–1990. Source: Cabinet Office

The examination thus far of the situation that prevailed at that time indicates, first, that it was becoming difficult to expect a rapid increase in private investment in plants and equipment after the end of the high-growth era with the slowing down of the growth rate, and, second, that, in light of the deteriorating fiscal position, it also became difficult to further expand government expenditures that had already been expanded to make up for the decline in the growth contribution by private investment. It is questionable whether private consumption, a major remaining component of domestic demand, could have become a driver of growth when the rate of economic growth was decelerating and the share of private consumption in GDP was declining after the two oil crises and subsequent recession.

If this were the case, it might have been difficult from the beginning to drastically reduce external imbalances (current account surpluses) that had been largely exogenously created, through expansion of domestic demand on the side of Japan.[27] It is possible that, in the process of politically pursuing goals difficult to achieve economically from the outset, serious problems emerged in the management of relevant economic policies.[28]

Bank Behavior under Financial Liberalization

In this subsection, we will look at the second factor that may have been responsible for the formation of the bubble, that is, the bank behavior under financial liberalization. As shown in Table 2.8, real estate-related loans by banks significantly increased from around the mid-1980s.

[27] There may well be an argument that adjustments in the exchange rate or liberalization of domestic markets will contribute to correcting external imbalances through changes in exports and imports. However, effectiveness of the market opening depends largely on reactions of companies and households and is therefore uncertain. Adjustments in foreign exchange rates were actually implemented, and the external imbalance of both Japan and the United States declined. As is shown in Fig. 2.18, however, the decline in current account deficits of the United States took place in conjunction with the decline in the size of excess investment in investment/savings balance, implying that the US external imbalance was a domestically driven phenomenon after all.

[28] It may be said that this is an outcome of external consideration taking precedence over the stabilization of the domestic economy and society, given the circumstances that Japan depends on a foreign country for its national security.

Table 2.8 Developments in real estate-related loans by banks (%, trillion yen)

	Outstanding loan balance as of end fiscal year						*Average rate of increase from FY 1985 to 1989*
	1984	*1985*	*1986*	*1987*	*1988*	*1989*	
Total outstanding amount of loans	229.3 (100)	249.6 (100)	273.3 (100)	297.6 (100)	322.3 (100)	356.8 (100)	9.2
Real estate sector	17.4 (7.6)	22.2 (8.9)	30.2 (11.1)	33.5 (11.3)	37.3 (11.7)	43.3 (12.1)	19.9
Non-bank financial institutions	23.2 (10.2)	29.6 (11.9)	36.9 (13.5)	45.1 (15.2)	50.9 (15.8)	59.6 (16.7)	20.7

Source: Fiscal and Monetary Research Institute, Ministry of Finance, Japanese Government (1993)

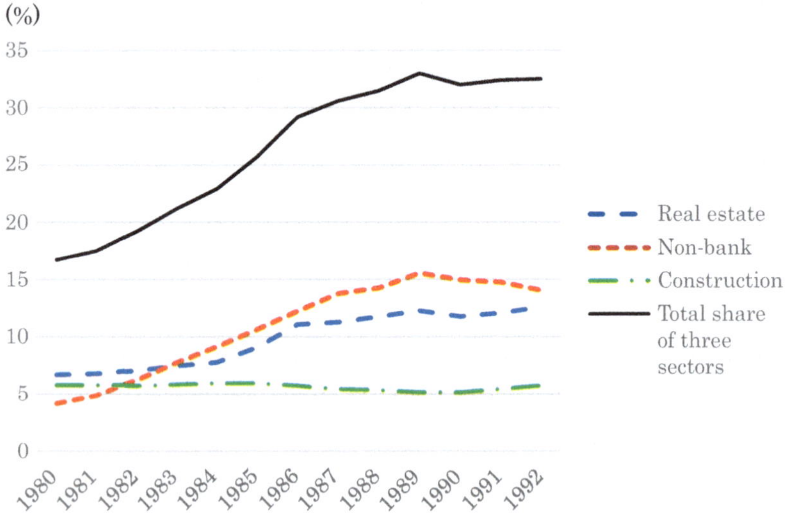

Fig. 2.25 Share of loans to three real estate-related sectors in total outstanding loans. Source: Tabulated based on Komine (2011a, 77)

Figure 2.25 shows that the shares held by three real estate-related sectors (real estate, non-bank financial institutions, and construction) in total loans significantly increased from the first half of 1980s.

We need to determine why banks increased real estate-related loans in this period. Behind such behaviors, there were two pressures at work. First was the erosion of the traditional client base of banks (particularly, big manufacturing companies). This was due to such factors as the decline in investment needs of companies with the end of high-speed growth era, accumulation of their own funds, and financial liberalization that had made financing through capital markets easier, particularly for big companies. Second was the shrinking profit margin of banks, also due to financial liberalization, which had made competition harder for banks in both funding and lending markets. These factors pushed banks to new profitable markets, including real estate-related loans, longer term loans, and loans to medium- and small-sized companies and individuals.

Let us look at these factors in some more detail.

Declining Dependence of Companies on Borrowing from Financial Institutions

Dependence of manufacturing companies on borrowing from financial institutions started to decline from the mid-1970s under "downsizing" with the transition from high-speed growth to the stable growth after the oil crises (Table 2.9). Financial institutions were faced with the erosion of an important client base.

Decline of Profit Margins of Banks under Financial Liberalization

Japan's financial system after the war was characterized by, one, control of deposit interest rates and, two, the specialized financial institutions system, under which securities and banking, and short-term and long-term lending, were separately conducted by different groups of financial institutions (by banks and securities companies and by commercial banks and long-term credit banks, respectively).

Table 2.9 Dependence of manufacturing companies on borrowing from financial institutions (%)

End of FY	*1975*	*1976*	*1977*	*1978*	*1979*	*1989*
Dependence on borrowing	38.4	37.8	37.4	36.1	32.5	25.2
Dependence on long-term borrowing	21.4	21.4	20.6	19.2	15.8	11.7

Note: Dependence on borrowing = long-term and short-term borrowings/total financing

Source: Tabulated from data from the Fiscal and Monetary Research Institute, Ministry of Finance, Japan (1993)

Control on deposit interest rates provided stability to the management of banks, particularly small- and medium-sized banks, because as long as these banks could collect deposits (at a low interest rate), they could profitably provide those funds to big commercial banks, which in turn lent the funds to big companies, short of funds under high-speed growth. The branching regulation, under which the opening of new branches were controlled by the authorities, also helped this mechanism (the system was sometimes called the "Convoy system"). From around the latter half of 1970s, liberalization progressed, however, and this system started to change. Driving forces were, first, deterioration of the fiscal position (again), and, second, liberalization of controls on international capital flows.

Deterioration of the Fiscal Position

Deterioration of the Fiscal Position Forced Liberalization of Interest Rates.

With the deterioration of the fiscal position, beginning around the mid-1970s, the government started issuing a large amount of government bonds Japanese Government Bonds (JGBs). Previously, all the JGBs were held by financial institutions and resale was regulated (sold to BOJ), and therefore, there was no secondary market. However, as banks could not continue to hold large amounts of JGBs with low interest, resale regulation was relaxed in 1977, and a secondary market was created, that is, a product with a liberalized interest rate became available. As most of JGBs that had been issued were 10-year bonds, banks worried that JGBs with liberalized interest rates, maturing in two years, would come into the market in 1983 (i.e., eight years after the start of large issuance), and that regulated two-year time deposits would lose competitiveness in the markets and a large outflow of funds from these deposits could occur.

Given the banks' worries, products with liberalized interest rates were allowed, but these changes eventually squeezed the banks' profit margins. In 1979, Certificates of Deposit (CDs, i.e., transferrable deposits of large amounts) with liberalized interest rates were allowed. In 1985, the interest rate on large amount deposit was liberalized.

The share of deposits with liberalized interest rates in the amount of banks' total funding sharply increased from 7.5% at the end of FY1984 to 53.4% at the end of FY1989,[29] squeezing the banks' profit margins. Banks

[29] Ministry of Finance (1993).

sought business providing high profits in new markets, such as small- and medium-sized enterprises (SMEs), individuals, and real estate-related loans.

Liberalization of International Capital Flows
Another Driving Force Was the Relaxation of International Capital Controls.

The 1980 reform of the Foreign Exchange Law, in principle, liberalized cross-border capital transactions. The "real demand rule" for forward foreign exchange transactions, which had required underlying facts such as trade contracts, was abolished in 1984, in the negotiations of the Yen–Dollar Committee with the United States, making hedging of exchange rate risks far easier. Companies raised funds overseas by issuing securities, avoiding regulated domestic markets, and placing another competitive pressure on interest rates of loans by banks.

"Tochi Shinwa" (Mythical Trust in Landholding)
Under these circumstances, banks turned toward high-profit, and seemingly, low-risk real estate-related loans. Entering the securities business was not easy, given legal restrictions governing the separation of banks from securities businesses (Article 65 of the Securities Law, in principle, prohibited banks from engaging in the business of securities business, similar to the US Glass–Steagall regulation). Therefore, banks sought profit opportunities in lending to SMEs, long-term loans that were more profitable than short-term loans, and real estate-related loans. Banks had to rely on real estate collateral in lending to SMEs or real estate sectors, as their ability to collect information for these new clients was limited. Real estate-related loans were traditionally unfavored by banks, but "Tochi Shinwa" (mythical trust in landholding)[30] and strong profit orientation by some

[30] "Tochi Shinwa," which literally translated means "land myth," is a perception that there is no asset more profitable than land. This perception held well until 1980s. For example, an estimate is made that, although investment of 3 million yen in deposits in 1955 would have increased to 22.83 million yen in 1985, investment of the same amount in land in one of the six largest cities would have increased to 402 million yen, 17.6 times more in 1985 (Ministry of Finance 1993). Price of land continued to rise after the Second World War, with an exceptional fall in 1974, after the oil crisis. There had been land price surges twice (early 1960s and around 1972–73) after the war, but neither of them were later found to be a bubble. In the 1980s, the asset price surge was generally not considered as a bubble at that time. Noguchi (1992) counted the number of the articles that appeared in the media, such as *Nihon Keizai Shimbun,* which have the word "bubble" for each year from 1985 to 1992. He found that

banks and the spillovers to other banks helped spur this transformation of what had been a traditionally conservative business model for banks.[31]

"Zai-Tech" (Financing Technology)

Also notable is that companies engaged in financial activities. Active involvement in financial activities, called "Zai Teku" (financing technology), spread among companies, partly due to positive reporting by media. Companies raised more funds than necessary to invest in financial assets. From 1985 to 1989, while the net shortage of funds of the corporate sector as a whole was about 62 trillion yen, the sector raised as much as about 233 trillion yen, nearly four times as much as the shortage. Typically, they raised funds by Commercial Papers (CPs), or overseas issuance of equity-linked securities at low cost, and invested these funds in "large amount deposits", offered by banks with higher interest rates, or stocks through accounts managed by financial institutions.[32]

Summary

In this chapter, we have examined that the two factors that affected the formation of the bubble—economic policy management and bank behaviors in the 1980s. The trade disputes with the United States and the deterioration of the fiscal position imposed constraints on the management of economic policies in the 1980s.

Under these constraints, the government tried to stimulate the economy through deregulation, including urban redevelopment, which seems to

the number was 1–8 in each year from 1985 to 1988, 11 in 1989, the peak year of the bubble, 194 in 1990, and then a dramatic increase to 2,546 in 1991, and 3,475 in 1992. These numbers suggest the asset price developments started to be recognized as a bubble only after those prices had started to fall.

[31] In the 1980s, aggressive profit-seeking by banks was under way. One famous phrase that was spoken by the chairman of one of the biggest city banks in the early 1980s conveys well the thinking of the era; "Mukou Kizu ha Towanai" (literally, frontal scar will not bother). "Mukou Kizu" is a scar that one receives from a frontal assault, when fighting an enemy, while "Ushiro Kizu" (a scar on the back) is the kind one would suffer when trying to escape from the enemy. Samurai regarded Ushiro Kizu as a shame. This phrase indicates that the management of banks at the time accepted or even encouraged aggressive profit-seeking by their staff (see Kusu [2005]). Presumably, raising objections to such profit-seeking activities meant dropping out from internal competition in the institution.

[32] Ministry of Finance (1993).

have planted seeds for the formation of a bubble in the early 1980s although there was a real factor for asset price increases in the very initial stage. Under continued disputes with the United States, the government accepted the appreciation of the yen (Plaza Accord) and also tried to transform Japan's economy into a more domestic demand-led one. However, with the sharper-than-expected appreciation of the yen, the BOJ was motivated to ease monetary policy repeatedly to promote the expansion of the domestic economy and to stabilize the yen rate in the late 1980s. Furthermore, in the process of formulating international consensus for exchange rate stabilization, the government committed to use fiscal policy to expand the domestic economy, which all created the conditions for the development of a bubble. Furthermore, the policy idea to transform the Japanese economy to a domestic demand-led one regrettably produced laws that promoted unsustainable land-related development projects throughout the country.

Another factor that might have been responsible for the bubble was the banks' behaviors during the financial liberalization. With the erosion of traditional client base and shrinking profit margins under liberalization, banks tried to enter new markets and sharply increased their real estate-related loans, which spurred the increase in land prices. Companies' aggressive engagements in financial activities also contributed to the stock market surge.[33]

These activities, taken together—heavy involvement by banks in real estate-related loans and aggressive financial activities by companies—were inevitably accompanied by high risk. With hindsight, strengthening of risk management by banks and tightening of regulation and supervision to that end was needed, but the issues were not sufficiently addressed at the time. Why were these risky (in hindsight) activities left unchecked? Who should be held responsible? Bank and company managers? Bank and company shareholders? Government? Mass media? We need to ask what could have been done when all these agents had strong confidence in the Japanese economy, and yet, were trapped by the "Tochi Shinwa" and accordingly, could not see the risk of land price collapse?[34]

[33] The number of individual shareholders increased by around 10% each year in this period, from over 16 million in FY1985 to over 24 million in FY1989 (Ministry of Finance 1993). Privatization of government-owned Japan Telegram and Telephone Corporation and sales of its shares to the public in 1987 attracted nationwide attention.

[34] See Kusu (2006).

However, we should note that all these actions occurred amid fierce disputes with, and strong pressures from the United States, on which Japan was (and still is) dependent for its national security. It is most regrettable that, under the circumstances, policy focus shifted from domestic issues to external problems, and the evolving problems, that is, the formation of a huge bubble, went unchecked, and necessary actions (i.e., giving priority to the consideration of domestic economy over external considerations, or at least limiting external considerations within the range of what was compatible with the stability of the domestic economy) were not taken.

3 Supplement

Theoretical Price of an Asset

Definition of an Asset Price Bubble

A asset price bubble is a phenomenon wherein the price of an asset rises to a level that is not based on fundamentals.

Fundamental Price and Its Derivation

Fundamental Price

The price based on fundamentals (=theoretical price) is expressed as below:

If the asset has no risk and the return is fixed:

$$P = R / i, \tag{2.1}$$

where R = return (office or housing rent, interest, etc.) to an asset, P = price of asset, i = long-term, risk-free interest rate (typically, long-term government bond yield in a secondary market).

If the asset has a risk and the return to the asset grows each period at a fixed rate of g, the fundamental price is rewritten as follows:

$$P = R / \left(i + \alpha - g\right), \tag{2.2}$$

where α is the risk premium (an additional return that is required for a risk asset to be held, on top of the return to a risk-free asset)

Derivation

Risk-free Case

Derivation of theoretical price (price based on fundamentals)

Assumption: There is no difference in risk profile across assets

Formulation: The rate of return will be equalized across different assets via arbitrage, so that we have

$$R / P = i \tag{2.3}$$

Note: Arbitrage may be defined as a simultaneous purchase and sale of assets to make profits from price discrepancy.

Then, we have:

$$P = R / i \tag{2.4}$$

Risk Asset Case

If the asset has a risk, then its rate of return has to be higher than that of risk-free assets (this additional part is called the risk premium (α) as explained before). Then, instead of (2.4), we have

$$P = R / (i + \alpha) \tag{2.5}$$

The aforementioned assumes that the asset price is constant. If the asset price changes, then, the formulation changes as follows.

The rate of return for buying the asset in period 1 for P_1 and selling it in period 2 for P_2 is shown in the left-hand side of Equation (2.6). and it will be equal to the rate of return of the risk-free asset on the right-hand side of the equation.

$$(R + (P_2 - P_1)) / P_1 = i \tag{2.6}$$

Or,

$$P_1 = (R + P_2) / (1 + i) \tag{2.7}$$

In the same way, the asset price in period 2 (P_2) may be expressed as follows.

$$P_2 = (R + P_3)/(1 + i) \tag{2.8}$$

By inserting (2.8) into (2.7), we have

$$P_1 = (R + (R + P_3)/(1 + i))/(1 + i) \tag{2.9}$$

Or,

$$P_1 = R/(1 + i) + R/(1 + i)^2 + P_3/(1 + i)^3 \tag{2.10}$$

By repeating this, we obtain;

$$P_1 = R/(1 + i) + R/(1 + i)^2 + R/(1 + i)^3 + \cdots, \tag{2.11}$$

which means that P_1 is equal to the discounted present value of future returns

Growth of Return

If we assume that the return (R) grows every period at a fixed rate of g, then we have

$$P_{11} = R/(1 + i) + R(1 + g)/(1 + i)^2 + R(1 + g)^2/(1 + i)^3 + \cdots \tag{2.12}$$

As this is the sum of geometrical series, assuming g < i, it can be written as:

$$P_1 = R/(i - g) \tag{2.13}$$

If the asset has a risk, then we use $i+\alpha$ instead of i:

$$P_1 = R/(i + \alpha - g) \tag{2.14}$$

Note: The above explanation is from Chapter 2 of *Nenji Keizai Hokoku* (Annual Economic Report) (1991).

Interest Rate-Adjusted PER and the Ratio of the Actual to Theoretical Stock Price

The theoretical price of stock is expressed by Eq. (2.1) (i.e., $P = R/(i + \alpha - g)$).

If we assume no risk and no growth in return, the theoretical stock price is expressed by Eq. (2.2) (i.e., $P = R/i$).

Assuming the return (R) in Eq. (2.2) can be replaced with profit per one unit of stock (ρ), then the theoretical stock price (P) is expressed as

$$P = \rho / i \tag{2.15}$$

The interest rate- adjusted PER (i × (Actual stock price/profit per one unit of stock (ρ))) corresponds to the ratio of Actual stock price to Theoretical stock price:

$$\text{iPER} = i \times (\text{Actual stock price} / \rho) = \text{Actual price} / (\rho / i) = \text{Actual stock price} / \text{Theoretical stock price} \tag{2.16}$$

The theoretical price rises if the risk premium decreases, and/or the expected growth rate of return increases

Note: PER = price/earning ratio, that is, stock price divided by profit per one unit of stock

Bibliography

English References

Flath, David (2005) *The Japanese Economy*, 2nd ed. Oxford: Oxford University Press.

Kosai, Yutaka (1986) *The Era of High-Speed Growth – Notes on the Postwar Japanese Economy.* Tokyo: University of Tokyo Press.

Okina, Kunio, Masaaki Shirakawa, and Shigenori Shiratsuka (2001) "Asset price bubbles and monetary policy: Japan's experience in the late 1980s and the lessons: Background Paper." *Monetary and Economic Studies* 19 (S1): 395–450.

Okina, Kunio, and Shigenori Shiratsuka (2002) "Asset price bubbles, price stability, and monetary policy: Japan's experience" *Monetary and Economic Studies* 20 (3): 35–76.

Japanese References

Bank of Japan (1990) *Chosa Geppo* (Monthly Research Report), April 1990.

Cabinet Office (2012) "Choki Keizai Tokei Heisei 24 Nendo" (Long-term economic statistics FY 2012), http://www5.cao.go.jp/j-j/wp/wp-je12/h10_data00.html (accessed on October 7, 2018).

Economic Planning Agency (1984) *Nenji Keizai Hokoku* (Annual Economic Report) 1984.

Economic Planning Agency (1991) *Nenji Keizai Hokoku* (Annual Economic Report) 1991.

Economic Planning Agency (1993) *Nenji Keizai Hokoku* (Annual Economic Report) 1993.

Fukao, Kyoji (2002) "Nihon no Chochiku Choka to 'Baburu' no Hassei" (Japan's Excess Savings and the Emergence of the 'Bubble'), In *Heisei Baburu no Kenkyu I* (Study of the Heisei Bubble I), edited by Michio Muramatsu and Masahiro Okuno, Tokyo: Toyo Keizai Shimpo Sha.

Funabashi, Yoich (1988) *Tsuka Retsu Retsu*, Asahi Shimbun Sha (English translation: *Managing the Dollar: From the Plaza to the Louvre* 1989 Washington, DC: Institute for International Economics).

Japan–US Joint Working Group of Special Meeting on Yen–Dollar Exchange Rate and Financial and Capital Markets (1984) "Nichi Bei Kyodo En-doru Reto Kinnyu Shihon Shijo Tokubetsu Kaigo Sagyo Bukai Hokoku Sho," (Report of the Japan–US Joint Working Group of Special Meeting on Yen–Dollar Exchange Rate and Financial and Capital Markets: Report of the Yen–Dollar Committee), May 1984.

Jinushi, Toshiki, Yoshihiro Kuroki, and Ryuzo Miyao (2001) "1980 nendai Kohan iko no Nihon no Kinnyu Seisaku- Seisaku Taio no Okure to sono Riyu" (Monetary Policy in Japan from the Latter Half of the 1980s – Delay in Policy Response and its Background). In *Nihon no Kinnyu Kiki – Beikoku no Keiken to Nihon heno Kyokun* (Monetary Policy in Japan – US Experience and Their Lessons for Japan), edited by Ryoichi Mikitani and Adam A. Posen. Tokyo: Toyo Keizai Shimpo Sha.

Kanagawa, Toru (1987) *Boeki Masatsu to Kokusai Keizai no Shomondai-Nihon to Amerika no Boeki Masatsu wo Chusin ni-* (Trade Frictions and Issues in International Economy–Centering on Trade Frictions between Japan and the US-) 1987, Keibun Sha.

Kanagawa, Toru (1989) *Nichi Bei Boeki Masatsu-Tairitsu to Kyocho no Kozu-* (Japan–U.S. Trade Frictions-Structure of Confrontation and Cooperation). Keibun Sha.

Kano, Tadashi (2006) *Doru En Soba no Seiji Keizaigaku – Kawase Hendo nimiru Nichibei Kankei* (Political Economy of the Yen–Dollar Exchange Rate—Japan–US Relationship Observed in the Foreign Exchange Movements). Nihon Keizai Shimbun Sha.

Katz, Richard (1999) *Kusariyuku Nihon toiu Sisutemu* (Japan, the System that Soured). Tokyo: Toyo Keizai Shimpo Sha.

Komine, Takao, ed. (2011a) *Nihon Keizai no Kiroku – Dai Niji Sekiyu Kiki heno Taio kara Baburu Hokai made* (1970 nendai~1996 nen) (Record of Japanese Economy From Responses to the 2nd oil shock and the Collapse of the Bubble [1970s to 1996]) ("Baburu/defure kino Nihon Keizai to Keizai Seisaku Rekisi hen dai 1 kan" (Japanese Economy and Economic Policy in the Period of Bubble and Deflation – History Vol. 1)), Economic and Social Research Institute, Cabinet Office, Japanese Government.

Komine, Takao, ed. (2011b) *Nihon Keizai no Kiroku – Kinnyu Kiki, Defure to Kaifuku Katei (1997 nen~2006 nen)* (Record of Japanese Economy - Financial Crisis, Deflation and Recovery Process [1997 to 2006] ("Baburu/defure kino Nihon Keizai to Keizai Seisaku Rekisi hen dai 2 kan" (Japanese Economy and Economic Policy in the Period of Bubble and Deflation – History Vol. 2)), Economic and Social Research Institute, Cabinet Office, Japanese Government.

Kosai, Yutaka, Osamu Ito, and Ritsuko Arioka (2001) "*Baburuki no Kinnyu Seisaku to sono Hansei*" (Monetary Policy in the Bubble Era and Its Reconsideration). In *Baburu to Kinnyu Seisaku – Nihon no Keiken to Kyokun* (Bubble and Monetary Policy – Japan's Experience and Lessons), edited by Yutaka Kosai, Masaaki Shirakawa, and Kunio Okina. Nihon Keizai Shimbun Sha.

Kubota, Isao (2008) *Shogen : Miyazawa Daiichiji [1986-1988] Tsuka Gaiko* (Testimony – First Currency Diplomacy [1986–1988] by Miyazawa). Nishi Nihon Shimbun Sha.

Kuroda, Haruhiko (2005) *Zaisei Kinnyu Seisaku no Seiko to Shippai* (Success and Failure of Fiscal and Monetary Policy). Nihon Hyoron Sha.

Kusu, Toshiharu (2005) "Baburu no Gennin Saiko (jo)" (Re-examining Causes of the Bubble [1]). In Yokin Hoken Kiko (Deposit Insurance Corporation) *Yokin Hoken Kenkyu*, October.

Kusu, Toshiharu (2006) "Baburu no Gennin Saiko (ge)" (Re-examining Causes of the Bubble [2])). In Yokin Hoken Kiko (Deposit Insurance Corporation) *Yokin Hoken Kenkyu*, November.

Kondo, Takehiko (1999) "Puraza Goi no Kenkyu" (A Study of the Plaza Accord). Tokyo: Toyo Keizai Shimpo Sha.

Land Economy and Construction Industries Bureau, Ministry of Land, Infrastructure, Transport and Tourism (2012) "Fudosan Shijo niokeru Shisan Kakaku Hendo ni kansuru Kenkyu Kai Hokoku Sho" (Report of the Study Group on Asset Price Developments in Real Estate Markets) 2012.

Matsuzaki, Masahiro (1988) *Nichi Bei Masatsu no Seiji Keizai Gaku* (Political Economy of Japan–U.S. Frictions) 1988. Yachiyo Shuppan.

Ministry of Finance (1984) "Kinnyu no Jiyuka oyobi En no Kokusaika nitsuiteno Genjo to Tenbo" (Current conditions and future prospect of financial liberalization and internationalization of the yen), May.

Ministry of Finance, Japan (1993) "Shisan kakaku hendo no mekanizumu to sono keizai koka" (The Mechanism of Asset Price Movements and its Economic Impacts) November 1993 Finansharu Rebyu Fiscal and Monetary Research Institute.

Noguchi, Yukio (1992) *Baburu no Keizaigaku – Nihon Keizai ni Nani ga Okotta noka* (Economics of the Bubble: What happened to the Japanese Economy?) Nihon Keizai Shimbun Sha.

Okita, Yoichi (2010) *Sengo Nihon Keizai Ron – Seicho Keizai kara Seijuku Keizai heno Tenkan* (Post-War Japanese Economy – Transition from a growing to a matured economy). Tokyo: Toyo Keizai Shimpo Sha.

Sakurai, Ryoji (1993) *Baburu Keizai no Hokai to Nihon Keizai no Honshitsu* (Collapse of the Bubble Economy and the Real Nature of the Japanese Economy). Hokei Ronshu Dai 71 Go.

Shimizu, Hironori (2001) "Goso Sendan Kisei, Ginko Keiei to Nihon no Kinnyu Kiki" (Convoy-based Regulations, Management of Banks and Financial Crisis in Japan). In *Nihon no Kinnyu Kiki – Beikoku no Keiken to Nihon heno Kyokun*, edited by Ryoichi Mikitani and Adam A. Posen. (Monetary Policy in Japan – US Experiences and Their Lessons for Japan). Tokyo: Toyo Keizai Shimpo Sha.

Shirakawa, Masaaki (2011) "Kodo Seicho kara Antei Seicho he –Nihon no Keiken to Shinkokoku Keizai heno Ganni" (From the high-speed to stable growth – Japan's Experiences and Their Implications to Emerging Economies) May 5, Bank of Japan.

Study Group on Structural Economic Adjustments for International Coordination (1986) "Kokusai Kyocho no tameno Keizai Kozo Chosei Kenkyu Kai Hokoku Sho" (Report of the Study Group on Structural Economic Adjustments for International Coordination) (Maekawa Report), April 7. (Viewed on August 17, 2018, at http://worldjpn.grips.ac.jp/documents/texts/JPUS/19860407.O1J.html)

Takenaka, Harukata (2005) "Chika Baburu heno Taio ha Naze Okureta ka – Tokyo no Mondai ga Nihon no Mondai ni Naru made" (Why was the response to the land price bubble delayed? – When the problem in Tokyo became the problem of Japan). In *Heisei Baburu - Saki Okuri no Kenkyu*, edited by Michio Muramatsu. (Heisei Bubble – A Study of Forbearance). Tokyo: Toyo Keizai Shimpo Sha.

Takita, Yoichi (2006) *Nichibei Tsuka Kosho – 20 nenme no Shinjitsu* (Japan US Currency Negotiations – Real Story after 20 Years) Nihon Keizai Shimubun Sha.

Volker, Paul, and Toyoo Gyoten (1992) *Tomi no Kobo – En to Doru no Rekisi* "(Rise and Fall of Wealth – History of the Yen and Dollar"). Tokyo: Toyo Keizai Shinpo Sha.

Yoshikawa, Hiroshi (1992) *Nihon Keizai to Makuro Keizai Gaku* (Japanese Economy and Macroeconomics). Tokyo: Toyo Keizai Shimpo Sha.

Yoshikawa, Hiroshi (1997) *Kodo Seicho – Nihon wo Kaeta 6000 Nichi* (High Speed Growth — 6000 days That Changed Japan). Yomiuri Shimbun Sha.

Yoshitomi, Masaru (1998) *Nihon Keizai no Shinjitsu* (Truth of the Japanese Economy) 1998, Toyo Keizai.

CHAPTER 3

Collapse of the Bubble and the Start of the Long Stagnation

In this chapter, we will first provide an overview of how the bubble collapsed at the beginning of the 1990s and what happened to the Japanese economy during the subsequent decades after the collapse of the bubble. Then, to identify the mechanism of the long stagnation, a division of the stagnation period of about two decades until Abenomics (i.e., 1991–2012) into four subperiods is proposed. After the division into subperiods, this chapter focuses on the first subperiod, that is, around seven years from the beginning of the 1990s to just before the financial crisis that broke out in late 1997. This period can be characterized as the starting period of the long stagnation and, therefore, is very important in that its examination should be able to give clues for the fundamental mechanism of the stagnation.

1 Collapse of the Bubble

The Government's Response to the Bubble

As we have seen in Chap. 2, the asset price inflation that occurred in the latter half of the 1980s was generally not regarded as a bubble, even at the end of the 1980s. The asset price inflation was considered as a problem not because of its risk of collapse and consequent negative impacts on the economy, but mainly from social and equity viewpoints.

K. Aramaki, *Japan's Long Stagnation, Deflation, and Abenomics*,
https://doi.org/10.1007/978-981-13-2176-4_3

Mounting Nationwide Criticism, Particularly toward the Land Price Surge
As we saw in Chap. 2, asset prices started to rise rapidly from the first half of the 1980s, and by the latter half of the 1980s, criticism of asset price inflation became stronger, particularly, in relation to the land price surge. The price rise was thought to have had a decisive impact on inequality, between the "Haves" and "Have Nots," and the price of a house in big cities like Tokyo rose to a level equivalent to ten times as high as the annual income of average income earners, making it impossible for them to own a house throughout their lifetime.

Around that time, many nasty incidents were reported in relation to such land-related activities as "Ji-age" (literally, land lifting), in which bullying or even violent actions were taken to force residents from their land, which potential buyers or their commissioned agents (sometimes, gangsters) targeted to purchase, and the government was strongly criticized for letting the land prices surge.

Government Responded by Various Measures
It was not true that the government did nothing to cope with the situation. For example, in July 1985, an administrative circular was issued from the Ministry of Finance (MOF) to banks. The circular requested that banks refrain from lending for speculative land transactions, and similar circulars were issued in April and December 1986, October 1987, and October 1989, to address the issue from the financing side. Notably, however, the objectives of these circulars were not to restrain land-related lending itself, which was necessary from a risk control viewpoint, but to contain lending to speculative land transactions (Kusu 2006).

Measures Implemented in the Land Use Regulation and Taxation Areas
Under the continued rise in asset price, in October 1987, the Cabinet decided on "Outline of Emergency Land Measures," which included such measures as flexible operation of monitoring zones under which certain land transactions were placed under prior registration requirements to the authorities, guidance on banks, suspension of sale of lands owned by the ex-National Railway, and the review of relevant taxation issues.

In October 1989, the Basic Land Law was enacted, stipulating principles applied to land including priority of public welfare and restraint on speculative transactions.

Monetary Policy Stance Changed in 1989

As we have seen in Chap. 2, monetary policy management was bound by considerations for external factors (i.e., correction of external imbalances and arresting further yen appreciation). However, from around mid-1987, as the wholesale prices started to show signs of increase, reflecting a recovery of the economy, the Bank of Japan (BOJ) began to place a greater emphasis on monitoring price developments. In August 1987, the BOJ let the short-term interest rate rise, and a shift toward monetary policy tightening came into sight. However, in October 1987, the world economy experienced a sharp global fall of stock prices ("Black Monday"), and the monetary policy shifted again toward easing. In January 1988, the joint statement by Prime Minister Takeshita and President Reagan stated, "To achieve sustained growth as well as to foster exchange rate stability, the Bank of Japan agrees, under the present stable price conditions, to continue to pursue the current policy stance and to make efforts to accommodate declining short-term interest rates" (Okina et al. 2001). While the Deutsche Bundesbank raised the discount rate in July 1988 and the Federal Reserve Board (FRB) in the United States raised the discount rate in August 1988, the BOJ's policy change had to wait until 1989.

BOJ Started to Sharply Raise the Discount Rate

In May 1989, the BOJ raised the discount rate by 0.75% from 2.5% to 3.25% for the first time in nine years. This was explained as a preemptive step to stem inflation under yen depreciation, which had started around May 1989 (Komine 2011, 303). In October 1989, the BOJ raised the discount rate by 0.5 to 3.75%. In December 1989, Mieno took the BOJ governor position. He stated in a press interview after inauguration, "we cannot ignore increase in land price in the sense that it can trigger an inflation expectation .... If there were not for financing, land prices will not rise, so, we cannot say it is unrelated .... We have not tightened monetary policy to lower land prices, but it is included in there when we make an overall judgments" (Komine 2011, 306–7. Author's translation), making it clear that land price developments were included in the overall judgment of the management of monetary policy. In December 1989, the BOJ raised the discount rate by 0.5 to 4.25%. In March 1990, the BOJ raised the discount rate by 1.0 to 5.25%. In August 1990, BOJ raised the discount rate by 0.75 to 6.0%. Thus, in around one year and three months, the BOJ rapidly raised the discount rate five times by 3.5% points from 2.5% to 6.0%.

Aggregate Lending Limit Imposed by the Ministry of Finance on Land-Related Loans and Other Measures Enforced

In March 1990, the MOF issued a circular that asked banks to limit the rate of increase in loans to real estate-related sectors,[1] to a level equal or less than the rate of increase in total loans (what is called "an aggregate lending limit"). This stayed in effect until December 1991. In April 1991, land price tax (tax on big landholdings) was introduced.[2] In May 1991, relevant laws were amended to strengthen regulations on land-related loans by non-bank financial institutions. In this way, a range of policy measures was put into force to cope, directly or indirectly, with problems of land price surge.

2 The Bubble Started to Collapse

As the discount rate was raised in May 1989, the transaction volume in the stock market started to decline. The Nikkei Stock Average, which peaked at 38,915 at the end-1989, started to weaken from the beginning of 1990 and had a collapse in February 1990, beginning a long decline. Land prices in Tokyo had already peaked in 1987 and became fairly stabilized, before starting to fall in 1990.

Long Stagnation

The asset price finally began declining at the beginning of the 1990s. Nobody knew at that time that it was going to be the start of a two-decade-long stagnation of the Japanese economy. In this section, we briefly look first at what happened to the Japanese economy by comparing economic performances before and after the burst of the bubble. Then, we will list major arguments and counterarguments on the causes of the long stagnation. Next, we will consider, in a more detailed manner, characteristics of the stagnation, giving particular attention to their changes

[1] Real estate-related loans to construction and non-bank sectors were excluded.

[2] Yoshimasa Nishimura, who was director-general of the Banking Bureau, Ministry of Finance, in 1994–1996, later stated that the Banking Bureau at the time was very reluctant to intervene in the banks' lending activities in such a direct way as to set an aggregate lending limit when the Bureau was pushing forward with financial liberalization, but had to introduce it under the mounting criticism from the ruling Liberal Democratic Party (LDP)'s committees and media on surging land prices (Matsushima and Takenaka 2011, pp. 308–314).

over the time span of about two decades, that is, from 1991 to 2012 (we denote these two decades as the period of long stagnation). Based on this examination, we will present our view that we need to divide the whole period of two decades into four subperiods, in order to find out the real mechanism of stagnation.

What Happened to the Japanese Economy after the Burst of the Bubble

GDP Growth: Comparison with the Past

Real GDP growth stagnated for more than two decades after high growth in the bubble period. Figure 3.1 shows real GDP growth rate for the period from 1956 to 2017. We divide the whole period of more than half a century into the following five periods and show the average growth rate for each of these periods (Table 3.1).[3]

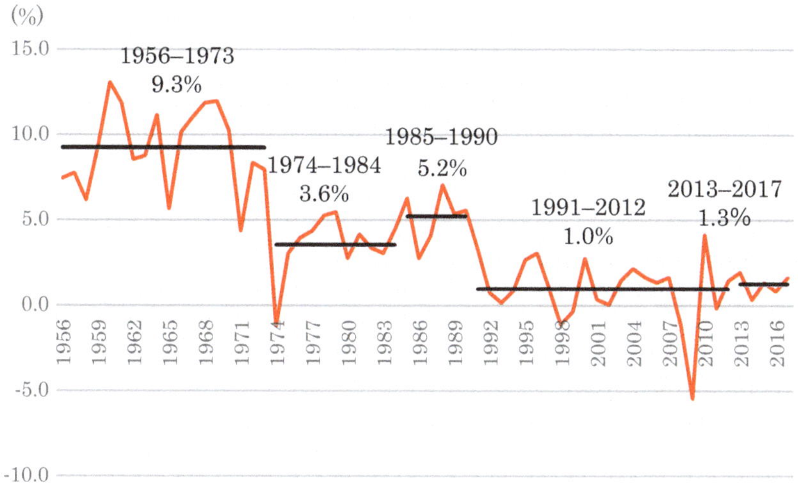

Fig. 3.1 Real GDP growth rate: Japan 1956–2017. Note: Data for 1956–1980 are from GDP statistics with base year = 1990, data for 1981–1994 are from statistics with base year = 2000, data for 1995–2016 are from statistics with base year = 2011, and data for 2017 are from the preliminary quarterly estimate basis. Source: Cabinet Office, GDP statistics

[3] The years from 2013 onward are examined as the Abenomics period in Chap. 7.

Table 3.1 Five periods of the Japanese economy since the high-speed growth era

High-speed growth period	1956–1973
Stable growth period	1974–1984
Bubble period	1985–1990
Long stagnation period	1991–2012
Abenomics period	2013–2017

Table 3.2 Comparison of real GDP growth rate: Japan and other advanced countries, 1980–2012

	1980–1989 (%)	*1990–1999 (%)*	*2000–2012 (%)*
Japan	4.4	1.5	0.8
Simple average of the US, UK, Germany, and France	2.5	2.4	1.6

Source: International Monetary Fund (IMF), World Economic Outlook April 2018 database

Growth rate during the long stagnation is about one-tenth of that in the high-speed growth era and less than one-fifth of that in the bubble period.

GDP Growth: Comparison with Other Countries

Table 3.2 shows a comparison of the growth performance with other advanced countries. After the burst of the bubble, Japan consistently underperformed in contrast to other major advanced countries, whereas Japan had substantially outperformed them in the 1980s.[4]

Unemployment Rate

Japan's unemployment rate was fairly low, staying in the range of 1–3% for nearly four decades after the Second World War. After the collapse of the bubble, it sharply increased, rising over 5%, and then remaining at an elevated level that averaged 4% in the long stagnation period (Fig. 3.2).

[4] In terms of growth rate of real GDP per capita, the Japanese economy also underperformed. A simple average of the rate of growth of GDP per capita in national currency (constant price base) for Japan over 1991 to 2012 is 0.8%, while the simple average for the other four advanced countries (the United States, Germany, France, and the United Kingdom) is 1.4%.

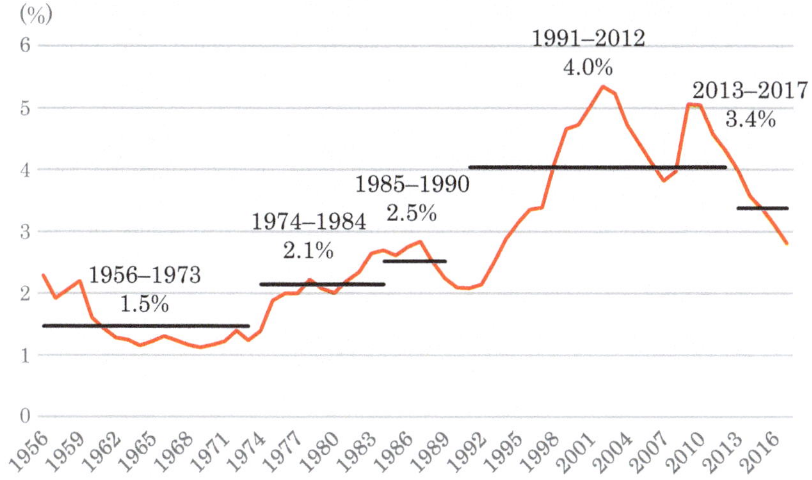

Fig. 3.2 Unemployment rate. Source: Statistics Bureau, Ministry of Internal Affairs and Communications

Why Did the Japanese Economy Stagnate So Long?: Major Arguments
As we have seen in the previous subsection, macroeconomic performance of the Japanese economy significantly deteriorated after the burst of the bubble, and the stagnation on average continued for two decades. Why did it happen? This is the biggest question that we address in this book. In this subsection, we briefly look at major arguments regarding the causes of the long stagnation.

Major arguments on the causes of the long stagnation can be classified into three groups:

1. Supply-side views, which regard structural factors, including low TFP growth, loss of competitiveness, and an aging and shrinking population, as responsible for the long stagnation.
2. Demand-side views, which regard demand shortage as a cause; they tend to focus on policy mistakes in fiscal and monetary areas that failed to provide sufficient demand stimuli.
3. Financial sector-problem views, which regard deficiency of the financial sector, ceasing to appropriately perform an intermediary function due to non-performing loan problems, as responsible for stagnation.

Let us briefly look at each of these views.

Supply-Side Views

There was always a certain number of people, if not many, who took the supply-side view. To quote some examples of such arguments from their books or articles:[5]

> Demand shortage arguments are inappropriate in explaining the lost 1990s .... The Keynesian economics that emphasize aggregate demand ... may be effective in explaining short-term economic developments such as business cycles, but cannot explain such a long stagnation as experienced by Japan in the 1990s. (Hayashi 2003, 3)

> The problem ... is a low productivity growth rate. Growth theory ... accounts well for the Japanese lost decade of growth. (Hayashi and Prescott 2002, 206)

> The fundamental cause of economic stagnation is in the enterprises .... Big structural changes (major contents of which are said to be "industrialization of China" and "progress of IT revolution") occurred in the global economy in the 1990s. Stagnation of the Japanese economy from the 1990s was due to the fact that the Japanese corporations could not properly respond to such changes. (Noguchi 2005, 7, 70) (Explanation in the parenthesis is added by the author based on Noguchi 2005, 10)

> As the working age population continues to decline, the domestic demand-type industries, which account for a large part of employment, constantly suffer from excess supply, and their business performance will never improve. (Motani 2010, 140)

Let us briefly examine these supply-side arguments in light of relevant data. It is true that the trend of real GDP growth changed after the burst of the bubble, as we see in Fig. 3.3, indicating there may have been structural factors at work.

However, developments in the nominal GDP give an entirely different impression. The nominal GDP experienced an abrupt change around the burst of the bubble (Fig. 3.4).

In terms of the growth rate, Japan's nominal GDP growth sharply slowed down from the average of 7.3% during 1988–1991, to 1.6% over

[5] For Hayashi (2003), Noguchi (2005), and Motani (2010), quoted sentences are translations, by the author of this book, of the Japanese original texts.

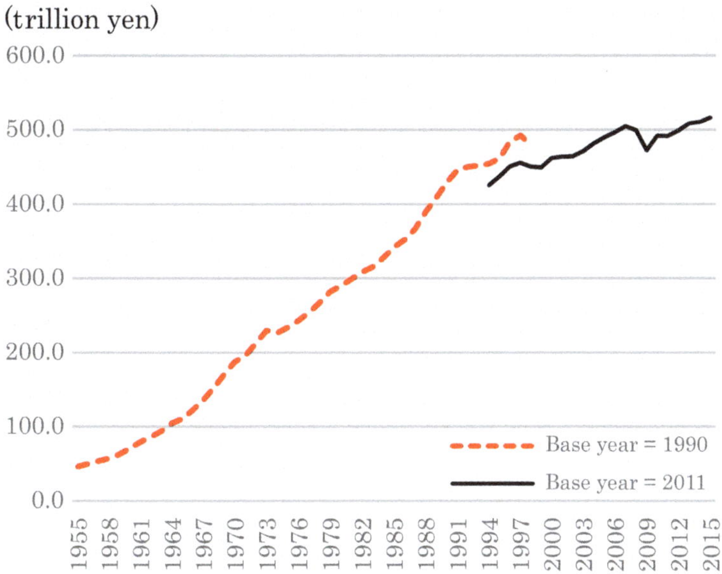

Fig. 3.3 Amount of real GDP: Japan 1955–2015. Source: Cabinet Office, GDP statistics

1992–1997.[6] In absolute amount terms, the nominal GDP peaked at 534 trillion yen in 1997, and it was 495 trillion yen in 2012, which is 7.3% lower than the level in 1997.

From such developments in nominal GDP, two questions are posed:

First, can such an abrupt change be caused by structural factors that take time to be formed and change only slowly and, therefore, make the economy difficult to change in a short period of time? In other words, was it something cyclical or something of abrupt nature that played a crucial role in causing such an abrupt change in nominal GDP?

Second, however, why did such an abrupt change continue for the long period of two decades? If caused by some abrupt factor, did it become structuralized in the process? If yes, when and how?

[6] The economy peaked in February 1991, but the real growth rate still recorded a relatively high level of 3.3% in 1991, as compared with the below 1% growth in the subsequent three years.

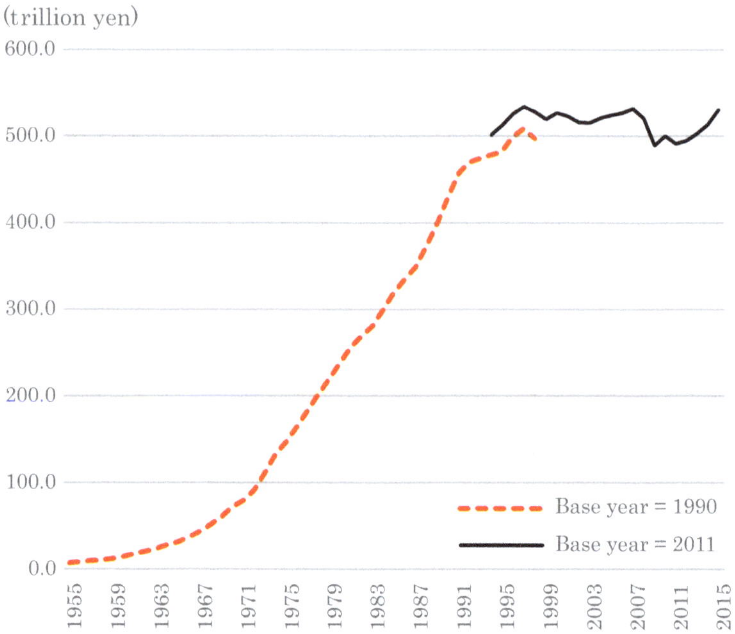

Fig. 3.4 Nominal GDP. Source: Cabinet Office, GDP statistics

Can the supply-side view give a satisfactory answer to the first question? Such structural factors as productivity growth, erosion of competitiveness, and demography all proceed only gradually and, therefore, are unlikely to cause such an abrupt change as in the development of nominal GDP that we saw.

Another point that should be explained by the supply-side view is that the Japanese economy generally suffered from a deflationary gap (supply > demand) during the long stagnation (Fig. 3.5); therefore, it is difficult to consider that inefficiency on the supply side, such as low productivity growth or shortage of supply capacity, was a problem. Supply capacity was sufficient.

Demand-Side Views

Next, let us look at demand-side views. As the Japanese economy primarily suffered from demand shortage during the long stagnation, as touched upon in the preceding subsection, and also, because demand level can be

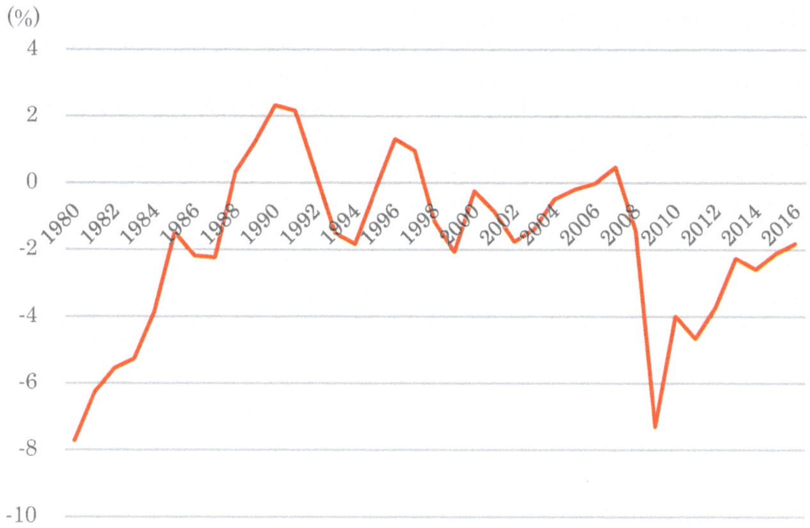

Fig. 3.5 Output gap (in GDP ratio). Source: IMF World Economic Outlook Database. October 2017

changed quickly by cyclical factors, there are many people who support the demand-side view. With respect to the cause of demand shortage, many arguments focus on the mistake or inappropriate handling of policies, in the fiscal or monetary areas.

Fiscal Policy Mistake

Some of the demand-side arguments focus on fiscal policy. For example, the consumption tax hike from 3% to 5% in April 1997 and other fiscal tightening measures, including the discontinuation of special income tax cut implemented in 1994–1996 and decrease in public work expenditure from the mid-1996 are blamed for interrupting the recovery and bringing about the long stagnation. However, as will be explained later, fiscal stimulus packages were repeatedly formulated to support the economy after the collapse of the bubble, resulting in a huge government debt. Considering that it is not possible to support the economy forever by fiscal demand injection, although the appropriateness of the timing of fiscal tightening in 1996–1997 may be questioned, the fiscal stance cannot be considered as the fundamental cause of the long stagnation.

Inappropriate Monetary Policy

It was the monetary policy that was criticized most severely, by those who saw problems in policies of the government. Many argued that inappropriate management of monetary policy was responsible for the long stagnation. We will examine this issue in Chap. 5 in more detail, but let us just look now at Fig. 3.6. Money stock (M2 + CD) growth rate, which recorded a level higher than 10% in the latter half of 1980s, took a nosedive around the beginning of 1991, recording negative growth in September 1992 for the first time since 1968, when the statistics were first published. The response to the bubble by the BOJ and the government from the end of the 1980s to the beginning of the 1990s, through the sharp and substantial increase in the discount rate and the introduction of the aggregate lending limit, may be described as "too much, too late" (rather than "too little too late"). Overkilling the economy with policy measures in response to strong social criticism on surging land prices and the inequality between "Haves" and "Have Nots" apparently played an extremely important role at the beginning of the two-decade-long stagnation.

Fig. 3.6 Money stock (M2 + CD) (year-on-year change): Japan, 1985–1998. Source: Bank of Japan

Financial Sector-Problem Views

The third argument, the financial sector-problem views, typically, contend that the financial sector problem, or the deterioration of the financial sector soundness due to non-performing loans (NPLs), brought about the credit crunch, which depressed the economy. However, the lending stance of financial institutions was generally not tight in the major part of the 1990s, except for relatively limited periods right after the burst of the bubble and in the height of the financial crisis in 1997–1998, as shown in Fig. 3.7. This indicates that financial tightening does not seem to be a cause of the stagnation, at least in the early stage of stagnant decades, that is, from the beginning of the 1990s until the financial crisis in the late 1990s, which, as argued later in this subsection, seems to be the most important period in the process of the long stagnation (Fig. 3.7).

The Need to Divide the Whole Period into Subperiods

When we looked at major arguments regarding the causes of stagnation in the preceding subsection, we saw that the performance of nominal GDP experienced an abrupt change at the beginning of the 1990s. We argued that such an abrupt change could not have been caused by structural

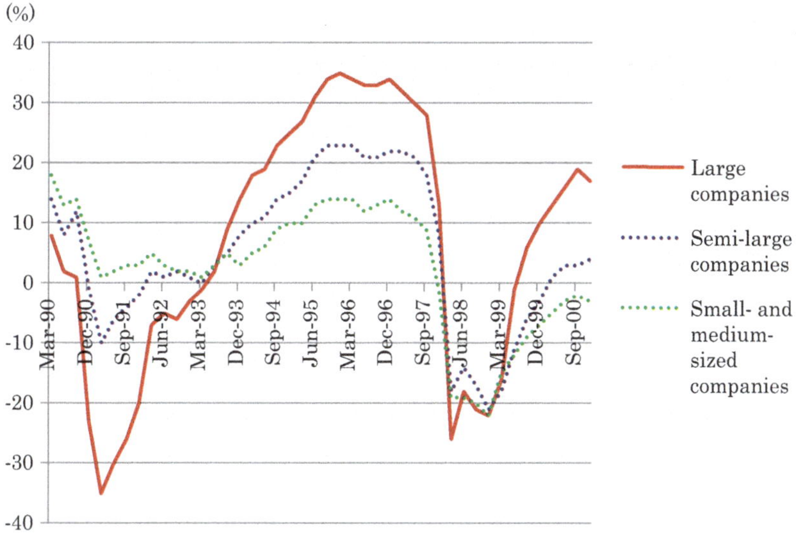

Fig. 3.7 The lending stance of financial institutions (share of "Eased" – share of "Tight"): Japan 1990–2000. Source: Bank of Japan, "Tankan Survey"

factors that normally change slowly and, therefore, affect the economy only gradually. So, it may be that some cyclical or other discontinuous factors caused such an abrupt change. At the same time, we also noted that such an abrupt change remained for many years and entirely altered the trend of nominal GDP. In other words, the abrupt change was perpetualized. So, the stagnation may have been caused by discontinuous elements but seems to have been structuralized as years went by. This fact implies that the mechanism of stagnation changed from the one that is of an abrupt nature to the one that is of a sustainable nature. If this is the case, we will not be able to see the real mechanism of stagnation if we lump the two decades together and try to find a single stagnation mechanism. Rather, we may be able to get closer to the real cause of the stagnation if we seek to find what factors played an important role in causing stagnation in what subperiod and examine whether and how such factors changed over time in the whole process of stagnation.

Thus we need to divide the whole process into appropriate subperiods in such a way that each subperiod is governed by its unique stagnation mechanism, which may be different across subperiods. Then, the question is how we can identify such subperiod, which was governed by a specific stagnation mechanism. As we do not or rather cannot know the answer beforehand, we take a two-staged approach; we first make a tentative division of the whole period into subperiods by looking at changes in the characteristics of economic performance during the two decade-long stagnation, and then try to identify the mechanism of stagnation in respective subperiods, and, second, drawing on the findings of the first-stage analysis, we try to capture the whole picture of the stagnation mechanism in the second stage.[7] Here, we will look at economic performance in the stagnation period in light of various indicators, so as to make tentative subdivisions of the entire stagnation period.

Characteristics of the Stagnation Period

First, let us look at the distinctive features of the long stagnation period in contrast with other periods. Decomposition of real GDP growth into contributions by major demand components shows that the contribution

[7] Chapters 3 and 4 conduct mainly the first-stage analysis, based on four subdivisions of the whole period that is introduced in this chapter. Drawing on the findings of these analyses, Chap. 6 conducts the second-stage analysis to find the real mechanism of stagnation. As a result, the four subperiod analyses will develop into the three-staged evolution of stagnation mechanism that focuses on corporate behavior.

Table 3.3 Contribution to real GDP growth by major demand components

	High growth period 1956–73 (%)	*Stable growth period 1974–84 (%)*	*Bubble period 1985–90 (%)*	*Long stagnation 1991–2012 (%)*
Real GDP growth	9.3	3.6	5.2	1.0
Private consumption	5.5	1.9	2.5	0.6
Housing investment	0.8	−0.1	0.4	−0.1
Private investment in plants and equipment	1.6	0.3	2.0	0.0
Government expenditure	1.5	0.7	0.6	0.3
Net exports	−0.3	0.7	−0.3	0.2

Source: Cabinet Office, GDP statistics

by private investment[8] to GDP growth is zero during the stagnation period (Table 3.3). Such a null contribution of private investment is the most distinctive feature in the stagnant period.

Growth Contribution of Private Investment Varied During the Long Stagnation Period

In the two decades, performance of private investment was not unchanged. After the burst of the bubble, private investment and also GDP growth itself experienced four dips as shown in Fig. 3.8. Private investment recorded a negative growth contribution in 1992–1993 after the bubble burst, in 1998–1999 during the financial crisis, in 2001–2002 after the collapse of the dot-com bubble, and in 2008–2009 when the Global Financial Crisis (GFC) broke out. These changes in private investment significantly affected GDP growth performance during the stagnation period, and therefore, we should take note of the performance of private investment when dividing the two decades into subperiods.

Developments in Diffusion Index

We also need to look at cyclical indicators. During the stagnant two decades, the Japanese economy went through five economic cycles (Table 3.4).

Cumulated Diffusion Index (an indicator of economic cycles) shows that after the bubble burst, there were two short recoveries interrupted,

[8] The words "private investment" and "private investment in plants and equipment" are used interchangeably in this book.

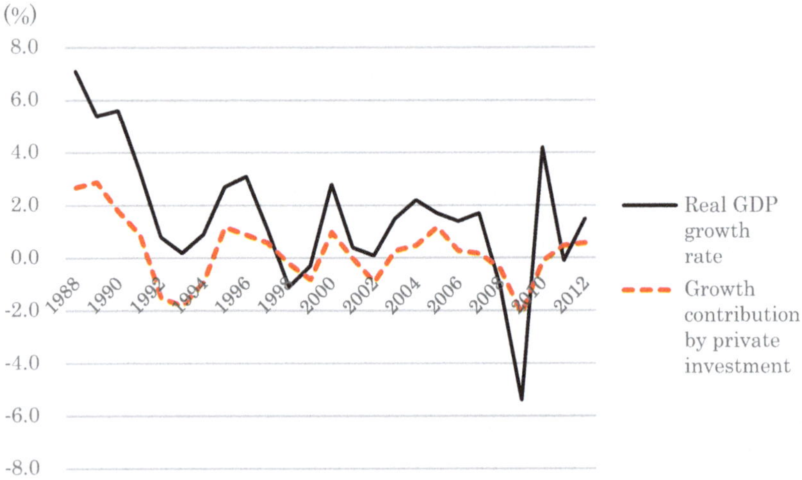

Fig. 3.8 Real GDP growth rate and contribution by private investment: Japan, 1991–2012. Note: Data for 1988–1994 are from GDP statistics, with 2000 as the base year; and for 1995–2012 from statistics, with 2011 as the base year. Source: Cabinet Office, GDP statistics

Table 3.4 Economic cycles during the long stagnation period

Cycle	*Trough*	*Peak*	*Trough*
11th	November 1986	February 1991	October 1993
12th	October 1993	May 1997	January 1999
13th	January 1999	November 2000	January 2002
14th	January 2002	February 2008	March 2009
15th	March 2009	March 2012	November 2012

Note: Cycles are counted after the Second World War.
Source: Cabinet Office

respectively, by the financial crisis and by the dot-com bubble collapse, and one long recovery interrupted by the GFC (Fig. 3.9).

The average growth rate in the expansion phase over 1994Q1–1997Q2 (2.1% on a year-on-year basis) was markedly weak, compared with the preceding expansion in the bubble period (5.5% over 1987Q1–1991Q1). The expansion phase after the financial crisis in the late 1990s was also weak (1.5% over 1999Q2–2000Q4) and short (less than two years). In this way, two expansions in the first 10 years after the burst of the bubble

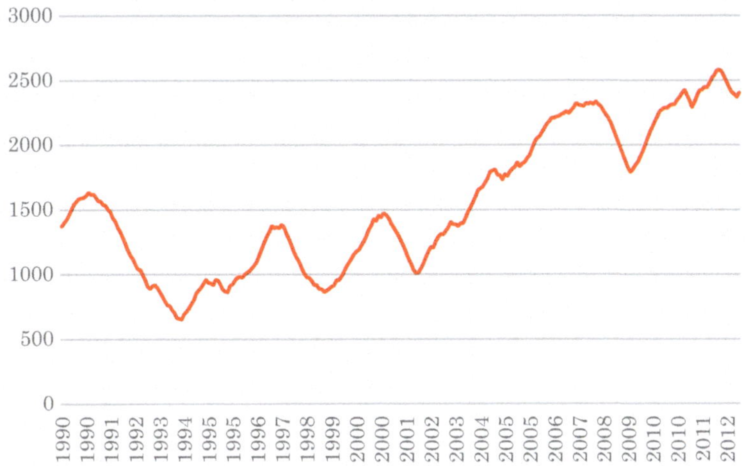

Fig. 3.9 Cumulated Diffusion Index. Source: Cabinet Office

were weak (and short in the case of the second expansion phase). By contrast, the recovery from the early 2000s was fairly long, extending over more than six years (the longest after the war), while the average growth rate over 2002Q2–2008Q1 was 1.5%, that is, the same as in the preceding expansion phase (Fig. 3.10).[9]

Unemployment Rate

Figure 3.11 shows developments in the unemployment rate. A difference from the previous chart (Fig. 3.2) is that the long stagnation period (1991–2012) has been divided into two periods: the pre-financial crisis period (1991–1997) and the post-financial crisis period (1998–2012). The unemployment rate was not very high until 1997, that is, before the financial crisis, averaging 2.8%, but it sharply increased after the financial crisis to a level near 5%.

[9]The expansion phase in this growth rate calculation is defined as starting from the first full quarter after the quarter in which the preceding bottom was identified, and ending in the quarter in which subsequent peak was identified.

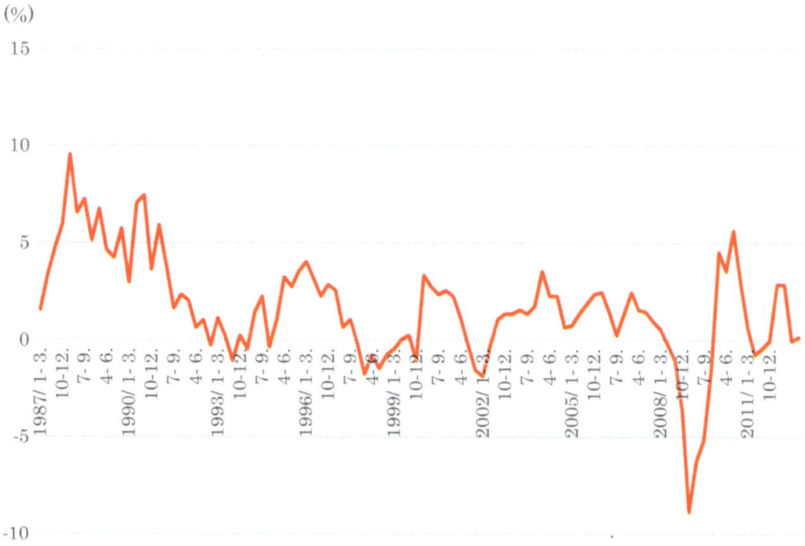

Fig. 3.10 Quarterly growth rate of real GDP (year-on-year): Japan, 1987Q1–2012Q4. Source: Cabinet Office

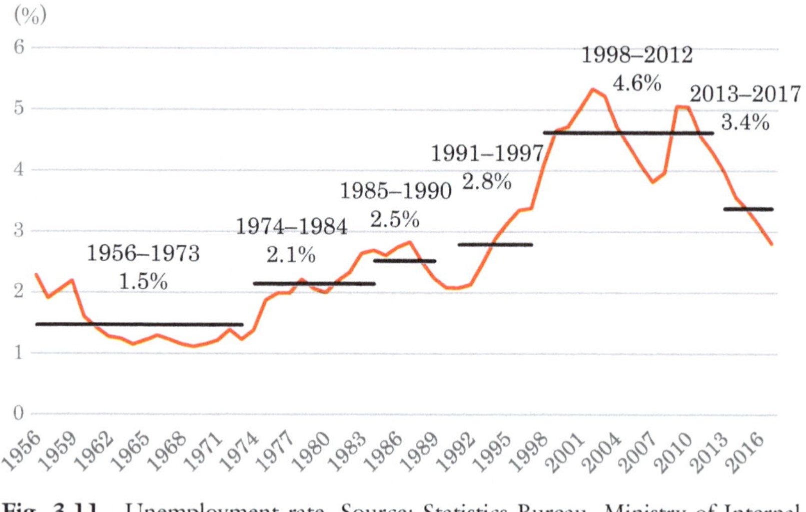

Fig. 3.11 Unemployment rate. Source: Statistics Bureau, Ministry of Internal Affairs and Communications

Non-Uniformity of the Economic Performance during the Long Stagnation and a Need to Divide the Whole Period into Four Subperiods

The foregoing indicates that the two decades of the stagnation period were not uniform, that is, economic characteristics (symptoms) were different across the years. Let us summarize what we have seen:

Behavior of private investment is significantly different on average in the long stagnation period, as compared with that in other periods, recording zero growth contribution on average during the stagnation.

Private investment dipped four times; that is, after each of the following incidents—the burst of the bubble, the financial crisis, the collapse of the dot-com bubble, and the GFC.

There were two weak recoveries in the first decade of stagnation and one long recovery in the second decade of stagnation.

The unemployment rate was not significantly high before the financial crisis, but it sharply increased thereafter.

These differences in characteristics of the economic developments or the difference in the symptoms of the disease (stagnation) suggest that, in our examination, it may be useful to divide the whole two decade-long period in the following way:

The first dividing line may be the financial crisis. The unemployment rate was moderate up to 1997, but it was elevated from 1998. The economy apparently suffered serious impacts during the financial crisis and underwent a substantial change.

Another dividing line may be the start of the long recovery in the early 2000s. There were two weak recoveries before the early 2000s and one long recovery after that.

One more dividing line may be the outbreak of the GFC. The long recovery was interrupted in 2008, and the economy was thrown into a turbulent era due to a series of external shocks.

Based on these considerations, we may divide the stagnant period of two decades into the following four subperiods:

Period I 1991–1997: After the burst of the bubble to just before the financial crisis. This subperiod may be called "Initial adjustment period"

Period II 1998–2002: From the financial crisis and to just before the long recovery. This subperiod is called "Financial Crisis and its impacts"
Period III 2003–2007: This period covers most of the long recovery and is termed "Long recovery"
Period IV 2008–2012: This subperiod covers the turbulent era from the GFC to just before the period of Abenomics that substantively started in 2013 and is called "Global financial crisis and after."

Table 3.5 shows growth contribution of major demand components in the aforementioned four subperiods in the long stagnation period, separated by aforementioned dividing lines. The bubble period is shown for comparison purpose.

In these subperiods, major characteristics of the economy seem to be distinctively different.

Period I 1991–1997: Initial adjustment period

Growth rate became less than one-third of the rate in the preceding bubble period (from 5.2% to 1.7%).

Table 3.5 Contribution to GDP growth by major demand components (bubble period and four subperiods in the long stagnation periods)

	Bubble period 1985–1990 (%)	*Period I Initial adjustment 1991–1997 (%)*	*Period II Financial crisis and its impacts 1998–2002 (%)*	*Period III Long recovery 2003–2007 (%)*	*Period IV Global financial crisis and after 2008–12 (%)*
Real GDP growth	5.2	1.7	0.4	1.7	−0.2
Private consumption	2.5	1.0	0.6	0.6	0.3
Housing investment	0.4	−0.1	−0.2	−0.1	−0.1
Private investment in plants and equipment	2.0	−0.1	−0.2	0.5	−0.3
Government expenditure	0.6	0.8	0.2	−0.3	0.3
Net exports	−0.3	0.2	0.1	0.8	−0.2

Source: Calculated based on GDP statistics provided by Cabinet Office

The most important negative factor for growth was private investment in plants and equipment (its growth contribution declined by 2.1% points, from +2.0% points in the bubble period to −0.1% points in Period I).

Period II 1998–2002: Financial crisis and its impacts

The growth rate further fell to 0.4%. Private investment stagnation aggravated (its growth contribution further declined to −0.2% points).

Period III 2003–2007: Long recovery

The growth rate recovered to 1.7%. Private investment recovered, with a positive contribution to growth (0.5% points).

Period IV 2008–2012: GFC and after

The growth rate became negative, again (−0.2%). Private investment recorded a negative contribution again (−0.3% points).

We would like to reiterate a need to divide the two decades into subperiods with different characteristics. In many analyses of Japan's stagnation, more than 20 years, after the burst of bubble, are often lumped together and called the "Lost Decades." Arguments are presented to explain a single "long stagnation." However, problems with the economy seem to have changed over the period of two decades. In this book, we divide the long stagnation period into subperiods based on characteristics of the economy and aim to identify the real mechanism of the Japan's long stagnation.

3 Initial Adjustment after the Collapse of the Bubble (Period I: 1991–1997)

In this section, we will look at Period I that spans from 1991 to 1997, that is, a period from the collapse of the bubble up to just before the financial crisis in the late 1997, which brought about far-reaching impacts on the economy, as we see later. We start with fact findings, that is, we will see what happened to the Japanese economy in this period and examine possible causes of the stagnation, with particular focus on the decline in private investment (that played the most important role in the stagnation in Period I). We also will see what the government did to find out what should (could) have been done to prevent such a long stagnation, as the economy actually experienced.

What Happened in Period I?

The economic expansion that started after November 1986 ended, hitting a peak in February 1991, more than one year after the stock price began its fall at the beginning of 1990, and the economy entered a contraction phase, as shown in developments in Cumulated Diffusion Index (Fig. 3.12).

The most distinct feature of this contraction phase is the severity of the contraction. In terms of quarterly growth rate (year-on-year basis), the growth rate of real GDP sharply decelerated from the average of 6.0% in the preceding three years over 1988Q1–1991Q1 to 1.0% over a contraction phase from 1991Q2–1993Q4 that followed. The growth rate in a subsequent expansion phase was also low at 2.1% over 1994Q1–1997Q2 (Fig. 3.13). The length of the contraction phase (32 months, which is the second longest contraction phase after the war) is another characteristic of this contraction phase.[10]

The main cause of the contraction was private investment. Decomposition of real GDP growth into contribution by major demand components

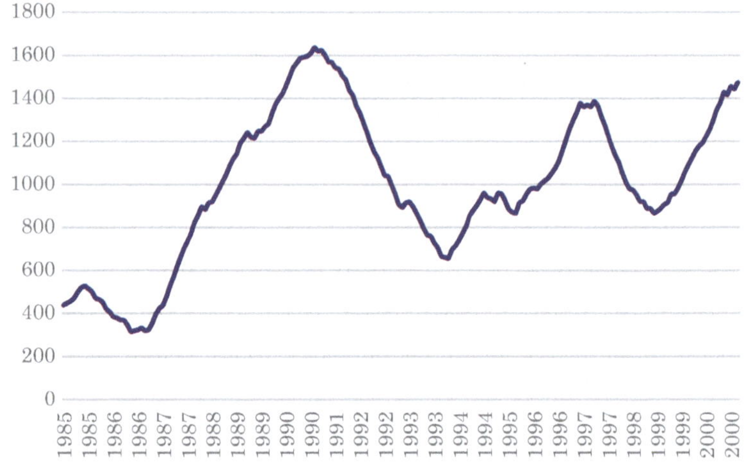

Fig. 3.12 Cumulated Diffusion Index. Source: Cabinet Office

[10]The longest contraction phase is 36 months from February 1980 (peak) to February 1983 (trough) after the second oil crisis.

Fig. 3.13 Quarterly growth rate of real GDP (year-on-year): Japan, 1985Q1–2000Q4. Source: Cabinet Office

confirms that the most important negative factor was private (corporate) investment in plants and equipment, recording negative growth contribution in many years in the first half of 1990s. By contrast, government expenditure and private consumption supported the growth in the initial adjustment period in 1991–1997 (Fig. 3.14).[11]

Why Was Private Investment Depressed So Severely and So Long?

We have seen that the biggest drag to growth in Period I was a decline in private investment. We would like to know why private investment was depressed so severely and so long. We will list three factors: (1) the accumulation of excessive capital stocks in the bubble period and their prolonged adjustment by corporations; (2) continuous decline in expected growth rate; and (3) the balance sheet damage made to corporations by

[11] Growth contributions by each of demand components tend to fluctuate, and therefore in Fig. 3.14, the three-year moving average of growth contributions of each demand component is shown, so as to see the basic trend.

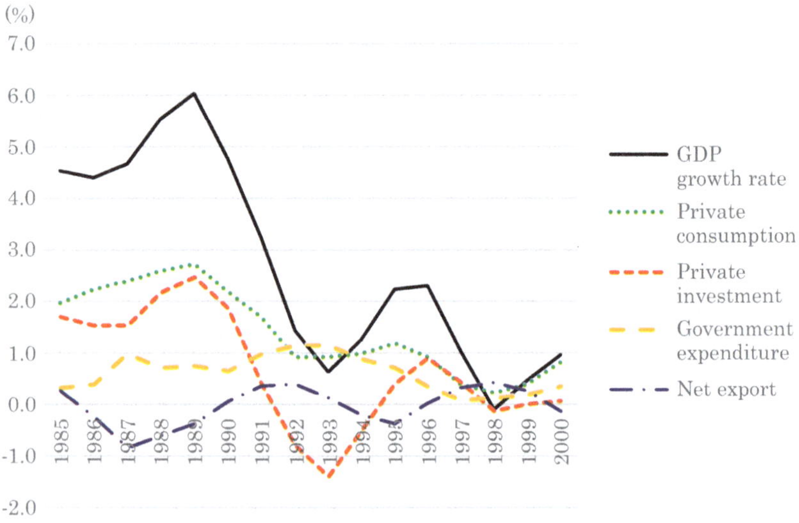

Fig. 3.14 Growth contribution of major demand components (three-year moving average): Japan, 1985–2000. Source: Cabinet Office

asset deflation. The former two factors played a fundamental role, and the third factor provided an extra burden.

Stock Adjustments

Stock Adjustments Conducted

We can see from Fig. 3.15 that private investment surged in the bubble period. The average share of private investment in real GDP was really high at 17.1% in 1988–1992, as compared with 12.5% in the stable growth period (1974–1984).[12] So, it is natural that excess assets created by overinvestment in the bubble period were downward adjusted (stock adjustment) as the economy slowed down after the burst of the bubble. However, the stock adjustment continued for a very long period of time. The share of private investment in real GDP stayed flat from mid-1990s to the first half of 2000s, and private investment was unable to act as a driving force for growth.

[12] As implementation of investment tends to have a lag, the peak of investment comes later than the peak of economic cycle.

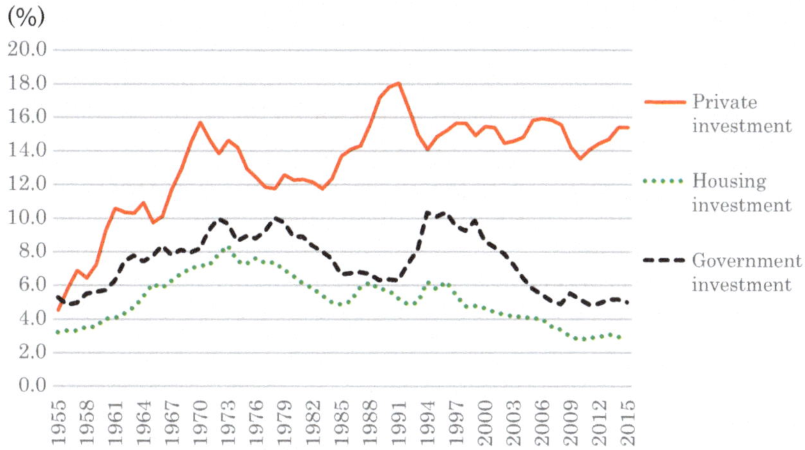

Fig. 3.15 Share in real GDP of private investment, housing investment, and government investment. Source: Cabinet Office

Why Was the Stock Adjustment Not Completed Sooner

While stock adjustments were inevitable, we would like to know why stagnation of private investment continued for such a long time and why the subsequent recovery was also slow. In fact, although the economy started to expand in late 1993 and private investment recovered a positive contribution to growth, the recovery at that time was weak, and private investment did not have its previous strength.

The background of this weakness can be found in Fig. 3.16. This figure shows developments in total assets, liabilities, and net assets of all profit-making companies (excluding financial and insurance companies) in Japan. It clearly shows the bubble period left Japan with excess assets accompanied by excess liabilities. The pace of increase in assets and liabilities in the second half of the 1980s was far higher than that in the preceding period. The existence of such excess assets seems to have placed a downward pressure on private investment.

Furthermore, Fig. 3.17 shows developments in total sales of all companies (excluding financial and insurance companies) in Japan and their breakdown into manufacturing and non-manufacturing sectors. The total amount of sales suddenly stopped growing after the burst of the bubble at the beginning of 1990s and started to absolutely decline in the 1990s. This is particularly the case for non-manufacturing industries.

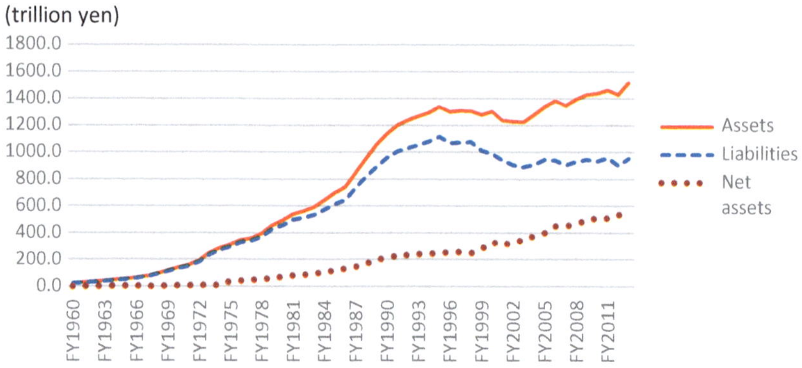

Fig. 3.16 Assets, liabilities, and net assets of companies (all industries excluding financial and insurance companies): FY 1960–2013. Source: Ministry of Finance "Financial Statements Statistics of Corporations by Industry"

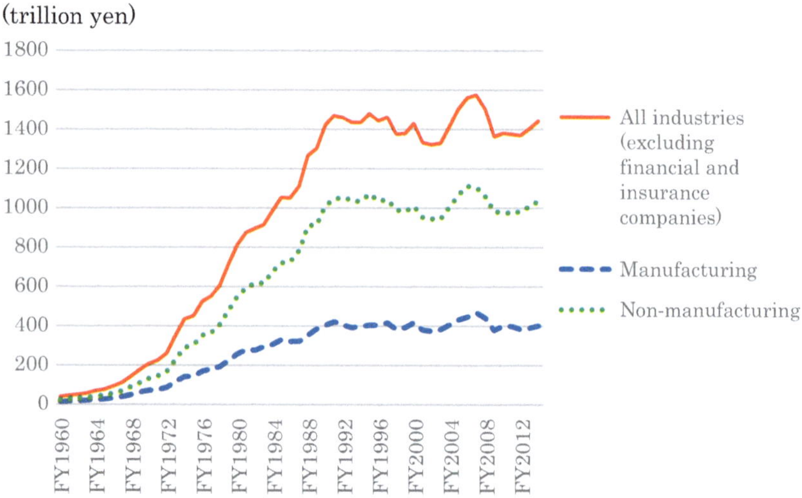

Fig. 3.17 Total sales of companies (all industries excluding financial and insurance companies) and their breakdown between manufacturing and non-manufacturing sectors. Source: Ministry of Finance "Financial Statements Statistics of Corporations by Industry"

Due to the sudden halt of sales growth, the size of physical assets, such as buildings, machineries, and equipment, became excessive relative to the sales volume.[13] The fact that companies had such assets, for which the companies could not expect sufficient sales, surely imposed another depressing impact on investment.

Continuous Downward Adjustment of Growth Expectation

Expected Growth Rate Declined with Declines in Actual Growth Rate

This mechanism may be looked at from a different angle in Fig. 3.18. The growth rate expected by companies (listed manufacturing and non-manufacturing companies) for the immediate three years into the future fell from an average of 3.4% in the bubble period (1985–1990) to 2.2% in the initial adjustment period (1991–1997), and then to 1.0% in the financial crisis and its impacts period (1998–2002), before rising to 1.8% in the recovery period (2003–2007).

The downward adjustments of growth expectation until the beginning of the 2000s seem to have reflected the continued decline in growth performance, provided in Fig. 3.18, and this decline in expectation reduced the required level of private investment by companies.[14]

What matters to companies may be expected sales growth rather than expected growth of the economy, but the expected growth rate may well act as a proxy for expected sales growth rates for companies. Figure 3.19 shows that the sales growth rate in the immediate past significantly affected private investment. In particular, after the bubble burst, the decline in sales growth negatively affected private investment.[15]

Why Did the Growth Rate or Sales Growth Continue to Decline?

From these observations, we can see that the formation of excess assets on the one hand, and the halt of growth and subsequent decline in sales on the other hand, significantly affected company behavior, and also, the economy as a whole. Excess assets were the negative legacy of the bubble, and therefore, their disposition was inevitable. Why then did sales continue to decline for long?

[13] This point is examined in detail, based on combined financial statements of companies in Chap. 6.

[14] See Footnote 25 in Chap. 2.

[15] Note that both sales and investment are in nominal terms in the figure.

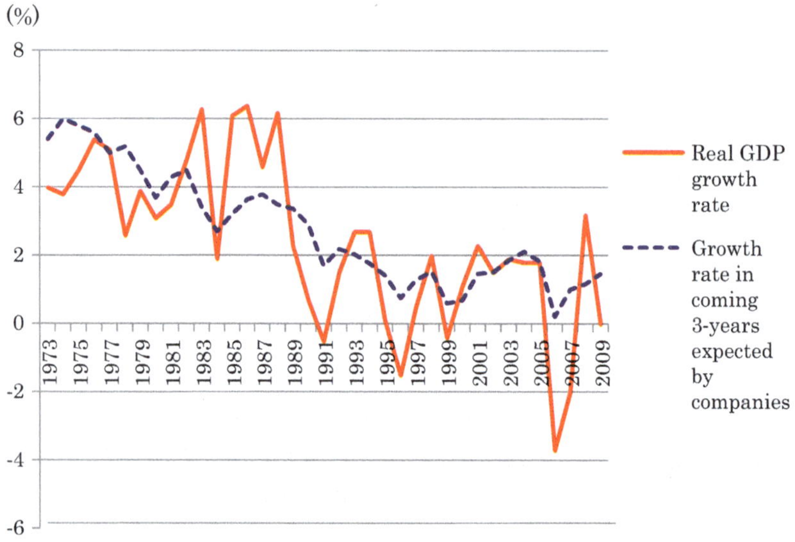

Fig. 3.18 Real GDP growth rate and expected growth rate held by companies for the next three years. Source: Cabinet Office "Survey on company behavior"

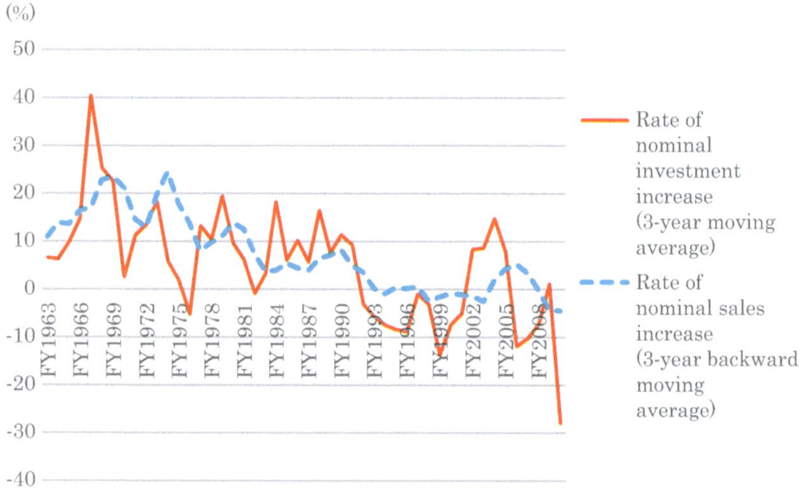

Fig. 3.19 Growth rate of nominal sales and growth rate of nominal investment (both in three-year moving average). Source: Ministry of Finance "Financial Statements Statistics of Corporations by Industry"

Prolonged Investment Restraint

One reason may be found in the prolonged stock adjustment. Due to the hangover of excess assets, stock adjustment, and therefore, investment restraint became a prolonged process, depressing the economy. It was in the mid-2000s when excess assets were finally removed, and in the intervening 15 years from the burst of the bubble, investment could not become a driver of economic growth.

Sharp Yen Appreciation

Another depressing factor on the growth was the rapid yen appreciation in the mid-1990s.The yen appreciated from 125 yen to the dollar in January 1993, when the first term of the Clinton administration started, to 79.75 yen to the dollar on April 19, 1995, representing some 57% appreciation of the yen vis-à-vis the US dollar in just little more than two years.[16] Rapid yen appreciation, together with the Great Hanshin-Awaji Earthquake in January 1995, hurt exports and dampened business confidence (Fig. 3.20).

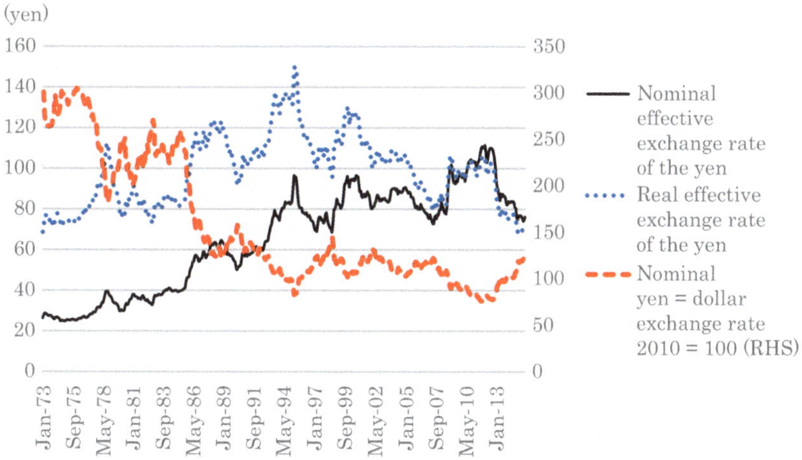

Fig. 3.20 The exchange rate of the yen to the dollar and real and nominal effective exchange rate (2010 = 100). Source: Bank of Japan

[16]A Ministry of Finance official in charge of international financial matters, including exchange rates, later wrote as follows: "Bickering over trade between Japan and the United States, which was intensively covered by the mass media, regrettably helped convince market players that the yen's surge would not be halted unless Japan's current account surplus was brought down" (Sakakibara 2000, 174).

In real effective terms, which is more relevant to the competitiveness of Japanese exporters, the yen rate in the mid-1990s, when Japan was struggling with the aftereffects of the bubble, was the highest in more than 40 years since the collapse of the fixed exchange rate system.

In this way, the economy was deprived of two important private demand components, investment and exports, in the initial adjustment period. So, as we have seen, in the initial adjustment period, major contributors to growth were government expenditures (0.8% of 1.6% average growth) and private consumption (1.0% of 1.6%). However, government expenditures could not support the economy forever. Private consumption may be able to support the economy for a short time under an economic contraction, as it is a relatively stable component in the aggregate demand. However, in the case where the economy stagnates for as long it actually did, the growth contribution of consumption is most likely to decline proportionately to the decline in the growth rate of the economy as a whole. Therefore, it was difficult for consumption to continue to be a driver of recovery under the prolonged stagnation.

Balance Sheet Damage

In the initial adjustment period, one more factor depressing investment and growth was at work. It is the damage to the balance sheets of companies, reducing the capacity for risk-taking.

Capital Losses Incurred by the Collapse of the Bubble

In Chap. 2, we saw the formation of a huge bubble in the 1980s. To repeat the data, urban land price Index (commercial use in six largest cities) rose 4.9 times in seven and a half years from 107.8 in October 1982 to 525.4 in April 1990. Thereafter, it declined continuously for 14 years from October 1990 to 67.2 (−87.0%) in April 2004, which was the level in 1972–1973, before it showed a minimal increase of 0.2% in October 2004.

Stock prices (Nikkei 225 [monthly average]) also increased 5.4 times in seven years and four months, from 7,042 in August 1982 to 38,130 in December 1989. It started to fall in January 1990, hit the then bottom of 15,790 (−58.6%) in August 1992, that is, in less than three years, and then became stabilized basically in the range of 16,000–21,000, before it resumed a fall in late 1997.

GDP statistics provide estimates of capital gains and losses (both realized and unrealized), arising from price developments in stocks and land for each year (Fig. 3.21).

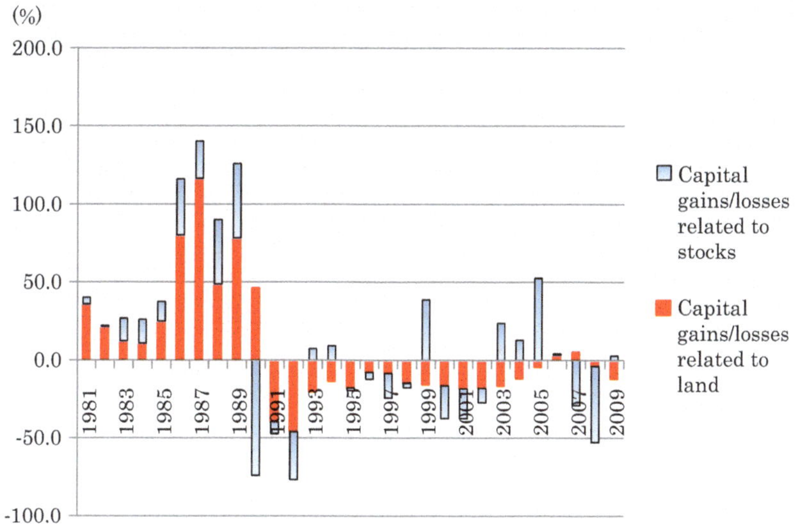

Fig. 3.21 Capital gains and losses accruing to land and stocks (in GDP ratio). Note: Bars show the combined amount of realized and unrealized capital gains and losses. Source: Cabinet Office, GDP statistics

According to these estimates, while the cumulative capital gains accrued to the economy as a whole over 1986–1989 amounted to 4.7 times the average GDP in that period, the cumulative capital losses accrued over 1990–2002 was 3.2 times the average GDP in the period, with 69% of these losses accrued in 1990–1997, a period overlapping Period I. As more than 90% of land and stocks were held by the private sector,[17] these capital losses were surely to damage balance sheets of companies and also financial institutions, discouraging their positive risk-taking behaviors, such as investment.

Some evidence of such intimidated behaviors are found in developments in companies' borrowings (Fig. 3.22). The outstanding balance of long-term debt of companies became almost flat after FY 1994, when the balance was 384 trillion yen, likely reflecting companies' efforts to repair their balance sheets. The balance hit a slightly higher peak of 406 trillion yen in 1998, after which the long-term debt fell sharply.

[17] As of 1990, 91.4% of land and 93.6% of stocks were held by the private sector (FY 2009 GDP statistics, Cabinet Office).

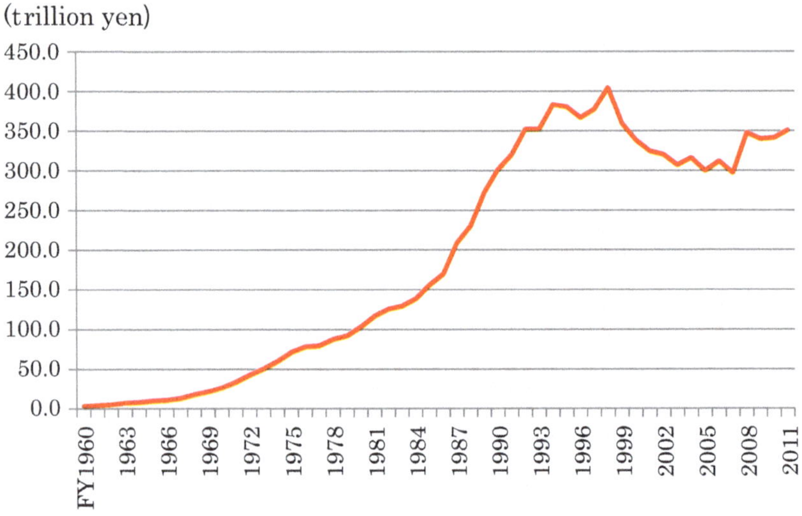

Fig. 3.22 Outstanding balance of long-term debt of companies (all industries excluding financial and insurance companies). Source: Ministry of Finance "Financial Statements Statistics of Corporations by Industry"

Continued Decline of Land Prices

Among these damages, it was capital losses accruing to landholdings that continued to arise for a long period of time after the collapse of the bubble. Annual rates of decline in land prices were in the range of 20% for three years, from 1992 to the beginning of 1995, and then around 10% for the subsequent seven years until 2003. These declines continued to impose additional damages to the balance sheets of companies and depressed positive economic activities.[18]

A question arises as to why the land price continued to decline for such a long period of time, more than three times as long as the average correction period after a housing price boom (which usually includes land prices), as found by the IMF.[19] As shown in Fig. 3.23, it is possible that the

[18] These price declines aggravated non-performing loan problems for banks, as examined in Chap. 4.

[19] IMF (2003) examined the historical experiences of booms and busts in equity and housing prices. The study covered equity prices in 19 industrial countries, for which equity price indices were generally available from 1959, and housing prices for 12 countries, for which housing price indices generally started in 1970. A bust was defined as a peak-to-trough

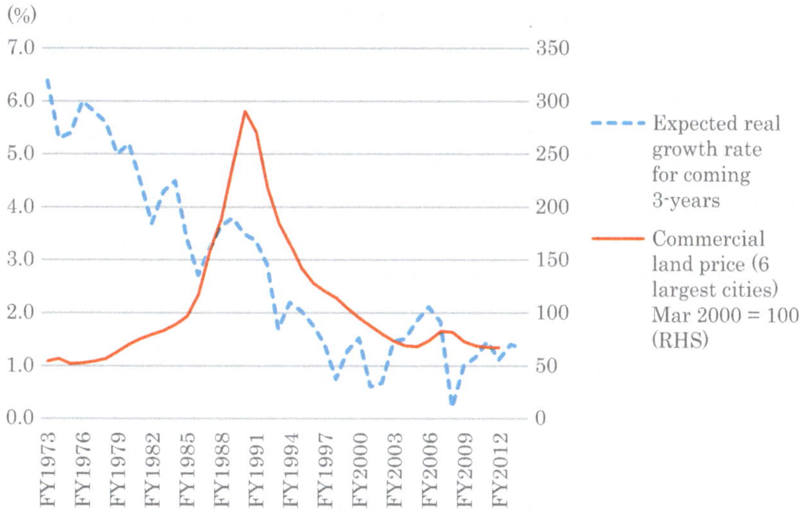

Fig. 3.23 Expected growth rate and land price. Note: Urban land price is calculated as of April 1 of each respective year. Source: Japan Real Estate Institute, Cabinet Office "Survey on company behavior"

continued decline in the expected real growth rate, which may well have reflected continued stagnation, reduced the expected rate of return to landholdings and thus depressed demand for land. This process continued until the early 2000s and then was temporarily suspended as the expected growth rate started to rise, most probably reflecting the long recovery. Land prices started to rise in the latter half of the 2000s, but this positive process did not continue for long with the impacts of GFC.

Thus, companies continued to incur realized/unrealized capital losses due to the collapse of the bubble and subsequent asset deflation, continuing for more than a decade until the beginning of the 2000s. During the excess capacity hangover, profits stagnated (as will be examined in Chap. 6 in more detail), and the balance sheets of companies continued

decline where the price change fell into the top quartile in all declines during bear markets (both indices were deflated by the Consumer Price Index (CPI). The study identified 52 equity price busts between 1959:Q1 and 2002:Q3 (one bust per country for every 13 years). On average, busts involved a price decline of about 45% and unfolded over a period of 10 quarters. The study identified 20 housing price crashes between 1970:Q1 and 2002:Q3 (one bust per country every 20 years). Price correction in the busts averaged 30% and lasted about 4 years, about a year and a half longer than equity price busts.

to deteriorate in the 1990s. Therefore, risk-taking behaviors of companies continued to be heavily discouraged, restraining investment for a long time.

How Did the Government Respond?

Let us look at how the government responded. In the face of economic contraction after the bubble burst, the government repeatedly implemented extensive expansionary measures.

Fiscal Policy

The government implemented as many as 12 large economic stimulus packages in less than 10 years between August 1992 and December 2001, and 6 out of 12 packages were implemented in Period I (Table 3.6). A new package was announced every year after the contraction started, except in 1996–1997, when no package was compiled, reflecting a short recovery and a fiscal consolidation policy that was pursued in that period but aborted shortly thereafter. The scale of eight packages were over 2% of the GDP.[20]

Table 3.6 Economic stimulus packages after the burst of the bubble (trillions of yen)

	August 1992	*April 1993*	*September 1993*	*February 1994*	*April 1995*	*September 1995*
Package volume (percent of GDP)	10.7 (2.2%)	13.2 (2.7%)	Approx. 6.0 (1.2%)	15.3 (3.1%)	Approx. 7.0 (1.4%)	14.2 (2.8%)
Amount of public investment in the package	8.6	10.6	5.2	7.2		11.4

	April 1998	*November 1998*	*November 1999*	*October 2000*	*October 2001*	*December 2001*
Package volume (percent of GDP)	Over 16.0 (3.2%)	Over 20.0 (4.7%)	Approx. 18.0 (3.5%)	Approx. 11.0 (2.1%)	Approx. 5.9 (1.2%)	Approx. 4.1 (0.8%)
Amount of public investment in the package	5.2	8.0	7.2	4.2		2.5

Source: Summarized from Table 1 in Nakao (2002)

[20] The largest stimulus package in 1998 was over 4.7% of GDP.

Reflecting fiscal stimulus efforts, government investment (in GDP ratio) significantly increased over the 1990s, making up, in part, for the decline in private investment (see previous Fig. 3.15).

As a result of fiscal stimulus, as well as revenue-reducing and expenditure-increasing effects of economic stagnation and the impacts of the population aging on welfare expenditure, the government deficit dramatically expanded (Fig. 3.24), and government debt (in GDP ratio) sharply increased.

Deterioration in fiscal balance was very significant relative to other advanced countries (Fig. 3.25).

Japan's government debt sharply increased and reached a high level that is far larger than other advanced countries (Fig. 3.26).

Monetary Policy

The discount rate, which was among the major tools of monetary policy at the time, was raised five times from the level of 2.5% to 6.0% in a year and three months from May 1989 to August 1990. Then, from July 1991, only 10 months later, it was lowered seven more times to reach 1.75% in September 1993. In 1995, the discount rate was further reduced twice to reach 0.5%, a level close to zero (Fig. 3.27).

Fig. 3.24 Fiscal balance of general government (in GDP ratio). Source: IMF, World Economic Outlook Database, October 2017

Fig. 3.25 General government deficit (in GDP ratio): Japan, US, the United Kingdom, Germany, and France. Note: General government net lending/borrowing (in percent of GDP). Source: IMF, World Economic Outlook October 2013 database

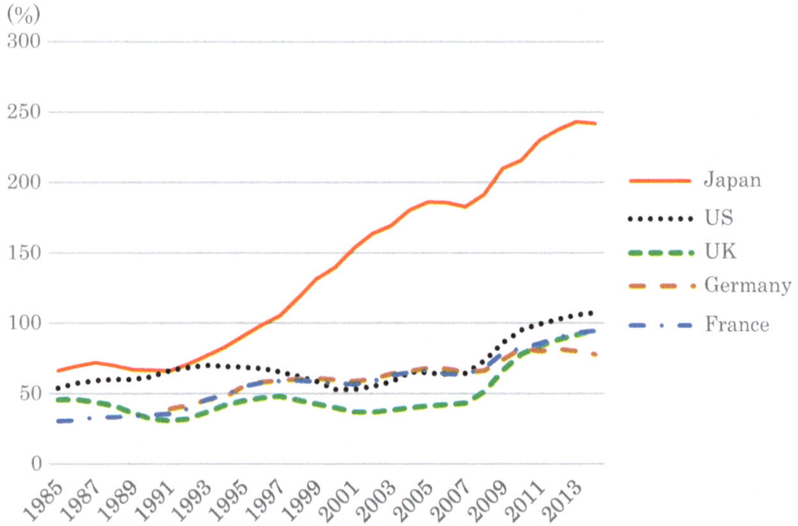

Fig. 3.26 Outstanding balance of general government debt (in GDP ratio). Source: IMF World Economic Outlook Database, October 2013

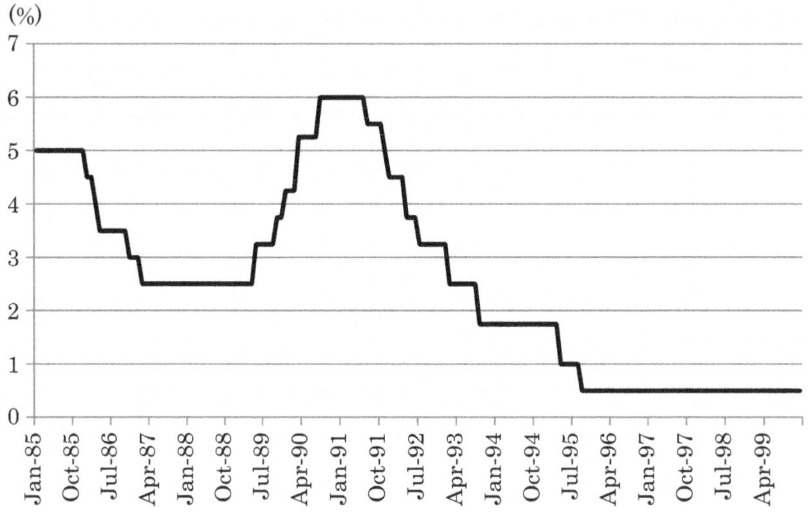

Fig. 3.27 Official discount rate. Source: Bank of Japan

Under these policy efforts, the economy started to recover in 1994–1996, but as we have seen, the recovery was weak and the stagnation did not end. On the contrary, the Japanese economy was eventually faced with an unprecedented financial crisis in the late 1990s, which we will look at in Chap. 4.

Summary of the Initial Adjustment Period

The trouble with the Japanese economy started with the collapse of the bubble. The sudden brake on the bubble by aggressive monetary policy tightening and the introduction of direct limits on real estate-related lending, as was evidenced by the nosedive in the growth rate of money stock, ushered in the collapse of the bubble and led the economy into a recession. As the economy decelerated, excesses formed in the 1980s in both assets and liabilities became a heavy burden for companies.

Fig. 3.16 clearly shows that the bubble era left Japan with excess assets, coupled with excess liabilities. The pace of growth in both assets and liabilities in the latter half of the 1980s was notably faster than in preceding periods. The problem with these excesses was that these assets were not accompanied by sustainable demand (sales), or in other words, they were not profitable. So, what was needed most in the initial adjustment period was the disposition of these excesses. However, the removal of these excesses by the corporate sector took a long time. The reason for the long time of disposition may be as follows. Initially, there was some delay in recognizing that assets were in excess and had to be downward adjusted, even after the collapse of the bubble and the halt of sales growth. Next, the excess itself expanded as the actual growth rate, and therefore, the expected economic growth rate (which leads to the expected sales growth rate) fell. (This point will be examined in detail in Chap. 6). Lastly, after the problem of excess assets came to the surface, the magnitude of the excess (to be discussed in Chap. 4 and its Supplement 2), and therefore, the expected negative impacts of their disposition when swiftly disposed of may have lengthened the disposition.

Furthermore, the sharp appreciation of the yen rate around the mid-1990s hurt exports and also imposed dampening effects on business confidence.

Worsening balance sheet conditions imposed an additional burden. Substantial capital losses incurred by nonfinancial and financial corporations due to sharp asset deflation imposed damages to their balance sheets, making these corporations cautious toward investment and debt assumption.

Continued decline in growth rates also reduced expected return to landholding and therefore reduced demand for land, depressing the land prices and further creating capital losses each year.

In this way, in the initial adjustment period, the Japanese economy was deprived of two major important drivers of economic recovery: private investment and exports.

The government supported the economy, and private consumption provided certain stabilizing effects to the economy, but sustainability of their growth contribution could not be expected under the prolonged stagnation.

With hindsight, Period I seems to be of critical importance. The problem of overinvestment in the bubble period and balance sheet damages by the collapse of the bubble were addressed by companies through their curtailing of investment and refraining from additional borrowing, so as to adjust production capacity downward and repair their balance sheets. Meanwhile, the government implemented very extensive stimulus and macroeconomic policies to support the economy. However, external developments, particularly sharp appreciation of the yen during trade disputes with the United States, limited the scope of more export-led recovery. Under these circumstances, the weakness of economic performance continued for a long time, which in turn lowered growth expectation held by companies for the future, leading to continued, self-fulfilling low growth.

Costs of lengthened adjustments of excess capacity of the corporate sector were gradually shifted to the financial sector and surfaced as the worsening of non-performing loan problems. This culminated in the late 1990s in the form of the first systemic financial crisis after the Second World War. Despite huge (realized and unrealized) losses arising from excess (unprofitable) assets formed during the bubble, Japan did not have a social or political crisis per se during the two decade-long stagnation, largely due to extensive government support. The lengthened adjustment process left Japan with negative legacy, however, including sharply elevated government debt and a downward shift of growth, trending to a very low level.

If the disposition of excess assets had been swiftly completed in the first half of 1990s, the economy would have been rapidly freed from the overhang of the adjustment burden and could have made a fresh start relatively early, with such strength as in the past. The magnitude of necessary adjustment, however, seems to have made this choice difficult. The fact that we could not or did not solve the problem in Period I turned out to be most crucial in the subsequent two-decade developments. After all, the Japanese economy, while avoiding swift adjustment, could not avoid in-depth adjustment (disposition of excesses), and in the end, there developed a crisis. The topic of the financial crisis, including reasons for non-disposal of excesses in a short period of time, is covered in the next chapter.

Supplement

Table 3.7 Chronology of relevant events

October 1987	Black Monday
May 1989	BOJ raised the discount rate for the first time in nine years
June 1989	Prime Minister Takeshita resigned amid a scandal (current Prime Minister Abe is the 17th prime minister after Takeshita)
January 1990	Stock prices started to fall
March 1990	MOF imposed an aggregate lending limit on real estate-related loans
1990	Land prices started to fall
August 1990	Iraqi troops invaded Kuwait
January 1991	The Gulf War started
February 1991	The Japanese economy peaked and started to slow down
August 1993	Non-LDP administration formed (Prime Minister Hosokawa)
October 1993	The Japanese economy hit a bottom
February 1994	Japan–US dispute over the "numerical target" for market opening demanded by the Clinton administration
April 1995	Yen recorded the then historic high at of 79.75 yen to the dollar
November 1996	Prime Minister Hashimoto instructed Finance Minister Mitsuzuka and Minister of Justice Matsuura that a reform of Japan's financial system had to be examined
November 1996	Finance Minister Mitsuzuka requested the chairmen of five advisory councils on securities transactions, accounting, the financial system, insurance, and foreign exchange to prepare as soon as possible a plan to complete a reform of Japan's financial system by 2001, and subsequently each of these councils started examination of the issues, so as to prepare a reform plan by June 1997
December 1996	The Cabinet decided on the fiscal consolidation target of reducing the fiscal deficit to equal or less than 3% of GDP at the earliest before fiscal 2005
January 1997	Prime Minister Hashimoto declared a start of drastic reforms in six areas, including fiscal structure and the financial system
January 1997	A report on a reform bill of Foreign Exchange and Foreign Trade Management Act was approved by the advisory council on foreign exchange
April 1997	Consumption tax rate was increased from 3% to 5%
June 1997	BOJ law amended (its independence strengthened)
June 1997	Comprehensive financial liberalization (Japan's financial "Big Bang") authorized by four relevant advisory councils (securities transactions, accounting, the financial system, and insurance) to MOF
July 1997	Thai baht recorded a sharp fall (start of the Asian currency crisis)
November 1997	Sanyo Securities filed an application for protection under the Corporate Rehabilitation Law, causing a default in the interbank market
November 1997	Hokkaido Takushoku Bank announced its inability to continue
November 1997	Yamaichi Securities announced closure of business
November 1997	Fiscal Structure Reform Act enacted

(*continued*)

(continued)

April 1998	Comprehensive Economic Measures decided
May 1998	Fiscal Structure Reform Act amended (in December 1998, its implementation was suspended)
October 1998	Government decided to nationalize the Long-term Credit Bank of Japan (first nationalization of private bank after the war)
November 1998	Emergency economic measures decided (historically largest size)
December 1998	Nippon Credit Bank nationalized

Bibliography

English References

Hayashi, Fumio, and Edward C. Prescott (2002) "The 1990s in Japan: A Lost Decade," *Review of Economic Dynamics* 5 (1): 206–235.

IMF (International Monetary Fund) (2003) *World Economic Outlook April 2003*. Washington, DC: IMF.

Mori, Naruki, Shigenori Shiratsuka, and Hiroo Taguchi (2001) "Policy Responses to the Post-bubble Adjustments in Japan: A Tentative Review." *Monetary and Economic Studies,* Institute for Monetary and Economic Studies, Bank of Japan, 19 (S1): 53–102.

Nakao, Takehiko (2002) "Japan's experience with fiscal policy in the 1990s in the aftermath of the bubble economy." Presentation at the 4th Banca d'Italia Workshops on Public Finances, "The Impact of Fiscal Policy, Perugia," March 21–23, 2002.

Okina, Kunio, Masaaki Shirakawa, and Shigenori Shiratsuka (2001) "Asset price bubble and monetary policy: Japan's experience in the late 1980s and the lessons." Background Paper, February. *Monetary and Economic Studies* (Special Edition): 395–450.

Okina, Kunio, and Shigenori Shiratsuka (2002) "Asset Price Bubbles, Price Stability, and Monetary Policy: Japan's Experience" *Monetary and Economic Studies*, Institute for Monetary and Economic Studies, Bank of Japan, 20 (3): 35–76.

Sakakibara, Eisuke (2000) "US-Japanese economic policy – conflicts and coordination during the 1990s." In *Japan's Financial Crisis and Its Parallels to U.S. Experience*, edited by Ryoichi Mikitani and A.S. Posen. Washington, DC: Institute for International Economy.

Shirakawa, Masaaki (2012a) "Deleveraging and Growth: Is the Developed World Following Japan's Long and Winding Road?" Lecture at the London School of Economics (LSE) and Political Science, co-hosted by the Asia Research Center and Suntory and Toyota International Centres for Economics and Related Disciplines (STICARD), LSE, January 10, 2012, Bank of Japan.

Shirakawa, Masaaki (2012b) "Japan's economy and monetary policy." June 4, 2012, Bank of Japan.

Japanese References

Bernanke, Ben (2001) "Mizukara kino mahi ni ochiitta nihon no kinnyu seisaku" ("Japanese monetary policy – A case of self-induced paralysis?). In *Nihon no Kinyu Kiki – Beikoku no Keiken to Nihon heno Kyokun* (Monetary Policy in Japan – "US Experiences and Their Lessons for Japan), edited by Ryoichi Mikitani and Adam A. Posen. Tokyo: Toyo Keizai Shimpo Sha.

Fukao, Mitsuhiro (2002) "1980 nendai kohan no shisan kakaku baburu hassei to 90 nendai no fukyo no gennin" ("Causes of asset price bubble in the late 1980s and recession in the 1990s"). In *Heisei Baburu no Kenkyu I* (Study of the Heisei Bubble I), edited by Michio Muramatsu and Masahiro Okuno. Tokyo: Toyo Keizai Shimpo Sha.

Fukao, Mitsuhiro (2009) "Choki Fukyo to Kinnyu Seisaku Kawase Reto Ginko Shinnyo" ("The long stagnation and monetary policy, foreign exchange rate and bank credit). In *Furyo Saiken to Kinnyu Kiki*, edited by Kazuo Ikeo, (Cabinet Office "Baburu/defure kino Nihon Keizai to Keizai Seisaku 4" (Japanese Economy and Economic Policy in the Period of Bubble and Deflation 4), Economic and Social Research Institute, Cabinet Office).

Fukuda, Shin-ichi (2009) "Baburu Hokai gono Kinnyu Shijo no Doyo to Kinnyu Seisaku" (Instability of Financial Markets after the Collapse of the Bubble and Monetary Policy). In *Defure Keizai to Kinnyu Seisaku* (*Deflationary Economy and Monetary Policy*), edited by Hiroshi Yoshikawa, (Cabinet Office Baburu/defure kino Nihon Keizai to Keizai Seisaku 7 (Japanese Economy and Economic Policy in the Period of Bubble and Deflation 7), Economic and Social Research Institute, Cabinet Office).

Hamada, Koichi, and Akiyoshi Horiuchi (2004) *Ronso: Nihon no Keizai Kiki – Choki Teitai no Shin-in wo Kaimei suru* (Debates: Japan's Economic Crisis – Examining Real Cause of the Long Stagnation). Nihon Keizai Shimbun Sha.

Hayashi, Fumio (2003) "Kozo Kaikaku Nakushite Seicho Nashi" (No growth without structural reform"). In *Usinawareta 10 nen no Shin-in ha Nanika* (What is the Real Cause of the Lost Decade?), edited by Kikuo Iwata and Tsutomu Miyagawa. Tokyo: Toyo Keizai Shimpo Sha.

Hori, Masahiro (2009) "Ajia no Hatten to Nihon Keizai – Gaiju Doko Kawase Reto to Nihon no Kyoso Ryoku-" ("Growth of Asia and Japan's economy – Evolution of foreign demand, foreign exchange rate, and Japan's competitiveness"). In *Makuro Keizai to Sangyo Kozo* (Macroeconomy and Industrial Structure), edited by Kyoji Fukao, (Cabinet Office, Baburu/defure kino Nihon Keizai to Keizai Seisaku 1 (Japanese economy and economic policy in the period of bubble and deflation 1), Economic and Social Research Institute, Cabinet Office).

Horioka, Charles Yuji (2007) "Nihon no 'Ushinawareta 10 nen' no Gennin" ("Cause of Japan's 'Lost Decade'") In *Keizai Teitai no Gennin to Seido* (Causes of Economic Stagnation and Institutions), edited by Fumio Hayashi. Keiso Shobo

Ito, Mitsutoshi (2002) "Choki teikinri seisaku no seiji keizai gaku" ("Political economy of the prolonged low interest rate policy.") In *Heisei Baburu no Kenkyu II* (Study of the Heisei Bubble II), edited by Michio Muramatsu and Masahiro Okuno. Tokyo: Toyo Keizai Shimpo Sha.

Iwata, Kikuo (1993) *Kinnyu Seisaku no Keizai Gaku – "Nichigin Riron" no Kensho* (Economics of Monetary Policy – Examination of the "BOJ Theory"). Nihon Keizai Shimbun Sha.

Iwata, Kikuo and Economic and Social Research Institute, Cabinet Office, eds. (2011) *Baburu/Defure ki no Nihon Keizai to Keizai Seisaku – Ware Ware ha Nani wo Mananda noka-* (Japanese Economy and Economic Policy in the Period of Bubble and Deflation – What Have We Learned?), Economic and Social Research Institute, Cabinet Office.

Iwata, Kikuo and Miyagawa Tsutomu, eds. (2003) *Ushinawareta 10 nen no Shin-in ha Nanika* (What is the Real Cause of the Lost Decade?), Economics Series. Tokyo: Toyo Keizai Shimpo Sha.

Kawai, Masahiro, and Shinji Takagi (2009) "Kawase reto to kokusai shushi – puraza goi kara heisei fukyo no makuro keizai gaku" ("Foreign exchange rate and balance of payments – Macroeconomics of the Plaza Accord to Heisei stagnation"). In *Kokusai Kankyo no Henka to Nihon* Keizai (Changes in International Environments and the Japanese Economy), edited by Motoshige Ito, (Cabinet Office Baburu/defure kino Nihon Keizai to Keizai Seisaku 3 (*Japanese Economy and Economic Policy in the Period of Bubble and Deflation* 3), Economic and Social Research Institute, Cabinet Office).

Kojo, Yoshiko (2009) "Kokusai seiji to nihon no kisei kanwa, kozo kaikaku" ("International politics and deregulation and structural reform in Japan"). In *Kozo Mondai to Kisei Kanwa* (Structural Problems and Deregulation), edited by Juro Teranishi, (Cabinet Office Baburu/defure kino Nihon Keizai to Keizai Seisaku 7 (Japanese Economy and Economic Policy in the Period of Bubble and Deflation 7) Economic and Social Research Institute, Cabinet Office).

Komine, Takao, ed. (2011) *Nihon Keizai no Kiroku Dai Niji Sekiyu Kiki heno Taio kara Baburu Hokai made (1970 nendai~1996 nen)* ("Record of Japanese Economy From Responses to the 2nd Oil shock and the Collapse of the Bubble (1970s to 1996)"). Baburu/defure kino Nihon Keizai to Keizai Seisaku Rekisi hen dai 1 kan (Japanese Economy and Economic Policy in the Period of Bubble and Deflation – History, Vol. 1), Economic and Social Research Institute, Cabinet Office, Japanese Government.

Kusu, Toshiharu (2005) "Baburu no Gennin Saiko (jo)" (Re-examining cause of the bubble (1)). In Yokin Hoken Kiko (Deposit Insurance Corporation) *Yokin Hoken Kenkyu* October.

Kusu, Toshiharu (2006) "Baburu no Gennin Saiko (ge)" ("Re-examining causes of the bubble (2)"). In Yokin Hoken Kiko (Deposit Insurance Corporation) *Yokin Hoken Kenkyu*, November 2006.

Matsushima, Shigeru, and Harukata Takenaka, eds. (2011) *Nihon Keizai no Kiroku – Jidai Shogen Shu (oraru Hisutori)* ("Record of Japanese Economy – Collection of Testimonies of the Period (Oral History)"). (Baburu/Defure ki no Nihon Keizai to Keizai Seisaku – Rekishi Hen dai 3 kan (Japanese Economy and Economic Policies in the Period of Bubble and Deflation, – History, Vol. 3)), Economic and Social Research Institute, Cabinet Office, Japanese Government.

Mieno, Yasushi (2000) *Ri wo Mite Gi wo Omou* (When Seeing profits, Thinking about Justice). Chuo Koron Sha.

Miyagawa, Tsutomu (2003) "'Ushinawareta 10 nen' to Sangyo Kozo no Tenkan" ('Lost Decade' and changes in industrial structure). In "*Ushinawareta 10 nen no Shinn-in ha Nanika*" (What is the Real Cause of the Lost Decade?), edited by Kikuo Iwata and Tsutomu Miyagawa, Economics Series. Tokyo: Toyo Keizai Shimpo Sha.

Miyazaki, Giichi (1992) *Fukugo Fukyo – Posuto Baburu no Shohosen wo Motomete* (Complex Recession – Seeking Prescriptions in Post-Bubble Era). Chuo Koron Sha.

Motani, Kosuke (2010) *Defure no Shotai –Keizai ha Jinko no Nami de Ugoku* ("The real origin of deflation: The economy moves by the demographic waves"). Kadokawa One Tema 21.

Noguchi, Asahi (2005, 2006) "Heisei keizai seisaku ronso" ("Heisei economic policy debates") in Nihon Hyoron Sha *Keizai Seminar*, April 2005 – March 2006.

Noguchi, Asahi and Yasushi Okada (2003) "Kinnyu seisaku no kino teishi ha naze shojita noka" ("Why was the dysfunction of monetary policy brought about?") In *Ushinawareta 10 nen no Shinn-in ha Nanika* (What is the Real Cause of the Lost Decade?), edited by Kikuo Iwata and Tsutomu Miyagawa, Economics Series. Tokyo: Toyo Keizai Shimpo Sha.

Noguchi, Yukio (2005) *Nihon Keizai Kaizo Ron* (Arguments for Fundamental Reform of Japan's Economy) Tokyo: Toyo Keizai Shimpo Sha.

Ogawa, Kazuo (2009) '*Ushinawareta 10 nen' no Shinjitsu – Jittai Keizai to Kinnyu Shisutemu no Sokoku* (Truth of the "Lost Decade" – Conflict between Real Economy and Financial System). Tokyo: Toyo Keizai Shimpo Sha.

Okada, Yasushi, and Hamada Koichi (2009) "Baburu Defure ki no Nihon no Kinnyu Seisaku" (Monetary policy in Japan during the period of bubble and deflation). In *Defure Keizai to Kinnyu Seisaku* (Deflationary Economy and Monetary Policy), edited by Hiroshi Yoshikawa. (Cabinet Office Baburu/defure kino Nihon Keizai to Keizai Seisaku 2 ("Japanese Economy and Economic Policy in the Period of Bubble and Deflation 2"), Economic and Social Research Institute, Cabinet Office).

Okina Kunio (2009) "Baburu no seisei hokai no keiken ni terashita kinnyu Seisaku no Ayumi – FED view to BIS view wo fumaete" (Evolution of monetary policy in light of experience of the formation and collapse of the bubble – Drawing on FED views and BIS views) In *Defure Keizai to Kinnyu Seisaku* (Deflationary Economy and Monetary Policy), edited by Hiroshi Yoshikawa. (Cabinet Office Baburu/defure kino Nihon Keizai to Keizai Seisaku 2 ("Japanese Economy and Economic Policy in the Period of Bubble and Deflation 2") Economic and Social Research Institute, Cabinet Office).

Tanaka, Takayuki (2002) *Gendai Nihon Keizai – Baburu to Posuto Baburu no Kiseki* (Current Japanese Economy – Trajectory of the Bubble and Post-Bubble). Nihon Hyoron Sha.

Tanaka, Takayuki (2009) *Kinnyu Kiki ni Do Tachi Mukau ka –Ushinawareta 15 nen no Kyokun* (How to Cope with Financial Crises? Lessons from 'the Lost 15 years'). Chikuma Shobo.

Yoshikawa, Hiroshi (2009) "Defureshon to kinnyu seisaku" ("Deflation and monetary policy") In *Defure Keizai to Kinnyuu Seisaku* (Deflationary Economy and Monetary Policy), edited by Hiroshi Yoshikawa. (Cabinet Office Baburu/defure kino Nihon Keizai to Keizai Seisaku 7 (Japanese Economy and Economic Policy in the Period of Bubble and Deflation 7), Economic and Social Research Institute, Cabinet Office).

Yoshikawa, Mototada (1998) *Mane Haisen* ("Defeat in monetary war."), Bunshun Bunko.

CHAPTER 4

The Financial Crisis and Its Impacts, Long Recovery, and Afterward

In this chapter, we cover three periods that follow Period I (1991–1997): Period II (1998–2002: financial crisis and its impacts), Period III (2003–2007: long recovery), and Period IV (2008–2012: Global Financial Crisis (GFC) and after). The focus is on the financial crisis that began in late 1997 and its impacts on the Japanese economy. The subsequent two periods will be examined more briefly.

1 Period II (1998–2002) Financial Crisis and Its Impacts

In this section,[1] we will examine Period II that covers 1998–2002. First, we look at how the financial crisis unfolded and was addressed; second, why non-performing loan (NPL) problems, which were the fundamental cause of the crisis, were not solved sooner; and third, the far-reaching impacts of the crisis on the Japanese economy.

The Unfolding of the Financial Crisis and Its Resolution

Overview

Financial Crisis Breaks Out

Seven years after the collapse of the bubble, a financial crisis broke out. In early November 1997, a medium-sized securities firm, called Sanyo Securities,

[1] Description in this chapter owes much to Nakaso (2001).

K. Aramaki, *Japan's Long Stagnation, Deflation, and Abenomics*,
https://doi.org/10.1007/978-981-13-2176-4_4

applied for a legal restructuring procedure, which led to an issuance by the court of an order to protect the firm's assets and a resultant default in obligations in the interbank market for the first time in postwar history. This event had grave impacts on interbank market participants, causing them to be more selective with respect to borrowers, and it became difficult for some financial institutions to obtain financing in the interbank market.

In mid-November 1997, Hokkaido Takushoku Bank, one of the largest banks in Japan, announced its inability to continue its business operations, which was the first failure of a large bank in Japan since the Second World War, and then, in late November, Yamaichi Securities, one of the "Big Four" securities firms in Japan, announced closure of its business. A few days later in the same month, the regional bank Tokuyo City Bank failed, making it apparent that the financial system was faced with serious systemic pressure. While the financial markets recovered some stability after new safety net measures were introduced (to be explained later), the crisis resurfaced in the mid-1998 with the problems of the Long-Term Credit Bank of Japan (LTCB) which was the second largest LTCB. Under the newly introduced, more comprehensive safety net measures, the LTCB and then, the Nippon Credit Bank (NCB), the third largest and smallest LTCB were nationalized in October and December 1998, respectively. Instability of the financial sector continued until the NPL problems were finally resolved by the mid-2000s.

Bank Failures

Under the severe systemic stress, failures of financial institutions reached an unprecedented level. In total, 181 financial institutions failed in the 1990s and the first half of 2000s. A total of 161 (89%) of 181 failed in five years from 1997 to 2001, and more than two-thirds were credit cooperatives (Fig. 4.1).

The number of financial institutions dramatically decreased by 500 (−44.9%) from 1,080 at the end of March 1990 to 580 at the end of March 2014. More than 42.4% (212 institutions) of these 500 closures occurred in five years from the end of March 1997 to the end of March 2002, with the outbreak of the financial crisis of 1997–1998, and 84.0% (178 institutions) of these 212 institutions were either credit banks or credit cooperatives. While the decline reflects not only closure due to failures but also mergers under changing business environments, such a rapid decline in the number of banks illustrates how serious the impacts of the crisis were to the Japanese economy.

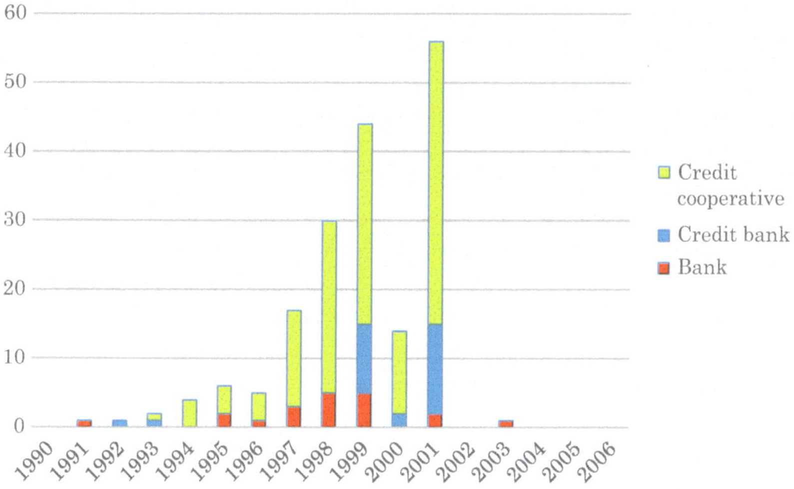

Fig. 4.1 Number of failed deposit-taking financial institutions. Source: Financial Services Agency

Background of the Non-Performing Loan Problems

Behind the crisis were the NPL problems. Even further behind was an excess capital stock formed in the bubble era in the corporate sector, followed by sales stagnation after the collapse of the bubble.

Excess Assets and Sales Stagnation

As we saw in Chap. 3, the corporate sector, by the early 1990s, had amassed physical assets far greater than implied by the preceding trend (see Fig. 3.16 in Chap. 3). So, in order to be profitable, the corporate sector needed a sufficiently large amount of sales. However, sales of corporations suddenly stopped growing after the burst of the bubble and instead declined during the 1990s (Fig. 3.17 in Chap. 3).

As a result, the Return on Assets (ROA: operating profits/total assets, %), which was on a declining trend from the high-speed growth period, further fell in the 1990s (Fig. 4.2).

Earned profits, that is, the accumulated profits stopped growing after the beginning of the 1990s until the end of 1990s (Fig. 4.3).

Thus, after the collapse of the bubble, the corporate sector was faced with a difficult problem of low profitability brought about by a combination of excessively large asset size and sales stagnation. If the sales were expected

Fig. 4.2 Return on Assets (ROA: operating profits/total assets). Source: Ministry of Finance "Financial Statements Statistics of Corporations by Industry"

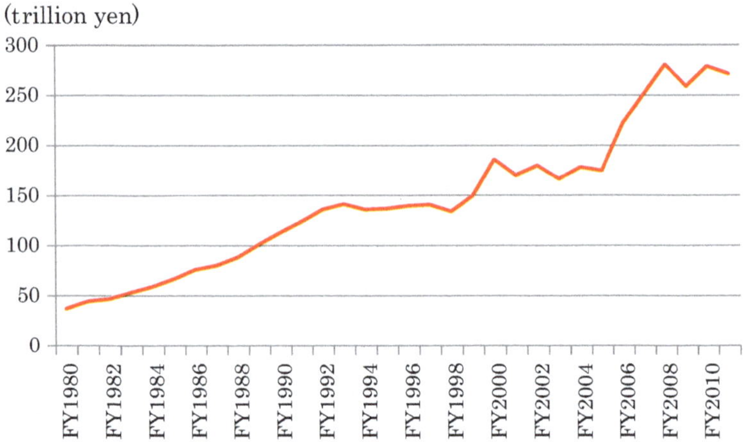

Fig. 4.3 Earned profits. Source: Ministry of Finance "Financial Statements Statistics of Corporations by Industry"

to recover, companies could continue to hold the assets and wait for the recovery of sales. If not, that is, if sales could not be expected to recover, companies should dispose of these assets to avoid low profitability for an extended period of time. What happened in reality was a prolonged sales stagnation (see Fig. 3.17 in Chap. 3), so, the right choice in hindsight was to dispose of the excess of unprofitable assets promptly.[2] However, the corporate sector took time to address the problem of excess assets, which made low profitability linger, gradually eroding the financial strength of the corporate sector.

From the financial sector's point of view, the erosion of financial soundness of the borrowing companies was a cause for their declining ability to repay their debts. The value of collateral was also being eroded after the burst of the bubble. This was particularly true with commercial mortgage loans, which were aggressively provided during the bubble. The financial sector came to have an increasingly difficult problem with their NPLs as years went by in the 1990s.[3]

Damage to the Balance Sheet of Borrowers and Lenders

Furthermore, the collapse of the bubble caused damage to the balance sheet of both borrowers and lenders, as explained in Chap. 3. Land prices continued to decline, reducing the land-related asset value, while burden of debts were kept unchanged. Stock prices also continued to decline, compressing unrealized capital gains that banks and companies had through stock holdings. Deterioration in the balance sheet soundness must have discouraged risk-taking behaviors, such as investment and debt assumption, which in turn placed an additional depressing effects on the economic recovery.

Increase in the Amount of NPLs

Reflecting lingering sales stagnation and the gradual approach by companies to cope with the excess (unprofitable) assets, the amount of NPLs incessantly increased from a range of over 10 trillion yen in the first

[2] In this case, disposition of assets does not necessarily mean demolition or destruction of the assets concerned. Typically, disposition of assets is conducted in such a way that the assets are sold at a price lower than the acquisition cost, entailing losses, and these losses are shared by relevant parties. It may be possible for the assets to become profitable, as the acquisition costs are low for the acquirer. Through the sale of assets at a lower price, the combined amount of assets of the corporate sector will decline.

[3] A report by the Deposit Insurance Corporation (DIC) (2005), which analyzed causes of the failures of 180 financial institutions to which DIC extended financial assistance, concluded that, for 165 (91.7%) of the total 180 failures, the NPL problem was listed among the causes of the failure (multiple listing). Out of these 165, 83 (46.1%) listed concentration of credit to real estate-related sector, 49 (27.2%) listed other factors including economic stagnation, and 47 (26.1%) listed concentration of credit to sectors other than the real estate-related sector as causes of failure.

half of 1990s to around 30 trillion yen in the latter half of 1990s. Against the background of prolonged stagnation and the break-out of the financial crisis, the amount of NPLs hit the peak of 42 trillion yen (NPL ratio equal to 8.4%) in the period ending in March 2002 (Table 4.1).[4,5,6,7]

[4]As the definition of NPL was gradually expanded, there is an issue whether a rigorous time-sequential comparison is possible.

[5]The amount of NPL and the resultant losses arising from the resolution of NPL tend to increase with the lapse of time if economic stagnation continues. This is because economic stagnation typically means sales stagnation, and therefore, revenue and profit stagnation of borrowing companies.

[6]The outstanding balance of NPLs is that of "risk-monitoring assets." There are three concepts of NPLs: "risk-monitoring assets," "disclosed assets under the Financial Recovery Act," and "NPLs under self-assessment." "Risk-monitoring assets" is a concept prescribed by the Banking Act and covers a longer period of time than data under the other two concepts do. It started to be disclosed from the year ending March 1993 and at that time covered only those **loans to failed borrowers** [①] and **past due loans** (loans for which unpaid interest is not recorded as revenue for six months or longer) [②]. Past due loans were disclosed only by major banks. From the year ending March 1996, disclosure under this concept was extended to cover **loans for which interest was reduced or waived** [③] and **loans to those borrowers for which such support as debt waiver had been extended** [④]. Furthermore, from the year ending March 1998 (for regional banks from the year ending September 1998), the aforementioned Type ② loans **were extended to cover loans past due three months or longer** [⑤], and a new type, **"loans for which lending conditions had been eased"** [⑥] was introduced to include, but was broader than loan types ③ and ④ (the term "risk-monitoring assets" began to be used from this point in time) (Watanabe 2001; Nakagawa 1996). The second concept, "disclosed assets under the Financial Recovery Act," was introduced by the Financial Recovery Act, enacted in October 1998. The act imposed a disclosure obligation under which major banks were required to disclose credit to legally bankrupt or de facto bankrupt borrowers (Type ①), credit in danger (Type ②), credit that needs to be monitored (Type ③), and normal credit (Type ④). It was implemented for major banks from the year ending March 1999, and for regional banks, from the year ending September 1999. The third concept, "NPLs under self-assessment" was made necessary by the Early Corrective Measures implemented from April 1998, under which, if the capital–asset ratio of an individual financial institution (to be calculated based on the self-assessment of loan quality) was lower than the prescribed level (8% for international criterion banks, and 4% for domestic criterion banks), authorities ordered the financial institutions to take corrective measures such as the strengthening of capital base. In the self-assessment, borrowers are classified into five categories: "failed," "in danger of failing," "risk of failure," "to be monitored," and "normal." Furthermore, respective assets are classified into four groups, from Class I (normal credit) to Class IV (credit impossible to recover or of no worth), depending on the degree of risk of recovery. Financial institutions were not required to disclose the amount of NPLs under the self-assessment and only the aggregate amount by type of financial institution and by classification of NPLs from Class I (normal credit) to Class IV (credit impossible to recover or of no worth) were disclosed by the authorities (Watanabe (2001)).

[7]The NPL ratio is the ratio of "disclosed assets under the Financial Recovery Act" (credit to legally bankrupt or de facto bankrupt borrowers [①], credit in danger [②], and credit that

Table 4.1 Outstanding non-performing loans (NPLs) and NPL ratio

	1993	*1994*	*1995*	*1996*	*1997*	*1998*	*1999*	*2000*	*2001*	*2002*	*2003*	*2004*	*2005*
Outstanding NPLs (bank) (trillion yen)	12.8	13.6	12.5	28.5	21.8	29.8	29.6	30.4	32.5	42.0	34.8	26.2	17.5
NPL ratio (bank) (%)							6.2	5.9	6.3	8.4	7.4	5.8	4.0
NPL ratio (major bank) (%)							6.1	5.4	5.3	8.4	7.2	5.2	2.9

Note:

1. Data are for the period ending in March of each year
2. Evolution of disclosure requirements of NPLs is explained in detail in footnote 6
3. The concept of the NPL ratio is explained in footnote 7
4. "Bank" consists of city banks, long-term credit banks, trust banks, and regional banks

Source: Financial Services Agency (FSA)

How Was the NPL Problem Addressed?

In this subsection, we will look at how the crisis surfaced and was resolved in a time-sequential manner, drawing on Nakaso (2001).[8]

needs to be monitored [③]) to the total credit. The basic concept of both the risk-monitoring assets and the disclosed assets under the Financial Recovery Act is same as is shown by the fact that both include failed loans, loans past due for three months or longer, and loans for which lending conditions had been eased. However, the two concepts adopt different classification methods, that is, while the starting point for risk-monitoring assets is the past due interest payments and then loans concerned are classified into those to failed borrowers and other loans (past due loans), under the disclosed assets of the Financial Recovery Act, division is between credit to failed borrowers and credit to borrowers that have not failed but have a high probability of non-recovery. In addition, risk-monitoring assets cover only loans, but disclosed assets under the Financial Recovery Act cover total credit including securities lending. Also, risk-monitoring assets are based on an asset-by-asset classification but disclosed assets under the Financial Recovery Act are based on a borrower-by-borrower classification).

[8] Nakaso (2001) gives a most detailed and clear chronological explanation of the unfolding of the financial crisis and authorities' responses.

Traditional Approach to the Troubled Banks

Until around the 1980s, troubled banks were acquired by healthy banks, mostly via intermediation by the Ministry of Finance (MOF), and all business, such as deposits and loans of failed banks, was in principle transferred to acquiring banks. This was possible because the acquisition brought to the acquiring banks such benefits as branch networks of the troubled banks, which were not easily obtained under the regulations then.

However, from around the late 1980s, it gradually became difficult to find a healthy bank that was willing to acquire a troubled bank, as the previous benefit had disappeared under liberalization.

Early Efforts and the Introduction of Full Deposit Guarantee

In the early 1990s, troubles with small- and medium-sized banks started to surface. In April 1992, financial assistance (a grant) within the payoff cost[9] from the DIC was extended for the first time to a bank that acquired a troubled regional bank, and the excess of burden over the payoff costs was covered by external assistance from the local government and other financial institutions.

In December 1994, two urban credit cooperatives failed, and a new bank (Tokyo Kyodo Bank [TKB]) was established as an assuming bank of the two failed banks by equal contributions from the Bank of Japan (BOJ) and private financial institutions.

Then, in 1995–1996, "Jusen" trouble became a major issue. Jusen were non-bank financial institutions established in the 1970s by banks and other financial institutions, originally for housing loans to households, for which banks did not have expertise at that time. As banks themselves became engaged in housing loans in the 1980s, Jusen was heavily involved in loans to real estate sectors, and with the burst of the bubble, they were left with huge NPLs. As the government could not find a solution under which all the losses of seven Jusen companies could be covered by founder banks and other creditor financial institutions, the government decided to use taxpayers' money to resolve these Jusen companies. This resulted in very strong public resentment, making further use of public funds politically taboo until the crisis broke out later in the 1990s.[10]

[9] Even before the 1996 amendment of the Deposit Insurance Law, DIC had the power to give financial assistance to the acquiring banks of failed banks, so as to make a deal possible, but the assistance was limited to the so-called payoff cost. Payoff cost usually refers to the amount of funds necessary to pay depositors the full insured amount (10 million yen per person, per bank) when a bank failed, less the remaining value of the failed bank (Nakaso 2001, 4).

[10] Nakaso (2001, 6–7)

In June 1996, the Deposit Insurance Law was amended to improve the safety net, and under the amendment, the payoff cost limit on DIC assistance was removed temporarily until March 2001.

Outbreak of the Financial Crisis in 1997 and 1998 and the Introduction of a Comprehensive Framework

The financial crisis broke out in autumn of 1997. As stated in the overview in this subsection, major financial institutions, Sanyo Securities, Hokkaido Takushoku Bank, Yamaichi Securities, and Tokuyo City Bank, collapsed in the same month of November 1997.

With the outbreak of the crisis in November 1997, discussions started on the possible use of public funds to cope with the unprecedented difficulties. In February 1998, the Law Regarding Emergency Measures for Financial Stability (the "Emergency Law") was enacted, under which a public fund injection scheme to strengthen the capital base of banks via purchase of preferred stocks, and so forth, was introduced with a limited duration until end March 2001. A total of 30 trillion yen of public funds, including those for capital injection, were made available as a temporary measure until March 2001.[11] As banks were generally reluctant to be singled out as weak and requiring capital injection, all major banks collectively applied for capital injection. As a result, all major 21 banks received a capital injection on March 30, 1998, totaling 1.8 trillion yen, but the amount was regarded as far too small, and it did not generate a very positive response in the market.

While the measures had some effects on calming the market turmoil temporarily, in June 1998, problems with the LTCB became evident.[12] In light of the size and complexity of its operation, purchase by new investors was sought to achieve an orderly wind down, rather than through liquidation. However, mechanisms that enabled winding down of such a large bank were non-existent at that time. The Diet discussion in the summer of 1998 produced significant legislation.

First, a law, the Law Concerning Emergency Measures for the Reconstruction of the Financial Functions (the "Reconstruction Law") was enacted in October 1998, which introduced a comprehensive framework for resolution of failed banks.

[11] A total of 30 trillion yen of public funds, including those for capital injection, were made available, with 17 trillion yen assigned to the Special Account of the DIC to cover the losses of failed financial institutions and 13 trillion yen allocated for capital injection into banks.

[12] This was just when the supervisory power of the MOF was taken over by the newly created Financial Supervisory Agency (FSA).

Under the law, a failed bank could either be placed under the Financial Reconstruction Administration (FRA), or temporarily nationalized. Under the FRA, the authorities designate an administrator who replaces existing management of a failed bank and tries to find a healthy bank to purchase the business of a failed bank. When the administrator cannot find buyer, he can transfer the business of a failed bank to a bridge bank, which the DIC establishes. Under nationalization, large-scale banks with systemic risk can be purchased by the government, and the authorities will designate a new management. It was generally conceived that financial institutions with more systemic implications would be nationalized. For both institutions under FRA and nationalized banks, business operations were to be continued, with liquidity provision directly from BOJ in the case of institutions under FRA and with liquidity support provided by the DIC in the case of nationalized banks. In the latter case, the DIC was to borrow from the BOJ to finance such liquidity support. Pursuant to the Reconstruction Law, the LTCB was nationalized in October 1997, and NCB, which was heavily exposed to the real estate industry and suffering from a large amount of NPLs, was nationalized in December 1980.

Second, the other law that was newly introduced was a strengthened capital injection scheme (again, effective through March 2001) tied into the early correction measure.[13] This measure was introduced by the Financial Function Early Strengthening Law ("Early Strengthening Law") that replaced the Emergency Law in October 1998, and some 7.5 trillion yen was injected into 15 banks in March 1999. The capital injection was a significant step to address the undercapitalization of Japanese banks. The amount injected was more than four times as large as the previous injection in March 1998 (1.8 trillion yen), after which the Japan premium (extra interest that Japanese banks were required to pay when they sought overseas funding) began to decline. Under the Reconstruction Law, the LTCB was nationalized in October 1998. The size of public funds made available for the new framework was doubled from 30 trillion yen to 60 trillion yen. With the new comprehensive safety net framework in place, the authorities were able to deal with a failed bank directly, without necessarily finding an assuming bank beforehand. For viable but undercapitalized banks, large-scale injections also became possible. The authorities quickly embarked on a systematic clean-up operation, fully utilizing the new framework.

[13] The early correction measure introduced in April 1998 is the scheme under which the authorities order a bank to take corrective measures, such as the submission of a management improvement plan or strengthening of its capital base, based on its capital–asset ratio.

Government-led Promotion of NPL Resolution Pursued in the First Half of 2000s under Prime Minister Koizumi

After such a comprehensive scheme for strengthening viable banks through capital injection and for smooth resolution of unviable banks was placed into operation, Koizumi became the president of the Liberal Democratic Party (LDP) and started the Koizumi administration in April 2001, under which resolution of the NPL problem was actively pursued:

In April 2001, a strong encouragement for writing off NPLs was stated in the Emergency Economic Package adopted by the government. Major banks were required to remove from their balance sheets the existing NPLs classified as "in danger of bankruptcy" or worse,[14] in principle, within two years and those NPLs newly classified as such, in principle, within three years ("Two Year–Three Year Rule"). "The Financial Revival Program" was announced by the government in October 2002, aimed at halving the NPL ratio of major banks by March 2005 from the level at the time (8.4% as of March 2002).

In January 2002, equity holdings by banks were restricted, and an entity was established to purchase equities held by banks and firms (the BOJ also started to purchase equities from banks).

In April 2003, the Industrial Revitalization Corporation was established, which bought NPLs from non-main financing banks and endeavored to revive the borrowers through cooperation with the main financing bank (existed from April 2003 to June 2007).

In May 2003, public funds were injected into a large financial group, Resona Group, to strengthen its capital base, and this became a turning point for the NPL problems.[15]

Although a large regional bank (Ashikaga) was found to be insolvent and nationalized in November 2003, the goal of halving the NPL ratio of major banks was achieved as of the end March 2005, and the NPL problem was finally resolved.

[14] Refers to "Bankruptcy," "De facto bankruptcy," and "In danger of bankruptcy."

[15] Nakaso (2014) wrote that, triggered by public funds injection into Resona Bank, stock prices gradually started to rise, and it was finally felt that the crisis was gradually waning. Nishimura (2011) pointed out that public funds injection into Resona Bank with no writing off of stocks shows a clear example of a soft landing approach, which the administration of the time was taking, despite its hard pressures on banks to dispose of NPLs.

In April 2005, the full deposit protection, in principle, was terminated, and the crisis came to an end.[16]

Why Was the NPL Problem Not Resolved Sooner?

Why Did the Private Sector Take So Long to Resolve the NPL Problem?

Adoption by the Corporate Sector of Gradual Resolution
The crisis broke out seven years after the burst of the bubble. Why did the crisis break out so late? As we have seen, the fundamental problem was the hangover of the excess (low-profitability) assets in the corporate sector. What was needed is a prompt resolution to these excesses. However, the corporate sector did not swiftly dispose of the excesses and chose to take time to deal with the issue. The reason for the gradual approach included initially an optimistic expectation for the future course of the economy (from another perspective, delay in recognizing the seriousness of the problem). Later in the process, there was a possibility that concern for the acute shock that could result in the economy by prompt resolution of the excesses might have affected the pace of the resolution.[17] The collective decision-making system, under which a decision tends to be made based on prior consensus incorporating interests of related parties, and the corporate governance system, under which it is difficult to reflect views of people outside the management of companies, may have been also behind the gradual approach.

Financial Sector Also Took a Gradual Approach
Two Methods of Disposition of NPLs
The financial sector seems to have followed the similar gradual approach to the problem. The financial institutions have two options in coping with NPLs.[18] One is indirect disposition, registering loan loss reserves on the lia-

[16] The full deposit protection, which was introduced in 1996, was scheduled to be terminated by end March 2001 but was extended to end March 2002 for time deposits and to end March 2003 for checkable deposits. The full protection of checkable deposits was extended further to end March 2005.

[17] Supplement 2 in this chapter gives a very rough estimate of the size of the excess assets (it is estimated that excesses accounted for nearly three-tenths of all assets), and an estimate of an increase in the number of unemployed people and a rise in the unemployment rate if excesses were promptly disposed of.

[18] In the case where loans with the total face value of 100 incurred a loss of 10, there are two types of disposition.

bility side of the balance sheet. In this case, the troubled assets continue to be held. The other is direct disposition, removing the troubled assets from the balance sheets, and at the same time, reducing capital. In the case of direct disposition, the troubled assets may be seized, and in a more serious case, the borrower might be liquidated, leading to an increase in unemployment, reduction in wages, and a fall in investment. Banks generally favored indirect disposition and continued to hold relevant assets on their balance sheets.[19,20]

What Is the Cost of Holding NPL?

Under the gradual approach to the NPL problem, the troubled assets continued to stay on the banks' balance sheets. What sort of problems did this bring about? A possibility of credit crunch and negative effects on efficiency are among the costs frequently mentioned.

Indirect disposition (registering loan loss reserves)
(Asset) Loans 100
(Liabilities & Capital) Debt 80, Capital 20
→(Asset) Loans 100
(Liabilities & Capital) Debt 80, Loan loss reserve 10, Capital 10
Direct disposition (removing the troubled asset)
(Asset) Loans 100
(Liabilities & Capital) Debt 80, Capital 20
→(Asset) Loans 90
(Liabilities & Capital) Debt 80, Capital 10

Direct deposition can be done through such measures as seizing and selling collaterals (factory, office, machines, etc.) or resolving the debtor.

[19] Financial institutions tended to regard it as their mission to assist those borrowing companies, which were considered viable but experiencing temporary difficulties, through reduction of interest rates or the rescheduling of loan repayments, and such loans were not regarded as NPLs. This approach was later modified in the process of the resolution of NPL problems, and those loans for which conditions were alleviated were included in the category of NPLs.

[20] The introduction of the BIS capital–adequacy ratio, agreed to in the late 1980s, may have acted as another constraint on banks. Under the agreement, banks were required to clear the minimum capital–asset ratio of 8% by end March 1993. Himino (2005) pointed out that, the capital–asset ratio of Japanese city banks was as low as 3%, if calculated based on the original proposal of the United States and the United Kingdom in 1987. Japanese authorities requested that unrealized capital gains of securities held by banks had to be included in capital, and it was agreed in late 1987 that 45% of unrealized capital gains could be included in capital. Most of Japanese banks cleared the requirement by end March 1990, partially helped by this treatment. After the burst of the bubble, however, continuous decline in stock prices continued to depress banks' capital, increasing the instability of bank operations (Komine 2011, 324–26).

① Credit Crunch

It is argued that if NPL continues to be held on a bank's balance sheet, it reduces available resources for new lending, thus bringing about a credit crunch. As for the possibility of this negative effect, we need to know if the problem of lending (or investment) stagnation observed after the burst of the bubble was due to the banks' unwillingness to lend or due to the borrowers' unwillingness to borrow. In this regard, we should note that the lending stance of financial institutions was generally not tight, excepting a short period immediately after the burst of the bubble and the crisis periods in the late 1990s (see Fig. 3.7 in Chap. 3). Also, as Fig. 3.22 in Chap. 3 shows, the outstanding balance of long-term debt of companies started to stagnate after the collapse of the bubble and then fell sharply after 1998. So, it is possible that the tightening of the lending attitude after the crisis was responsible for the sharp decline in long-term debt beginning in 1998. However, it seems to be difficult to regard the eased lending attitude as causing stagnation of long-term debt in the period prior to the crisis. The credit crunch was generally not observed in the 1990s before the crisis.

② Negative Effects on Economic Efficiency

It is also argued that those companies with difficulty in serving their borrowings are inefficient and allowing them to survive will lower the efficiency of the whole economy (Zombie company arguments). For this argument, a counterargument similar to the credit crunch applies. If there was no credit crunch in Period I (initial adjustment period over 1991–1997), then the problem was not the existence of arguably inefficient companies but the insufficient demand for investment in productive and efficient areas. So, it is not the elimination of the allegedly inefficient companies but finding productive and risk-taking companies that was really needed at that time.

There may be some truth in the Zombie company argument, though. The corporate sector suffered long from the excess capacity overhang, and the sector recorded a very stagnant performance in investment. Positive risk-taking for the future by the corporate sector was contained for a long time after the burst of the bubble.

There were two types of problems. One relates to the case where a company itself is solvent but suffers from redundant unprofitable capacity. The other relates to the case where the company holding assets itself is insolvent. In the former case, early recognition and disposition of the unprofitable assets is needed from the viewpoint of efficiency. If this is not done, those assets that are not profitable continue to place burden on the company, depressing risk-taking. Banks could have encouraged companies to dispose of excess assets more promptly. However, the corporate sector took time to resolve the excess capacity overhang; as is explained later (in detail in Chap. 6), it took about 15 years to get rid of the excess assets, lengthening investment stagnation. While postponing resolution is not beneficial to the company, why did it opt for delaying the decision? The answer may be found in the structure of governance of a company that makes a drastic decision difficult to take without a crisis.

In the latter case of an insolvent company, usually it cannot continue to obtain funding if its financial position is properly assessed. Figure 4.4 shows that operating profits of the companies with capital less than 10 million yen nearly disappeared after the collapse of the bubble. These companies counted as many as 1.6 million (78.7% of total 2.0 million at that time) and accounted for 29.9% of total employment by the corporate sector as of 1990 (but only 10.8% of total investment as of 1990).[21] Stagnation of wages (and to a lesser extent investment) is partly accounted for by these companies' poor performance. How could these companies with no profits stay in the market? In the long stagnation period, the government provided a loan insurance scheme for small- and medium-sized enterprises (SMEs), under which 100% (later reduced to 80%, in principle) of loans were covered by government-subsidized funds, if defaulted. This scheme may have helped those SMEs that temporarily had difficulty in funding while remaining basically viable. It is also possible this scheme may have saved unprofitable and unviable companies, depressing the efficiency of the economy, at the cost of the taxpayers.[22]

[21] The number of companies with capital less than 10 million yen declined to 1.3 million (i.e., 54.4% of total 2.4 million) in 1997, and their share in total employment declined to 15.9%. This decline reflects changes in capital requirements under the 1991 amendment of the Commercial Law, which raised the minimum capital to 10 million yen for stock companies, with the transition period lasting until end March 1996.

[22] This scheme is under the jurisdiction of the SME Agency of the Ministry of Economy, Trade and Industry and is widely supported by political circle. The ratio of insurance has been in principle reduced to 80%. As of February 2016, 2.8 million cases of loans are insured and the outstanding balance insured amounts to as much as 25.8 trillion yen.

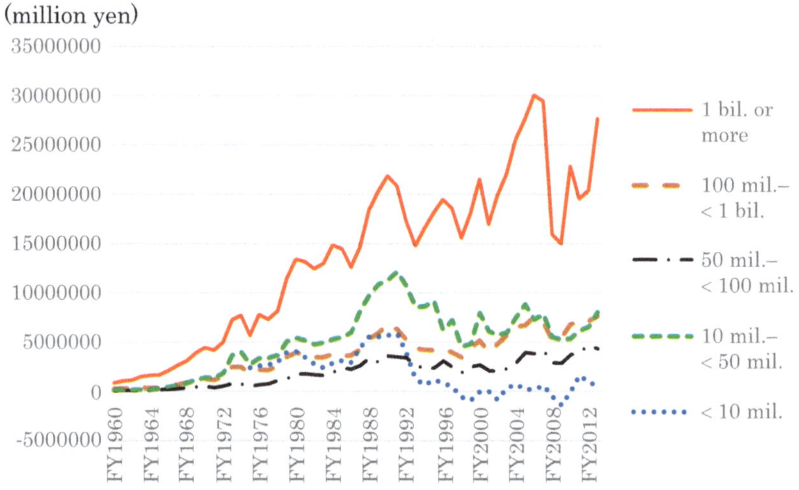

Fig. 4.4 Operating profits by companies' capital size. Source: Ministry of Finance, "Financial Statement Statistics of Corporations by industry"

Why Did the Government Take So Long to Solve the NPL Problem?

Adoption of a "Step-by-Step" Approach and Its Background

Adoption of a Gradual Approach for Resolution

We have seen that the private sector took a gradual approach to the NPL problem. Now, let us see why the government took so long to solve the NPL problem.

The government also took a step-by-step approach to the NPL problem.

In August 1992, administrative guidelines[23] were issued by the MOF, the supervisory authority for the financial sector at that time. The guidelines stated that, while encouraging financial institutions to promptly formulate their NPL resolution policy, NPLs should be actively resolved in a planned and staged manner, prescribing a gradual approach to resolution. The stance of the government became more proactive later in the 1990s. For example, in April 1995, the government stated in "The Emergency Economic Measures under the Yen Appreciation" that NPLs should be disposed of within about next five years so that the resolution of the problem could be seen. However, the government approach was still based on

[23] Ministry of Finance, "Kinnyu gyosei no tomen no unnyo hoshin" (On the current policy of the financial sector supervision), August 18, 1992.

promotion or encouragement, and the initiative was basically expected to come from the financial institutions' side.

Non-availability of a Comprehensive Resolution Framework

This approach may have reflected the expectation of economic recovery (particularly, the expectation of bottoming out of land prices) and the government's concern over the negative impacts on the economy of rapidly resolving the NPL problem (e.g., increase in bankruptcy and unemployment). The more fundamental constraint that hindered the government from a swift resolution, however, may have been the lack of an institutional framework for resolution of unviable banks and for a capital injection scheme for viable banks.

Without capital injection, the government cannot pressure viable banks to dispose NPLs beyond banks' capabilities. Without a comprehensive framework for failed bank resolution, including nationalization of large banks, the government cannot actively pursue the goal of dissolving unviable banks, as it would push the situation out of control.[24]

Then, the next question is why the comprehensive resolution framework and the capital injection scheme were not introduced earlier? An MOF staff member who served as director-general of the Banking Bureau of the MOF, which was in charge of banking sector oversight, in the early 1990s, later stated that, after having studied the case of the prewar financial crisis of 1927 (Showa Kinnyu Kyoko), he concluded that, unless banks become insolvent and unable to pay, provision of public funds for banks will never be accepted by general public. Provision of funds will be regarded not for the protection of depositors but for the rescue of banks, resulting in confusion and an increase in costs to the taxpayers.[25] This may explain part of the delay in

[24] Fukao (2009) pointed out that the estimated combined amount of net business profits (inclusive of losses due to disposition of NPLs) of banks (city banks, long-term credit banks, and regional banks), a concept similar to operating profits, was negative for 10 straight years from FY 1993 to FY 2002; that is, after the burst of the bubble, banks could not cover credit risk by their profits from their main business operations. Banks recorded surplus in terms of final profits in 5 out of the 10 years, through sales of assets. He also pointed out that the accumulated losses of banks arising from disposition of NPLs amounted to 96.8 trillion yen over 14 years from March 1992 to March 2006, equivalent to 19% of GDP in 2006.

[25] Matsushima, and Takenaka (2011, 225–6). "*Nihon Keizai no Kiroku Jidai Shogen Shu Oraru Hisutori*" (Records of the Japanese Economy—Testimony of the Era—Collection of Oral History) 2011 Economic and Social Research Institute, Cabinet Office, Japanese Government ("Baburu/ Defure ki no Nihon Keizai to Keizai Seisaku (Rekisi Hen) 3" ("the Japanese Economy and Economic Policy in the Period of Bubble

fundamental responses by the MOF. In fact, earlier attempts for the introduction of public funds faced fierce criticism. In August 1992, then Prime Minister Miyazawa mentioned a need to use public funds to solve the NPL problem, but he soon withdrew it in the face of objections from all fronts, including banks themselves.[26] In December 1995, when the government decided to use public funds to resolve unviable housing loan companies ("Jusen"), criticism throughout the nation mounted.[27]

Insufficiency of Disclosure Requirements

The lack of or the late introduction of the comprehensive resolution framework was a product of various relevant factors. We have seen that the general public or the political circle did not regard the use of public funds for the financial sector as appropriate, at least by mid-1990s. Since perception is basically formed by available information, an important question is whether the authorities in charge of NPL problem, that is, the MOF and BOJ at the time, recognized the seriousness of the NPL problem as of the first half of the 1990s and, also, what information was made available to the public?

As for the first question, the starting point is disclosure requirements imposed on banks regarding NPLs. Until the beginning of the 1990s, there was virtually no disclosure on NPLs. From the business year ending end of March 1993, banks started to disclose NPLs, but the coverage of the initial disclosure was limited to loans to borrowers who had become legally bankrupt (in the case of major banks, loans past due for six months or longer were disclosed as well).[28] So, by disclosure alone,

and Deflation Vol. 3 (History)") 2011 Economic and Social Research Institute, Cabinet Office, Japanese Government) pp. 225–226.

[26] See Komine (2011, 473–6); Nishino (2003); and Nihon Keizai Shimbun Sha (2000).

[27] When dissolving Jusen, public funds were used to avoid negative impacts on the financial system by imposing loan loss onto agriculture-related financial institutions that had lent heavily to Jusen. However, according to a book written by a journalist (Nishino 2003), the agricultural sector demanded that saving the agricultural-related financial institutions should not be used in the explanation as objectives of the use of public funds. In the absence of a clear and easily understandable explanation, the general public, and therefore, political circle, considered that the public funds were used to bail out Jusen, for which cases of fraudulent activities were widely reported in the media.

[28] Disclosure requirements were gradually strengthened. See footnotes 6 and 7 in this chapter.

it would have been impossible to make a comprehensive assessment of the NPL problem in the early 1990s.

Nakaso (2001) wrote "the Bank of Japan had detected by early 1993 that potential risk in the financial system could be larger than it had been widely believed." A banking Bureau official later stated that, even prior to that, that is, as of summer of 1992, the Banking Bureau of the MOF recognized that if the stock price fell to around 12,000 yen (it was about 14,000 yen around that time), some banks could become insolvent, and that if it happened, the Bureau would enact a special law to introduce public funds while liquidity was being provided by the BOJ. If the enactment of such a special law was delayed, an emergency law for moratorium could be enacted.[29] However, because stock prices temporarily stabilized soon afterwards, such a response was not placed into operation.

As for the size of NPLs, it is stated that, in August 1992, the Banking Bureau was informed by the BOJ that the size of NPLs would exceed 40 trillion yen, and in early 1994, the Banking Bureau itself estimated the size of NPLs to be 42 trillion yen.[30] However, they thought that if the land prices stopped falling (land prices had fallen by some 50% by that time), it would be possible for banks to dispose of the NPLs using their business profits.[31]

If these statements are correct, then both the MOF and the Bank of Japan recognized the seriousness of the NPL problem as of 1992–1993. If a crisis broke out due to a further fall in stock prices, then the Banking Bureau thought that public funds would be introduced to resolve the problem; and if a crisis did not happen and if land prices stopped falling, then the NPLs could be disposed of by using banks' business profits. One possible reason why, despite such a recognition, a fundamental response was not taken is that the government held an optimistic expectation for the

[29] Matsushima and Takenaka (2011, 225).

[30] The Ministry of Finance announced that the size of NPLs of large banks was 7–8 trillion yen in April 1992 and around 12 trillion yen in October 1992. However, this covered only major banks and did not cover all financial institutions. Also, the assets covered were limited to bankrupt or past due claims. As for claims on non-bank financial institutions, including Jusen, creditor financial institutions did not grasp the actual situation, and therefore, they were not classified as bankrupt or past due.

[31] Matsushima and Takenaka (2011, 220–1).

future course of stock and land prices (and the economy as a whole), which was a crucial factor in the NPL problem. In fact, in the early stage after the collapse of the bubble, there was a serious concern that the land price surge might return if policy response was eased.[32] Even after the land price dropped substantially, it was difficult even to imagine that the land prices would continue to fall for more than a decade. The government, banks, corporations, media, and people at large were still trapped by "Tochi Shinwa" (land myth), and it might have delayed an appropriate response.

By contrast, Nakaso (2001) referred to a dilemma that the authorities including the BOJ faced. Nakaso argued, if the BOJ called for introduction of a comprehensive safety net framework, it could trigger a financial crisis. Without a clear strategy on how to address the issue, the authorities continued with a piecemeal approach to the NPL problem. This is a logical argument, but with hindsight, postponing a comprehensive response only aggravated the situation, leading to a serious financial crisis in the late 1990s.[33]

As has been repeatedly pointed out, the core problem was excess (unprofitable) assets in the corporate sector. Unless the corporate sector removed these excesses, the economy could not recover fully. What was needed for the financial institutions was to help borrowing companies remove these excesses, not to help them continue to hold these excesses. The financial sector, however, did not act in this way.

What could have been done then, under the circumstances, when a much needed comprehensive framework did not exist? If we are to make a mere

[32] The official discount rate, which was raised to 6.0% in June 1990, but was lowered beginning in July 1991. The aggregate lending limit, which was introduced in March 1990, was lifted in December 1991. A Banking Bureau executive at that time said later, "When we lifted the aggregate lending limit, most of the newspaper articles criticised (it), by writing 'If policy reaction is eased, land price will never fail to rise again'" (Matsushima and Takenaka 2011, 313).

[33] In January 1997, Prime Minister Hashimoto (LDP) declared the intention to start drastic reforms in six areas, including fiscal structure and the financial system. Directed by Prime Minister Hashimoto, the Ministry of Finance, then the supervisory authority of banks and securities firms, started examination of comprehensive liberalization of the Japanese financial system called "Japan's Financial Big Bang," and reform plans were authorized by advisory councils attached to the MOF in June 1997. Those reforms were surely necessary for Japan, but their timing was not right. With hindsight, when the financial sector was fragile, as evidenced by series of failures of financial institutions, the greatest care should have been paid to maintain stability of the sector and markets without embarking on drastic reforms.

theoretical argument with hindsight, probably we should have had a financial crisis or extensive bank and company failures in the early 1990s. If a crisis was unavoidable, we should have had one while Japan's banking sector, corporate sector, and also the government still held far more strength to cope with a crisis, as compared with five years later. If a crisis had happened, Japan could not have avoided sharp deterioration of the economy and instability of the society, at least for some time.[34] However, if a comprehensive framework for strengthening the financial system, including a capital injection scheme introduced during the crisis, it could have been possible to restore a sound financial system and economy more swiftly than actually happened. Then, Japan's economy might have recovered from the shock of the collapse of the bubble in a relatively short period of time and could have returned to a relatively high-growth path similar to the one in the period before the bubble. In reality, all relevant parties made their maximum efforts to containing a risk of crisis (it is their duty), and it was unfortunate that Japan still had sufficient strength to delay a crisis for some time. Japan succeeded in controlling the pending problem that they faced, but left a more serious problem for the future. This point will be highlighted by the analysis of the case of Scandinavia in the next subsection.

How Were Banking Crises Handled by Other Countries? (Scandinavian Case)

In order to find out what should have been done, let us look at cases in other countries.[35] Response to the collapse of the bubble by the Scandinavian countries is sometimes referred to as a success, so in this subsection, we examine these cases.

The Scandinavian countries had a banking crisis in the early 1990s, which had substantive commonalities in background but big differences in outcomes with Japan.

Under financial liberalization, started by the 1980s and favorable economic conditions, rapid credit expansion and an asset bubble emerged in Scandinavian countries in the 1980s. With the burst of the asset price bubble

[34] Supplement 2 in this chapter gives a very rough estimate of impacts on employment of a prompt resolution of excess assets. According to the estimate, if the total excess assets had been disposed of in fiscal 1991, the number of unemployed people would have increased by more than 12 million, and the unemployment rate would spiked by more than 10 times, increasing from an actual 2.1% to an estimated 21.2%.

[35] Explanation in this part is based on IMF (1995).

in the late 1980s (Norway) and at the beginning of 1990s (Finland and Sweden), these countries were faced with severe banking crises in the early 1990s (started in Norway in the late 1980s) (Figs. 4.5, 4.6, and 4.7).

As the NPL problem developed into a systemic banking crisis rather quickly, the three governments responded by decisive measures.

In Norway, the loan loss problem surfaced in late 1980s, first with financial companies, spreading to banks, and even large banks were placed in serious difficulty by the end of 1990. Substantial funds were injected, and

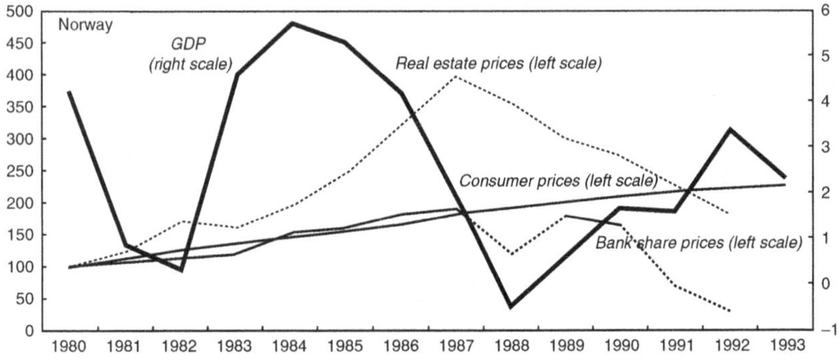

Fig. 4.5 Real GDP growth rate and asset price (1980 = 100): Norway. Source: IMF (1995) "The Nordic Banking Crises: Pitfalls in Financial Liberalization?" IMF Working Paper WP/95/61

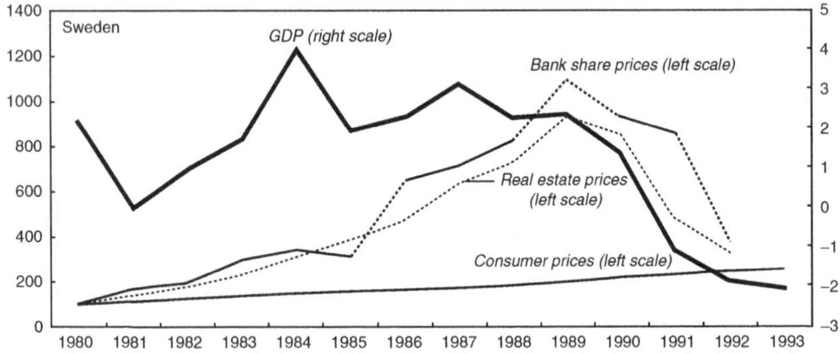

Fig. 4.6 Real GDP growth rate and asset price (1980 = 100): Sweden. Source: IMF (1995) "The Nordic Banking Crises: Pitfalls in Financial Liberalization?" IMF Working Paper WP/95/61

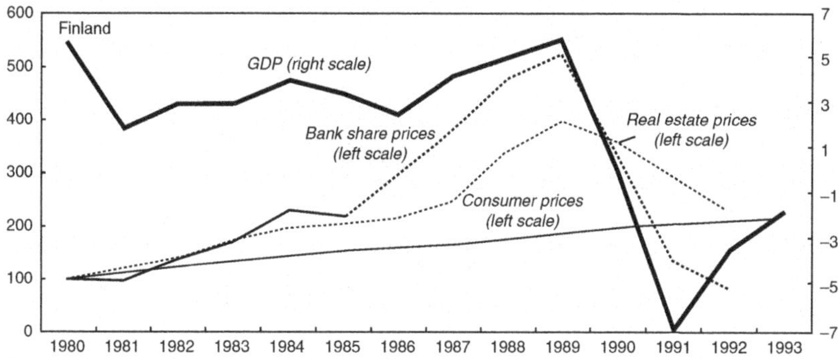

Fig. 4.7 Real GDP growth rate and asset price (1980 = 100): Finland. Source: IMF (1995) "The Nordic Banking Crises: Pitfalls in Financial Liberalization?" IMF Working Paper WP/95/61

by the end of 1991 the government had become the sole or majority owner of the three largest commercial banks in Norway.

In Sweden, while problems surfaced with financial companies in 1990, large banks faced with financial difficulties in 1991. The Swedish government injected funds into these large banks (including the largest bank which was government owned), by way of such measures as direct purchase of new equities and provision of loan guarantees from 1991.

In Finland, as the saving banks were most severely hit, most support was directed to Skopbank (the central institution for the saving banks). Faced with a liquidity crisis in September 1991, the Bank of Finland (BOF) took over Skopbank. In April 1992, a fund, Government Guarantee Fund (GGF), was established, and the GGF acquired Skopbank from the BOF in September 1992 and injected capital. Forty-one savings banks were merged into the Savings Bank of Finland (SBF), which was subsequently taken over by the GGF, which then made capital injections.

Furthermore, Sweden and Finland used explicit blanket guarantees on bank liabilities (Norway did not explicitly announce it). In Sweden, a technique to split a troubled bank into a "good bank" and a "bad bank" (an asset management company handling NPLs of the troubled bank) was used.

By mid-1990s, GDP growth recovered, and the Scandinavian cases were generally regarded as successes in handling banking crises (Fig. 4.8).

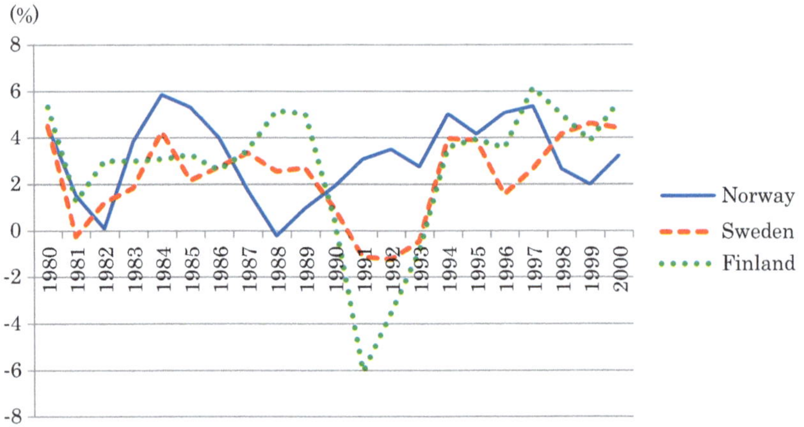

Fig. 4.8 GDP growth rate: Norway, Sweden, and Finland. Source: IMF (2014) World Economic Outlook database Oct. 2014

Scandinavia vs. Japan: Why the Difference?

There is a big difference between Scandinavian case where solid growth returned soon after the crisis and Japan's case where a long stagnation followed after the collapse of the bubble and the financial crisis. Why this difference?

It seems that strong government intervention into the financial sector, including capital injection and nationalization, is necessary in order to effectively deal with a problem of the financial sector facing a systemic risk. Such intervention can be made possible only when there is a strong political will to rescue financial system using tax money. How can such a political will be formed? Only through a crisis, as was learned by a MOF official from the Showa financial crisis? If that is the case, why the difference? While Scandinavian countries faced a crisis very shortly after the collapse of the bubble, Japan did not have a crisis soon after the collapse of its bubble. In Japan, all the parties concerned made maximal efforts to avoid an early eruption of a crisis under a situation in which a comprehensive legal framework for orderly resolution of a crisis was lacking. These actions delayed the formation of a political will that would be necessary to take drastic measures to fundamentally strengthen the financial system. After all, Japan experienced a worst scenario to face a serious financial crisis after seven years of stagnation.

Summary of the Financial Crisis

The financial crisis broke out seven years after the burst of the bubble. The government's macroeconomic policy supports, in terms of repeated economic measures and monetary easing after the bubble collapse, might have given relief to troubled corporations and banks. However, with continued sales stagnation, the continued fall in asset prices, particularly land prices, and a weak economic recovery, the financial position of corporations and, therefore, of banks deteriorated, causing NPL problems to grow more and more serious year by year. The problem behind the NPLs was an excess assets hangover, so it was necessary to dispose of these excessive assets swiftly in order to avoid prolonged profit stagnation and recover positive risk-taking behaviors of companies. However, companies took time to address the problem. Banks typically did not press companies to dispose of these excesses promptly. Behind these behaviors were optimistic expectations for the future and a problem with governance. At the same time, there seems to have been growing concern about the hugely negative impacts on the economy if a rapid resolution was conducted.

The government let banks take the initiative and, as a result, took a gradual approach to the problem. In tackling the NPL problem, the lack of a comprehensive framework for resolution of unviable banks including nationalization and capital injection for viable banks, seem to have placed a fundamental constraint on the way government dealt with the problem. It may have been possible to introduce these policy tools sooner and resolve the NPL problem more quickly, but duties of all relevant parties were to prevent a crisis, and Japan unfortunately had sufficient strength to delay a crisis at that time. With hindsight, Japan probably needed a strong will to resolve the problems of both corporate and banking sectors—when the country had more strength to cope—through strong government interventions, even if such action could have triggered a crisis. If the parties had acted in that way, the Japanese economy could have returned to a reasonably high–growth path after a relatively short period of time, and would not have experienced the lost decade or decades.

Impacts of the Financial Crisis

Fundamental Changes That Were Brought about by the Financial Crisis

Fundamental changes were brought about in the Japanese economy by the financial crisis. In this section, we will first look at what changes took place, and we note that most of these changes were related to company behaviors. As a further analysis of company behaviors will be conducted in Chap. 6, we take just a brief look at what happened in this subsection.

On the macro level, the economic conditions deteriorated. The real growth rate dropped further, from 1.7% in 1991–1997 (Period I: Initial Adjustment) to 0.4% in 1998–2002 (Period II: Financial Crisis and Its Impacts), although this decline also reflected effects of the dot.com bubble collapse in 2000–2001. In this deceleration process, the growth contribution of private investment further dropped from −0.1% in 1991–1997 to −0.2% in 1998–2002.[36]

The number of corporate bankruptcies, which had started to rise after the start of the 1990s, further went up and stayed high in and after the financial crisis (Fig. 4.9).

Business conditions, as judged by the enterprises, plummeted, going below the level recorded immediately after the collapse of the bubble (Fig. 4.10).

The lending stance of financial institutions also dramatically changed, sharply shifting from excess of "eased" over "tight" to excess of "tight" over "eased" (Fig. 4.11 [reproduction of Fig. 3.7 in Chap. 3]). A similar tightening of lending stance occurred immediately after the collapse of the bubble. However, at that time, tightening of lending stance was not so

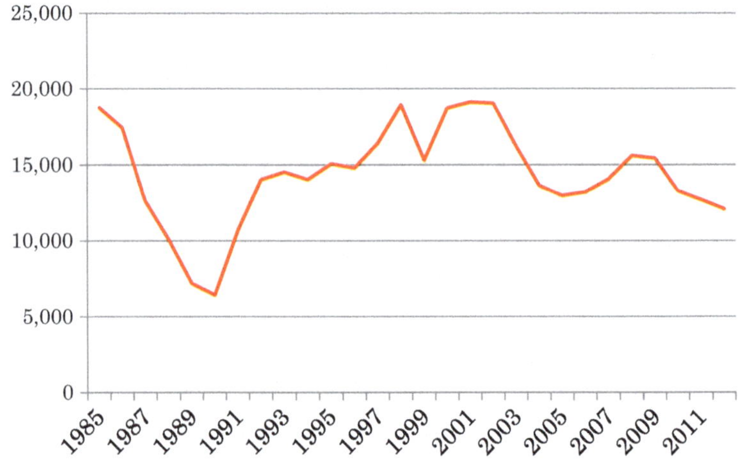

Fig. 4.9 Number of corporate bankruptcies. Source: Tokyo Shoko Research

[36] The expected growth rate held by companies for the next three years declined further from 2.2% in Period I (Initial Adjustment Period, 1991–1997) to 1.0% in Period II (Financial Crisis and Its Impacts Period, 1998–2002), as explained in Chap. 3.

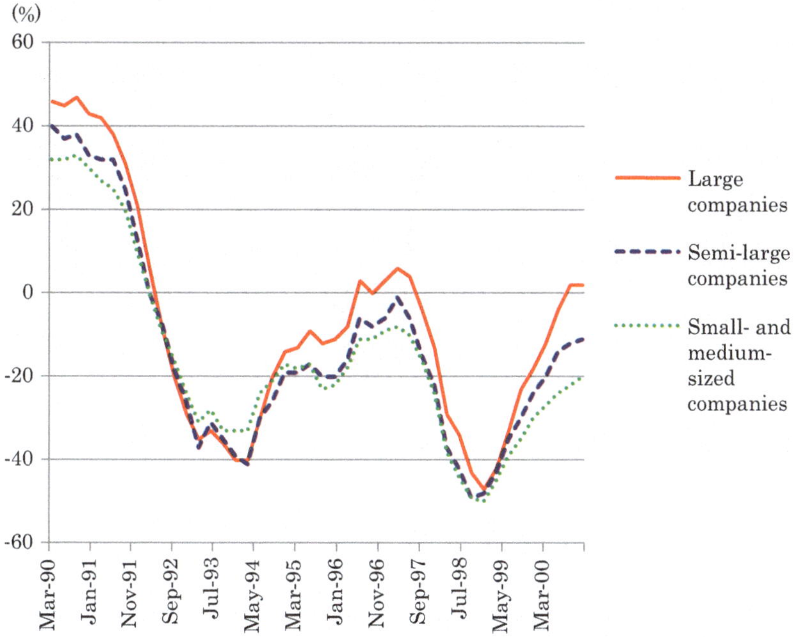

Fig. 4.10 Economic conditions, as judged by companies. Note: The chart shows the share of "good"-the share of "bad." Source: Tankan Business Survey, BOJ

strong for SMEs, which were more dependent on lending than for larger companies but, after the financial crisis, the sharp tightening of lending stance was observed across company size.

Against the background of the sharp deterioration of the economy, fundamental changes took place in employment and company behaviors, and deflation started at the same time.

Fundamental Change ①: Unemployment Rate Climbed Up

Although the unemployment rate was increasing in Period I (1991–1997), after hitting the bottom of 2.0% in February 1992, it stopped rising briefly from late 1995 to mid-1997. However, it started to rise sharply from 3.5% in October 1997, shortly before the failure of large financial institutions, to 4.0% in April 1998, 4.5% in November 1998, and 4.8% in June 1999. It reached 5.5% in 2002–2003 (Fig. 4.12 [reproduction of Fig. 3.11 in Chap. 3]). The number of unemployed increased by 0.86 million in a year and eight months from 2.38 million in October 1997 to 3.24 million in June 1999.

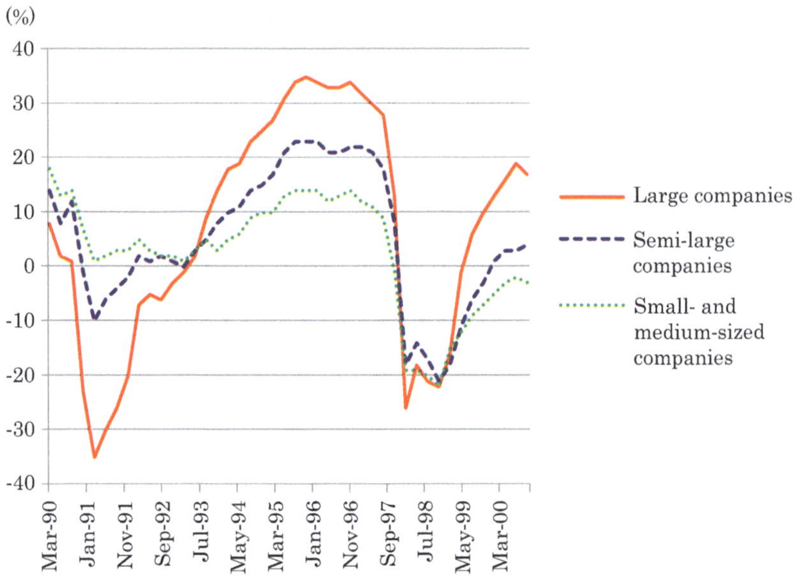

Fig. 4.11 Lending stance of financial institutions, as judged by companies, Japan 1990–2000. Note: The chart shows the share of "eased"-the share of "tight." Source: Tankan Business Survey, BOJ

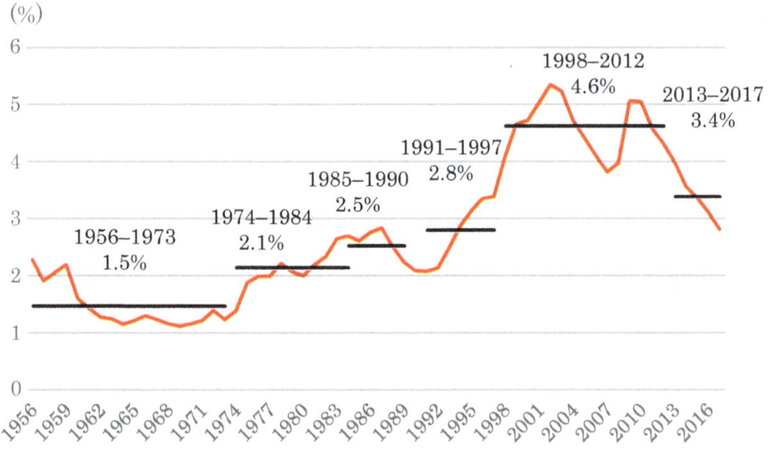

Fig. 4.12 Unemployment rate. Source: Ministry of Internal Affairs and Communications

Fundamental Change ②: Nominal Wages Started to Decline

After the financial crisis, nominal wages started to decline from the beginning of 1998. Since then, the nominal wages has shown a declining trend over a long period, and the average of year-on-year change on a monthly basis in 15 years, from January 1998 to December 2012, was –0.8%. The cumulative decline of the index (2010 = 100), from 113.6 in 1997 to 98.9 in 2012, is –12.9% (Fig. 4.13).

Fundamental Change ③: Shift of Employment toward Non-Regular Work Accelerated

The share of non-regular workers of total employees stayed fairly flat in the first half of 1990s but switched to a rising trend in the second half of the 1990s, and continued to rise thereafter at a rather high pace (Fig. 4.14).

At the same time, the number of regular employees started to decline rapidly after the financial crisis. After hitting a peak of 38.1 million in February 1997, the number of regular employees declined by 1.7 million (–4.5% from February 1997) to 36.4 million in February 2001. The pace

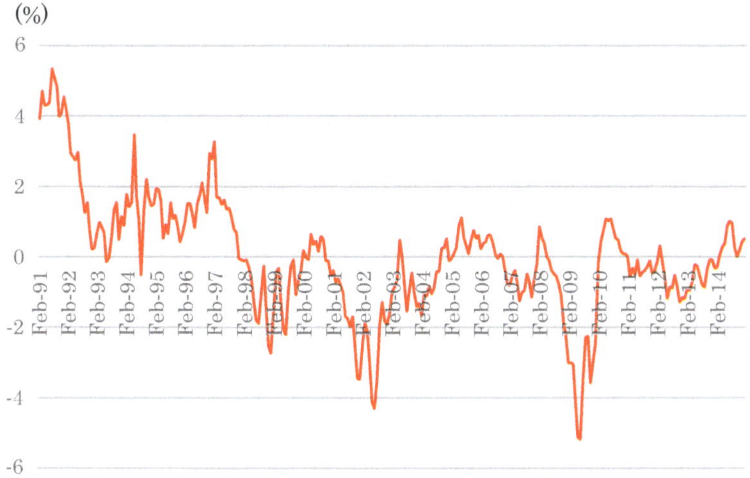

Fig. 4.13 Nominal wages (year-on-year change, three-year moving average). Note: Nominal wage is the total monthly cash earnings per employee (three-month moving average of the year-on-year growth rate in establishments with five employees or more). Source: Ministry of Health, Labor, and Welfare, "Monthly labor survey"

Fig. 4.14 Share of non-regular employees in total number of employees, excluding executives. Source: Statistics Bureau, Ministry of Internal Affairs and Communications "Labor force survey"

of decline accelerated from January to March in 2002, losing another 3.1 million (−8.0% from February 2001) before hitting a bottom of 33.3 million in the period January–March 2005. As a whole, 4.8 million (12.6% of the peak in 1997) regular employment positions were lost in the eight-year period from February 1997 to January–March 2005 (Fig. 4.15).

Fundamental Change ④: Switch of Companies from Financial Deficit to Financial Surplus Sector

Furthermore, a change took place in saving and investment behaviors of companies. Companies (nonfinancial enterprises) had been reducing the size of financial deficit after the burst of the bubble, but they switched to a financial surplus sector from 1998.[37] The amount of financial surplus hit a peak in 2003, and thereafter, started to decrease but still stayed positive even in recent years (Fig. 4.16).

[37] Financial surplus/deficit corresponds to the difference between the amount of financial investment and the amount of fundraising, which is conceptually equal to net lending/net borrowing (formerly called "the difference between savings and investment") in the national account.

Fig. 4.15 Number of regular workers. Source: Statistics Bureau of Japan, "Labor Force Survey—Special Survey"

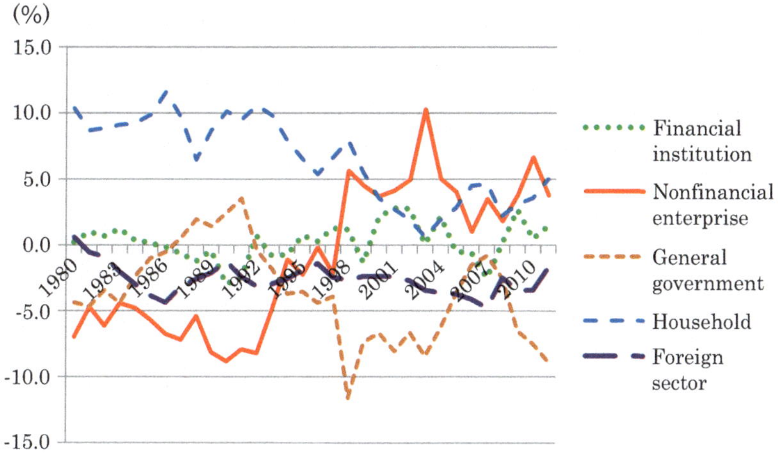

Fig. 4.16 Financial surplus/deficit by sector (in percent of GDP). Note: Years are fiscal year. Source: Bank of Japan, "Flow of Funds"

Fundamental Change ⑤: Deflation Started

Among significant changes that occurred in Japan, the decline in price level (deflation) has attracted the biggest attention. The Consumer Price Index (CPI) (excluding fresh foods) hit a peak in 1997–1998, and started to gradually decline. On a year-on-year change basis, CPI (excluding fresh food) started to record a decline from July 1998, and excepting short periods of global price hikes of food and natural resources before the GFC and in more recent years, it continued to record a fall, that is, basically for nearly 15 years from July 1998 to April 2013—but it was a mild deflation. The average rate of changes of CPI (excluding fresh food) from the previous year in the period July 1998 to April 2013 was −0.3%, and the cumulative price decline over the 15-year period was −3.6% (Fig. 4.17).

Response by the Government

Faced with the financial crisis, the focus of policy was shifted from pre-crisis long-term, structural measures, such as fiscal consolidation and the financial big bang, to full-fledged crisis management measures, which were composed of the following, as explained before:

Fig. 4.17 Consumer Price Index (excluding fresh food) (year-on-year change). Source: Statistics Bureau, Ministry of Internal Affairs and Communications

Introduction of a Comprehensive Resolution Framework for Financial Crisis

A framework for resolution of failed (unviable) banks and for capital injection to viable banks was introduced.

Macroeconomic Policy

In fiscal policy, six economic stimulus packages were implemented after the financial crisis (April and November 1998, November 1999, October 2000, October and December 2001).

As for monetary policy, a reduction of policy rate (uncollateralized overnight call rate) to 0.25% (September 1998) and the adoption of a zero interest rate policy (February 1999–August 2000) were implemented, and a Quantitative Easing (QE) policy was put into force (March 2001–March 2006).

With these supportive policies, the economy started to recover beginning in April 1999, but the recovery was weak and soon started to contract again starting November 2000, with the stagnation of the world economy triggered by the collapse of the dot.com bubble and the sudden deceleration of the US growth from the second half of 2000. In Japan, production substantially shrank, and the unemployment rate reached a historic high of over 5% in 2001. In this way, the stagnation of the Japanese economy further aggravated and entered the second decade with the impact of the financial crisis.

2 Period III (2003–2007) Long Recovery

Long Recovery

The economy, which entered the contraction phase in November 2000, finally started to recover from the beginning of 2002, and this time the recovery was not as short-lived as previous ones, and recorded the longest expansion, after the Second World War, of six years and one month (Fig. 4.18 (reproduced from Fig. 3.9 in Chap. 3)).

Background of the Long Recovery

Why did the economic expansion last so long this time? The recovery in 2002–2007 (Period III: Long Recovery), averaging 1.7%, was driven, by (1) private investment growth, with a growth contribution of 0.5% on average; and by (2) net exports, with a growth contribution of 0.8%. We will first look at private investment.

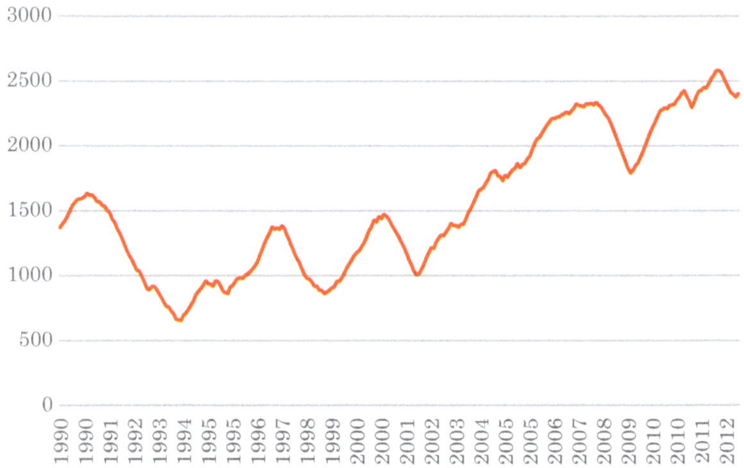

Fig. 4.18 Cumulated Diffusion Index. Source: Cabinet Office

Elimination of Three Excesses

We have seen in Chap. 3 that stagnation in private investment in Period I was brought about, first, by the continued stock adjustment of supply capacity, under the prolonged sales stagnation and downward adjustment of growth expectation, and, second, by deterioration of balance sheets of companies due to the collapse of the bubble. Both these factors related not to the "flow" side but to the "stock" side (i.e., assets and liabilities) of company behaviors. There is an argument with a similar viewpoint called the "three excesses" argument. The contention is that companies in Japan developed "three excesses," as a result of the formation and collapse of the bubble, that is, the assumption of excessive capital stock (excess assets), excessive debt, and excessive employment. These excesses had depressing impacts on positive activities of companies such as investment. These excesses were eliminated during the first half of 2000s, and it is said that the removal of such a longstanding burden led to the recovery of a positive growth contribution of private investment, which made the long recovery possible.

Elimination of Excessive Capital Stock

Excessive production capacity, as indicated by company response to a survey (Tankan) by BOJ, was almost eliminated during the first half of 2000s (Fig. 4.19).

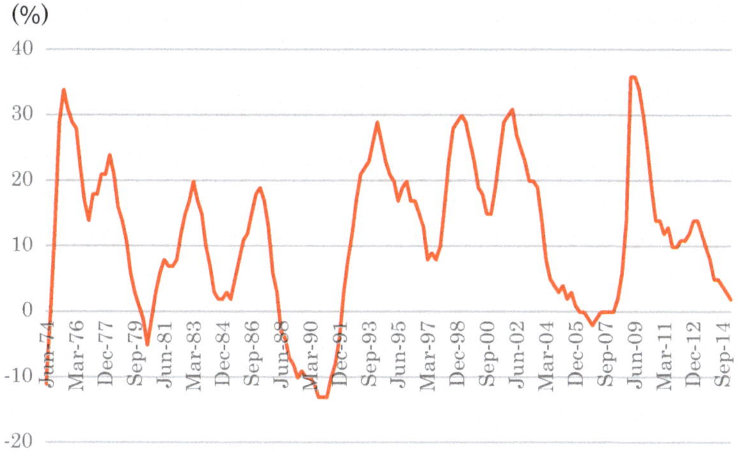

Fig. 4.19 Production capacity ("excessive"–"insufficient"). Source: Bank of Japan, "Tankan Survey"

Elimination of Excessive Debt

Interest-bearing debt relative to cash flows also decreased in the first half of the 2000s, to the level in the pre-bubble era, indicating that excess debt has been eliminated (Fig. 4.20).

Figure 4.21 (reproduction of Fig. 3.22 in Chap. 3) also shows that the outstanding balance of long-term debt of companies fell sharply after 1998.

Elimination of Excessive Employment

Employment conditions as judged by companies showed that excessive employment which they had kept for a long time beyond the collapse of the bubble, was also eliminated, and employment conditions turned to insufficient employment by the mid-2000s (Fig. 4.22).

Companies also strengthened their balance sheets by accumulating profits after the financial crisis (see Fig. 4.3 in this chapter) and gradually enhanced their liquidity position (Fig. 4.23). These developments seem to have promoted positive behavior of companies.

Favorable External Environments

The second background of the long recovery from the beginning of the 2000 was the favorable external economic environments. The world economy experienced a fairly long period of high and stable growth, which was

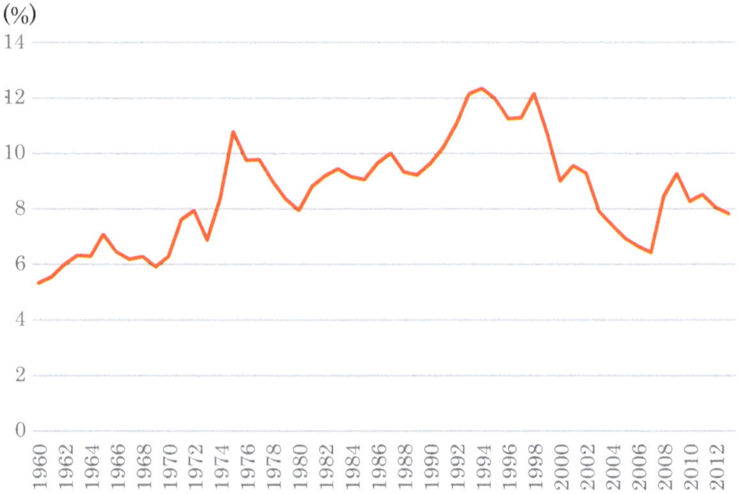

Fig. 4.20 Interest-bearing liabilities/cash flow. Note: Interest-bearing liabilities = short-term and long-term borrowings + bond, cash flow = current profits × (1/2) + depreciation. Source: Ministry of Finance, "Financial Statements Statistics of Corporations by Industry"

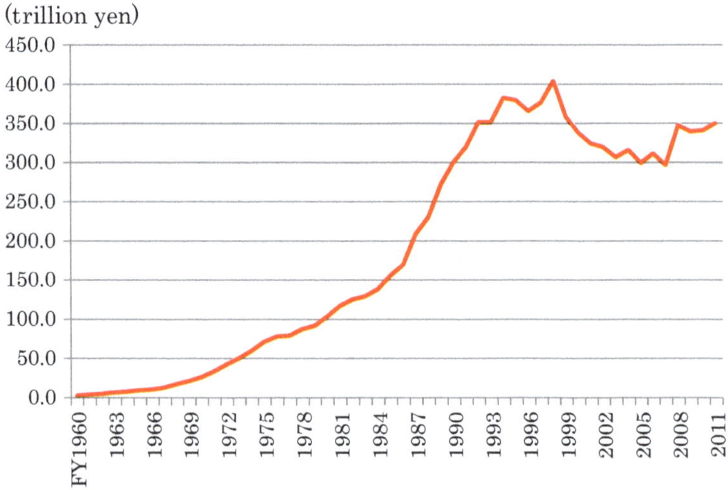

Fig. 4.21 Long-term debt of companies. Source: Financial Statements Statistics of Corporations, Ministry of Finance

Fig. 4.22 Employment conditions as judged by companies ("excessive employment"—"insufficient employment"). Source: Bank of Japan, "Tankan Survey"

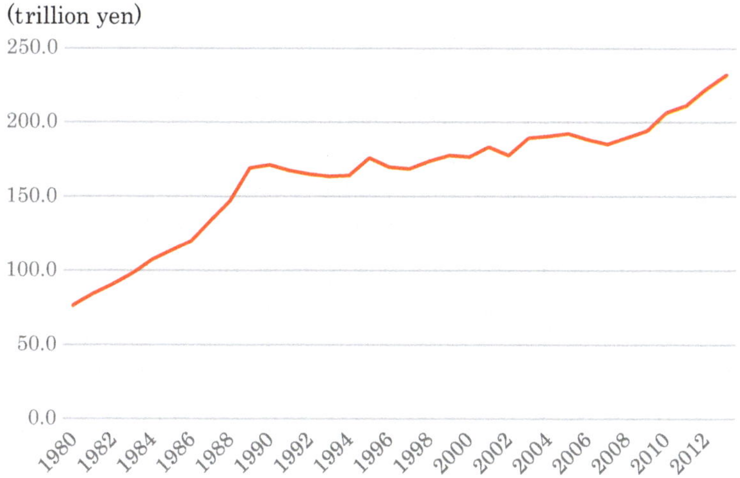

Fig. 4.23 Cash and deposit holdings by nonfinancial companies. Source: Bank of Japan, "Flow of Funds"

once later called the "Great Moderation," after bottoming out in 2002 until the eruption of the GFC in 2008 (Fig. 4.24). Thanks to such external environments, growth contribution of net export to the Japanese economy significantly rose from 0.2% in Period I and 0.1% in Period II to 0.8 in Period III.

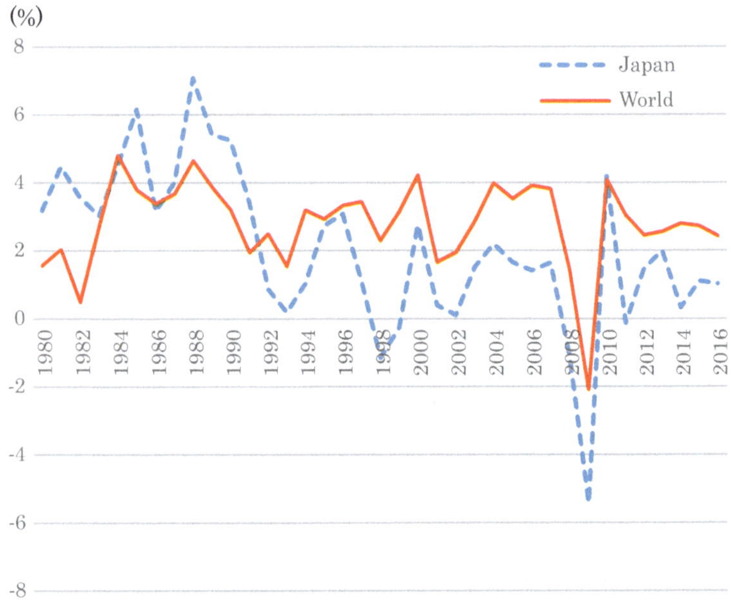

Fig. 4.24 Real GDP growth rate of the world and Japan. Source: IMF (2017) World Economic Outlook database, October 2017

Fundamental Changes Remained

In this way, in the long recovery period in 2003–2007, because companies had overcome the aftereffects of the collapse of the bubble through improvements of their balance sheets and also due to the favorable external environments, the growth rate recovered to 1.7% in Period III, from 1.7% in Period I and 0.4% in period II. The growth contribution by private investment switched to positive (0.5%) in Period III from −0.1% in Period I (1991–1997) and −0.2% in Period II (1998–2002).

However, despite these favorable developments during the long recovery period, fundamental changes that occurred in the behaviors of corporations continued.

The unemployment rate started to decline from the peak of 5.5% in April 2003 to a level just below 4.0% in 2007. The level was still far higher, however, than the pre-crisis average of 2.8% (see Fig. 4.12).

Nominal wages recovered a positive growth only in 2005 and 2006 (Fig. 4.10).

Increase in the share of non-regular workers somewhat decelerated from around the mid-2000s but basically maintained its rising trend (Fig. 4.14).

The excess of savings over investment in the corporate sector declined, but the sector continued to be the net saver (Fig. 4.16).

CPI (excluding fresh food) stayed in the neighborhood of zero inflation (Fig. 4.17).

These developments show persistence of what may be called defensive behaviors of companies, such as restraining investment and cutting labor costs. The declining trend of the ratio of investment to cash flow, which became clear after the burst of the bubble, continued at a moderate pace, even in the long recovery period (Fig. 4.25).

Why do the companies continue to restrain investment? We should note that companies strengthened foreign direct investment (FDI) relative to domestic investment after entering the 2000s. The ratio of FDI to private investment (nominal) increased from the average of 3.8% in the 1990s to an average of 7.9% in the 2000s, more than twice as high as in the 1990s (Fig. 4.26).

Figure 4.27 provides an example. The electric machinery and appliances sector, which recorded a level of domestic investment that was higher than

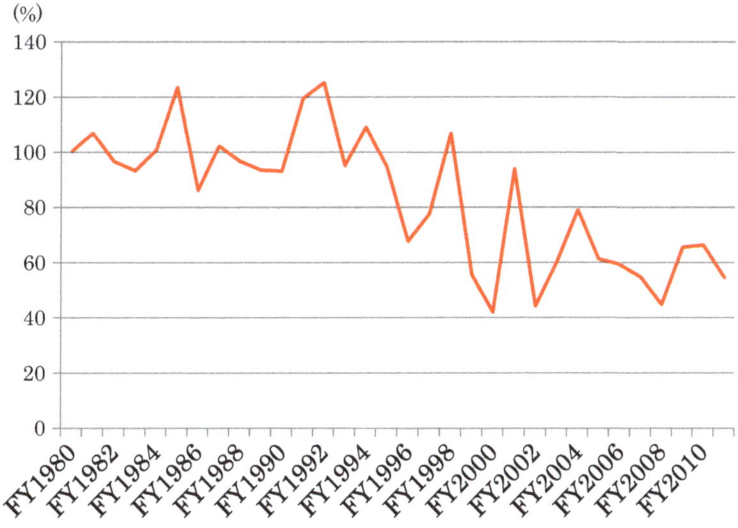

Fig. 4.25 Investment/cash flow. Source: Ministry of Finance, "Financial Statements Statistics of Corporations by Industry"

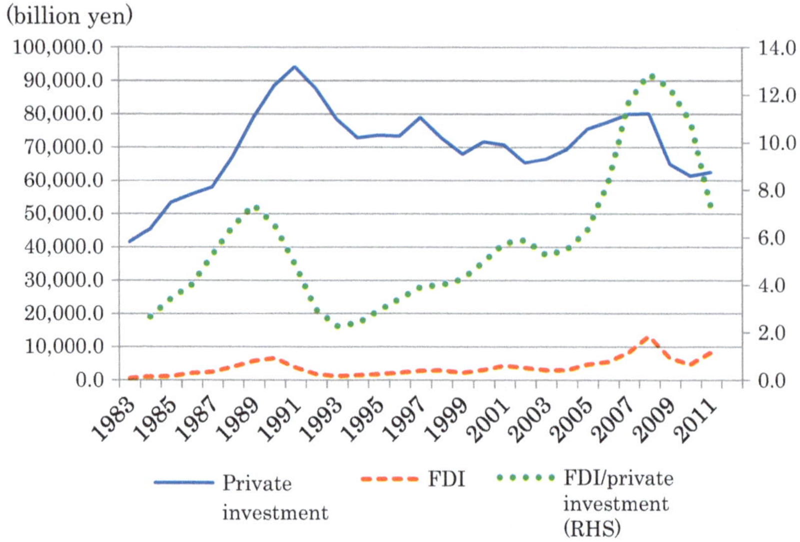

Fig. 4.26 Private investment and Foreign Direct Investment. Note: Private investment is in nominal terms. Foreign direct investment, in terms of yen, is obtained by converting the FDI, in terms of dollars, using the period's average exchange rate. FDI/Private Investment is the ratio of two values, both in three-year moving average. Source: Tabulated using relevant data from Cabinet Office, JETRO, and IMF

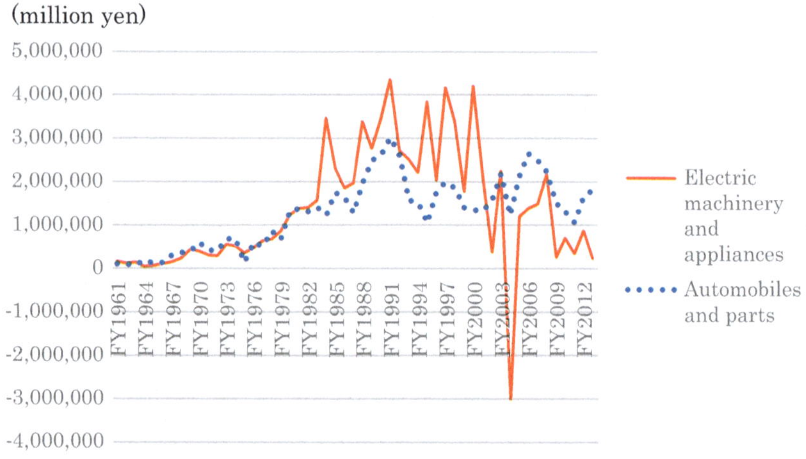

Fig. 4.27 Nominal investment by the electric machinery and appliances sector and the automobiles and parts sector. Source: Ministry of Finance, "Financial Statements Statistics of Corporations by Industry"

that of the automobile and parts sector throughout the 1980s and 1990s, significantly reduced the level of domestic investment, particularly after entering the 2000s. By contrast, the automobile and parts sector maintained a relatively high level of investment, even after the financial crisis.

Another example of defensive behaviors of companies is found in the labor cost reduction. Restraint of labor cost (salary and bonus) in terms of labor share in value added (Fig. 4.28), which became clear after the financial crisis, was strengthened after entering the 2000s and continued until the GFC. Thereafter, the share of labor cost in value added increased, as the value added sharply shrank after the GFC, but thereafter it started to decline again.

What Did the Government Do in the Long Recovery Period? Characteristics of Economic Policies in the Long Recovery Period under the Koizumi Administration (April 2001–September 2006) and the First Abe Administration (September 2006–August 2007)

How were economic policies managed in Period III when the economy underwent a long recovery. Most of the economic policies in this period focused on the long-term agenda and were not, in general, friendly to short-run growth.

First, policy returned to fiscal consolidation. The total size of the initial budget decreased by 3.6% in five years under the Koizumi administration. Expenditure related to public works was cut by 23.7% from 9,435 billion yen in FY 2001 (before Koizumi) to 7,201 billion yen in FY 2006 (when Koizumi left) on an initial budget basis. The share of public fixed capital formation in GDP was halved in a decade from an average of 7.8% in the latter half of 1990s to an average of 3.8% in the latter half of 2000s (Fig. 4.29).

Second, government-led promotion of the resolution of NPLs was strongly pursued, as explained before. The "Financial Revival Program" (the so-called Takenaka Plan) (October 2002), which aimed at halving the NPL ratio of major banks (8.4% at that time) by March 2005, was enforced (the goal was achieved in 2005).

Third, promotion of structural reform was strongly promoted under slogans such as "Structural reforms that do not allow any sanctuaries" or "No growth without reform."

Fourth is the "Great Intervention," which should have had short-term economic impacts. About 35 trillion yen in total were used for intervention in the foreign exchange market from January 2003 to March 2004. However, the yen appreciated from 119.37 yen /dollar on December 30,

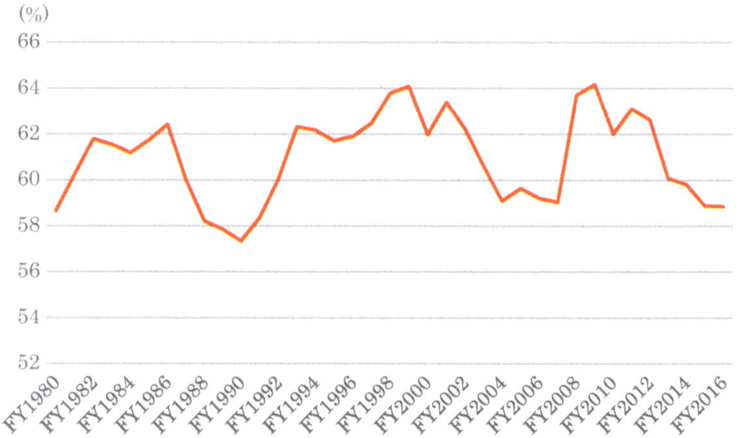

Fig. 4.28 Labor cost/value added. Note: Value added = salaries and bonuses for employees and executive members + expenses for fringe benefits + rental fees + taxes and other official charges + operating profits; labor costs = salaries and bonuses for employees + expenses for fringe benefits. Source: Ministry of Finance, "Financial Statements Statistics of Corporations by Industry"

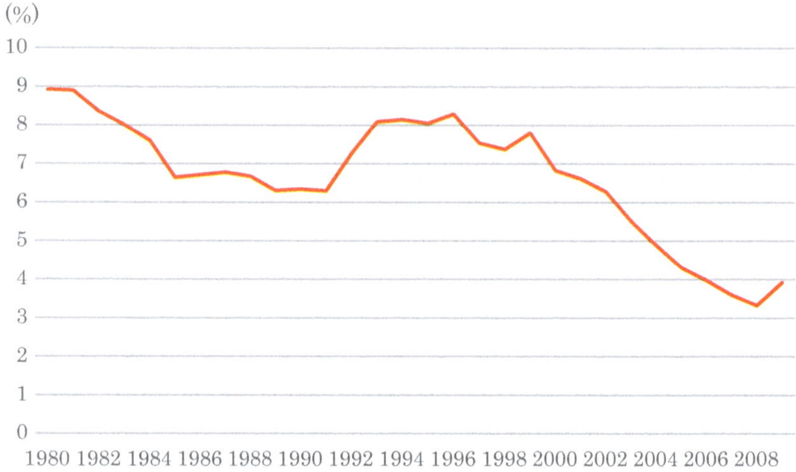

Fig. 4.29 Share of public fixed capital formation in real GDP. Source: Cabinet Office

2002, to 105.77 yen/dollar on March 31, 2004. The Great Intervention did not bring about yen depreciation but worked to prevent further appreciation of the yen.

Japanese Economy Started to Show Other Significant Changes

Thus, the Japanese economy finally overcame the negative legacy of the collapse of the bubble, eliminating excesses, by the mid-2000s, but it became clear that the corporate sector continued to show defensive behaviors. Furthermore, the Japanese economy started to show other significant changes from the 2000s.

First, the growth contribution by consumption started to decline. Contribution to growth by consumption was relatively high in Period I (1991–1997) at an average of 1.0% in 1991–1997, when the average growth rate over the period was 1.7%, accounting for nearly two-thirds of the growth. The growth contribution of consumption declined to 0.4% in Period II (1998–2002), when the average growth rate fell to 0.4%. In Period III (2002–2007), while the growth rate recovered to 1.7%, the contribution of consumption stayed at 0.6%, accounting for just over one-third of the entire growth rate (Fig. 4.30).

Behind the declining growth contribution by consumption was a continued fall in real wages since the financial crisis (Fig. 4.31).

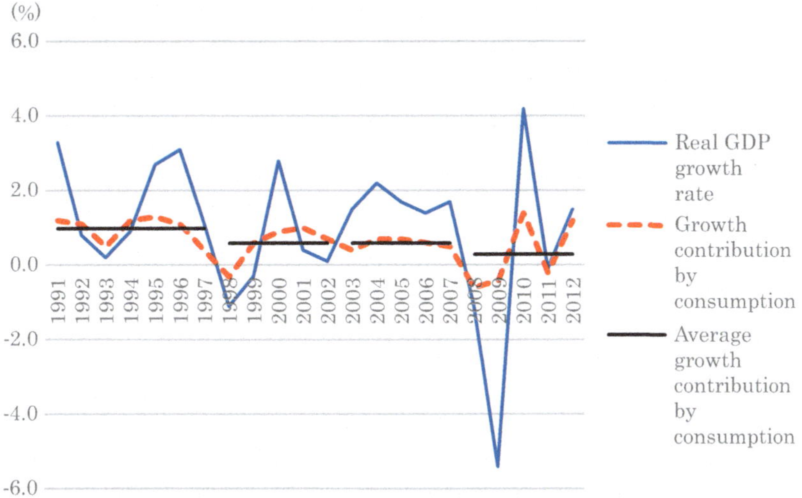

Fig. 4.30 Real GDP growth rate and growth contribution of private consumption. Source: Cabinet Office

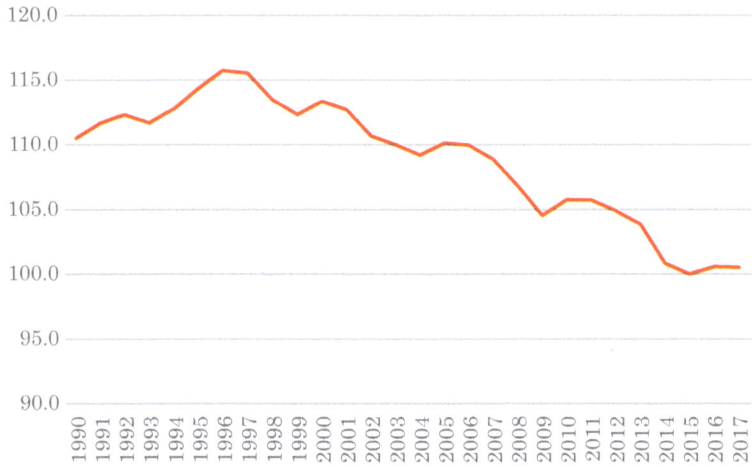

Fig. 4.31 Real wage (2015 = 100). Note: Real wage is obtained by deflating total cash earnings in establishments with five or more employees by CPI. Source: Ministry of Health, Labor, and Welfare, "Monthly labor survey"

As the nominal wages kept falling, the household savings ratio continued to fall after the financial crisis and finally fell below zero in 2013 (Fig. 4.32).

Another change in the Japanese economy was an increasing dependence on trade. The trade dependency ([exports + imports]/GDP) consistently rose after the war, then became flat from the mid-1970s, and in the 1980s stayed at a slightly lower level. However, the trade dependency rate significantly rose from the mid-1990s through the long recovery period (from 15.4% in 1990 to the average of 24.4% in 2003–2007) (Fig. 4.33). This development implies that the economy's vulnerability to external shocks has increased, posing a threat to the stability of economic performance.

One additional change to note is the growth potential of the Japanese economy. The corporate sector continues to be a net saver (Fig. 4.16). On the basis of Financial Statement Statistics, the amount of investment in nominal terms is smaller than the amount of depreciation, that is, net investment is negative, in 13 out of 15 years from fiscal 1998 to fiscal 2012 (Fig. 4.34). By contrast, the government sector continues to be the biggest user of the savings. The fact that the government sector, not the private sector, has been a net investor for a long time, since around the time of the financial crisis, poses a concern over the future growth potential of the Japanese economy.

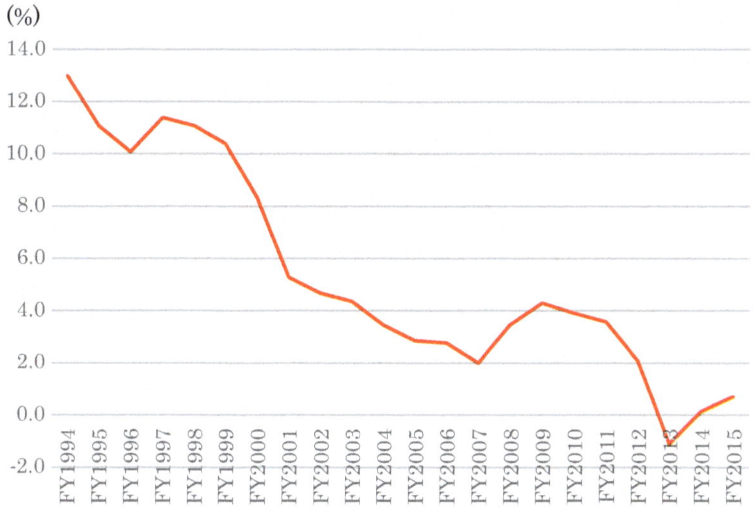

Fig. 4.32 Household savings ratio. Source: Cabinet Office

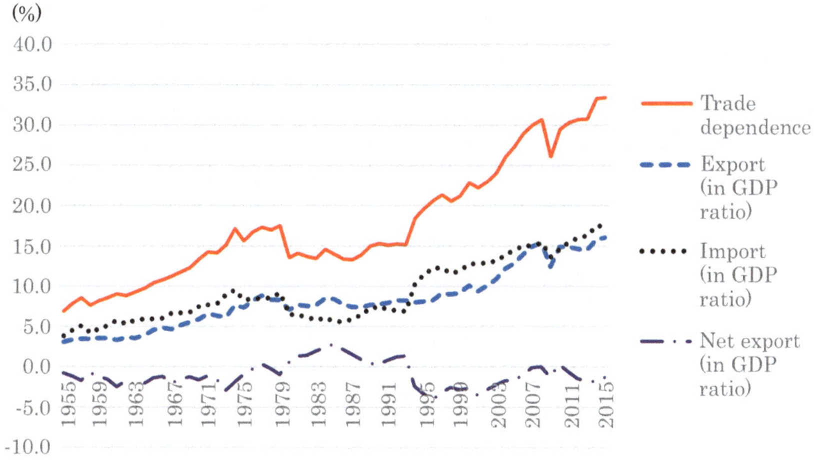

Fig. 4.33 Trade dependence, export, import, and net export (in GDP ratio). Source: Cabinet Office

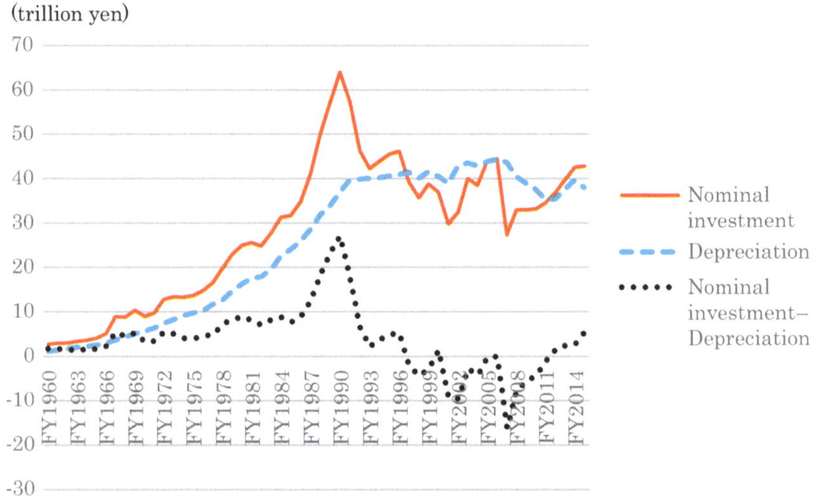

Fig. 4.34 Nominal investment, nominal amount of depreciation, and nominal net investment. Source: Ministry of Finance, "Financial Statements Statistics of Corporations by Industry"

Summary of Period III (Long Recovery Period)

The expansionary macroeconomic policies to support the economy were placed into force to their full extent, under the sharp deterioration of the economy after the financial crisis that erupted in the late 1990s. Then, the long recovery started in 2002 and lasted for more than six years. The background of the long recovery included, first, the fact that the corporate sector had finally got rid of the excesses that it had assumed in the bubble period ("three excesses") and restored sound balance sheets, and second, favorable external environments. However, even under the long recovery, the corporate sector continued to contain investment relative to cash flow, squeeze labor costs (the unemployment rate stayed high and a shift to non-regular employment continued), accumulate profits, strengthen the liquidity position, and remain an excess saving sector, maintaining a defensive stance. At the same time, deflation continued.

During the long recovery, some additional changes in the Japanese economy became more apparent. One is a structural shortage of domestic demand. In addition to the continued restraint on investment, consumption gradually reduced its growth contribution, reflecting the continued fall in real wages. In parallel, the trade dependence has increased, possibly raising external vulnerability.

Furthermore, the restraint on investment by the corporate sector and the use of savings by the government sector pose a concern for the long-term growth prospects of the Japanese economy.

3 Period IV (2008–2012): GFC and After

In this section, we briefly look at Period IV (2008–2012), the GFC, and after.

External Shocks and Their Impacts on the Japanese Economy

The Japanese economy underwent a series of shocks in Period IV (2008–2012).

In 2008, the GFC broke out, and Japan, together with Germany, was most severely hit among the major advanced countries by the subsequent global recession. In 2009, the European debt crisis started. Furthermore, Japan was hit by the East Japan Great Earthquake in March 2011, and due to the interruption of production networks and the increase in imports of energy due to the nuclear power plant accident, Japan's goods and services account fell into deficit (Fig. 4.35). However, the yen rate surged, hitting a record high of 75.32 yen to the dollar in the New York market on October 31, 2011, allegedly due to the global search for safe assets. Despite weakening economic conditions, the yen rate stayed high, frequently recording a historic level below 80 yen to the dollar in 2011 and 2012 (Fig. 4.36).

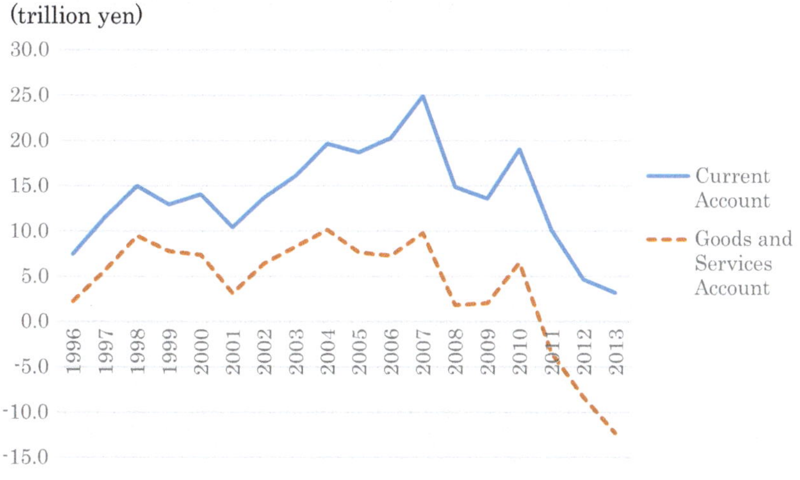

Fig. 4.35 Current account and goods and services account. Source: Ministry of Finance

Fig. 4.36 Yen to dollar nominal exchange rate. Note: Spot rates at 17 pm, monthly average. Source: BOJ

Under the sharp yen appreciation, the overseas/domestic investment ratio of manufacturing industries increased sharply from 2010. Thus, Period IV was a time when Japan's external vulnerability was severely felt (Fig. 4.37).

4 Problem with the Japanese Economy, after Overcoming Aftereffects of the Bubble and the Shock of the Financial Crisis (Demand Structure and Growth Potential)

This chapter has examined the process of the financial crisis that broke out in the latter half of the 1990s and its impacts on the Japanese economy. After the bubble burst, while the corporate sector took time to dispose of excess assets and liabilities, cost and risk of excess (unprofitable) assets gradually shifted to the banking sector, and a financial crisis broke out seven years after the collapse of the bubble. The government was unable to promptly resolve the NPL problem. The background for this includes optimistic expectations held by the government for the future course of economy and land prices in the initial stage, concern in the subsequent stage for the huge negative impacts on the economy that could arise from prompt resolution of the excesses, and also non-existence of a comprehensive framework necessary to resolve the financial crisis. With the breakout of the

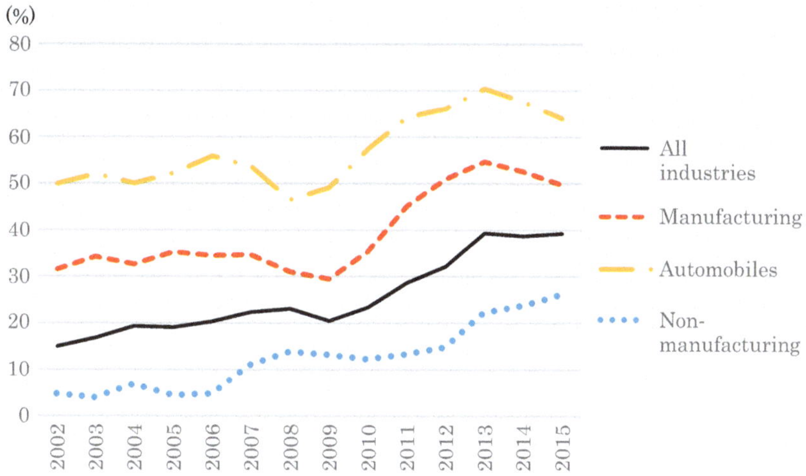

Fig. 4.37 Overseas investment/domestic investment. Note: Overseas investment is on a consolidated basis, and domestic investment is on an unconsolidated basis. Source: Development Bank of Japan, "Investment plan survey fiscal years 2015 · 2016 · 2017", August 4, 2016

crisis, fundamental changes took place in the Japanese economy, such as a surge of the unemployment rate, expansion of non-regular employment, decline of nominal wages, switch of the corporate sector to a net saver position, and emergence of deflation. These changes, in principle, stayed with the economy even during the long economic recovery that started in the early 2000s.

After reviewing economic developments from Periods II through IV, we have found the following characteristics and problems with the current Japanese economy after it overcame the negative legacy of the bubble.

First, private investment increased in recent years, but its level continued to be constrained relative to cash flow.

Second, companies continued to restrain labor costs through reduction in nominal wages and a shift from regular to non-regular employment.

Third, the growth contribution of consumption declined against the background of continued fall in real wages.

Fourth, dependence on foreign demand rose, possibly raising Japan's vulnerability to external shocks.

Fifth, the government continued to be the biggest user of savings, with possible negative effects on potential growth.

To put everything together, the Japanese economy seems to have had two problems after overcoming the aftereffects of the formation and collapse of the bubble and the financial crisis, that is, insufficiency of domestic demand coupled with growing dependence on external demand, and possible decline in growth potential. The background of these problems is the continuation of defensive behaviors of companies, as is observed in their restraint on investment and labor costs. What has caused such a defensive stance of companies? How should we tackle them? These are the key questions and challenges that the Japanese economy currently faces after it has overcome the aftereffects of the bubble and the direct impacts of the financial crisis.

Supplement 1

Chronology in Period II (1998–2002), Period III (2003–2007), and Period IV (2008–2012)

1997	
January	Prime Minister Hashimoto (LDP) declared intention to start drastic reforms in six areas, including fiscal structure and the financial system
April	Consumption tax rate increased from 3% to 5%
June	BOJ law amended (its independence strengthened)
June	Comprehensive financial liberalization (Japan's "Financial Big Bang") authorized by advisory councils to MOF
July	Thai baht recorded a sharp fall (start of the Asian currency crisis)
November	Sanyo Securities filed a petition for protection under the Corporate Rehabilitation Law, causing default in the interbank market
November	Hokkaido Takuchoku Bank announced its inability to continue
November	Yamaichi Securities announced closure of business
November	Fiscal Structure Reform Act enacted
1998	
April	Comprehensive economic measures decided
May	Fiscal Structure Reform Act amended
October	Government decided to nationalize the Long-Term Credit Bank of Japan (first nationalization of private bank after the war)
November	Emergency economic measures decided (historically largest size)
December	The Nippon Credit Bank nationalized
1999	
February	BOJ introduced the zero interest rate policy
2000	
August	BOJ lifted zero interest rate policy
2000–2001	
	Collapse of the dot.com bubble
2001	
March	Government declared Japanese economy was under moderate deflation for the first time after the war
March	BOJ introduced Quantitative Easing Policy (QEP)
April	Koizumi administration started (return to the fiscal consolidation and policy orientation for structural reform)
2002	
January	The economy hit a bottom (start of the long economic recovery)
October	Financial Services Agency (FSA) formulated financial revival program (aimed at halving the NPL ratio of major banks by end March 2005)

(*continued*)

(continued)

2003	
January 2003–March 2004	Great intervention
2008	
September	Lehman Brothers collapsed (start of the GFC of 2008–2009)
2009	
September	The Democratic Party took the power
October	Misreporting of fiscal position by Greek government uncovered (start of the European debt crisis)
2011	
March	East Japan Great Earthquake
2012	
December	Second Abe administration and Abenomics started

Supplement 2

Impacts on Employment of Prompt Disposition of Excess Assets

In this supplement, we will conduct a very rough estimate on what impacts would have been imposed on employment if excess assets had been speedily disposed of.

Fig. 4.38 shows developments in total assets of corporations (excluding financial and insurance companies), based on Financial Statement Statistics of Corporations by Industry (MOF). We can see that there is a bump (excess assets) in the period from the mid-1980s to the first half of 2000s. The figure also shows an approximate line (a trend line) for the entire period, except for the years from fiscal 1985 to 2004 when there was a bump, that is, a trend line for the period from fiscal 1960 to 1984 and then the period from fiscal 2005 to 2016. If we regard the difference between the actual size of the total assets and the amount indicated by the trend line as excess assets, then the excess assets account for nearly three-tenths of the total assets in the first half of 1990s as indicated in Fig. 4.39 which shows the ratio of the excess of total assets over the amount implied by the trend line to the total assets.

Now, let us assume that the whole personnel resources—the combined number of executive members and employees—of companies (excluding financial and insurance companies) in the Financial Statement Statistics of Corporations by Industry) are deployed evenly and proportionately to the assets and that, if an asset is disposed of, then the whole personnel staff

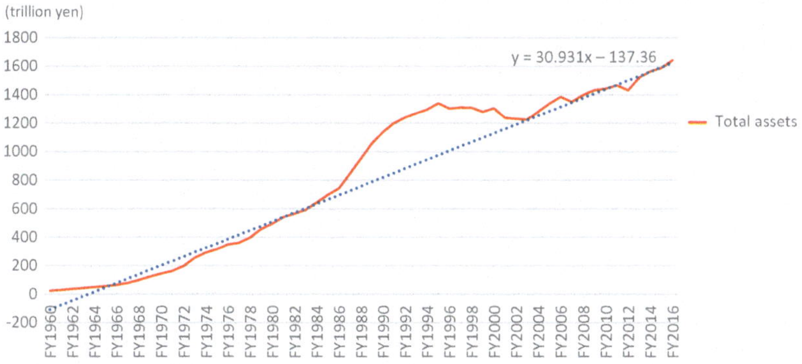

Fig. 4.38 Total assets of corporations (excluding financial and insurance companies) and their trend line. Total assets (for the red line). Trend line for the entire period except for 1985–2004. Source: Ministry of Finance, "Financial statement statistics of corporations by industry"

Fig. 4.39 Share of excess assets in total assets: FY1985~FY2010. Source: Ministry of Finance, "Financial statement statistics of corporations by industry"

deployed to the asset are entirely dismissed and become unemployed. Fig. 4.40 shows, for each year from fiscal 1985 to 2010, first, the number of additional people that would have become unemployed if all the excess assets estimated for the year had been disposed of in that year and if the entire personnel staff deployed to these assets had become unemployed; second, the resultant (elevated) unemployment rate; and third, the actual unemployment rate (as of December each year). For example, if all the

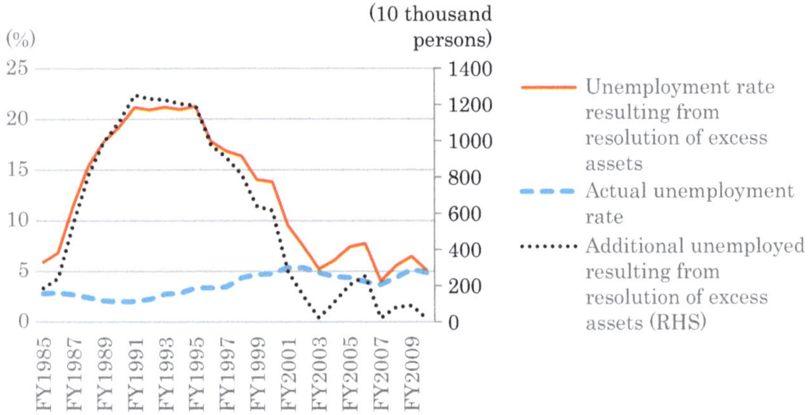

Fig. 4.40 Additional number of people unemployed and the unemployment rate resulting from prompt resolution of excess assets. Source: Ministry of Finance, "Financial statement statistics of corporations by industry"

excess assets had been disposed of in fiscal 1991, additional unemployment amounting to more than 12.5 million would have occurred, and the unemployment rate would have risen to 21.2%, that is, 10 times as high as the actual unemployment rate that year of 2.1%. The figure shows that similarly huge negative impacts would have occurred in any year in the first half of the 1990s. Considering that the estimate assumes an extreme case—that the entire personnel staff deployed to an asset will be dismissed and become unemployed if the asset was disposed of—then, in reality, the resultant direct impacts would have been smaller than estimated. On the contrary, in the case where disposition of excess assets led to abolition of relevant business operations, and indirect impacts spread to other parties such as business partners, secondary effects could have been added to the aforementioned direct impacts, producing an upward risk. No matter what the case may be, the magnitude of excess assets created in the 1980s seems to have been of such a scale that their rapid disposal would have seriously shaken the basis of the Japanese economy. It is unrealistic just to criticize delays in disposing excesses, as is done in the many arguments. It is implied that very strong intervention by the authorities was necessary, if extreme confusion and a sharp increase in the instability of the society was to be avoided.

Considering that the aforementioned total assets included such assets as liquid assets and securities held for investment purposes, we would like to conduct another estimate that uses physical assets (excluding land) instead of total assets. Fig. 4.41 shows developments in physical assets (excluding

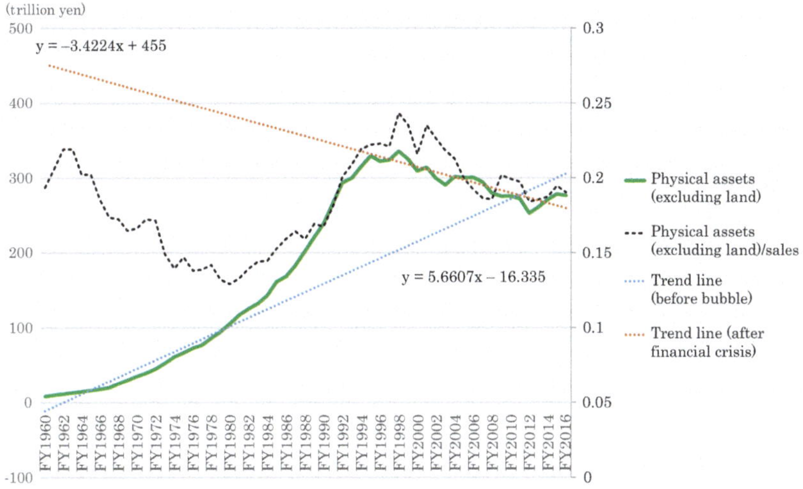

Fig. 4.41 Physical assets (excluding land) of corporations (excluding financial and insurance companies), their trend lines, and the ratio of physical assets to sales. Source: Ministry of Finance, "Financial statement statistics of corporations by industry"

land) and an approximate line (trend line) for the period from fiscal 1960 to 1984. If we regard the difference between the actual amount of physical assets (excluding land) and the amount calculated by the trend line as excess, then it can be shown that the size of excess assets amounted to greater than four-tenths of the entire physical assets (excluding land) around the mid-1990s. This implies that prompt disposal of excesses would have created negative impacts greater than calculated in the preceding estimate.

Fig. 4.41 shows an approximate line (trend line) for the period from fiscal 1998 onward. The trend of physical assets (excluding land) is entirely different for the period between before the bubble and after the financial crisis. The figure also shows the ratio of physical assets (excluding land) / sales. The ratio swiftly rose from the 1980s, hit a peak in fiscal 1998, sharply fell until the mid-2000s, and stabilized thereafter. It is implied that in the 1990s, two processes were simultaneously ongoing, one, efforts to overcome the collapse of the bubble (disposition of excess assets) and, two, adjustment to new environments where sales do not grow (restraint on asset size or its downward adjustments). In other words, going forward from some point in time in the 1990s, possibly from the financial crisis, companies began to exhibit investment behavior that assumes that the domestic economy will not expand in the future.

Bibliography

English References

International Monetary Fund (IMF) (1995) "The Nordic Banking Crises: Pitfalls in Financial Liberalization?" IMF Working Paper WP/95/61, IMF, Washington, DC.

Nakaso, Hiroshi (2001) "The financial crisis in Japan during the 1990s: How the Bank of Japan responded and the lessons learnt." BIS Papers No. 6, BIS, Basel.

Nakaso, Hiroshi (2014) "What the lost decades left for the future." Keynote speech, 2014 International Conference of the International Association of Deposit Insurers, Asia–Pacific Regional Committee, Bank of Japan, April 23.

Shirakawa, Masaaki (2012) "Japan's economy and monetary policy" June 4, 2012, Bank of Japan.

Japanese References

Asahi Shimbun (2009) "Henten Keizai" (Economy in Transition) News Collection Group *Ushinawareta '20 nen'* (Lost '20 years'), Iwanami Shoten.

Bank of Japan (1993) "Heisei 5 nendo no Kinnyu oyobi Keizai no Doko" (States of Finance and Economy in FY 1993), in BOJ *Chosa Geppo*, June.

Bank of Japan (2001) "Saikin no Ginko Kashidashi Shijo no Doko nitsuite" (Recent Developments in Bank Credit Markers), October, *Market Review* 2001-J-10.

Bank of Japan (2003a) *Keizai Bukka no Shorai Tenbo to Risuku Hyoka* (Future Outlook of the Economy and Price and Risk Assessment), April.

Bank of Japan (2003b) *Keizai Bukka no Shorai Tenbo to Risuku Hyoka* (Future Outlook of the Economy and Price and Risk Assessment), October.

Bank of Japan (2004a) *Keizai Bukka no Shorai Tenbo to Risuku Hyoka* (Future Outlook of the Economy and Price and Risk Assessment), April.

Bank of Japan (2004b) *Keizai Bukka no Shorai Tenbo to Risuku Hyoka* (Future Outlook of the Economy and Price and Risk Assessment), October.

Bank of Japan (2005a) *Keizai Bukka no Shorai Tenbo to Risuku Hyoka* (Future Outlook of the Economy and Price and Risk Assessment), April.

Bank of Japan (2005b) "Wagakuni Kigyo niyoru Yurishi Fusai no Asshuku to Rieki Bunpai Saku" (Reduction of Interest-bearing Debt by Japanese Companies and Profit Distribution Policy) May, *Nichigin Review* 2005-J-7.

Bank of Japan (2005c) *Keizai Bukka no Shorai Tenbo to Risuku Hyoka* (Future Outlook of the Economy and Price and Risk Assessment), October.

Bank of Japan (2009a) *Kinnyu Keizai Geppo* (Monthly Financial and Economic Report), February.

Cabinet Office (2001) *Heisei 13 nendo Nenji Keizai Zaisei Hokoku – Kaikaku Nakushite Seicho Nashi-* (Heisei 13 Annual Report on the Japanese Economy and Public Finance–No Gains without Reforms), December.

Cabinet Office (2005) *Heisei 17 nendo Nenji Keizai Zaisei Hokoku* (Heisei 17 Annual Report on Japanese Economy and Public Finance), July.

Cabinet Office (2008) *Nihon Keizai 2008–2009* (Japanese Economy 2008–2009), December.

Deposit Insurance Corporation of Japan (2005) "Kinnyu Kikan Hatan ni kansuru Teiryo Bunseki" (Quantitative analysis of failures of financial institutions), *Yokin Hoken Kenkyu* September.

Economic Planning Agency (1993) *Heisei 5 nen Nenji Keizai Hokoku* (Heisei 5 Annual Economic Report).

Fujii, Mariko (2009) *Kinnyu Kakushin to Shijo Kiki* (Financial Breakthrough and Market Crisis), Nihon Keizai Shimbun Sha.

Fujii, Yoshihiro (2001) *Kinnyu Saisei no Gosan* (Miscalculations of Financial Recovery), Nihon Keizai Shimbun Sha.

Fukao, Mitsuhiro (2009) "Ginko no Keiei Akka to Hatan Shori" (Deterioration of performance of banks and their resolution). In *Furyo Saiken to Kinnyu Kiki* (Non-Performing Loans and Financial Crisis), edited by Kazuto Ikeo. ("Baburu/Defure ki no Nihon Keizai to Keizai Seisaku Vol. 4") (Japanese Economy and Economic Policies in the Period of Bubble and Deflation-Vol. 4). Economic and Social Research Institute, Cabinet Office.

Heisei Kinnyu Kiki heno Taio Kenkyu Kai (2005) "Hatan Shori Shuho no Shinka to Kanren Ho no Seibi (Kinnyu Saisei Ho Igo)" (Progress in Tools for Resolution of Failed Institutions and Provisions of Relevant Laws [Since the Financial Recovery Act]) *Yokin Hoken Kenkyu* Vol. 4, September.

Himino, Ryozo (2005) *Kensho BIS Kisei to Nihon* (Examining BIS regulations and Japan), Kinnyu Zaisei Jijo.

Hori Masahiro, and Hideaki Kitaki (2004) "Ginko kino teika genkyo setsu ha settoku ryoku wo mochiuruka" (Is the argument to blame declining bank function convincing?). In *Ronso: Nihon no Keizai Kiki – Choki Teitai no Shin-in wo Kaimei suru* (Debates: Japan's Economic Crisis – Examining Real Cause of the Long Stagnation), edited by Koichi Hamada and Akiyoshi Horiuchi. Nihon Keizai Shimbun Sha.

Horioka, Charles Yuji (2007) "Nihon no 'Ushinawareta 10 nen' no gen-in" (Cause of Japan's 'Lost decade'). In *Keizai Teitai no Gen-in to Seido*, (Causes of Economic Stagnation and Institutions), edited by Fumio Hayashi. Keiso Shobo.

Hoshi, Takeo, and Hugh Patrick, eds. (2001) *Nihon Kinnyu Shisutemu no Kiki to Henbo* (Crisis in Japan's Financial System and its Transition), Nihon Keizai Shimbun Sha.

Ikeo, Kazuto, ed. (2009) *Furyo Saiken to Kinnyu Kiki* (Non-Performing Loans and the Financial Crisis), Cabinet Office, "Baburu/defure kino Nihon Keizai to Keizai Seisaku 4" (Japanese Economy and Economic Policy in the Period of the Bubble and Deflation 4), Economic and Social Research Institute, Cabinet Office.

Ishii, Shigeru (1998) *Ketsudan naki Keiei* (Management without Decision). Nihon Keizai Shimbun Sha.

Ito, Motoshige, ed. (2009) *Kokusai Kankyo no Henka to Nihon Keizai* (Changes in International Environments and the Japanese Economy), (Cabinet Office, "Baburu/defure kino Nihon Keizai to Keizai Seisaku 3" (Japanese Economy and Economic Policy in the Period of the Bubble and Deflation 3), Economic and Social Research Institute, Cabinet Office).

Karube, Kensuke (2004) *Dokyumento Zero Kinri – Nichigin vs Seifu Naze Tairitsu Surunoka* (Documentary Zero Interest Rate – BOJ vs Government Why Do They Come into Collision?). Iwanami Shoten.

Karube, Kensuke, and Nishino Tomohiko (1999) *Kensho Keizai Shissei – Dare ga Nani wo Naze Machigaetaka* (Examining Economic Policy Mistakes – Who Made What Mistakes and Why?). Iwanami Shoten.

Kataoka, Goshi (2010) *Nihon no 'Ushinawareta 20 nen'* (Japan's 'Lost Two Decades'). Fujiwara Shoten.

Kawai, Masahiro, and Shinji Takagi (2009) "Kawase reto to kokusai shusi – Puraza goi kara heisei fukyo no makuro keizai gaku" (Foreign exchange rate and balance of payments – Macroeconomics of the Plaza accord to Heisei stagnation). In *Kokusai Kankyo no Henka to Nihon Keizai* (Changes in International Environments and the Japanese Economy) edited by Motoshige Ito (Cabinet Office, "Baburu/defure kino Nihon Keizai to Keizai Seisaku 3" (Japanese Economy and Economic Policy in the Period of the Bubble and Deflation 3)), Economic and Social Research Institute, Cabinet Office.

Komine, Takao, ed. (2011) *Nihon Keizai no Kiroku – Dai Niji Sekiyu Kiki heno Taio kara Baburu Hokai made (1970 nendai~1996 nen)* (Record of Japanese Economy From Responses to the 2nd Oil shock and the Collapse of the Bubble [1970s to 1996]) ("Baburu/defure kino Nihon Keizai to Keizai Seisaku Rekishi hen dai 1 kan"), (Japanese Economy and Economic Policy in the Period of Bubble and Deflation – History Vol. 1), Economic and Social Research Institute, Cabinet Office.

Komine, Takao (2005) *Nihon Keizai no Shin Kyokumen* (New Phase of Japanese Economy). Chuo Koron Sha.

Kusano, Atsushi (1998) *Yamaichi Shoken Hatan to Kiki Kanri – 1965 and 1998* (Failure of Yamaichi Securities and Crisis Management: Years of 1965 and 1997). Asahi Shimbun Sha.

Matsushima, Shigeru, and Harukata Takenaka, eds. (2011), *Nihon Keizai no Kiroku – Jidai Shogen Shu (oraru Hisutori)* (Record of Japanese Economy – Collection of Testimonies of the Period (Oral History)) ("Baburu/Defure ki no Nihon Keizai to Keizai Seisaku – Rekishi Hen dai 3 kan") (Japanese Economy and Economic Policies in the Period of Bubble and Deflation – History Vol. 3), Economic and Social Research Institute, Cabinet Office, Japanese Government.

Mikitani, Ryoichi, and Adam A. Posen, eds. (2001) *Nihon no Kinnyu Kiki – Beikoku no Keiken to Nihon heno Kyokun* (Monetary Policy in Japan – US Experiences and Their Lessons for Japan). Tokyo: Toyo Keizai Shimpo Sha.

Ministry of Finance (1992) "Kinnyu gyosei no tomen no unnyo hoshin" (Current policy of financial administration), August 18, 1992, in Banking Bureau, Ministry of Finance, "*dai 42 kai Ginko kyoku Kinnyu Nenpo Heisei 5 nen ban*" (42nd Annual Report of Banking Bureau Heisei 5).

Nakagawa, Satoshi (1996) "Wagakuni kinnyu kikan no furyo saiken no genjo nitsuite" (on the current status of non-performing loans of the Japanese financial institutions) Ministry of Finance *Fainansu*. October.

Nakahara, Nobuyuki (2006) *Nichigin ha Dareno Monoka* (Whom Is the BOJ for?). Chuo Koron Sha.

Nihon Keizai Shimbun Sha (2000) *Kensho Baburu – Han-i Naki Ayamachi* (Examining the Bubble—Fault without Intention). Nihon Keizai Shimbun Sha.

Nishimura, Kiyohiko (2005) *Nihon Keizai Miezaru Kozo Tenkan* (Japanese Economy – Invisible Structural Transition). Kansai Shakai Keizai Kenkyujo.

Nishimura, Kiyohiko, and Yoshiro Miwa (1990) *Nihon no Kabuka Chika Keisei no Mekanizumu* (Mechanism of Stock and Land Price Formation in Japan). Tokyo: Tokyo University Press.

Nishimura, Yoshimasa (1999) *Kinnyu Gyosei no Hai-in* (Cause of Defeat in Financial Administration). Bunshun Bunko.

Nishimura, Yoshimasa (2009) "Furyo Saiken Shori no Keii to Ronten" (Process and Issues of Disposition of Non-Performing Loans). In: *Furyo Saiken to Kinnyu Kiki* (Non-Performing Loans and Financial Crisis), edited by Kazuto Ikeo (Non-Performing Loans and the Financial Crisis), Cabinet Office "Baburu/defure kino Nihon Keizai to Keizai Seisaku 4" (Japanese Economy and Economic Policy in the Period of the Bubble and Deflation 4) 2009, Economic and Social Research Institute, Cabinet Office.

Nishimura, Yoshimasa (2011) *Kinnyu Shisutemu Kaikaku 50 nen no Kiseki* (50-Year History of Financial System Reform), Kinnyu Zaisei Jijo Kenkyu Kai.

Nishino Tomohiko (2001) *Kensho Keizai Meiso – Naze Kiki ga Tsuzuku noka* (Examining the Economy Straying off Course: Why Does the Crisis Continue?). Iwanami Shoten.

Nishino Tomohiko (2003) *Kensho Keizai An-un-Naze Sakiokuri Surunoka* (Examining Economy under Clouds—Why Is It Put Off?). Iwanami Shoten.

Noguchi, Asahi (2005) Ekonomisuto Tachi no Yuganda Suishodama (Distorted Cristal Balls of Economists). Tokyo: Toyo Keizai Shimpo Sha.

Ogawa, Kazuo, and Heizo Takenaka (2001) *Seisaku Kiki to Nihon Keizai* (Policy Crisis and Japanese Economy). Nihon Hyoron Sha.

Otake, Fumio, and Noriyuki Yanagawa (2004) *Heisei Fukyo no Ronten* (Issues in Heisei Recession). Tokyo: Toyo Keizai Shimpo Sha.

BOJ (2009) "Kigyo Shueki no Kaizen to sono Nihon Keizai heno Ganni" (Improvements in Corporate Profits and Its Implications to Japanese Economy), September 20. Research and Statistics Department.

Sakuragawa, Masaya (2003) "Furyo Saiken Mondai ga Nihon Keizai ni Ataeta Dageki" (Damage Made to Japanese Economy by Non-Performing Loan problems). In *Ushinawareta 10 nen no Shinn-in ha Nanika* (What is the Real Cause of the Lost Decade?), edited by Kikuo Iwata and Miyagawa Tsutomu, Economics Series. Tokyo: Toyo Keizai Shimpo Sha.

Sato, Takafumi (2003) *Sinnyo Chitsujo Seisaku no Saihen – Wakugumi Ikoki toshiteno 1990 nendai* (Reorganization of Policies for the Maintenance of Stable Financial System – 1990s as a Period of Framework Transition). Nihon Tosho Center.

Sato, Takafumi (2010) *Kinnyu Gyosei no Zahyo Jiku – Heiji to Yuji wo Koete* (Coordinate Axis for Financial Administration – Beyond Times of Peace and Crisis). Tokyo: Toyo Keizai Shimpo Sha.

Tanaka, Takayuki (2009) *Kinnyu Kiki ni Do Tachi Mukau ka –'Ushinawareta 15 nen' no Kyokun* (How to Cope with Financial Crises? – Lessons from 'the Lost 15 Years'). Chikuma Shobo.

Ueda, Kazuo (2001) "1990 nendai niokeru Nihon no Furyo Saiken Mondai no Gennin" (Cause of Non-Performing Loan Problems in the 1990s in Japan). In "*Nihon Kinnyu Shisutemu no Kiki to Henbo*" (Crisis in Japan's Financial System and its Transition), edited by Takeo Hoshi and Hugh Patrick. Nihon Keizai Shimbun Sha.

Ueda, Kazuo (2005) *Zero Kinri tono Tatakai* (Battle against Zero Interest Rate). Nihon Keizai Shimbun Sha.

Uemura Shuichi, and Sato Yoshiko (2000) "Saikin no Chika Keisei no Tokucho nituite" (On the Characteristics of Recent Land Price Formation), October, BOJ *Chosa Geppo*.

Watanabe, Takashi (2001) *Furyo Saiken ha Naze Kienai* (Why Have Non-Performing Loans Not Disappeared?). Nikkei BP Sha.

Yoshikawa, Hiroshi, ed. (2009) *Defure Keizai to Kinnyu Seisaku* (Deflationary Economy and Monetary Policy), (Cabinet Office "Baburu/defure kino Nihon Keizai to Keizai Seisaku 7") (Japanese Economy and Economic Policy in the Period of the Bubble and Deflation 7). Economic and Social Research Institute, Cabinet Office.

Yoshitomi, Masaru (1998) *Nihon Keizai no Shinjitsu* (Truth of the Japanese Economy). Toyo Keizai.

Yuasa, Shoyo, and Masahiro Tsujihiro (1996) *Dokyumento Jusen Hokai* (Documentary Collapse of Jusen). Diamond Sha.

CHAPTER 5

Deflation and Monetary Policy

In Chaps. 2, 3, and 4, we examined the mechanism of the three decade-long difficulties of the Japanese economy, basically in a time-sequential manner. In this and the next chapters, we will look at the issues that are more directly relevant to the current Japanese economy, that is, the long economic stagnation after the collapse of the bubble and deflation.

This chapter considers the issue of deflation and monetary policy. We will first look at the evolution of deflation in Japan and then list major arguments regarding the causes of deflation. In light of the fact that many arguments have been presented contending that deflation is a monetary phenomenon, we will assess monetary policy management with a view to finding causes of deflation, from the collapse of the bubble until just before the adoption of the Quantitative and Qualitative Monetary Easing (QQE) under Governor Kuroda, by dividing the whole period into two: first, the period from the collapse of the bubble to the adoption of the zero interest rate policy (ZIRP), which corresponds roughly to the period before the economy fell into deflation and was placed under the zero lower-bound constraint on interest rate; and second, the period from the lifting of ZIRP to the Quantitative Monetary Easing Policy (QEP) implemented from 2001 to 2006, which corresponds to the period under deflation and the zero lower-bound constraint. In Chap. 6, with a view to finding the mechanism of economic stagnation and deflation in the real sector, we

K. Aramaki, *Japan's Long Stagnation, Deflation, and Abenomics*,
https://doi.org/10.1007/978-981-13-2176-4_5

will analyze corporate behaviors, drawing mainly on the financial statement statistics that cover all the profit-making companies in Japan. Other factors, including external factors that may have relevance to the stagnation and deflation, will be briefly examined as well in Chap. 6.

1 Deflation in Japan from the 1990s

Changes in the Consumer Price Index (CPI, excluding fresh food) from the previous year were largely negative from July 1998 until 2013, except for a brief period of price rise in 2006–2008, which reflected energy and food price surge in the global market (Fig. 5.1, reproduced from Fig. 4.17 in Chap. 4). So, the Japanese economy was under deflation, defined as a continued decline in the general price level, basically for nearly 15 years from July 1998 to April 2013, but it was a mild deflation. The average rate of changes of CPI (excluding fresh food) from the previous year for the period from July 1998 to April 2013 was −0.3%, and the cumulative price decline over the 15-year period was −3.6%.

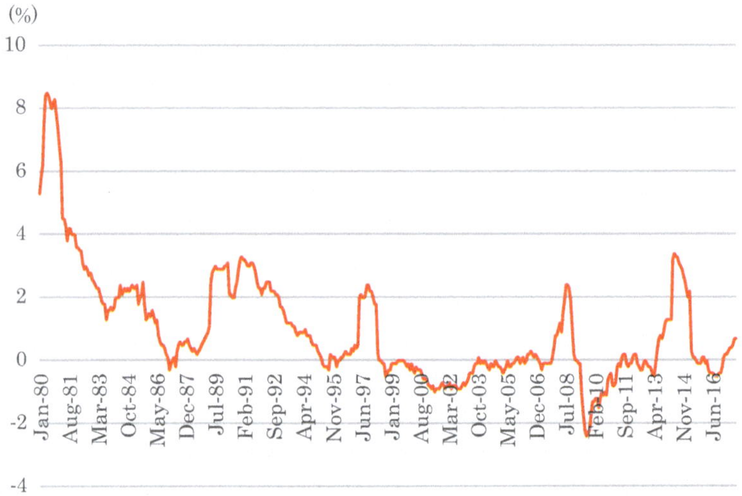

Fig. 5.1 The Consumer Price Index (excluding fresh food): Changes from the previous year. Source: Statistics Bureau, Ministry of Internal Affairs and Communication

Changes of the GDP deflator from the previous year have been almost consistently negative from the mid-1990s. The phenomenon of deflation is more clearly shown in the development of the GDP deflator, as compared with CPI (Fig. 5.2).[1]

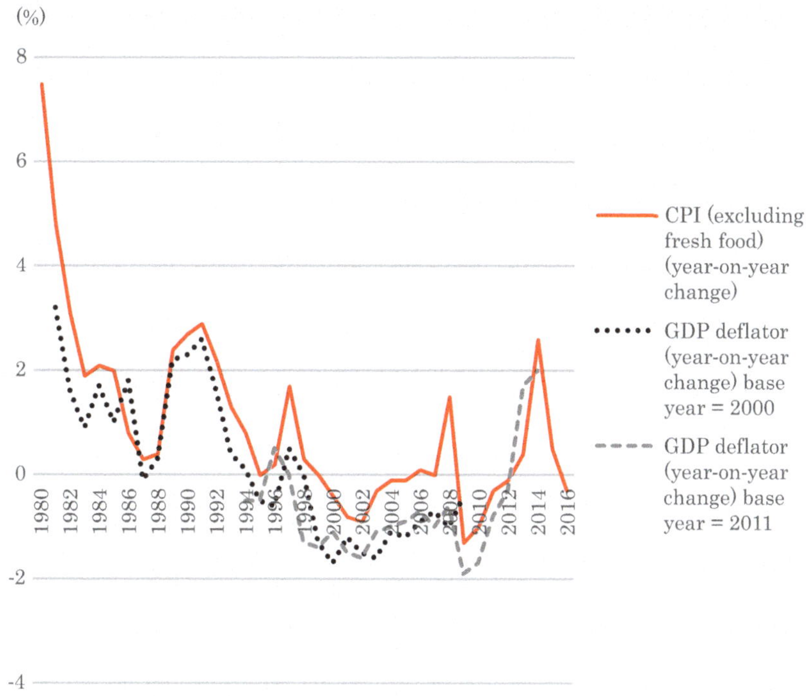

Fig. 5.2 The GDP deflator and Consumer Price Index (excluding fresh food) (year-on-year change). Source: Cabinet Office, Statistics Bureau, Ministry of Internal Affairs and Communications

[1] The GDP deflator is a deflator that covers the entire economic activities, including investment and exports, while CPI covers only private consumption. Two points should be noted. First, prices of investment goods such as machinery tend to reflect price-reducing technological progress. Second, price movements of imports are excluded from the calculation of the GDP deflator (i.e., if import prices rise at a higher pace than domestically produced goods, then the GDP deflator tends to be lowered more than otherwise), while rise in import prices are reflected in CPI (household sector consumes imported goods, too). Therefore, the GDP deflator tends to record a lower rate of increase than that of CPI, if prices of domestically produced goods, including those for exports, rise less than import prices.

2 Major Arguments on the Causes of Deflation

What caused such chronic but mild deflation? Cabinet Office (2001) lists three factors:

① Supply-side structural factors, such as inflow of low-priced imports from China and other emerging countries, IT, and other technological innovations (supply factor arguments)
② Demand factors caused by a lack of strength of the economy (demand factor arguments)
③ Financial factors, including declining intermediation function of banks due to excessive debts of corporations and the problem of non-performing loans (NPLs), and resultant stagnating money stock growth (financial sector- problem arguments)

In particular, as a type of argument that falls under the demand factor views, extensive arguments have been presented that blame the Bank of Japan's (BOJ) monetary policy management, some examples of which are as follows:[2]

Shinpo (2002) argued that the substantial fall in the inflation rate in Japan was due to the deterioration in macro supply/demand balance, that the deterioration in macro supply/demand balance was largely caused by a fall in the growth rate of money supply, and that the delay in interest rate reduction after the burst of bubble is responsible for a fall in the rate of increase in money supply (Shinpo 2002, 82).

Iwata (2001, 111) wrote, "The average rate of increase of money supply over 1991–2000 was 2.7%. In light of the long-term relationship between money supply and price, this [i.e., 2.7% increase] was low enough to let the Japanese economy fall into deflation from the mid-1990s." (The words in brackets were added by the author.)

Before assessing monetary policy in detail in the following sections, we will look at the aforementioned three factors briefly.

Supply Factor Arguments: Did Supply-Side Structural Factors Cause Deflation?

We look at supply-side factors drawing on Nishizaki et al. (2011).

[2] Translated by the author of this book into English from the original text.

Import Penetration

Japan's import penetration ratio significantly rose from 6% at the end of 1980s to around 12% in the latter half of 2000s (Fig. 5.3).

Changes from previous year of prices of imported and import-competing goods that are included in CPI were lower than the changes of prices of other goods in CPI from around mid-1990s, suggesting import penetration of low price products contributed to lowering price level (Fig. 5.4).

The Technological Progress and Deregulation

Cumulated changes in the GDP deflator by sector, from 1990 to 2009, show price decline was greater in IT-related fields where technological progress is thought to be most pronounced (Fig. 5.5).

Furthermore, it may be pointed out that, during 20 years from the 1990s, while CPI (excluding fresh food) on the whole increased moderately, prices of those goods that are in the deregulated sectors, such as communication, or in the area where import liberalization advanced, such as certain agricultural products, significantly decreased (Fig. 5.6).

The foregoing implies that supply-side structural factors played a role in reducing prices of certain categories of goods and services. Did these supply factors cause deflation?

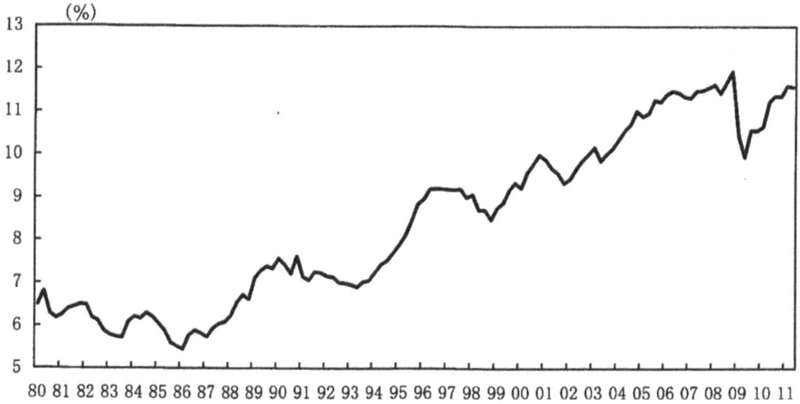

Fig. 5.3 Import penetration. Note: Import penetration rate = import/domestic demand (in real term). Source: Nishizaki et al. (2011)

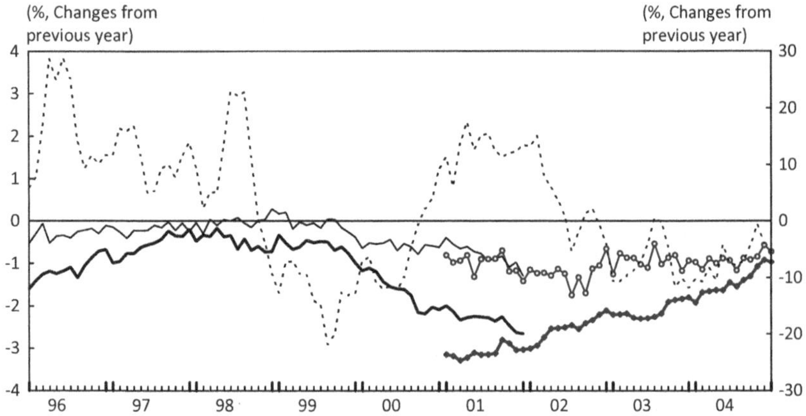

Fig. 5.4 Price developments in imports and import-competing products. Note: —•—Imports and import-competing products (GDP statistics with base year = 2000), —∘— other products (GDP statistics with base year = 2000), —— imports and import-competing products (GDP statistics with base year = 1995), —— other products (GDP statistics with base year = 1995), …… Yen—dollar exchange rate (RHS). Source: Nishizaki et al. (2011)

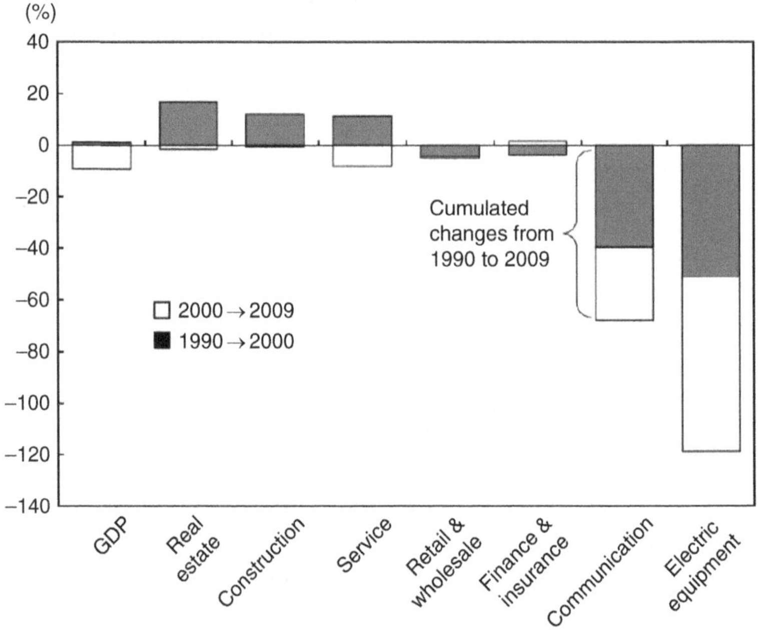

Fig. 5.5 Cumulated changes in GDP deflator from 1990 to 2009 by sector (%). Source: Nishizaki et al. (2011)

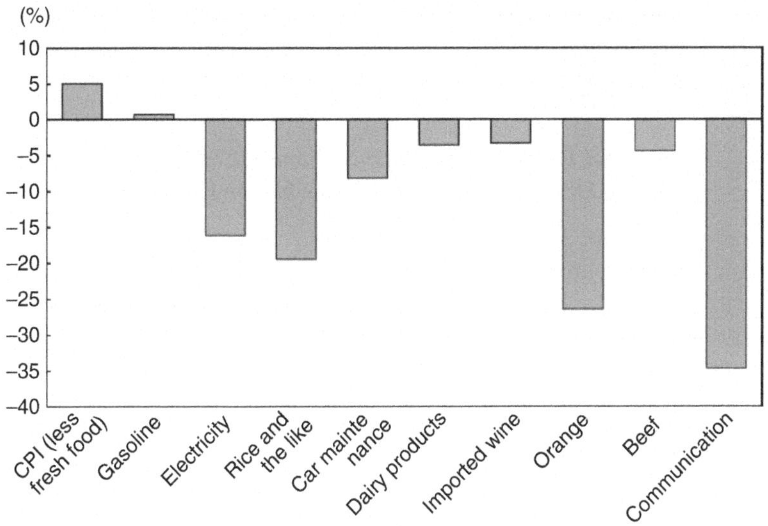

Fig. 5.6 Price changes from 1990 to 2009 of deregulation-related products. Source: Nishizaki et al. (2011)

There is a counterargument. It is theoretically possible for supply-side factors (increase in efficiency or cost reduction due to the availability of low cost inputs, technological progress, or deregulation) to bring about deflation. However, such structural changes are basically favorable to the economy and are expected to produce an expansion of production, which does not seem to be in line with Japan's case where the growth rate continued to decline from the 1990s.[3] So, even if we admitted the price-reducing effects of these (favorable) supply factors, this mechanism would not be

[3] Noguchi (2002) criticized the supply-side structural interpretation of deflation by contending that positive shocks on the supply side, such as technological progress and availability of less expensive materials from abroad, will shift the (upward sloping) short-term aggregate supply curve to the right, bringing about a reduction of price level, and that this shift is expected to produce an expansion of production, which does not seem to be in line with Japan's case in which the growth rate continued to decline from the 1990s. So, under this argument, even if we admit the effects of price decline due to these (favorable) factors on the general price level, it is clear that this mechanism was not dominant in the functioning of the Japanese economy during the stagnant decades. We need to find out what was a dominant

able to sufficiently explain developments in the Japanese economy during the stagnant decades. We need to find a mechanism under which both deflation and stagnation are simultaneously brought about.

Demand Factor Arguments: Is Economic Stagnation Due to Demand Shortage Responsible for Deflation?

As we saw in Chap. 3 (Fig. 3.5), the Japanese economy generally suffered from a negative output gap, that is, demand was in short of production capacity. When supply capacity is greater than demand, there can be two interpretations. One is that demand is in short relative to the sustainable demand level, and the other is that supply capacity is in excess relative to the sustainable demand level. In either case, resultant excess supply could produce downward pressures on price, and therefore, could contribute to deflation. Demand factor arguments for deflation seem to presuppose that demand is in short, that is, demand is lower than a sustainable level, and therefore, demand could (or should) be raised. So, under this argument, factors that have brought about such demand shortage are regarded as the ultimate cause of deflation. In preceding chapters, we have seen that the most depressing factor on the economy during the stagnation was private investment. Consumption has supported growth, while its contribution gradually declined. Government expenditure also has supported the economy until the beginning of the 2000s. Net exports played a relatively small role under the appreciation of the yen. So, demand shortage arguments seem to implicitly or explicitly assume the potential of macroeconomic policies for activating investment activities (and possibly net exports) and, based on that presumption, question the appropriateness of the actual macroeconomic policy management. From this viewpoint, those arguments that blame monetary policy management can be typically classified as demand factor arguments for deflation. We will assess the role of monetary policy in causing demand shortage and deflation in the next section.[4]

mechanism that operated through the Japanese economy, which produced both stagnation and deflation.

[4] There are some arguments that refer to the quantity theory of money in their understanding of deflation. However, the quantity theory of money, which advocates that the quantity of money supplied in the economy determines the general price level, may be relevant in the

Other demand factor arguments blame fiscal policy management. We have already seen, however, that fiscal supports were repeatedly injected into the economy during the stagnation, and as a result, the government debt deteriorated to the world's worst level. As the government cannot continue to support the economy forever, the real cause of stagnation (under this argument, demand shortage) needs to be found elsewhere.[5]

In contrast to the demand shortage argument, the excess supply argument contends that supply capacity was in excess and, therefore, what was needed was not policies to stimulate demand but policies to remove excess capacity. An examination focused on supply capacity (i.e., asset side) will be conducted in Chap. 6.

Financial Sector Problem Arguments: Was the Problem in the Financial Sector to Blame?

It is often argued that the deficiency in the financial sector's intermediation function due to the NPL problem was responsible for the stagnation of private investment and the economy at large. However, the lending attitude of financial institutions was generally not tight, excepting periods immediately after the burst of the bubble and around the financial crisis (see Fig. 3.7 in Chap. 3). The financial sector could not be responsible for the stagnant investment for the major part of the 1990s before the financial crisis.

Some empirical analyses confirm this observation.

Miyao (2004) wrote, "Judging from existing empirical analyses, the time of financial crisis in 1997–78 is the only occasion where credit crunch might have had significant effects on real investment, and therefore, credit crunch cannot be considered as a major cause of long stagnation in the 1990s."[6]

Motonishi and Yoshikawa (1999) also wrote, "an extremely poor performance of corporate investment is the most important factor to explain the long stagnation of the Japanese economy ... the effects of the real factor[7] on investment are much more significant than those of the financial

very long-term or under the extreme circumstances such as hyperinflation, but for other, more realistic cases, the theory does not seem to be of practical use.

[5] The timing of fiscal policy management may be questioned. Yoshikawa (1999) criticized the timing of fiscal consolidation efforts in 1997, on the grounds that they were undertaken, despite economic indicators showing that the economy might have entered a contraction phase by mid-1997, and argued that it is impossible to achieve fiscal consolidation under a recession.

[6] Translated by the author.

[7] Refers to the worsening real profitability, in particular.

factor … during the same period (i.e., 1992–94), the financial factor was supportive. However, beginning 1997 … the credit crunch finally occurred."

So, at least, as far as demand shortage or the stagnation in Period I (1991–1997) is concerned, the financial sector problem does not seem to be a major factor.

As we have seen here, neither the supply factor or financial sector problem arguments for deflation is sufficiently convincing. Therefore, in the next section, we will look at the issues of monetary policy management in the context of the demand factor arguments for deflation, which have been extensively debated for the last two decades.

3 Assessment of Monetary Policy Before Kuroda's QQE: Is Monetary Policy Responsible for Falling into Deflation and Being Unable to Get Out of Deflation?

In this section, we will look at the monetary policy management in the periods before the QQE, which was introduced by Governor Kuroda of BOJ in April 2013 as the first arrow of Abenomics (Abenomics will be examined in Chap. 7), by dividing the whole period into two, namely, the period up to the introduction of zero interest rate policy (1991–1999) (basically the period before the economy fell into deflation and was placed under the zero lower-bound constraint on interest rate) and the period thereafter (the period after the economy had been placed under deflation and the zero lower-bound constraint).

Brief Chronology prior to the Adoption of QQE: What Did the BOJ Do after the Bubble Burst?

How the monetary policy was handled after the burst of the bubble until the implementation of the QQE by Governor Kuroda is briefly shown below:

July 1, 1991–September 8, 1995—BOJ reduced official discount rate nine times (6.0→0.5%)

March 31, 1995–September 9, 1998—BOJ promoted decline in overnight, uncollateralized call rates three times (2.25%→0.25%)

February 12, 1999—BOJ introduced ZIRP (BOJ promoted decline in overnight call rates [0.25→0.15%] and later encouraged a further decline)

August 11, 2000—BOJ lifted ZIRP (BOJ promoted increase in overnight call rates [0→0.25%])
March 19, 2001—BOJ adopted the QEP
March 9, 2006—BOJ lifted the QEP and shifted to ZIRP. At the same time, the BOJ made public the Bank's thinking on price stability (price increase of 0~2% given as within the range of price stability, as indicated by members of the monetary policy meeting)
July 14, 2006—BOJ lifted ZIRP
October 31, 2008—BOJ promoted decline in overnight call rate (0.5→0.3%)
December 19, 2008—BOJ promoted decline in overnight call rate (0.3→0.1%)
February 14, 2012—BOJ introduced a "price stability goal for medium and long term," which was judged to be within the positive range of 2% or lower on a year-on-year basis and set a price stability goal at 1% for the time being
January 22, 2013—BOJ introduced a "price stability target" of 2% in terms of year-on-year change of the CPI (excluding fresh food)
April 4, 2013—BOJ introduced the QQE

How Should We Assess BOJ's Monetary Policy up to and including the Adoption of ZIRP in 1999: Is Monetary Policy Responsible for Stagnation and Falling into Deflation?

As stated before, we divide the whole period before the QQE into two, that is, the period up to the introduction of ZIRP and the period after that, and in this subsection, we assess management of monetary policy in the first period, drawing on the relevant research papers, including the work by Ahearne et al. (2002) and papers by BOJ.

Sufficiency and Swiftness of Monetary Policy Response

Before the adoption of ZIRP, the BOJ reduced the official interest rate nine times and promoted decline in the overnight call rate three times. As a result, both policy rates and long-term interest rates significantly declined, with the short-term interest rate approaching zero (Fig. 5.7). In 1998, then Governor Hayami (BOJ 1998b) stated that most of the available measures to support the economy had been put in place in the area of monetary policy, while

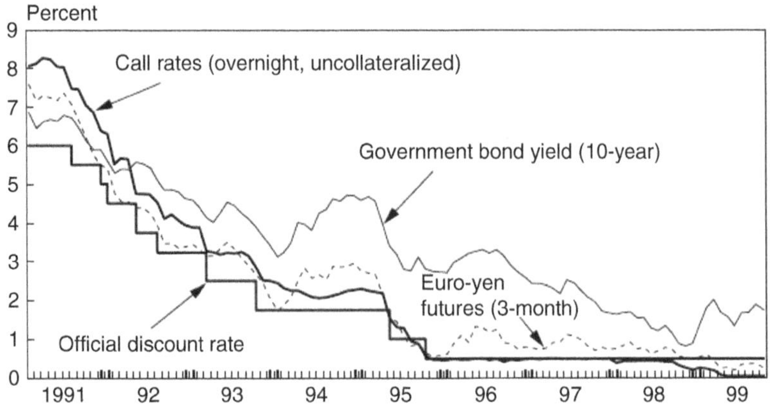

Fig. 5.7 Interest rates. Source: Mori et al. (2001)

stressing the importance of early restoration of financial system soundness and bold structural reforms.[8]

In assessing the monetary policy in the 1990s, with reference to the experience in the United States under the Great Depression, Mori et al. (2001), from the BOJ, wrote, "while Japan was faced with a tremendous decline in asset prices, which came close to that experienced in the US during the Great Depression, the CPI has so far remained stable. In other words, a rapid and self-sustaining price decline known as deflation, as was experienced in the US during the Great Depression … has been successfully avoided" (Figs. 5.8 and 5.9).

By contrast, Ahearne et al. (2002), of the Federal Reserve Board (FRB), presented a different view:

> Japanese monetary policy during 1991–95 appeared appropriate based on the expectations for the economy that prevailed at that time. However, inadequate allowance for downside risk was built into monetary policy, as evidenced by the fact that once actual inflation and growth numbers came in weaker than expected, interest rates ended up being higher than were called for under the Taylor rule. (Ahearne et al. 2002, 20)

[8] Hayami, Yu (1998) "Azia Keizai to Nihon no Yakuwari" (The Asian Economy and the Role of Japan), keynote speech by Governor Hayami of Bank of Japan, October 29. (BOJ Home Page, https://www.boj.or.jp/en/index.htm/).

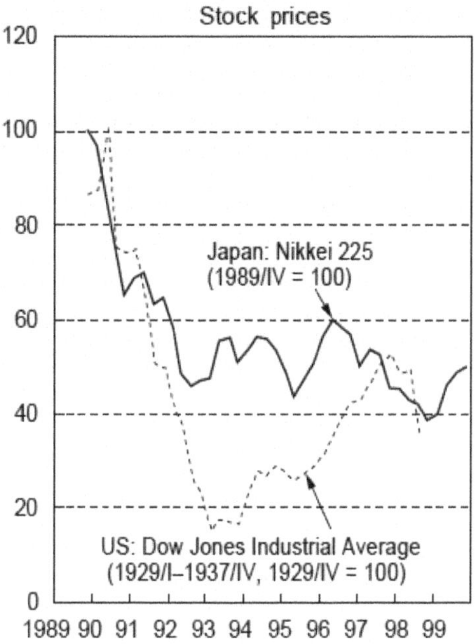

Fig. 5.8 Stock price: Japan in 1990s and US in the Great Depression. Source: Mori et al. (2001)

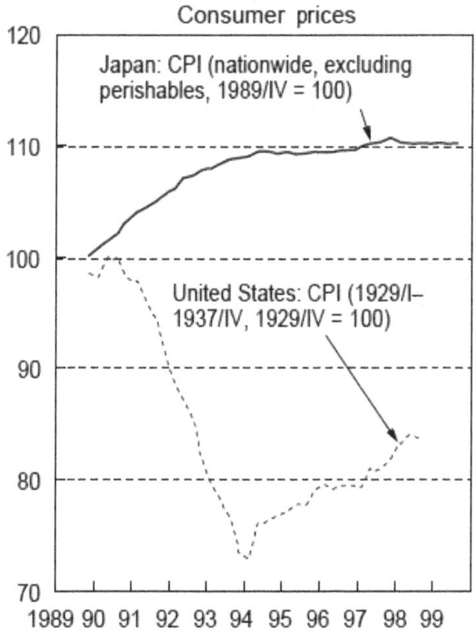

Fig. 5.9 Consumer Price Index: Japan in 1990s and US in the Great Depression. Source: Mori et al. (2001)

> ... had the BOJ loosened monetary policy to the extent modeled in the simulations[9] at any time up until early 1995, inflation could have been kept positive through the end of the decade. (Ahearne et al. 2002, 21)

> Given the inability of conventional monetary policy to stabilize an economy under deflation, ... there is a clear asymmetry of costs to deflation and inflation ... given the very low rate of inflation and negative output gap that existed in 1994–95, some precautionary further lowering of interest rates would have been valuable to reduce the probability of deflation. (Ahearne et al. 2002, 21–22)

> A more expansionary monetary policy in 1994 might have avoided the sharp increase in real long-term interest rates and hefty yen appreciation that occurred that year. (Ahearne et al. 2002, 38)

> Using real-time ... data, ... Japan was "too loose" on average from 1990 through 1994. Using revised data, Japanese policy was "too tight" over the same period (Ahearne et al. 2002, 19).

This argument is presented in Fig. 5.10. The figure gives three rates, the actual policy rate (Call Money Rate), the optimum policy rate calculated based on the Taylor rule, using data that were available when the policy was adopted (Real-time Taylor Rule), and the optimum policy rate calculated based on the Taylor rule using data that became available after the policy had been adopted (Revised Taylor Rule). The actual policy rate as of 1994 was sufficiently eased if assessed using data available at that

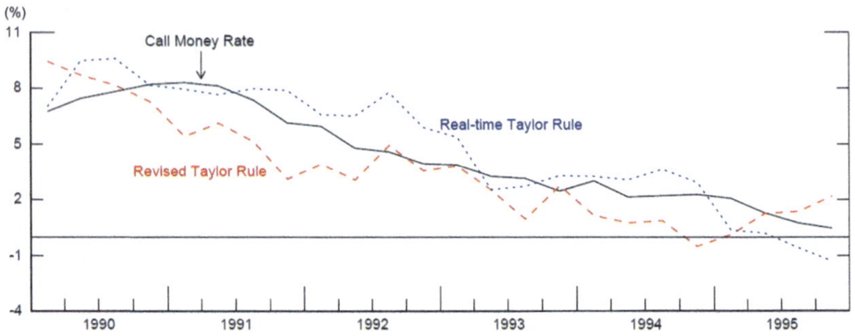

Fig. 5.10 Taylor rule analysis of US and Japanese interest rates. Source: Ahearne et al. (2002)

[9] Simulation using the FRB/Global model.

time, but it was too tight if assessed using data that became available afterward. This is an argument that, as Japan's economy was moving closer to deflation, we should have been prepared for a downside risk.

Jinushi et al. (2000) presented a similar analysis and argued that the actual call rate stayed high, as compared with the optimum call rate calculated using the Taylor rule.

It is true that, after the collapse of the bubble, the BOJ adopted "historically unprecedented accommodative monetary policy" (Mori et al. 2001, 80). However, it was not recognized by the BOJ nor by the government in general that the Japanese economy was faced with an unprecedented economic situation, that is, the formation and collapse of the huge bubble, with its potentially far-reaching and serious negative impacts on the economy, if not managed speedily and properly. Considering this, it can be argued, with some hindsight, that the BOJ should have and could have acted more aggressively with downside risk in mind, as argued in Ahearne et al. (2002). However, a question still remains: had the BOJ acted more aggressively, would the subsequent stagnation have been avoided? Drawing on the discussion in this chapter, the answer seems to be no. What is crucial when examining this point is how we interpret the deflationary gap that the Japanese economy experienced. In other words, the point is whether the Japanese economy was in a demand shortage or whether supply capacity was in excess in light of the sustainable demand level. Those arguments blaming the BOJ, including Ahearne et al. (2002), seem to presume that demand was in short, so monetary policy could have helped raising demand. If supply was in excess, however, what monetary policy could do seems to be more limited than generally assumed. Through lower interest rates and an eased liquidity provision, monetary policy could favorably stimulate lending and investment, support asset prices such as land and stocks, and affect foreign exchange rates. If supply capacity was in excess of sustainable demand, then the most important task should be the removal of such excess. More aggressive monetary easing could have prevented stagnation to some extent in the first half of the 1990s, but it could not have (or rather should not have) raised demand to such an unsustainable level that would make excessive assets profitable.

In this connection, we should rather remind ourselves of the fact that the monetary policy was aggressively tightened from 1989 to 1990, raising the discount rate five times, from 2.5% to 6.0% in little more than a year. Together with the introduction of the aggregate lending limit by the Ministry of Finance (MOF), this aggressiveness seems to have overkilled the economy, as is shown by the nosedive of money stock growth (Fig. 3.6 in Chap. 3). Such a tightening was reversed just one year later in 1991. The discount rate was lowered seven times from 6.0% to 1.75% in just over two years, between July 1991 and September 1993. A mishandling of monetary policy, if there ever was one, seems to be more relevant in the tightening phase (1989–1990), rather than in the easing phase (1991–1993, and 1995).

Whether or not the monetary policy management was appropriate, adjustments in the real sector that we saw in Chap. 4—disposition of excesses, particularly unprofitable supply capacity, and relevant debt in the corporate sector—had to be conducted in any event. So, the major problem was not with the financial sector but with the borrowing companies that had accumulated unprofitable assets. Unless such excesses formed during the bubble were removed, the economy could not have recovered its strength (including, particularly, the positive risk-taking behaviors such as investment). The BOJ could have done more to avoid stagnation, but unless policies targeting more prompt disposition of unprofitable assets and relevant debt in the corporate sector were taken, stagnation was bound to continue.[10] This mechanism is examined in detail in Chap. 6.

[10] Why could the removal of unprofitable assets from the balance sheets of corporate sector not be conducted more speedily? There is an argument that funding from financial institutions had an element of introducing capital rather than pure borrowing. Under this argument, when an investment project financed by financial institutions failed, financial institutions acted as if they were a provider of capital and shared responsibility of failure, through alleviation of repayment conditions and/or providing additional funds. Such behaviors helped delay the necessary adjustments and made it possible for companies to continue to hold the unprofitable project. Probably, the best solution was to remove unprofitable assets together with relevant debt from the rest of the borrower, that is, splitting a borrower into a "good company" and a "bad company," with the latter proceeding to a bankruptcy procedure. See Harashima (2005) for an interpretation of bank loans as provision of capital.

Interpretation of Price Stability: How Should We Assess the BOJ's Interpretation of "Price Stability," Prescribed in the BOJ Law as the Goal of Monetary Policy?

The second point made by Ahearne et al. (2002) in assessing BOJ's policy was its interpretation of price stability. Then Governor Hayami (BOJ 1998a) stated that "price stability" refers to "the absence of inflation or deflation."[11] However, Ahearne et al. (2002) pointed out "zero inflation on average over time will likely imply shorter periods of deflation as well as inflation. In the event, these risks [of deflation and the associated possibility that interest rates would hit their zero lower bound] became reality and the ability of conventional monetary policy to pull the economy out of recession was substantially undermined" (Ahearne et al. 2002, 15–16).

Here, again, it is pointed out that risk of deflation was not properly recognized at that time. This lack of sufficient risk awareness may have been common not only to the BOJ but also to other authorities, media, and the general public.[12]

[11] Manuscript of the press conference by Governor Hayami on July 21, 1998 (BOJ 1998a). The same statements were found in the manuscript of the press conference by Governor Hayami on August 13, 1998. Such statements are also found in press releases by the Monetary Policy Committee. For example, see Bank of Japan (1998c) "Kinnyu Shijo Chosetsu Hosin no Henko ni tuite" (On the Changes of Monetary Adjustment Policies, September 9, 1998).

[12] Around the beginning of the 2000s, an argument that distinguishes between "good deflation" and "bad deflation" attracted some attention. Under this argument, deflation caused by such factors as technological progress or structural reform is said to be beneficial to the economy. Then BOJ Governor Hayami contended in a press conference on March 10, 2000, that price declines arising from reductions in production and distribution costs due to technological progress and a distribution revolution were beneficial to consumers. This contention can be classified as a "good deflation" argument. The Annual Economic and Fiscal Report FY 2001, pp. 43–49, of the Cabinet Office argued that the good deflation arguments have problems: First, the arguments do not properly distinguish between changes of prices of specific items (relative price change) and deflation (decline in general price level). Second, decline in general price level does do harm to the economy. Under deflation, the burden of debt in real terms increases, depressing investment. If the nominal interest rates or nominal wages do not fall to the same extent as the general price level falls, the real interest rates or the real wages rise, depressing investment and employment. Deflation may be beneficial to the lenders for whom the real value of interest and principal repayments increase and those employees whose employment and wages are protected; it is disadvantageous to borrowers

Communication: How Should We Assess BOJ's Communication Technique, Especially in Relation to the BOJ's Discomfort with the Short-Term Interest Rate Close to Zero and Its Inclination for Structural Reforms?
The third point made by Ahearne et al. (2002) relates to the BOJ's communication.

Then Governor Hayami stated, shortly after the introduction of ZIRP, that in the area of monetary policy, the BOJ had been doing everything possible, and progress in structural reform was important,[13] showing his inclination toward structural reform, and thereafter gradually started to emphasize by-products of ZIRP, including reduction of interest income of households.[14] After entering 2000, Governor Hayami called the zero interest rate abnormal,[15] or an emergency measure to deal with an emergency situation, and started to mention that it should be normalized as soon as possible.[16] This line of comments were continued to be made by the Governor until ZIRP was lifted in August 2000.

and new entrants to labor markets who may be squeezed out. In total, deflation discourages investment and is detrimental to employment, bringing about significant damage to the economy. Some media favored the "good deflation" argument. For example, Mainichi Newspaper on March 17, 2001, in an article entitled "Deflation, Do Not Stop Prices from Falling," argued that price drops in recent years were due to import penetration or deregulation, and therefore desirable. The article criticized the government's interpretation of the price developments at that time as deflation, as stated in the government monthly economic report on March 16, 2001. The government report wrote that, if deflation is defined to mean continuous decline in prices, then the Japanese economy is under a mild deflation.

[13] The manuscript of the press conference by the Governor on May 20, 1999 (BOJ 1999a). Governor Hayami also stated in another press conference that the BOJ had been providing sufficient funds to the financial markets under the zero interest policy, and even if additional finance was provided, further monetary easing effects would not be expected. See the manuscript of the press conference, September 21, 1999 (BOJ 1999c).

[14] In a press conference on August 17, 1999, Governor Hayami stated that there were four by-products in relation to the zero interest policy: a distributional problem of reducing interest income of the household, a concern that structural reforms may be delayed, moral hazard of the market participants, and decline in market function. See manuscript of press conference by Governor Hayami on August 17, 1999 (BOJ 1999b). For similar comments, see manuscripts of press conference by the Governor on February 15, 2000 (BOJ 2000a).

[15] Manuscript of press conference by the Governor on March 10, 2000 (BOJ 2000b).

[16] Manuscript of a press conference on April 12, 2000 (BOJ 2000c). In a press conference on June 14, 2000, Governor Hayami said "(it) is an emergency measure adopted under an emergency situation. Interest rate is something that goes up and down under the demand/supply conditions like price; clearly, zero interest rate should not be continued limitlessly. We

Deputy BOJ Governor Yamaguchi (1999) stated that "monetary policy cannot replace the necessary structural policies or adjustments. The decisive monetary easing and active interventions to support the financial system by the Bank of Japan no doubt averted deflation or financial panic in Japan. On the other hand, those policy decisions might have dampened the restructuring efforts at Japanese financial institutions."

However, in this regard, Ahearne et al. (2002, 15) pointed out "Investors' sense that policymakers were eager to move rates off their zero floor no doubt kept longer-term interest rates elevated."

In this respect, probably, the problem was not with the communication itself but with the policy thinking. The BOJ was conducting monetary policy with a significant focus on nominal interest rate. Without keen awareness of the cost of deflation, the BOJ seems to have thought monetary policy tools had been thoroughly exhausted (and should be recovered as soon as possible), and there was not much for the BOJ to do to stimulate the economy.[17]

How Should We Assess Monetary Policy after the Japanese Economy Had Fallen into Deflation? (Assessment of Monetary Policy After ZIRP)

As we have seen, from around 1998, the Japanese economy fell into chronic but mild deflation, and the interest rate dropped to zero in the following year. A question for this subsection is what monetary policy can do when deflation has set in under a situation in which the nominal interest is zero (monetary policy options under the zero interest rate).

have always a desire to recover space of maneuvering of monetary policy. See manuscript of press conference by the Governor on June 14, 2000 (BOJ 2000d). In a press conference on July 19, 2000, Governor Hayami stated that as the interest rates adjust monetary conditions, the situation where interest rate is zero is a very distorted situation, while it may not be appropriate to refer to the degree of freedom of monetary policy. See manuscript of press conference by Governor, July 19, 2000 (BOJ 2000e).

[17] The thought that monetary policy tools had been exhausted was later denied by the policy actions of the BOJ itself, which included quantitative easing and its move to inflation targeting. However, whether these policy actions contributed to the removal of the fundamental cause of the long economic stagnation is a different matter.

Conventional Transmission Mechanism of Monetary Policy

In the case of monetary easing by the BOJ, traditionally, effects are expected to work in the following manner (effects flow from ① to ⑥).

① Purchase by the BOJ of bonds and bills in the market.
② Increase in the BOJ current account balances (i.e., part of base money) held by commercial banks
③ Decrease in the interest rates in the interbank market
④ Decrease in the other short-term market rates and the medium- and long-term interest rates (including securities yields)
⑤ Decrease in the bank lending rates
⑥ Increase in investment and consumption by enterprises and households

Proposed Options under the Zero Interest Rate

Once the short-term interest rates reach zero, this conventional channel ceases to operate: Then, what policy options do we have? There have been a lot of debates on the issue, and the proposed options include the following (not mutually exclusive):[18]

Type A: Measures to Reduce Long-Term (Nominal) Interest Rate

(a) Purchase of long-term government bonds
   - This affects demand and supply conditions in the market, raising the price and reducing the yields (interest rates) to these bonds.

(b) Commitment to maintain current accommodating policy for the future ("policy duration effect")
   - Long-term interest rates depend on the expected course of the short-term interest rate in the future, and therefore, the expected duration of the accommodating policy in the future affects the long-term interest rate.

(c) Purchase of other more risky assets

[18] The classification in the text basically followed Tanaka Takayuki, "Zero Kinri Seiyakuka niokeru Rifureshon Seisaku Rongi-Nichign ha Nani wo Okonai Nani wo Okonawa Nakattaka-"(Reflation Policy Debate under the Zero Lower Bound Constraint on Interest Rate—What Did the BOJ Do and Not Do?), downloaded on January 19, 2015, http://ir.acc.senshu-u.ac.jp/index.php?active_action=repository_view_main_item_detail&page_id=13&block_id=52&item_id=1426&it em_no=1

- The long-term interest rate consists of the expected short-term interest rate and the risk premium, and purchase of risky assets can lower the risk premium and the long-term interest rate.

(d) Provision of abundant base money (portfolio rebalancing effects)
- Purchase of assets by the central bank from the market with the consideration deposited in its current account held by private banks (i.e., base money increase) causes portfolio rebalancing in the private sector (the added base money will be disposed of through acquisition of other assets including stocks, real estates, and credit, thereby promoting investment).

Type B: Measures to Raise the Expected Rate of Inflation to Reduce the Real Interest Rate

(e) Inflation targeting (Krugman 1998)
Commitment by the central bank to achieve a positive rate of inflation helps raise the expected rate of inflation, reducing the real interest rate.

(f) Price level targeting (Swenson 2003)
If the target level of prices is missed, the required rate of inflation to achieve the target within a specified time frame becomes greater.

(g) Purchase of government bonds coupled with fiscal stimulus (helicopter money)
This action can create demand, but amounts to fiscal policy with monetization.

Type C: Measures for Other Purposes

(h) Currency depreciation by intervention in the foreign exchange market (Bernanke 2000)
- This action promotes exports.

BOJ Economists' Views
BOJ's economists were very skeptical of these unconventional policies at that time:

> Aggressive operations[19] should be regarded as a high-risk, high return policy option.
>
> An important question here is what would happen to the term premiums requested for long-term interest rates.
>
> A term premium might reflect both risk premium on uncertainty about future inflation and credit risk regarding government bonds.
>
> It is probable that a massive increase in the outright purchase of government bonds is seen by the public as a loss of fiscal discipline … it would likely result in the further downgrading of Japanese Government Bonds (JGBs), thus leading to the situation where government bond price formation is to a large extent determined from the viewpoint of credit risk.
>
> In addition, if uncertainty about the outlook for inflation increases due to the decisive outright purchase of government bonds, inflation risk premium also rises.
>
> The … risk is that the BOJ might incur a substantial capital loss, resulting in a serious burden on the government's budget in the future. (Fujiki et al. 2001, 111–12)

Okina and Oda (2000) also argued that the introduction of inflation targeting might hinder the flexibility of monetary policy operation.

Adoption of QEP by the Bank of Japan

In spite of these cautious views, the BOJ restarted reducing the policy interest rate on February 28, 2001, after a brief lifting of ZIRP from August 11, 2000, and further adopted QEP on March 19, 2001.

QEP had three distinctive characteristics:

(a) The policy target was changed from the overnight call rate to the amount of deposits held by private banks with the BOJ's current account (a component of the base money).[20]
(b) It was committed that this policy would be maintained until the change in CPI from the previous year stably recorded 0% or over.
(c) An increase in the amount of outright purchase of long-term government bonds was clearly indicated.

QEP lasted nearly five years before it was lifted on March 3, 2006. Meantime, the BOJ increased the targeted balance in BOJ's current

[19] The aggressive outright purchase of long-term government bonds.

[20] The base money is composed of deposits with the BOJ and cash (notes and coins in circulation). As of February 2001, the amount of base money was 68.4 trillion yen, with notes amounting to 56.4 trillion yen (87%), coins 4.2 trillion yen (6.4%), and deposits with the BOJ 4.2 trillion yen (6.5%).

account nine times (4 trillion yen →30~35 trillion yen), and also increased the amount of long-term JGB purchase four times (400 billion yen →1.2 trillion yen per month).

Although this policy is a novel step forward, some cautious comments are presented on the BOJ's QEP as follows (Adachi 2013):

Considering the upward bias of the CPI (as the weight is fixed, based on the share of the adopted items in consumption in the base year), a 0% increase is not sufficient for overcoming deflation.

The time schedule for overcoming deflation is not clear.

Furthermore, as implied by the subsequent emphasis on "policy duration effects" by BOJ executives, the BOJ apparently expected the commitment of the policy for the future to have an effect of flattening the yield curve and lowering the long-term interest rate. Under the classification mentioned previously, the BOJ was still working within the interest rate transmission channel categorized as Type A (i.e., nominal interest rate reduction).

How to Assess the Effects of the Bank of Japan's QEP?

Ugai (2007), who extensively surveyed empirical analyses of the effects of BOJ's QEP, concluded as follows:

> The survey confirm[ed] a clear effect whereby the commitment to maintain the QEP fostered the expectations that the zero interest rate would continue into the future, thereby lowering the yield curve centering on the short- to medium-term range. .... Portfolio rebalancing ... effect, if any, was smaller than that stemming from the commitment.
>
> The QEP contained financial institutions' funding costs and staved off financial institutions' funding uncertainties .... The QEP's effect on raising aggregate demand and prices was often limited, due largely to the then progressing corporate balance-sheet adjustment, as well as the zero lower bound constraint on interest rates. (Ugai 2007, 1)

Shirakawa (2002), who reviewed one year experience under Quantitative Easing (QE), stated that increase in reserve money did not give clear effects on prices of financial assets (long-term government bonds, stocks, and foreign exchange), and that it did not cause increase in money supply or in total assets of deposit-taking financial institutions.

As Ugai (2007) pointed out, while QEP might have contained funding uncertainty of the financial institutions, its effects on real economy (aggregate demand and supply conditions) and also price level seem to have been very much limited.

Now, let us look at some relevant data. Figure 5.11 shows developments in the rate of change in M2 and CPI (excluding fresh food) from the previous year. It appears that the rate of change in both CPI (excluding fresh food) and M2 declined after entering the 1990s, implying that movements in money stock and CPI may be related to each other.

However, Fig. 5.12 shows that the rate of change in base money, on which the BOJ has a substantial degree of influence, does not seem to be related to the rate of change in M2, casting doubts on the effectiveness of quantitative easing.

Loans by Banks Did Not Respond

Loans held by banks hit a peak of 493.0 trillion yen in December 1997, and then decreased to a bottom of 395.9 trillion yen in June 2005. After that, loans started to slowly recover, but the outstanding amount as of December 2012, that is, before the start of Abenomics, was 433.8 trillion yen, lower than the level in December 1997. Meanwhile, JGB holdings by banks increased by 5 times, from 31.1 trillion yen in December 1997 to 161.2 trillion yen in December 2012. Under QEP, the decline in the outstanding balance of loans ended, but the pace of increase in loan balance was rather slow (Fig. 5.13). We will look at developments after Abenomics started in Chap. 7.

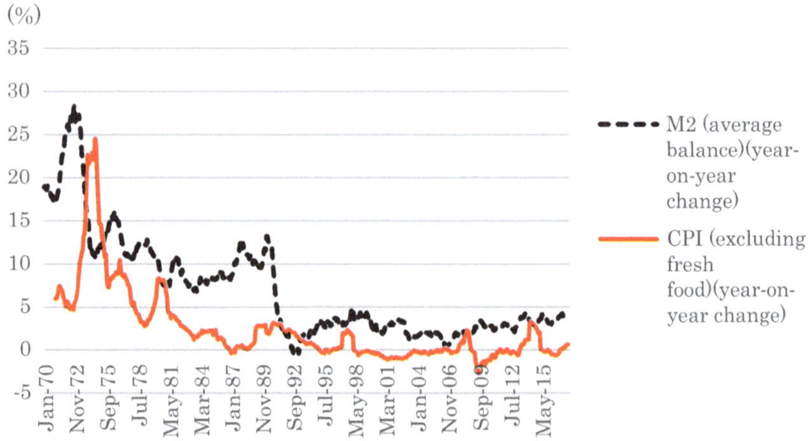

Fig. 5.11 M2 and Consumer Price Index (excluding fresh food) (year-on-year change). Source: Bank of Japan, Statistics Bureau, Ministry of Internal Affairs and Communications

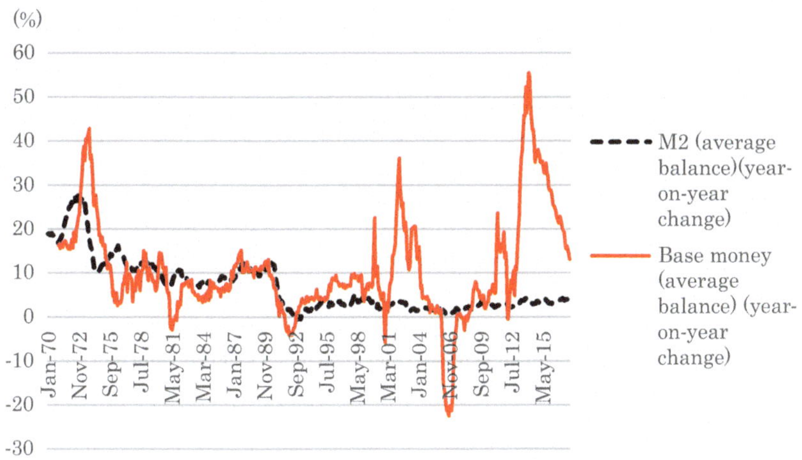

Fig. 5.12 Base money and M2 (year-on-year change). Source: Bank of Japan

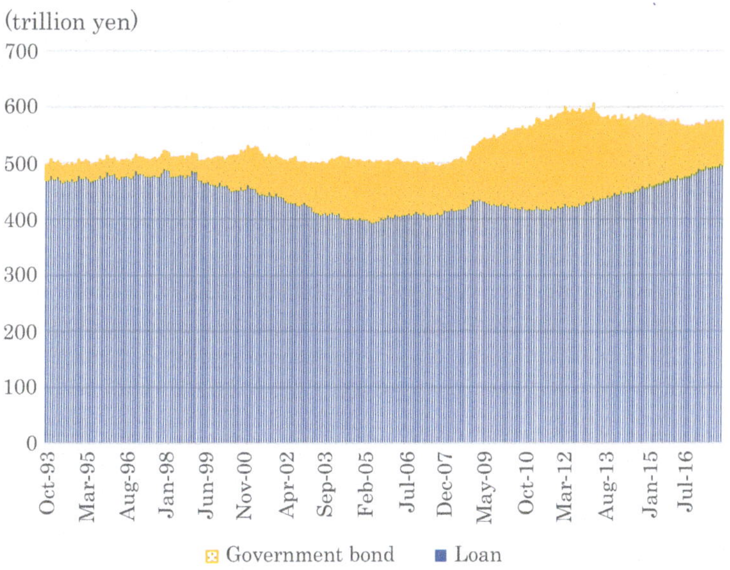

Fig. 5.13 Loans and government bonds held by domestic banks. Source: Bank of Japan

4 Summary of the Examination in This Chapter

Let us summarize what we learned on the issue of deflation and monetary policy, drawing on the analysis in this chapter.

As for the cause of deflation, there might have been some supply-side factors at work, such as penetration of low-priced goods from emerging economies, technological progress, and deregulation, but these supply-side factors[21] by themselves cannot explain why the Japanese economy experienced both deflation and economic stagnation. These supply-side factors may make production more efficient and bring about benefits to the economy. However, this is different from what actually happened. We need to explain the situation in which both economic stagnation and deflation emerge simultaneously.

Another argument on the cause of deflation contends that problems with the financial sector gave birth to a credit crunch and depressed investment. This may fall under the category of (broadly-defined) demand-side factor arguments. However, the lending attitude of the financial institutions was an eased one for the major part of the 1990s. This implies that investment stagnation was not due to shortage of supply of funds but due to shortage of investment demand; and the interpretation that financial sector problems caused demand shortage and deflation is not convincing.[22]

Another argument on the cause of deflation is related to demand-side factors. As we saw in Chap. 3, the most depressing effect on growth after the burst of the bubble came from stagnation of private investment. Although there are arguments that criticize the volume and the timing of demand injection through fiscal policy that was conducted on a very large scale over the first 10 years of stagnation, more extensive debates were made on the appropriateness of monetary policy. The analysis in this chapter made clear that there might have been some problems in monetary policy in relation to sufficiency and swiftness of the easing, its interpretation of price stability, and communication. So, if managed differently, it is possible that monetary policy could have given greater support to the economy.

[21] These factors must have been at work, albeit to a different degree, in other advanced economies.

[22] The situation changed with the outbreak of the financial crisis in the late 1990s, and the lending attitude of the financial institutions was suddenly tightened. This fact implies that we need to look at effects of the financial crisis on the behaviors of financial institutions and companies.

However, it is not clear whether we could have avoided the long stagnation, if the monetary policy had been more aggressive and speedy. This depends on whether we find the origin of the problem in the 1990s in demand shortage or in excess supply. The argument of this book is that the root cause of the investment (and economic) stagnation was in excess (non-profitable) assets in the corporate sector. Under this view, what was fundamentally needed was not to raise demand but remove these excesses. To this end, monetary easing could be of no more help than buying time.

It seems that mishandling of monetary policy was more significant in 1989–1990, when extremely aggressive monetary tightening was conducted, together with the introduction of an aggregate limit on real estate-related lending by the MOF, crushing the bubble and overkilling the economy. Those unprofitable investments in facilities and real estate-related projects, undertaken by companies and local authorities partly under the promotion by central government, which could not expect sufficient demand, were destined to fail. So, intentional crushing of the bubble was not necessary. Preventing the bubble from developing further was what was essentially needed. It may have been beyond the ability of human beings to contain (not crush) the bubble while keeping the economy on a stable growth path. It is regrettable that policies not from an economic efficiency or risk-control viewpoint but from an egalitarian viewpoint were adopted to cope with the bubble, with little concern or awareness of dangers of these policies to the economy.

After Period I passed, the Japanese economy experienced the financial crisis. Simultaneously, the economy fell into deflation. ZIRP and QEP by the BOJ could not bring the economy out of deflation. At this stage, on top of the overhang of excess assets, which was the origin of the problem, the economy may have become trapped in a vicious circle caused by deflation.

If deflation continues, deflation may be incorporated in expectations of enterprises. If a decline in nominal sales amount (nominal revenue) is expected, the real burden of expenses with fixed nominal value, such as wages, interest payments, and principal repayments, becomes heavier. Then, new investment or employment may be contained, resulting in a reduced investment and consumption demand. This may lead to a further decline in sales, and the whole process enters into a declining cycle, making deflation a chronic phenomenon. This process possibly acted as an extra depressing factor on the Japanese economy, in addition to the fundamental burden of excess assets and liabilities that the corporate sector continued to bear.

Bibliography

English References

Ahearne, Alan, J. Gagnon, J. Haltmaier, and S. Kamin (2002) Preventing Deflation: Lessons from Japan's Experience in the 1990s," Board of Governors of the Federal Reserve System, International Finance Discussion Paper Number 729.

Bank of Japan (1998) "Change of the Guideline for Money Market Operations" September 9.

Bernanke, Ben (2000) "Japanese monetary policy: A case of self-induced paralysis?" In *Japan's Financial Crisis and Its Parallels to U.S. Experience*, edited by Mikitani, Ryoichi and Adam S. Posen, 149–166. Washington, DC: Institute for International Economics.

Fujiki, Hiroshi, Kunio Okina, and Shigenori Shiratsuka (2001) "Monetary Policy under Zero Interest Rate: Viewpoints of Central Bank Economists." *Monetary and Economic Studies*/February 2001.

Jinushi, Toshiki, Yoshihiro Kuroki, and Ryuzo Miyao (2000) "Monetary policy in Japan since the late 1980s: Delayed policy actions and some explanations." In *Japan's Financial Crisis and Its Parallels to U.S. Experience*, edited by Mikitani, Ryoichi, and Adam S. Posen, 115–48. Washington, DC: Institute for International Economics.

Katz, Richard (1998) *Japan: The System that Soured: The Rise and Fall of the Japanese Economic Miracle*. Armonk, NY: M.E. Sharpe.

Krugman, Paul (1998) "It's Baaack: Japan's Slump and the Return of the Liquidity Trap." *Brookings Papers on Economic Activity* 2: 137–205.

Krugman, Paul (2000) "Thinking about the liquidity trap" *Journal of the Japanese and International Economies* 14 (4): 221–37.

Mori, Naruki, Shigenori Shiratsuka and Hiroo Taguchi (2001) "Policy Responses to the Post-bubble Adjustments in Japan: A Tentative Review." *Monetary and Economic Studies* 19 (S1): 53–112. (Institute for Monetary and Economic Studies, Bank of Japan, February).

Motonishi, Taizo, and Hiroshi Yoshikawa (1999) "Causes of the Long Stagnation of Japan During the 1990s: Financial or Real?" NBER Working Paper No. 7351, National Bureau of Economic Research, Cambridge, MA.

Nishizaki, Kenji, Toshitake Sekine, and Yuichi Ueno (2012) "Chronic deflation in Japan." *Bank of Japan Working Paper Series*, No.12-E-6, Bank of Japan.

Okina, Kunio, and Nobuyuki Oda (2000) "Additional Monetary Easing Options under the Non-negative Constraint of Interest Rate: Issues Drawing on Japan's Experience." *Kinnyu Kenkyu* 2000.12, Institute for Monetary and Economic Studies, Bank of Japan.

Shirakawa, Masaaki (2010) "Japan's economy and monetary policy." January 29, Bank of Japan.

Shirakawa, Masaaki (2012) "Japan's economy and monetary policy." June 4, Bank of Japan.

Swenson, Lars E. (2003) "Escaping from a Liquidity Trap and Deflation: Foolproof Way and Others." NBER Working Paper No. 10195, National Bureau of Economic Research, Cambridge, MA.

Ugai, Hiroshi (2007) "Effects of the Quantitative Easing Policy: A Survey of Empirical Analysis" *Monetary and Economic Studies/* March 2007, BOJ.

Yamaguchi, Yutaka (1999) "Monetary Policy and Structural Policy: A Japanese Perspective." Remarks by Yutaka Yamaguchi, Deputy Governor of the Bank of Japan, before Colloque Montaire International at Banque de France, October 8–9.

Japanese References

Adachi, Seiji (2013) "Kinnyu seisaku kettei purosesu to kinnyu seisaku ronso no keifu" (Process of monetary policy determination and developments in monetary policy debates). In *Mazu defure wo tomeyo* (Stop Deflation, First), edited by Kikuo Iwata. Nihon Keizai Shimbun Sha.

Bank of Japan (1990) *Chosa Geppo* (Monthly Research Report) April 1990.

Bank of Japan (1998a) Hayami Sosai Kisha Kaiken Yoshi (Manuscript of press conference by governor Hayami), July 21, 1998.

Bank of Japan (1998b) Hayami Sosai Kisha Kaiken Yoshi (Manuscript of press conference by governor Hayami), August 13, 1998.

Bank of Japan (1999a) Hayami Sosai Kisha Kaiken Yoshi (Manuscript of press conference by governor Hayami), May 20, 1999.

Bank of Japan (1999b) Hayami Sosai Kisha Kaiken Yoshi (Manuscript of press conference by governor Hayami), August 17, 1999.

Bank of Japan (1999c) Hayami Sosai Kisha Kaiken Yoshi (Manuscript of press conference by governor Hayami), September 21, 1999.

Bank of Japan (2000a) Hayami Sosai Kisha Kaiken Yoshi (Manuscript of press conference by governor Hayami), February 15, 2000.

Bank of Japan (2000b) Hayami Sosai Kisha Kaiken Yoshi (Manuscript of press conference by governor Hayami), March 10, 2000.

Bank of Japan (2000c) Hayami Sosai Kisha Kaiken Yoshi (Manuscript of press conference by governor Hayami), April 12, 2000.

Bank of Japan (2000d) Hayami Sosai Kisha Kaiken Yoshi (Manuscript of press conference by governor Hayami), June 14, 2000.

Bank of Japan (2000e) Hayami Sosai Kisha Kaiken Yoshi (Manuscript of press conference by governor Hayami), July 19, 2000.

Bank of Japan (2000f) "Wagakuni no Bukka Doko—90 nendai no Keiken wo Chushin ni" (Developments in Prices in Japan—Centering on the Experience in the 1990s), October, Department of Research and Statistics.

Cabinet Office (2001) *Heisei 13 nendo Nenji Keizai Zaisei Hokoku—Kaikaku Nakushite Seicho Nashi* (Heisei 13 Annual Report on the Japanese Economy and Public Finance—No Gains without Reforms), December.

Dai-Ichi Seimei Keizai Kenkyu Jo (2003) *Shisan Defure de Yomitoku Nihon Keizai* (Understanding Japanese Economy through Asset Price Deflation). Nihon Keizai Shimbun Sha.

Harashima, Motomu (2005) *Nihon Keizai Shippai Gaku* (Failure Theory of the Japanese Economy), V2 Solution.

Hattori, Shigeyuki (2008) *Kinnyu Seisaku no Gosan* (Miscalculations of Monetary Policy) 2008, NTT Shuppan.

Hayami, Masaru (1998) "Azia Keizai to Nihon no Yakuwari" (The Asian Economy and Japan's Role"), Keynote speech at 24th business conference for Japan and ASEAN countries, Bank of Japan, October 29.

Iwata, Kazumasa (2010) *Defure tono Tatakai* (Battle against Deflation). Nihon Keizai Shimbun Sha.

Iwata, Kikuo (1992) Nichigin Riron wo Hoki seyo (Give up the BOJ Theory). *Shukan Toyo Keizai*, September 12.

Iwata, Kikuo (1993) *Kinnyu Seisaku no Keizai Gaku – 'Nichigin Riron' no Kensho* (Economics of Monetary Policy – Examination of the "BOJ Theory"). Nihon Keizai Shimbun Sha.

Iwata, Kikuo, ed. (2000) *Kinnyu Seisaku no Ronten* (Issues on Monetary Policy). Toyo Keizai Shinpo Sha.

Iwata, Kikuo (2001) *Defure no Keizaigaku* (Economics of Deflation). Tokyo: Toyo Keizai Shimpo Sha.

Iwata, Kikuo (2009) *Nihon Ginko ha Shinnyo Dekiruka* (Is the Bank of Japan Trustworthy?). Kodansha Gendai Shinsho.

Iwata, Kikuo (2011) *Defure to Cho Endaka* (Deflation and Super High Yen). Kodansha Shinsho.

Iwata, Kikuo, ed. (2013) *Mazu defure wo tomeyo* (Stop Deflation, First). Nihon Keizai Shimbun Sha.

Iwata, Kikuo (2013) *Refure ha Tadasii* (Reflation is Right). PHP Kenkyu Jo.

Karube, Kensuke (2004) Dokyumento Zero Kinri – Nichigin vs Seifu Naze Tairitsu Surunoka (Documentary Zero Interest Rate – BOJ vs Government Why Do They Come into Collision?)

Kataoka, Goshi (2010) Nihon no 'Ushinawareta 20 nen' – Defure wo Koeru Keizai Seisaku ni Mukete (Japan's "Lost Two Decades" – For the Economic Policy Beyond Deflation). Fujiwara Shoten.

Kimura, Takeshi, Tsuyoshi Shimatani, Ken-ichi Sakura, and Hiroaki Nishida (2001) "Mane to Seicho Kitai : Bukka Hendo no Mekanizumu wo Megutte" (Money and Growth Expectation: On the Mechanism of Price Movements), August. Institute for Monetary and Economic Studies, BOJ *Kinnyu Kenkyu*.

Komiya, Ryutaro, ed. (2002) *Kinnyu Seisaku no Soten – Nichign Hihan to Sono Hanron* (Issues in Monetary Policy Debates—Criticism on BOJ and Counterarguments). Nihon Keizai Shimpo Sha.

Miyao, Ryuzo (2004) "Ginko Kino no Teika to 90 nendai Iko no Defure Teitai–'Kashi Shiiburi' Setsu to 'Oigashi' Setsu no Kento" (Deterioration of Banks' Function and Deflationary Stagnation since the 1990s–'Credit crunch' theory and 'Rescue loans' theory). In *Ronso Nihon no Keizai Kiki*, edited by Koichi Hamada and Akiyoshi Horiuchi, (Debate on Japan's Economic Crisis), Nihon keizai Shimbun Sha.

Nishizaki, Kenji, Yoichi Ueno, and Tanaka Masahiro (2011) "Nihon no Bukka Hendo no Haikei: Jijitu to Ronten Seiri" (Background of Price Developments in Japan: Facts and Issues) December, Bank of Japan, Working Paper Series No. 11-I-9.

Noguchi, Asahi (2002) "*Keizaigaku wo Shiranai Ekonomisuto Tachi*" (Those Economists Who Do Not Know Economics), Nihon Hyoron Sha.

Noguchi, Asahi (2006) "Ekonomisuto Tachi no Yuganda Suishodama" (Distorted Crystal Balls of Economists). Toyo Keizai Shimpo Sha.

Noguchi, Asahi (2013) "Kozo Mondai to Defureshon" (Structural Problems and Deflation). In *Mazu defure wo tomeyo* (Stop Deflation, First) edited by Kikuo Iwata, Nihon Keizai Shimbun Sha.

Noguchi, Yukio (2010) *Nihon wo Hametsu kara Sukuu Tameno Keizaigaku* (Economics to Save Japan from Catastrophe). Diamond Sha.

Okamoto, Naoki (2001) "Defure ni Chokumen suru Wagauni Keizai – Defure no Teigi no Saiseiri wo Fukumete" (Japanese Economy Facing Deflation – Including Redefining Deflation), Cabinet Office, Business Condition Judgement and Policy Analysis Discussion Paper DP/01-1.

Okina, Kunio (1992) "Nichigin Riron ha Machigatte inai" (BOJ Theory Is Not Wrong). In *Shukan Toyo Keizai*, October 10.

Otani, Satoshi, Shigenori Shiratsuka, and Masayuki Nakakuki (2004) "Seisan Yoso Shijo no Yugami to Kokunai Keizai Chosei" (Distortions in Production Factor Markets and Domestic Economic Adjustments), *IMES Discussion Paper* No. 20040J-1.

Shinpo, Seiji (2002) "Defure wo Motarashita noha Kozo Yoin ka Kinnyu Seisaku ka" (Is It a Structural Factor or Monetary Policy That Has Brought about Deflation?). In *Kinnyu seisaku ronso no soten–nichigin hihan to sono hanron* (Issues in Monetary Policy Debates – Criticism of the Bank of Japan and Counterarguments) edited by Ryutaro Komiya). Nihon Keizai Shimbun Sha.

Shirakawa, Masaaki (2002) "Ryoteki Kanwa Saiyo go 1 nenkan no Keiken" (One Year of Experience since the Introduction of Quantitative Easing). In *Kinnyu seisaku ronso no soten -nichigin hihan to sono hanron* (Issues in Monetary Policy Debates—Criticism on the BOJ and Counterarguments), edited by Ryutaro Komiya. Nihon Keizai Shimbun Sha.

Shirakawa, Masaaki (2008) "Gendai no Kinnyu Seisaku" (Current Monetary Policy). Nihon Keizai Shimbun Sha.

Shirakawa, Masaaki (2009) "Tokushu Sei ka Ruiji Sei ka? – Kinnyu Seisaku Kenkyu wo Meguru Nihon no Baburu Hokaigo no Keiken" (Uniqueness or Similarity?

Japan's Post-Bubble Experience in Monetary Policy Studies), September 16, 2010, Bank of Japan.

Shirakawa, Masaaki (2011) "Baburu, Jinko Dotai, Shizen Saigai" (Bubbles, Demographic Change, and Natural Disasters) June 1, Bank of Japan.

Shirakawa, Masaaki (2012) "Derebarejji to Keizai Seicho – Senshinkoku ha Kakoni Nihon ga Ayunda 'Nagaku Magari Kunetta Michi' wo Tadotte Ikunoka" (Deleveraging and Growth: Is the Developed World Following Japan's Long and Winding Road? January 10, Bank of Japan.

Takita, Yoichi (2002) *Nihon Keizai Fusakui no Tsumi* (Japanese Economy—A Crime of Omission). Nihon Keizai Shimbun Sha.

Tanaka, Hideomi, and Seiji Adachi (2003) *Heisei Dai Fukyo to Showa Kyoko – Purakutyikaru Keizaigaku Nyumon* (Heisei Great Stagnation and Showa Depression – Introduction to Practical Economics). Nihon Hoso Shuppan Kai.

Tanaka, Takayuki (2008) *Ushinawareta 15 nen to Kinnyu Seisaku – Nichigin ha Naniwo Okonai Naniwo Okonawa nakatta noka* (Lost 15 Years and Monetary Policy – What Did BOJ Do and Not Do?). Nihon Keizai Shimbun Sha.

Tatebe, Masayoshi (2010) "Kinnyu Kikika no Nichigin no Kinnyu Seisaku" (BOJ's Monetary Policy Under the Financial Crisis). Chuo Daigaku Shuppan Bu.

Ueda, Kazuo (2005) *Zero Kinri tono Tatakai* (Battle against Zero Interest Rate). Nihon Keizai Shimbun Sha.

Umeda, Masanobu (2011) *Nichigin no Seisaku Keisei 'Gijiroku' nado ni Miru Seisaku Handan no Doki to Seigosei* (Policy Formation of the BOJ – Motives of Policy Determination and their Coherence in Light of Committee Minutes). Toyo Keizai Shimbun Sha.

Wakatabe, Masazumi (2013) "Keizai Gakusha Tachino Tatakai – Datsu Defure wo Meguru Ronso no Rekishi" (Battle of the Economists – History of Debates over Exit from Deflation). Toyo Keizai Shimpo Sha.

Watanabe, Tsutomu (2009) "Shihan Seiki no Bukka Hendo" (Price Developments over a Quarter of a Century). In *Defure Keizai to Kinnyu Seisaku* (Deflationary Economy and Monetary Policy), edited by Hiroshi Yoshikawa ("Baburu/defure kino Nihon Keizai to Keizai Seisaku 7" (Japanese Economy and Economic Policy in the Period of Bubble and Deflation 7)), Economic and Social Research Institute, Cabinet Office.

Watanabe, Tsutomu (2012) "Zero Kinri kano Choki Defure" (Chronic Deflation under the Zero Interest Rate) *BOJ Working Paper Series* No.12 ~J~3 March.

Watanabe, Tsutomu (2013) "Defure Dakkyaku no Joken" (Conditions for Exit from Deflation) March 26, Canon Institute for Global Studies (viewed on August 17, 2018, http://www.canon-igs.org/research_papers/macroeconomics/20130326_1816.html).

Yoshikawa, Hiroshi (1999) *Tenkanki no Nihon Keizai* (The Japanese Economy at a Turning Point). Iwanami Shoten.

CHAPTER 6

Deflation and the Mechanism of Corporate Behavior

1 Mechanism of the Long Stagnation and Deflation Viewed through Corporate Behavior

In Chap. 5, we examined the causes of deflation mainly from the viewpoints of the appropriateness of the monetary policy. So far, however, we cannot say that we have obtained a convincing explanation of the causes of long stagnation and deflation after the burst of the bubble, including the continuation of the situation after the excesses of the corporate sector had been removed. We have been arguing that the fundamental problem was in the corporate sector. So, in this chapter, we examine company behaviors that lay behind the macroeconomic developments, through the analysis of financial statements of companies. As we have seen, during the long stagnation, particularly after the financial crisis, fundamental changes took place in the Japanese economy—a sharp increase in unemployment rate, a rapid decline in regular employment and a shift to non-regular work, a fall in nominal wage, a switch of the corporate sector from excess investment to an excess savings position, and a mild but chronic fall in the Consumer Price Index (CPI) (deflation). Almost all these changes (employment, wages, pricing, and investment) are related to company behaviors. So, in order to understand the mechanism of these phenomena, or the cause of the stagnation and deflation, we need to see what happened to companies.

Much of the following analysis is based on "the financial statement statistics of corporations by industry" (Ministry of Finance [MOF]). These statistics annually provide, based on a survey sample of about 36,000 companies,

K. Aramaki, *Japan's Long Stagnation, Deflation, and Abenomics*,
https://doi.org/10.1007/978-981-13-2176-4_6

estimated data for all of the profit-making companies (about 2.7 million companies) in Japan, such as sales, wages, profits, assets, liabilities, and capital. The statistics also give breakdowns by sectors and by company size classified by capital size. All data are in nominal terms. We first look at profit and loss, then assets and liabilities, and finally net assets. Drawing on these analyses, we then present our views on the whole mechanism of stagnation and deflation after the collapse of the bubble, and we further explore the reason why companies continued to restrain investment and wages even after the companies had eliminated excesses.

Profits and Losses of Companies

From the combined profit and loss statements of all the profit-making corporations, we see that the total amount of sales of companies in Japan suddenly stopped growing at the beginning of the 1990s, and started to show a declining trend from around the mid-1990s to the beginning of 2000s (Fig. 6.1). As sales stopped growing, wages also stopped growing

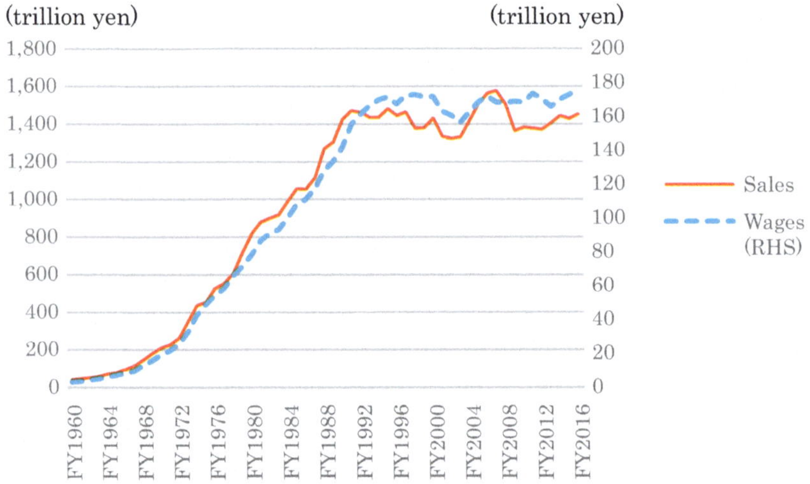

Fig. 6.1 Sales and wages (all industries excluding financial and insurance companies). Note: Wages = salaries + bonuses + expenses for fringe benefits for employees. Source: Ministry of Finance, "Financial Statements Statistics of Corporations by Industry"

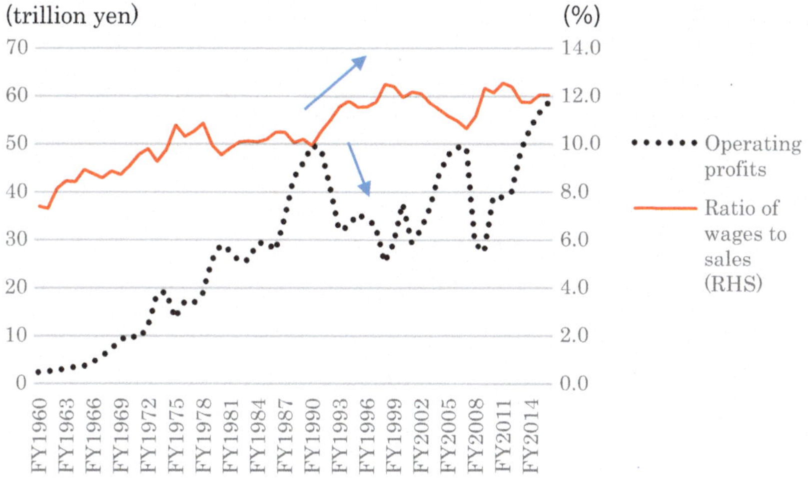

Fig. 6.2 Ratio of wages to sales and operating profits. Source: Ministry of Finance, "Financial Statements Statistics of Corporations by Industry"

by the mid-1990s. By the first half of the 1990s, however, wages continued to grow gradually, and they became more or less flat (did not decline) thereafter.[1]

Reflecting such developments in sales and wages, the ratio of wages to sales rose until the late 1990s, and the operating profits stagnated (Fig. 6.2). With the outbreak of the financial crisis, the ratio started to decline and it continued to do so until 2007. Then, the ratio jumped due to the sales collapse after the Global Financial Crisis (GFC), but subsequently started to decline again. Operating profits, which had been stagnating, started to rise after entering the 2000s, but drastically fell with the GFC, after which it resumed its rise. Over a quarter of a century after the burst of the bubble, the operating profits have not shown a stable rising trend, while developments in most recent years may show some upward movements.

Different from developments in operating profits, current profits (and net profits after tax) recovered a rising trend from the end of the 1990s, reflecting improvements in non-operational profits from the early 1990s, which cover such items as interest and dividends received and interest paid. Since then, current profits have been rising with substantial fluctuations (Fig. 6.3).

[1] Companies in Fig. 6.1 exclude financial and insurance companies. The same applies to all subsequent figures.

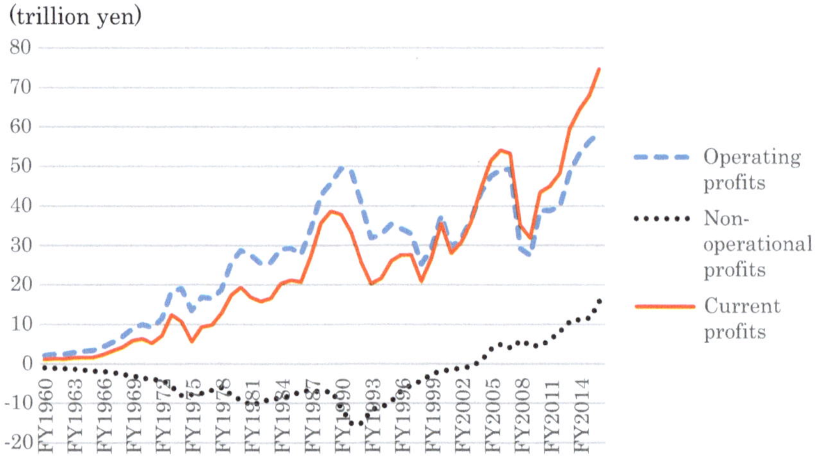

Fig. 6.3 Operating profits, non-operational profits, and current profits (all industries excluding financial and insurance companies). Source: Ministry of Finance, "Financial Statements Statistics of Corporations by Industry"

However, companies' behaviors have changed in an important respect, as compared with the period before the bubble. Until 1980s, an increase in current profits was accompanied by increase in wages. Since the mid-1990s, an increase in current profits is not reflected in an increase in wages (Fig. 6.4).

To summarize what we have seen in relation to developments in profits and losses of companies from the 1990s:

First, sales stopped growing from the beginning of 1990s and started to decline from around the mid-1990s.

Second, wages continued to grow for some time, but they became flat before the mid-1990s.

Third, the ratio of wages to sales rose substantially after entering the 1990s (after the financial crisis, the ratio started to decline but then rose again significantly, due to the GFC).

Fourth, the operating profits sharply declined and stayed low throughout the 1990s (they rose in the 2000s but declined due to the GFC).

Fifth, current profits recovered a rising trend from the end of the 1990s, reflecting improvements in non-operational profits.

Sixth, improvements in current profits, however, have not led to an increase in wages (improvements in current profits and wages have been de-linked).

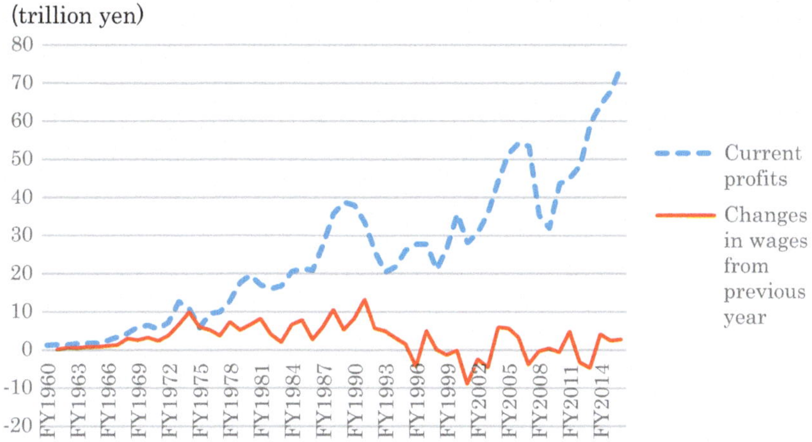

Fig. 6.4 Current profits and changes in wages from previous year. Source: Ministry of Finance, "Financial Statements Statistics of Corporations by Industry"

Assets and Liabilities of Companies

Next, we will look at the balance sheets of companies. Figure 6.5 shows developments in assets and liabilities of companies. We can see that there is a bump in both assets and liabilities in the latter half of 1980s and throughout 1990s. Both assets and liabilities started to expand from the mid-1980s at a pace that was much faster than the trend in the preceding years. The pace of expansion of both assets and liabilities slowed down after entering the 1990s, and they started to decline from the mid-1990s. The bump disappeared, and adjustments seem to have been completed in the early 2000s. While assets resumed growth in the early 2000s, liabilities continued to be stagnant.

Figure 6.6 shows developments in assets with their breakdown into fixed and liquid assets. The low growth (or shrinking) of total asset size mainly reflected decline in liquid assets, whereas fixed assets continued to grow, albeit at a lower rate from the 1990s until recent years (Fig. 6.6).

A breakdown of liquid assets shows that the shrinkage in liquid assets that we saw in Fig. 6.6 seems to reflect stagnation in business activities, as shown in the developments in notes and accounts receivables and inventory assets (Fig. 6.7). Cash and deposits started to decline after entering the 1990s, became flat in the 2000s, and then started to increase from around the GFC.

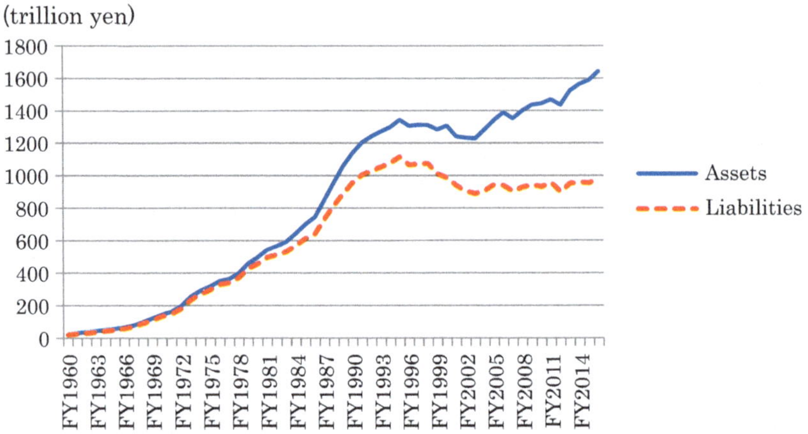

Fig. 6.5 Assets and liabilities of companies (all industries excluding financial and insurance companies). Source: Ministry of Finance, "Financial Statements Statistics of Corporations by Industry"

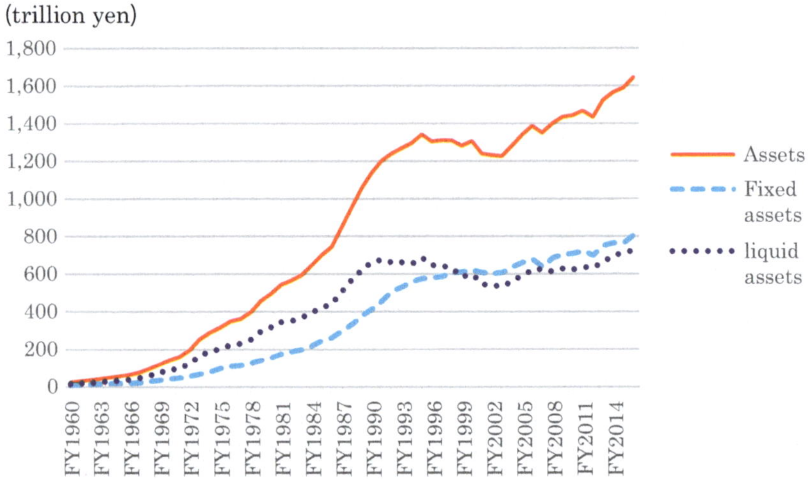

Fig. 6.6 Assets and their breakdown between fixed and liquid assets (all industries excluding financial and insurance companies). Source: Ministry of Finance, "Financial Statements Statistics of Corporations by Industry"

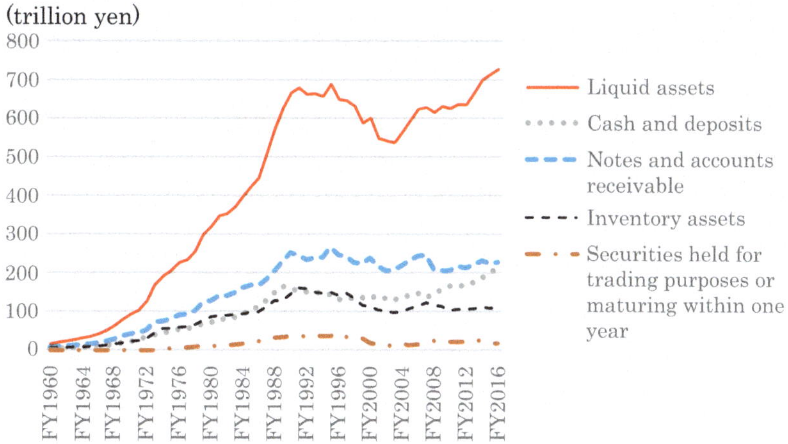

Fig. 6.7 Liquid assets and their components (all industries excluding financial and insurance companies). Source: Ministry of Finance, "Financial Statements Statistics of Corporations by Industry"

As opposed to liquid assets, fixed assets continued to grow even after entering the 1990s, at a lower rate than before. However, a breakdown of fixed assets shows that physical assets (excluding land),[2] such as buildings and machinery, continued to increase up to the mid-1990s, started to decline from around the financial crisis, and became flat recently. By contrast, securities held for investment purpose have been consistently increasing (Fig. 6.8).

Figure 6.9 shows securities held for investment purposes by companies, their breakdown into stocks and bonds, and the outstanding balance of foreign direct investment (FDI) (converted into yen using the year-end exchange rate). It shows that stocks account for most of the securities held for investment purpose, and the increase in FDI, particularly, since the early 2000s, seems to account for a substantial part of expansion of stock holdings (Fig. 6.9).[3]

[2] Physical assets (excluding land) is the sum of "expenditure for construction that is not completed" and "other physical assets (excluding land)" in the financial statement statistics of corporations by industry.

[3] The ratio of outstanding FDI (converted to the yen using the year-end exchange rate) to stocks held for investment purposes has been around between 30% and 40% from the latter half of 1990s to the beginning of 2010s. It showed a sharp increase since the first half of 2010s, reaching a level above 50% in fiscal 2016.

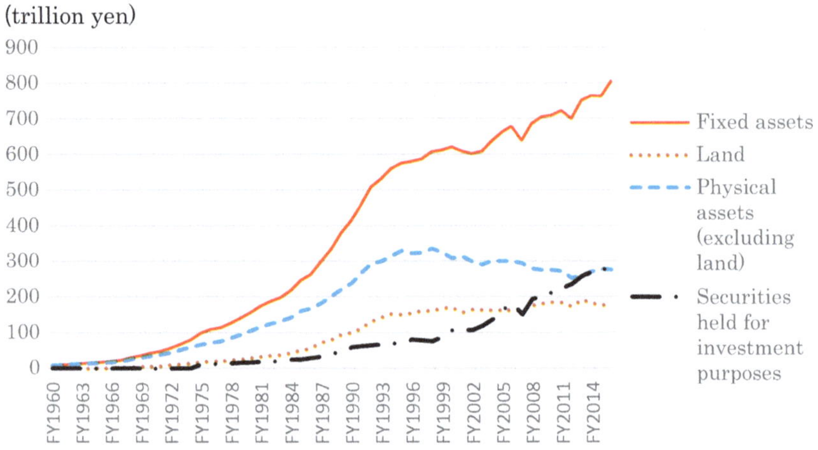

Fig. 6.8 Fixed assets and their major components (all industries excluding financial and insurance companies). Source: Ministry of Finance, "Financial Statements Statistics of Corporations by Industry"

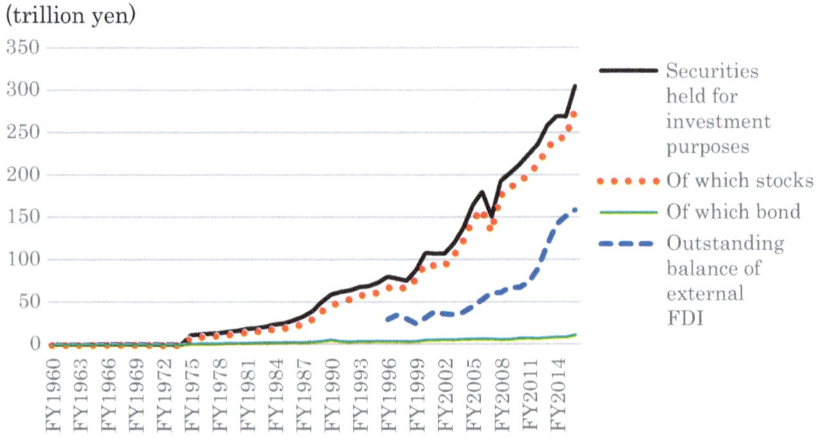

Fig. 6.9 Investment securities and Foreign Direct Investment. Note: Data for outstanding balance of external FDI are obtained by multiplying calendar year-end balance of FDI (in US dollars) by year-end yen–dollar exchange rate. As data for securities for investment purposes are as of the fiscal year end (that is, end March of the following year), there is a three-month discrepancy in timing between these two data. Source: Ministry of Finance, "Financial Statements Statistics of Corporations by Industry," Japan External Trade Organization (JETRO)

To summarize the developments in assets of profit-making corporations from the 1990s:

First, the decline in liquid assets after the collapse of the bubble reflects stagnation in business activities.

Second, by contrast, fixed assets continued to increase. This is because, while physical assets including buildings and machinery started to decline from around the time of the financial crisis, an increase in securities held for investment purposes more than made up for such a decline.

Third, it is possible that the increase in securities held for investment purposes from around the mid-2000s was substantially accounted for by an expansion of outward FDI.

Let us look at the liability side next. Liabilities consistently expanded from the 1960s, and the pace of expansion accelerated in the latter half of 1980s. Liabilities continued to expand after entering the 1990s but declined from the mid-1990s, becoming flat from the first half of 2000s. A breakdown shows that liquid liabilities became flat after entering the 1990s and started to decline from around the mid-1990s. Fixed liabilities started a decline in the latter half of the 1990s (Fig. 6.10).

A breakdown of liquid liabilities into major components shows that notes and accounts payable stopped growing after entering the 1990s and then followed a declining trend. This appears to reflect a stagnation of business activities, as is shown in the development in liquid assets. However, short-term borrowing (borrowing maturing within one year) continued to increase until the mid-1990s. This may be because companies coped with the general deterioration of business environments by resorting to short-term borrowing. This could also be related to the fact that physical assets kept rising up to the latter half of the 1990s, as we saw before. That is, investment planned in the 1980s may have taken years to be completed, and therefore, investments continued to be implemented even in the 1990s. Under the worsening investment environments, maturity shortening of funding may have occurred (Fig. 6.11).

Developments in fixed liabilities show that fixed liabilities continued to increase, albeit at a lowering pace, even after entering the 1990s, but started to sharply decline after the financial crisis. A breakdown of fixed liabilities shows that, as the amount of corporate bonds were more or less flat, developments in fixed liabilities almost solely reflected developments in long-term borrowing (Fig. 6.12).

To summarize developments in liabilities:

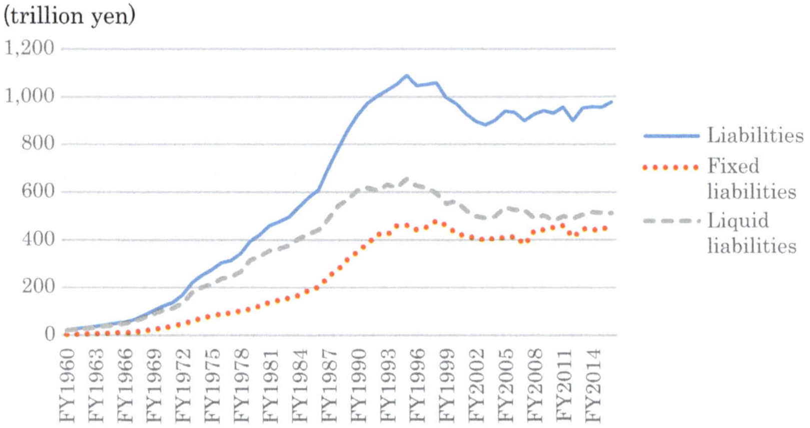

Fig. 6.10 Liabilities and their breakdown between liquid and fixed liabilities (all industries excluding financial and insurance companies). Source: Ministry of Finance, "Financial Statements Statistics of Corporations by Industry"

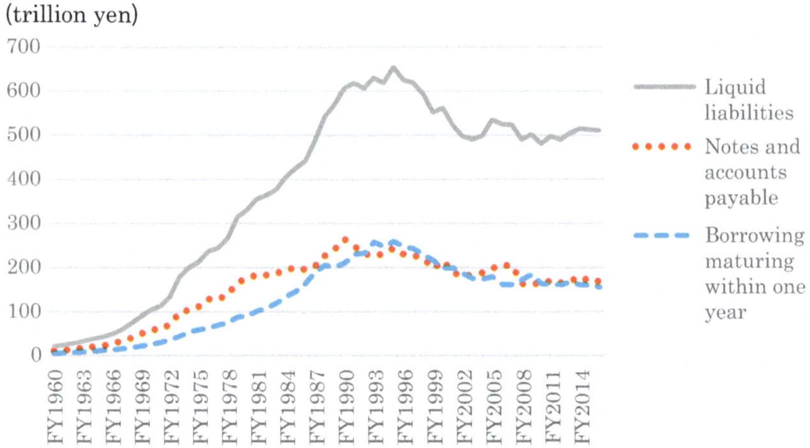

Fig. 6.11 Liquid liabilities and their major components (all industries excluding financial and insurance companies). Source: Ministry of Finance, "Financial Statements Statistics of Corporations by Industry"

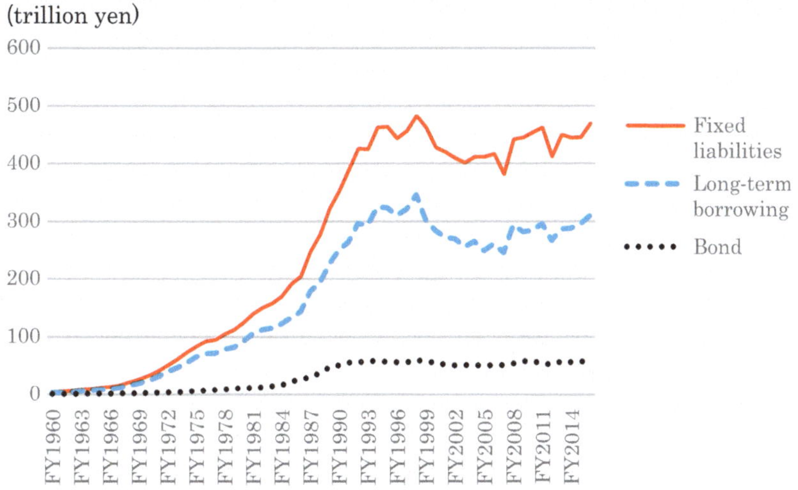

Fig. 6.12 Fixed liabilities and their components (all industries excluding financial and insurance companies). Source: Ministry of Finance, "Financial Statements Statistics of Corporations by Industry"

First, while the declining growth rate of liabilities reflects stagnation of economic activities, it should be noted that both short-term and long-term borrowing continued to increase until the mid-1990s, albeit at a decreasing pace.

Second, the decline in liabilities from the latter half of the 1990s was due substantially to the decline in borrowing, in particular, the sharp decline in the long-term borrowing after the financial crisis. This indicates that companies drastically changed their behavior in the direction of reducing borrowing after the financial crisis.

Net Assets of Companies

Finally, we take a look at developments in net assets. Net assets substantially changed in two phases: first, after entering the 1990s, and, second, after the financial crisis. Net assets gradually increased in the 1970s and 1980s, with the pace of the increase rising in the latter half of the 1980s. The pace of net asset growth slowed down after entering the 1990s, almost leveling off in the mid-1990s. However, the pace of growth of net assets suddenly accelerated after the financial crisis (Fig. 6.13). The

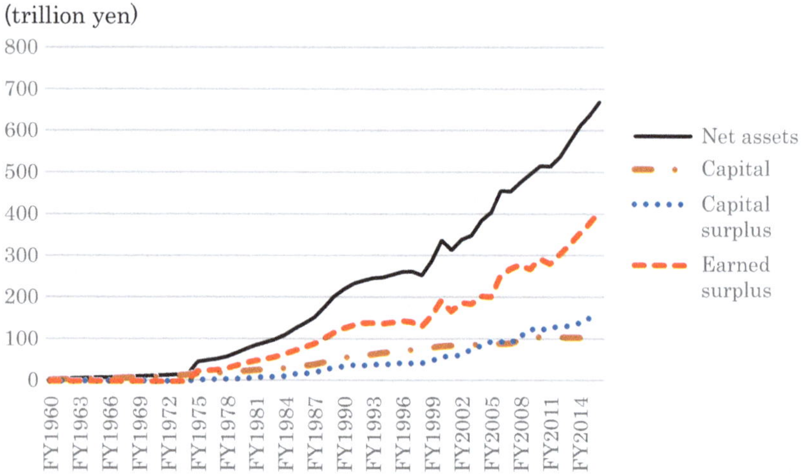

Fig. 6.13 Net assets and their components (all industries excluding financial and insurance companies). Source: Ministry of Finance, "Financial Statements Statistics of Corporations by Industry"

major factor behind the increase was an increase in earned surplus supported by an increase in profits, which was substantially supported by improvements in non-operational profits that we have seen in this chapter (Fig. 6.14).

Such a move to strengthen the net assets position can be found also in developments in the capital/asset ratio. The capital/asset ratio of companies was on a rising trend from the mid-1970s and throughout the 1980s. Then, it decelerated after entering the 1990s and almost stopped growing after the mid-1990s. However, it started to sharply rise after the financial crisis and has reached a historic high in recent years (Fig. 6.15).

We have looked at developments in profits and losses, assets and liabilities, and net assets of companies based on combined financial statements. What do they imply? Developments in these financial statement data indicate that the financial crisis seems to have fundamentally changed the behaviors of companies. It appears that priorities in the management of companies changed; strengthening their balance sheet position was given priority over other objectives. The reason behind this was the drastic change in financial environments. We have seen in Chap. 4 that the lending attitudes of financial institutions was sharply tightened at the outbreak of the financial crisis, across companies of all capital sizes, including small- and medium-sized enterprises (SMEs) that were

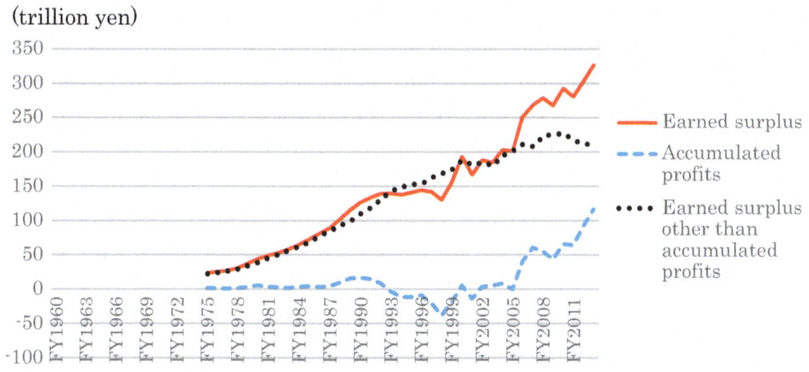

Fig. 6.14 Earned surplus and its components. Source: Ministry of Finance, "Financial Statements Statistics of Corporations by Industry"

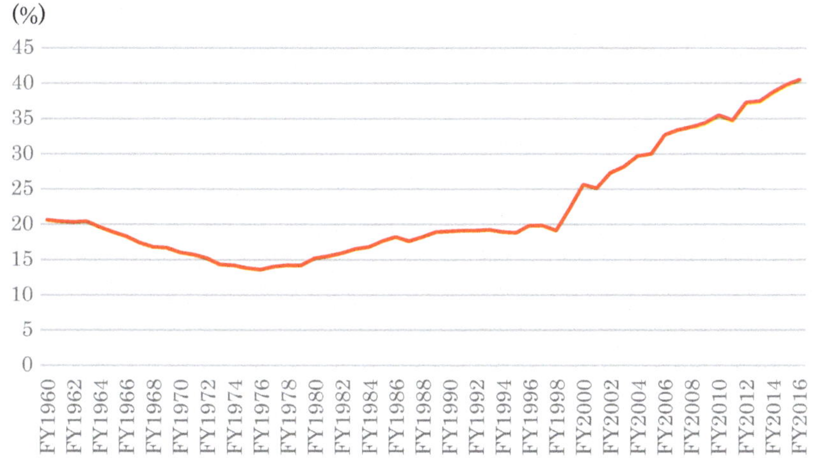

Fig. 6.15 Capital/assets ratio. Note: Capital/asset ratio = (net assets-right to purchase newly issued stocks)/(liabilities + reserves under special law + net assets). Source: Ministry of Finance, "Financial Statements Statistics of Corporations by Industry"

most dependent on borrowing (see Fig. 4.11 in Chap. 4). In addition to the rising uncertainty for the future caused by the failure of big financial institutions, the sharp deterioration of funding environments from outside made it necessary for companies to fundamentally review their business operations so that they could survive.[4] Figure 6.16 shows the number of manufacturing companies by capital size. We see that the number of smaller companies with capital less than 100 million yen hit a peak in 1995, and thereafter, was on a declining trend. Their numbers started to sharply decline after the financial crisis, particularly after entering the 2000s. The financial crisis seems to have had a greater impact on relatively smaller companies and reduced their viability. The number of companies with capital equal or greater than 100 million yen and less than 1 billion yen had been increasing until the 2000s, and thereafter, became flat and declined after the GFC. The number of big companies with capital 1 billion yen or greater was also slowly declining beginning around the GFC.

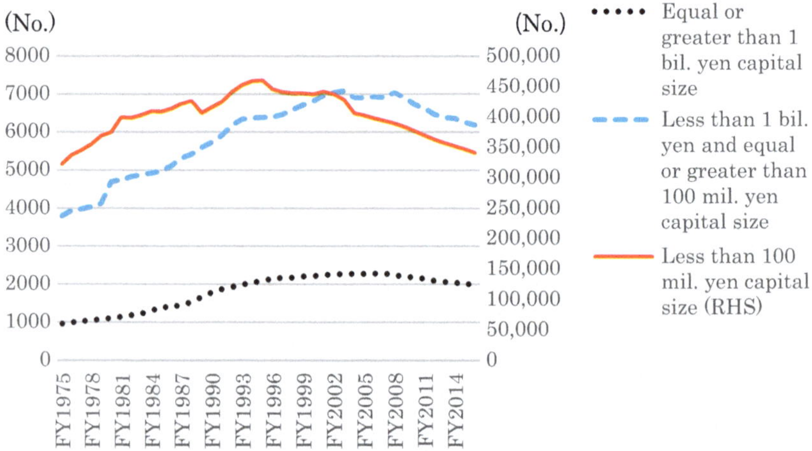

Fig. 6.16 Number of manufacturing companies by capital size (all industries excluding financial and insurance companies). Source: Ministry of Finance, "Financial Statements Statistics of Corporations by Industry"

[4] Particularly, for small- and medium-sized companies that were highly dependent on borrowing from financial institutions, borrowing from financial institutions had been functioning as funding similar to capital contributions for which only interest payments were required and repayment of principal was not expected. Therefore, faced with curbing of new loans (or possibly, forcible collection of outstanding loans) by financial institutions after the financial crisis, these companies had no choice other than trying to defend themselves by, for example, strengthening their net asset positions.

Changes in Assets/Liabilities and Net Assets and The Interpretation: Strengthened Defensiveness of Companies

Let us summarize once more how the asset and liability structure and net asset position have changed over the last three decades from the mid-1980s:

First, the size of assets and liabilities started to expand from the mid-1980s at a much faster pace than indicated by the trend in the preceding periods.
Second, the growth of both assets and liabilities slowed down after entering the 1990s and then declined from mid-1990s to early 2000s.
Third, after that, while assets resumed growth in early 2000s, liabilities showed little growth to date.
Fourth, stagnation of assets after entering the 1990s was due to the decline in liquid assets caused by stagnant business activities.
Fifth, fixed assets continued to grow, albeit at a slower pace even after entering the 1990s (they are growing even now).
Sixth, however, in the fixed assets, physical assets (excluding land) started to decline after the financial crisis, and this continued until recent years.
Seventh, on the other hand, in place of physical assets (excluding land), securities held for investment purposes significantly increased, making up for the decline in physical assets (excluding land), and became a driving force of supporting an increase in fixed assets or assets as a whole. Increase in cash and deposits also supported growth of assets after the GFC in 2008.
Eighth, stagnation of liabilities, after entering the 1990s, also reflected stagnation of economic activities. At the same time, both short-term and long-term borrowing continued to increase at least up to the mid-1990s (this corresponds to the fact that physical assets (excluding land) were on a rising trend until around the financial crisis).
Ninth, the decline in liabilities from around the mid-1990s reflects a decline in short-term and long-term borrowing (this has been particularly distinct after the financial crisis).
Tenth, the growth of net assets accelerated in the second half of the 1980s, slowed down after entering the 1990s, and halted around the mid-1990s. However, net assets suddenly started a sharp increase, reflecting an increase in earned surplus supported by an increase in profits.

How should we interpret these developments? One interpretation, which draws not only on what we found in this chapter but also on what we learned in the preceding chapters, is as follows:

The problem started with the rapid expansion of the asset size of the corporate sector from the mid-1980s and the sudden stop of sales growth and the subsequent fall of sales after the burst of the bubble at the beginning of the 1990s. These developments indicate that the corporate sector came to have a huge amount of assets for which they could not expect sufficient sales or demand, that is, excessive (unprofitable) assets. This lay at the heart of the difficulties of the Japanese economy after the collapse of the bubble.

Under the circumstances, the corporate sector initially took the following responses. First, they restrained investment but did not swiftly remove excessive assets. Second, they maintained existing employment (regular employment showed a moderate increase until the second half of the 1990s). Third, they restrained wage increases, but the combined amount of wages paid by the corporate sector continued to increase for some time (accordingly, the wage/sales ratio significantly increased in the 1990s). Fourth, as a result, operating profits stagnated, and companies tried to secure current profits by improving non-operational profits (interest payments, etc.). So, current profits started to increase from the end of the 1990s, but different from the pattern than existed until the 1980s; the improvements in current profits did not lead to an increase in wages (performance of companies and wage increases had become de-linked). Such response by the corporate sector, in the period from the collapse of the bubble but before the breakout of the financial crisis, may be regarded as a passive response in that they did not swiftly dispose of the excess assets and liabilities, maintained employment, and accepted a wage increase for some time. If we focus on the corporate behavior, this first stage of the economic stagnation may be termed "the period of passive response."

Although the corporate sector employed what may be called a traditional approach that placed importance on securing employment and took time to dispose of excessive assets, the costs and risk of holding excessive (unprofitable) assets started to be shifted to the financial sector, in the form of increasing non-performing loans (NPLs) and a financial crisis broke out in late 1990s. Faced with the crisis, the corporate sector addressed the problem of excessive assets in a dramatically different way, and with this change, the stagnation entered the second stage.

To explain the process, after the crisis broke out, the lending attitude of financial institutions was suddenly tightened, including for small- and medium-sized borrowers for which the tightening of lending was relatively moderate in the period immediately after the burst of the bubble. In the face of such adverse changes in funding environments, the corporate sector seems to have started to forcefully strengthen its capital base to survive. The net asset position and the capital asset ratio started to rise sharply after the financial crisis. Strengthening of the net asset position was achieved mainly through the accumulation of profits. Under the prolonged sales stagnation, the only options open to companies to secure profits were reduction of labor costs, cutback of interest payments through repayment of debts, and sales of assets. Therefore, the companies embarked on full-fledged labor cost reduction through nominal wage cuts and reductions in regular workers, replacing them with non-regular workers. They also started to make substantial repayments of debts and disposition of assets. Furthermore, companies strengthened their stance to restrain investment, with a result that the size of physical assets, such as buildings and machinery, started to decline. What these responses by companies in the second stage of stagnation indicate is that previous company behaviors that placed priority on securing employment and investing and holding physical assets had been significantly altered to the one that presumed continuation of stagnation, or low growth. Although current profits recovered a rising trend from the end of the 1990s, companies now gave first priority to strengthening their net asset position and pursued labor cost reduction, restraining investment and reducing physical assets. If we focus on corporate behavior, the second-stage economic stagnation in and after the financial crisis may be referred to as "the period of crisis response."

Thanks to such defensive behaviors, that is, restraint on wages and restraint on physical investment ("two restraints"), excessive assets and liabilities, as well as excessive employment that had been formed during the bubble period, were eliminated (as Fig. 6.5 indicates, the size of total assets returned to the level implied by the long-term trend line by the mid-2000s). However, even after the elimination of excesses, such defensive behaviors of companies continued and became long-lasting or perpetuated. It may be said that, with the continuation of defensive behaviors of companies, economic stagnation changed in nature and entered a third stage. If we focus on corporate behavior, this period could be called "the period of continued defensiveness." Such corporate behaviors placed downward pressures on consumption (through wage restraint) and investment (through sales stagnation), bringing about structuralized demand shortage.

If we interpret the mechanism of economic stagnation in this way, how should we explain the mild decline of general price levels (deflation), which has been another big issue of the Japanese economy? Our conclusion is that we should regard deflation as brought about by structuralized demand shortage under the long-lasting defensive attitude of companies. To expound, labor cost reduction through nominal wage cuts and replacement of regular employment with non-regular employment placed a downward pressure on general price levels. At the same time, defensive behaviors of companies imposed negative impacts on consumption through stagnant wages. Structuralized demand shortage due to such downward pressure on consumption and prolonged restraint on investment must have worked as a chronically depressing pressure on general price levels. If this is the case, it is likely that deflation is not the cause of the economic stagnation that Japan suffered for such a long time, but it is the outcome of the stagnation, or the consequence of the defensive behaviors of companies triggered by the financial crisis. This interpretation, however, does not deny the possibility that deflation may have added an extra burden on the economy through a mechanism that discouraged employment and borrowings, making an exit from the low-growth cycle more difficult.[5]

2 Mechanism Behind the Continued Defensive Attitude of Companies

In the preceding section, drawing on observed changes in corporate behavior since the latter half of 1980s, we have divided the period of long-term economic stagnation extending over more than two decades after the collapse of the bubble, into three periods, focusing on the responses of companies: "Period of passive response" (first stage of stagnation) from the collapse of the bubble in the beginning of the 1990s to the period before the financial crisis in the latter half of the 1990s, "Period of crisis response" (second stage of stagnation) from the financial crisis to the mid-2000s, when removal of excess assets and liabilities were completed, and "Period of continued defensiveness" (third stage of stagnation) since the mid-2000s, when the excesses had been eliminated.

[5] In addition to such behavioral changes of companies, however, it is possible that external factors contributed to the nominal wage decline and emergence of deflation. This issue is examined later in this chapter.

In this section, we will address the question of why companies continued to restrain investment and wages even in the period after the negative legacy of the collapse of the bubble was overcome (that is, in the third stage of stagnation: "Period of continued defensiveness"). There are two types of views on this issue. In the first view, companies' behavior is judged as irrational. The mindset of companies stand at the heart of the arguments. It is argued that, since it took as long as 15 years from the collapse of the bubble to the elimination of the excess assets and liabilities and because low growth and deflation continued for these years, the mindset or habitual mental attitude of companies changed irrationally into an excessively defensive one. From this viewpoint, it is most important to change such mindsets of companies. In contrast, the second viewpoint regards company behaviors as rational. Restraint on investment and wages is regarded not as the outcome of the defensive mindset but as the outcome of the rational choice made by companies in the internal and external economic environments. In this section, we examine whether the restraint on investment and wages that appears to be structuralized is due to an irrational deep-seated defensive mindset or based on rational considerations. We first look at investment restraint to be followed by wage restraint.

Mechanism of Investment Restraint

Mechanism of Investment Restraint in the First and Second Stages of Stagnation

Before examining investment restraint in the third stage of stagnation, let us look at the mechanism of investment restraint in the first and second stages of stagnation. As we have repeatedly emphasized, the most important background is the excess assets (and excess liabilities) of the corporate sector that resulted from the excessive investment in the bubble period from the mid-1980s (see Fig. 6.5). Almost as important is the sudden termination of sales growth of companies after the collapse of the bubble (see Fig. 6.1). Due to the sudden cessation of sales growth, physical assets such as structure, machinery, and equipment became excessive relative to the volume of sales. Figure 6.16 shows the ratio of physical assets (excluding land) to sales, which is an inverse of a type of total asset turnover ratio.[6] This ratio shows how much physical assets companies hold per unit of

[6] The total asset turnover ratio is usually defined as the value of sales divided by total assets. In the text, the term, physical assets (excluding land), is used instead of total assets.

sales. The ratio hit a bottom by the beginning of the 1980s, and then followed a rising trend. The pace of the rise accelerated after entering the 1990s, but it started to decline from the mid- through the second half of the 1990s (Fig. 6.17).

With these developments in mind, let us conduct a very rough estimate of the amount of excessive supply capacity (physical assets).[7] We first assume that a company has some criterion on the desirable physical assets/sales ratio, or how much physical assets it wishes to hold per unit of expected sales. As companies usually need physical assets in order to produce goods or services, it is realistic to assume that a company would wish to strike some balance between the size of physical assets and the volume of sales. As Fig. 6.17 shows, this ratio changes over time, and it is difficult to know what level of the ratio a company regards as appropriate. Figure 6.18 shows estimates of excess physical assets. Estimates of excess physical assets

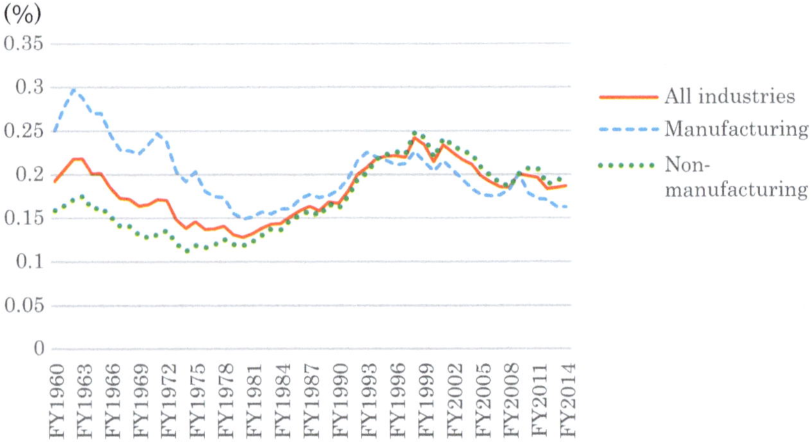

Fig. 6.17 Ratio of physical assets (excluding land) to sales. Note: Physical assets = expenditure for construction that has not been completed + other physical assets such as structure, machinery, and equipment (excluding land). Source: Ministry of Finance, "Financial Statements Statistics of Corporations by Industry"

[7] Estimation is conducted as follows. It is assumed that the physical assets/sales ratio was optimum and that there was no excess assets in FY 1990. The optimum size of physical assets is calculated for each of the subsequent years by multiplying the amount of sales in each year by the physical assets/sales ratio in FY 1990. That part of the actual size of physical assets that is greater than the estimated "optimum" size of physical assets in each year is regarded as excess assets.

Fig. 6.18 Estimated excess physical assets, investment, and depreciation (all industries excluding financial and insurance companies). Source: Ministry of Finance, "Financial Statements Statistics of Corporations by Industry"

are obtained by, first, assuming that the physical assets/sales ratio as of FY 1990 (0.16) was desirable (in other words, there was no excess supply capacity in FY 1990); second, calculating the optimum size of physical assets using the actual sales amount in each of the subsequent years (by multiplying sales amount by 0.16); and, third, subtracting the optimum from the actual size of physical assets. The size of estimated excess physical assets increased rapidly from FY 1990, hit a peak in FY 1998, and thereafter sharply declined. The actual amount of investment and the amount of depreciation are shown in the same figure. The figure shows that, during the period when excess physical assets were increasing and stayed at a high level, net investment declined, and that, after the financial crisis, the amount of investment dropped below the amount of depreciation, that is, net investment was negative. Investment started to increase from the beginning of the 2000s, catching up with the level of depreciation around the mid-2000s when the estimated excess physical assets declined substantially.

This calculation explains why stock adjustment was not finished swiftly after the collapse of the bubble. After entering the 1990s, while investment declined, net investment was still positive and supply capacity continued to be added. On the contrary, sales amount leveled off and then tended to decline, with the result that excess supply capacity did not decline, increasing rather until the latter half of the 1990s. The presence of such excess supply capacity brought about by sales stagnation and the growth of supply capacity placed a continuous downward pressure on investment, making the recovery in the first stage of stagnation weak.

After the financial crisis (or in the second stage of stagnation), companies' responses drastically changed, and disposition of excess assets and liabilities rapidly progressed. In this stage, restraint of investment was further strengthened and physical assets started to decline. Investment restraint in the second stage of stagnation was implemented in order to carry out disposition of excesses that had been delayed and, therefore, was an unavoidable process.

Mechanism of Investment Restraint in the Third Stage of Stagnation

Due to the positive disposition by companies of excess assets, they were eliminated by the mid-2000s, and against this background, real gross private investment, which had been stagnant in the 1990s, started to increase from the first half of the 2000s (later, it sharply declined due to the GFC, but began to rise afterward) (Fig. 6.19).

After the disposition of excess assets was completed, was the problem of investment restraint by companies that had lasted for more than 10 years

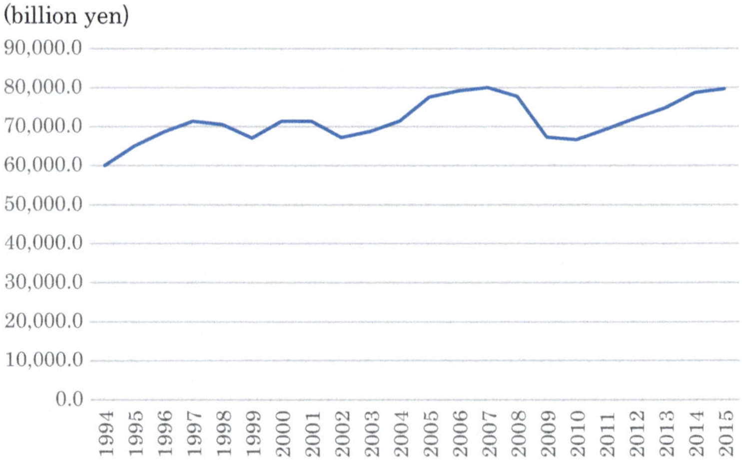

Fig. 6.19 Real gross private investment. Source: Cabinet Office

solved? Not necessarily. Figure 6.20 shows developments in cash flows and investment. While the level of private investment had been broadly the same as the level of cash flow for more than 30 years, until the beginning of the 1990s, the private investment/cash flows ratio substantially declined in the latter half of 1990s. The ratio hit the bottom and became flat thereafter. Even after the mid-2000s, when the negative legacy of the collapse of the bubble was finally eliminated, the level of private investment stayed substantially at a lower level than the level of cash flows. Why did the companies restrain investment in relation to the level of cash flows?

According to the first of the two interpretations previously mentioned on the cause of continued investment restraint, it is claimed that companies assumed an excessively defensive attitude and were strongly reducing risk-taking in response to both the shocks of the collapse of the bubble and the financial crisis, and that such defensiveness has led companies to give priority to liquidity holding and to restrain investment, even after their balance sheets have been normalized.

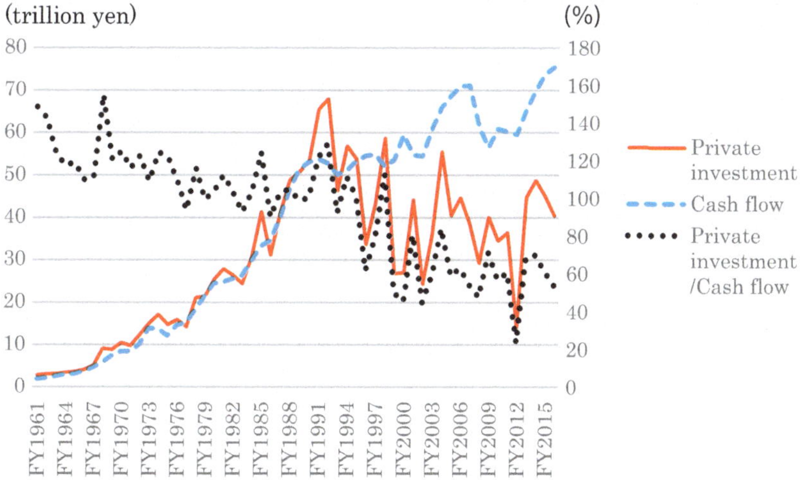

Fig. 6.20 Cash flow, private investment, and private investment/cash flow. Note: Private investment =①Difference from previous year in (a) expenditure for construction that has not been completed, (b) other physical assets (excluding land), (c) intangible assets other than software, and (d) software + ②depreciation. Cash flow = current profits × (1/2) + depreciation. Source: Ministry of Finance, “Financial Statements Statistics of Corporations by Industry”

If such a defensive mindset of companies is the fundamental cause of continued restraint on investment, in order to increase investment and growth, policy measures may be regarded as necessary and appropriate that would alter irrationally defensive attitudes. Such policies could include encouraging the industrial community politically to increase investment and to strengthen the governance structures of companies so as to enhance appropriate risk-taking instead of primarily defending the company.

However, the second of the two interpretations claimed that continued investment restraint after excessive assets and liabilities had been removed by the mid-2000s was the outcome of rational choices made by companies. In other words, there is a good reason for the caution exercised by companies toward domestic investment.

As we have already seen, companies started to reduce physical assets (excluding land) and expand security holding for investment purposes from the latter half of the 1990s. Most of the securities held for investment purposes that companies are increasingly holding are stocks. If we compare the outstanding balance of outward FDI (converted into yen by end-period exchange rate) with the outstanding amount of securities held for investment purposes, the former accounts for approximately 30–50% of the latter. The increase in security holding for investment purposes seems to reflect active FDI by companies (Refer to Fig. 6.9).

Figure 6.21 shows, first, the amount of dividends received from abroad in relation to FDI recorded in the Balance of Payments (BOP) statistics, and, second, the share of such dividends received from abroad in the amount of non-operational revenue of companies (all industries excluding financial and insurance companies). The ratio of dividends received in relation to outward FDI to the amount of non-operational revenue of companies (excluding financial and insurance companies) increased by 4.5 times from 4.2% in 1996 to 18.7% in 2014 (however, the share substantially declined in most recent years due to a sharp fall in dividends received) (Fig. 6.21).

These data indicate that companies placed a greater importance than before on foreign investment, as compared with domestic investment, and that they have been allocating cash flow accordingly after the financial crisis, particularly, after entering the 2000s. If so, why? First, after the burst of the bubble, the expected growth rate of domestic economy held by companies significantly declined and stayed at a

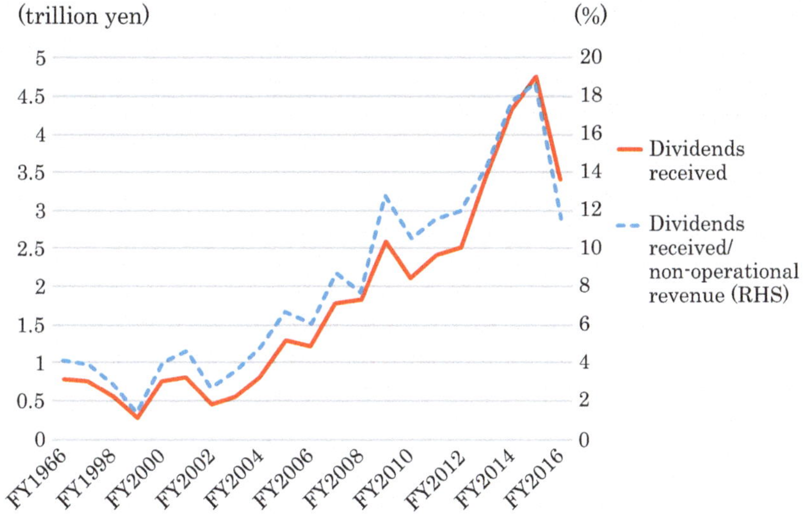

Fig. 6.21 Dividends received from abroad and their share in non-operational revenue. Note: Dividends received = "Dividends and withdrawals from income of quasi-corporations" in Ministry of Finance, "Balance of payments statistics." Non-operational revenue is for all industries excluding financial and insurance companies. Source: Ministry of Finance, "Financial Statements Statistics of Corporations by Industry"

low level since. If the domestic economy is expected to grow at a low rate, domestic investment is restrained (Fig. 6.22).[8]

Second, the difference in profitability between foreign and domestic investment may be making companies wary about domestic investment. Figure 6.23 indicates that the ratio of current profits to sales of foreign subsidiaries has been substantially higher than that of domestic companies (all industries excluding financial and insurance companies) after entering the 2000s, although it has declined sharply in recent years.

[8]The shrinking population or the expectation of the population shrinking is sometimes cited as a cause of the decline of expected growth rate. However, the number of people of working age in the population started to decline in the mid-1990s, and the total population started to decline in the latter half of the 2000s. It is probably since about 2010 that the economic effects of the population shrinking started to be widely recognized. Developments in expected growth rate do not seem to be in line with evolution of the demographic facts. Refer to the supplement to this chapter for information about the demography and the economy.

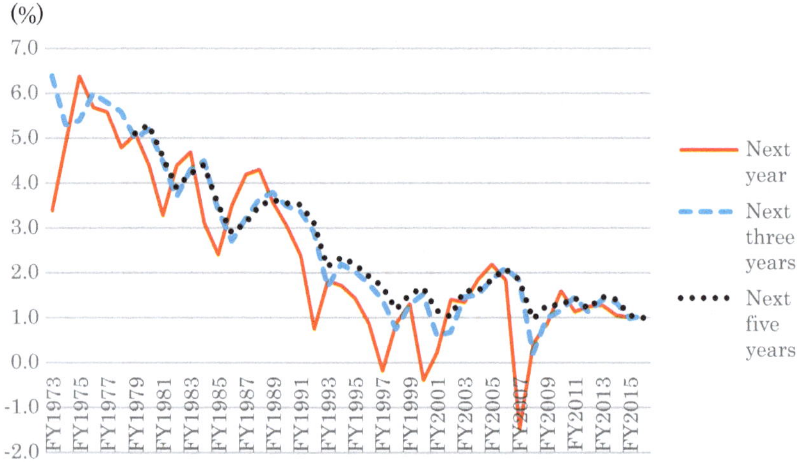

Fig. 6.22 Expected growth rate held by companies. Source: Cabinet Office, "Survey on company behavior"

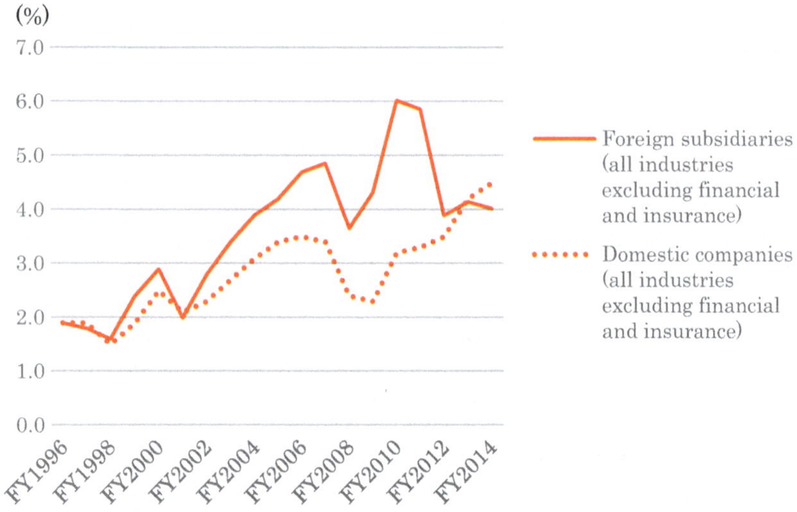

Fig. 6.23 Ratio of current profits to sales (%). Source: Ministry of Economy, Trade and Industry, "Basic survey on overseas business activities"

The ratio of outstanding balance of outward FDI to domestic physical assets (excluding land) has been consistently rising since around the end of the 1990s. Reflecting the depressed growth expectation of the domestic economy and relatively high profitability of overseas operations, companies seem to have been gradually shifting their business base to overseas, by increasing overseas investment and restraining domestic investment as a rational choice, particularly, since mid-2000s (Fig. 6.24).

Figure 6.25 shows that the overseas production ratio (sales of subsidiaries/[sales of subsidiaries + sales of domestic companies]) of the manufacturing sector has been largely rising consistently. For manufacturing companies with overseas subsidiaries, 38% of the total production was done abroad in FY 2014. Nominal yen appreciation tends to be followed by a further rise in overseas production ratio after a lag of a few years.

The foregoing indicates that companies seem to have been strengthening their position to place a greater emphasis on foreign operations year by year, and as a result, a gap has emerged between the amount of domestic investment and the amount of cash flow. In order to examine this situation, we have added FDI to domestic investment in Fig. 6.26. The combined amount of domestic and foreign investment comes close to the level of cash flow in

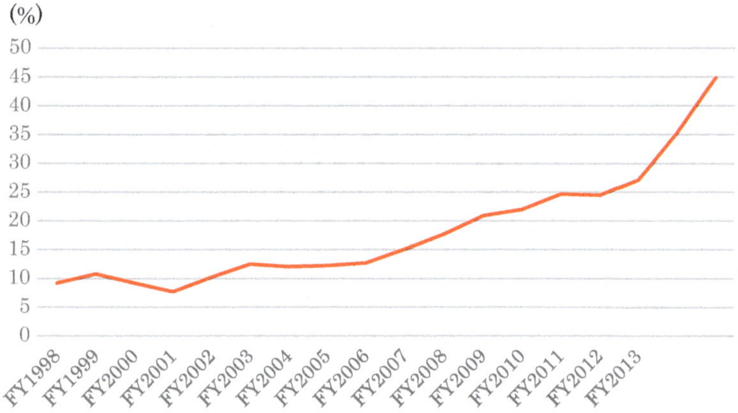

Fig. 6.24 Ratio of outstanding Foreign Direct Investment (all sectors) to physical assets (excluding land) (all industries excluding financial and insurance companies). Note: Outstanding FDI is obtained by converting the year-end outstanding balance of outward FDI (all sectors, in US dollars) to yen using the year-end exchange rate. Physical assets are the sum of "other physical assets (excluding land)" and changes from the previous year in "expenditure for construction that has not been completed" (all industries excluding financial and insurance companies). Source: Ministry of Finance, "Statistics of corporate financial statements," JETRO)

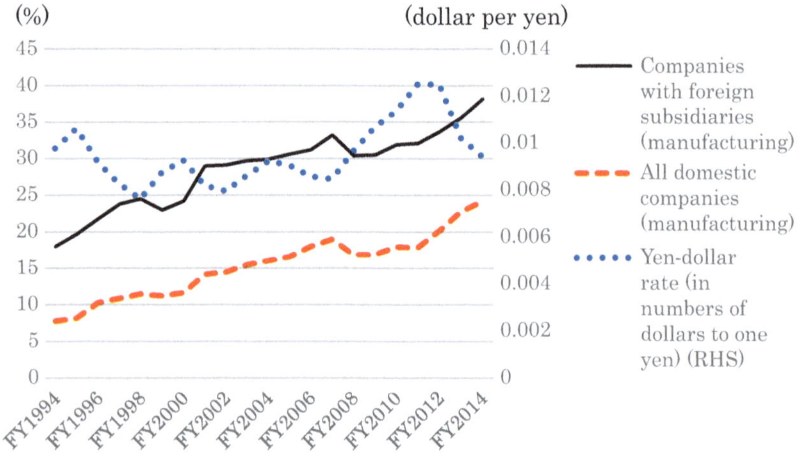

Fig. 6.25 Overseas production ratio (manufacturing). Source: Ministry of Economy, Trade and Industry, "Basic survey on overseas business activities"

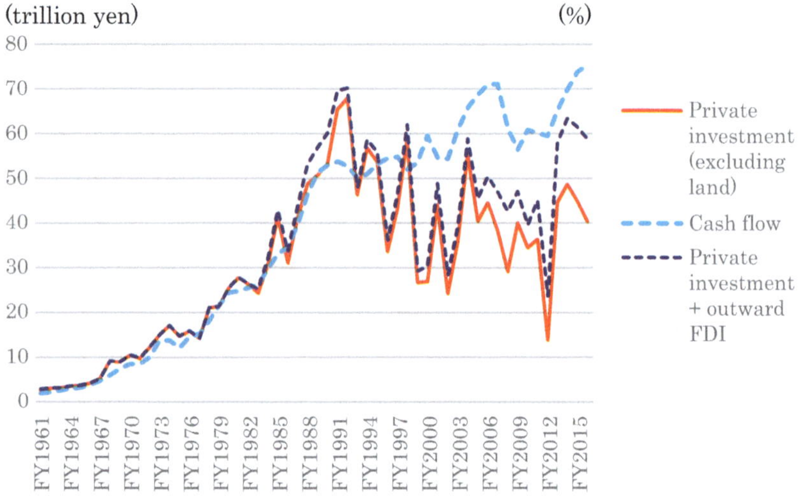

Fig. 6.26 Private investment, outward Foreign Direct Investment, and cash flow. Source: Ministry of Finance, "Financial Statements Statistics of Corporations by Industry"; JETRO "Direct Investment Statistics"; IMF, "International Financial Statistics"

most recent years, indicating that companies are starting to use their cash flows almost completely, but with a greater emphasis on overseas investment.

Let us summarize the outcome of the examination of investment restraint in this chapter:

First, the long-lasting investment restraint extended over more than 20 years after the burst of the bubble. The reason for the investment restraint in the first and second stages of the stagnation from the beginning of the 1990s through the first half of the 2000s, on the one hand, and the reason for the investment restraint in the third stage of stagnation from the mid-2000s, on the other hand, may be different.

Second, investment restraint (or reduction) in the first and second stages of stagnation was largely due to the hangover of excessive assets and liabilities.

Third, in the third stage of stagnation, domestic investment has been restrained relative to the amount of cash flow, despite the negative legacy of the bubble and the shocks of the financial crisis having been overcome and the balance sheets of companies normalized. This could be attributed to an irrationally defensive attitude of companies, with risk aversion having become deeply ingrained into mindsets during the shocks of the collapse of the bubble and the financial crisis.[9] However, this behavior could reflect that companies have become cautious about domestic investment and have started to place greater importance on overseas business, based on stagnant growth expectations about the domestic economy and expectations for relative profitability of overseas business. As is shown in Fig. 6.22, the settlement of low growth expectation of domestic economy prompted by the financial crisis provided an important background for such defensive attitude.

Mechanism of Wage Restraint

Next, taking into account the preceding analysis of investment, let us examine the mechanism of wage restraint.

[9] As Fig. 6.7 in this chapter shows, cash and deposits held by companies sharply increased from the latter half of 2000s. This is partly due to the shock of the GFC, but the fact that it continues to increase demonstrates the strength of defensive attitude or risk avoidance.

Developments in Wages

Developments in wages indicate that wages have been restrained for nearly 20 years. Year-on-year rate of changes in wages per worker (nominal index, 2015 average = 100) has been negative in 12 out of 19 years from 1998 to 2016 (a simple average of year-on-year rate of change over 19 years is −0.7%). The level of nominal wage per worker declined by 12.4% from the peak of 114.8 in 1997 to 100.6 in 2016 (Fig. 6.27).

Developments in real terms are almost the same. Real wages per worker (yearly average, deflated by CPI, 2015 = 100) have declined by 13.1% from the peak of 115.8 in 1996 to 100.6 in 2017 (a simple average over the first to third quarters) (Fig. 6.28).

How Did the Wage Restraint Start? Problems Brought about by Corporate Behaviors in the First Stage of Stagnation

As we have seen, wage reduction occurred after the financial crisis in 1997–1998. In the preceding period, after the collapse of the bubble, the total sales of companies (all industries excluding financial and insurance companies) suddenly stopped growing and followed a declining trend until the beginning of 2000s, yet the total amount of wages paid by companies continued to increase for the first half of 1990s. In consequence, the

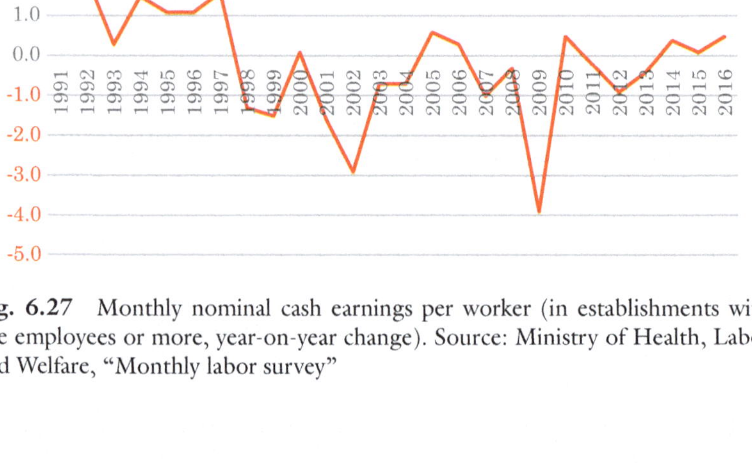

Fig. 6.27 Monthly nominal cash earnings per worker (in establishments with five employees or more, year-on-year change). Source: Ministry of Health, Labor and Welfare, "Monthly labor survey"

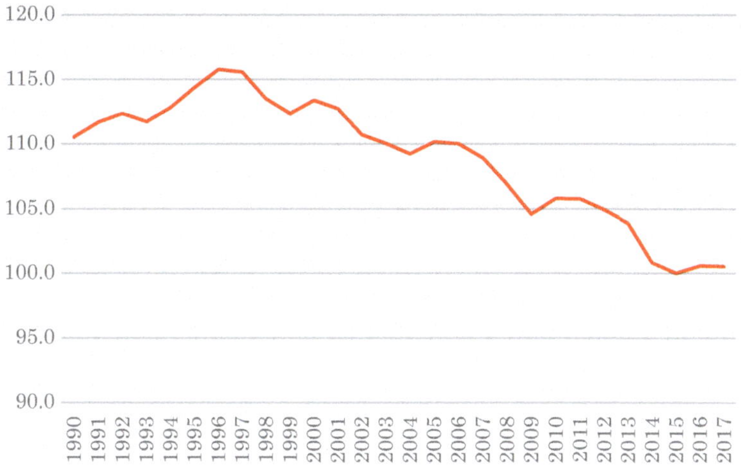

Fig. 6.28 Monthly real cash earnings per worker (in establishments with five employees or more [2015 = 100]). Source: Ministry of Health, Labor and Welfare, "Monthly labor survey"

ratio of total wages to total sales significantly increased after entering the 1990s, and the operating profits substantially declined and stagnated (see Figs. 6.1 and 6.2).

As previously mentioned, response by companies in the period after the collapse of the bubble but before the financial crisis was passive. During this period of passive response, companies maintained employment and wages, and accordingly, a rise in labor costs and reduction in operating profits resulted.

Figure 6.29 shows developments in real wages and labor productivity since the 1990s. It shows that the rise in real wages from 1990 exceeded the rise in labor productivity over the same period throughout the 1990s.

Reflecting such developments, as Fig. 6.30 indicates, the share of labor income (the labor share) in national income sharply increased in the 1990s.[10]

[10] Labor income share = (labor income in real GDP)/(real GDP) = (real wage per worker [w]) × (total number of workers [N]) / (real GDP [y]) = w/(y/N). Therefore, the rate of change in labor income share = the rate of change in real wages − the rate of change in labor productivity. So, if an increase in real wages exceeds an increase in labor productivity, as is the case shown in Fig. 6.29, the labor income share rises.

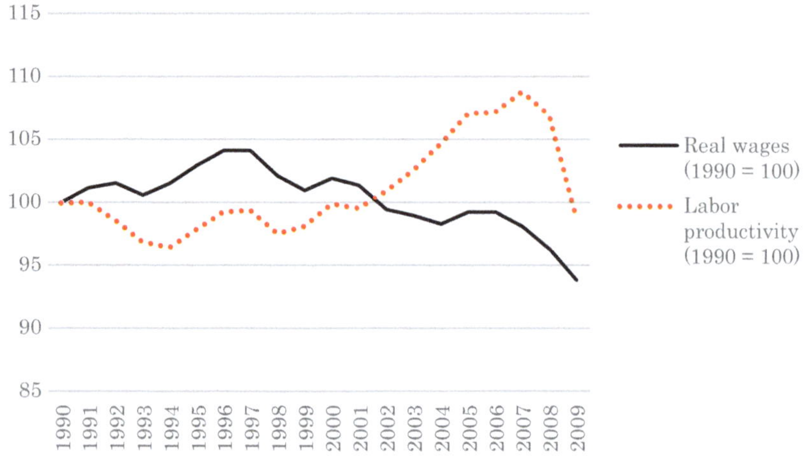

Fig. 6.29 Real wages and labor productivity (1990 = 100). Note: Real wages = real wages in Monthly Labor Survey, labor productivity = real GDP (all industries)/No. of employees in Labor Force Survey. Source: Ministry of Health, Labor, and Welfare, "Monthly labor survey"; Cabinet Office, Statistics Bureau, Ministry of Internal Affairs and Communications, "Labor force survey"

The rise in real wages and labor income share depressed return on assets (ROA) of companies. As we saw in Fig. 4.2, ROA continuously declined after entering the 1990s until near the end of the 1990s.[11]

In this way, in the first stage of stagnation until before the financial crisis, companies not only continued to hold excess (unprofitable) assets, as previously explained, but also accepted increases in labor costs, and as a result, incurred a further decline in ROA. However, the situation drastically changed with the breakout of the financial crisis in the late 1990s. The lending stance of financial institutions was sharply tightened. With the deterioration of funding environments, companies started to rapidly strengthen their net asset positions, as explained before. The "period of crisis response" previously mentioned then started. With little expectation for sales increase, companies aimed to strengthen their net asset positions by creating profits through labor cost reduction, in addition to repayment of debts (interest payment reduction), and sales of assets (realization of unrealized capital gains).

[11] The decline in ROA may have been another factor that contributed to the restraint on investment.

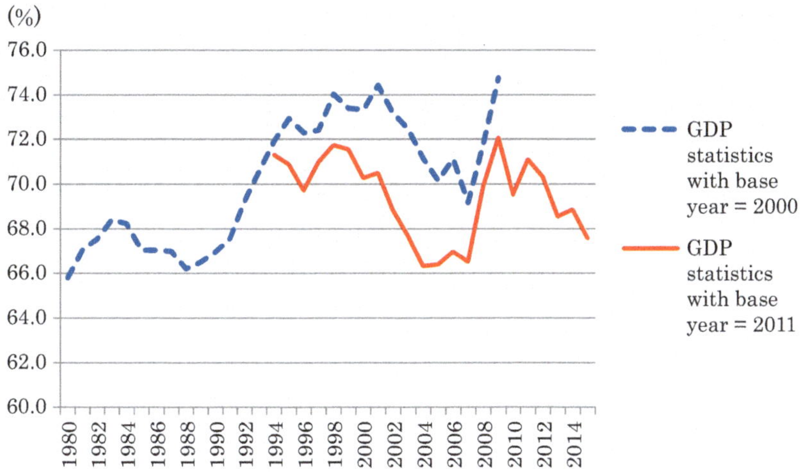

Fig. 6.30 Labor income share. Note: Labor income share = labor income/national income (in factor price base). Source: Cabinet Office, GDP statistics

Labor cost reduction after the financial crisis was pursued basically through a reduction in wages of regular workers and a reduction in the number of regular workers and their replacement with non-regular workers. As we saw in Fig. 4.15, the number of regular workers declined by 4.8 million in eight years from 1997 to 2005. It tended to decline beyond that, but it hit a bottom in 2014 and recovered an upward trend recently. Also, as we saw in Fig. 4.14, the share of non-regular workers sharply increased from 20.2% in 1990 and 20.9% in 1995 to 37.9% in 2014, subsequently declined somewhat thereafter.[12]

[12] Expanded use of non-regular workers has been in progress in almost all sectors from 2003 to 2015 (Ministry of Internal Affairs and Communications, "Labour Force Survey, Detailed Tabulation"). The share of non-regular workers is high in restaurants, hotels, wholesale and retail, real estate, and services, including medical and welfare. Also, the share of non-regular workers substantially increased in such sectors as transportation, restaurants, and hotels. At the same time, employment in manufacturing sector has been declining, and employment has been rising in such sectors as medical care and welfare and restaurants and hotels, showing a shift in industrial structure toward domestic demand-type services industries. Among the sectors in which increased employment has been provided, the wage levels in those sectors, such as medical care, welfare, and wholesale and retail are relatively low and the wage levels in information and communication are high. The wage levels in regulated sectors, such as railways and electricity, gas and water supply are high (Ministry of Health, Labor, and Welfare, "Basic Survey on Wage Structure").

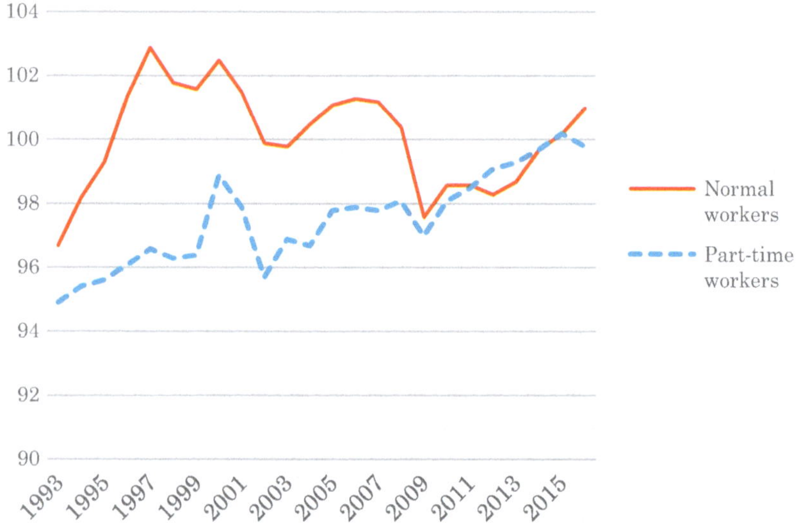

Fig. 6.31 Monthly cash earnings per worker for normal workers and for part-time workers (2015 = 100). Source: Ministry of Health, Labor, and Welfare, "Monthly labor survey"

Figure 6.31 shows developments in nominal wages (total cash earnings) for normal workers and part-time workers. The nominal wages of normal workers increased up to the financial crisis, but thereafter started to rapidly decline. By contrast, the nominal wages of part-time workers almost continuously followed a rising trend. Labor cost reduction by companies was conducted through cutting back the number and wages of regular workers and by their replacement with non-regular workers. Demand for non-regular workers consequently increased, and their wages followed an upward trend.

The ratio of wages of non-regular workers to those of regular workers has been rising from the level around 60% in the mid-2000s, but it remained at 63.9% in 2015. A reduction in the number of regular workers and their replacement with non-regular workers has produced substantial labor cost reduction effects for companies in the short run (Fig. 6.32).[13]

[13] If we include social security contribution borne by companies, costs of hiring a regular worker become further high as compared with hiring a non-regular worker.

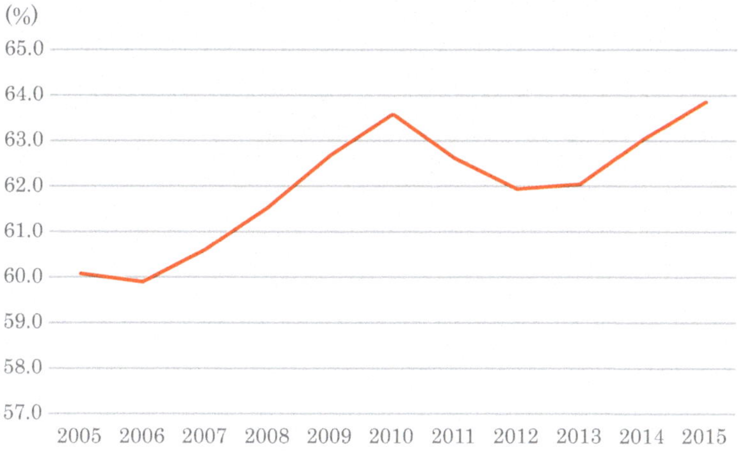

Fig. 6.32 Ratio of wages of non-regular workers to those of regular workers. Source: Ministry of Health, Labor, and Welfare, "Basic survey of wage structure"

It seems that the reduction in nominal wages and replacement of regular workers with non-regular workers on such a large scale was conducted only after the financial crisis. Behaviors of companies, which once considered the provision of stable employment as their social responsibilities, was dramatically altered upon the outbreak of the financial crisis.

Why Does Wage Restraint Still Continue?

The mechanism of wage restraint explained in the preceding subsection may not continue once the unsustainable situation created by a hike in labor costs and labor income share has been corrected through downward adjustments of labor costs (resolution of excess employment and wage reduction). However, the reality is different.

As a result of labor cost restraint, the labor share in Japan, which was internationally at a high level in the 1990s, significantly declined by mid-2000s, as shown in Fig. 6.33, and although it rose somewhat due to the GFC and is high to some extent in most recent years, it is broadly at a comparable level to those in other major advanced countries.

On the other hand, the share of labor costs to the value added dropped sharply after the financial crisis. Due to the sudden shrinking of the value added after the GFC, the share of labor costs went back to a high level but subsequently started to decline sharply, and there does not seem to be a fundamental change to the trend of labor cost restraint (Fig. 6.34).

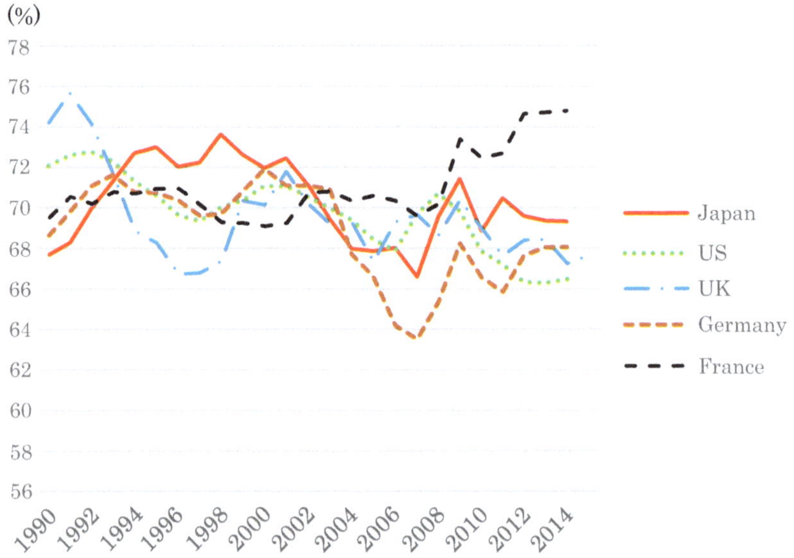

Fig. 6.33 Compensation of employees/net national income (at factor price). Note: Net national income (at factor price) = net national income (at market price) – taxes less subsidies on productions and imports. Compensation of employees is made up of two components, namely, wages and salaries, and the value of social contributions payable by employers, and does not include mixed income. Source: Organisation for Economic Co-operation and Development [OECD], data downloaded from OECD. Stat on May 28, 2016

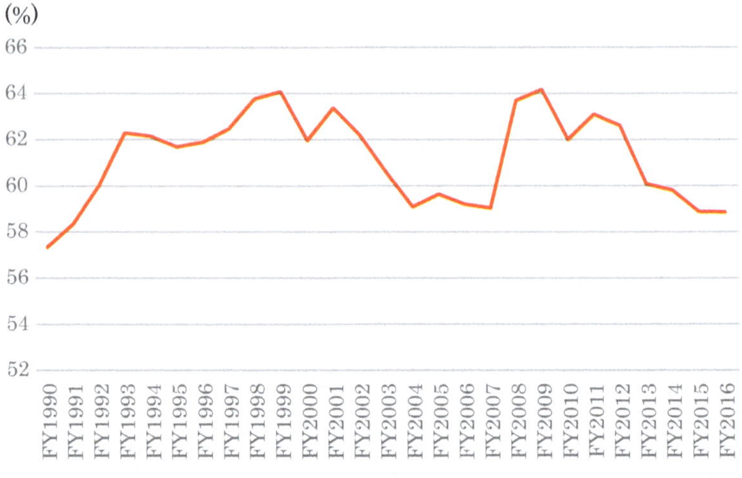

Fig. 6.34 Labor cost/value added. Note: Labor cost = wages + bonuses + expense for fringe benefits. Source: Ministry of Finance, "Financial Statements Statistics of Corporations by Industry"

In this way, despite companies having overcome the negative legacy of the bubble (excess assets and liabilities), with substantially reduced labor costs and greatly strengthened net asset positions after the financial crisis, they continue to restrain wages. While employment conditions in the labor market continue to improve, wage increases have been weak. The unemployment rate, which recorded a high of 5.5% in July 2009, declined to a yearly average of 3.6% in 2014, and then to 2.8% in October 2017. However, the average rate of increase (year-on-year) in the nominal wage per worker (total monthly cash earnings per worker in establishments with five or more workers from the "Monthly Labor Survey") for three years, from 2014 to 2016, was as low as 0.3%. As shown in the next chapter, the hourly wages of non-regular workers have been showing a rate of increase higher than that of regular workers for the last few years. Tightening of labor market conditions is reflected more clearly in wages of non-regular workers than in wages of regular workers.

Figure 6.35 shows developments in the amount of value added and the ratios to value added of three values: the amount of increase in wages from the previous year, the amount of increase in net assets from the previous year, and the amount of dividends paid out. After the amount of value

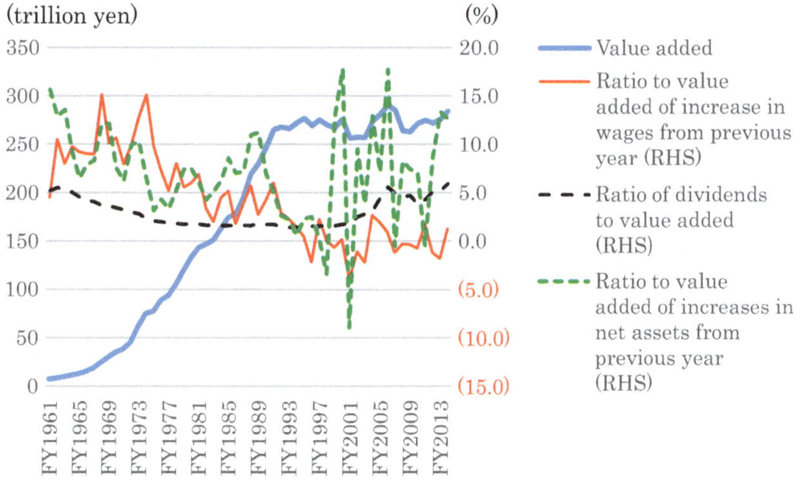

Fig. 6.35 Value added and ratio of wage increase, dividends, and increase in net assets to value added. Source: Ministry of Finance, "Financial Statements Statistics of Corporations by Industry"

added stopped growing following the collapse of the bubble, and, particularly, after the financial crisis, the amount of value added was allocated differently from the previous pattern—strengthening the net asset position and dividend payments, and curtailing increases in wages. Companies' priorities for the allocation of value added changed greatly with the outbreak of the financial crisis, and the change may have become irreversible.

Are Effects of External Factors Relevant to the Continuation of a Defensive Attitude Concerning Labor Cost Restraint?

What is the reason for the stance of companies toward restraining labor costs, which appears to be almost unceasing? Is it because of an irrational excessively defensive mindset? Or is it the outcome of rational choice? As with investment restraint, let us look at the effects of external factors.

Predisposition to Low Inflation of the Japanese Economy

Figure 6.36 shows developments in average nominal wage (1990 = 100) for five advanced countries. It is only Japan, among these advanced countries, which has experienced stagnation and decline in nominal wages. The rate of increase in hourly earnings (manufacturing) for Japan, as shown in

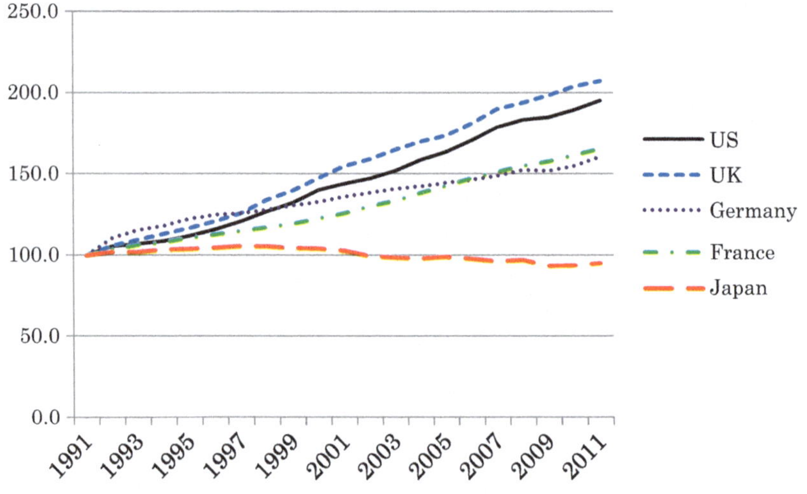

Fig. 6.36 Annual average wage (1991 = 100). Source: OECD Economic Outlook Database

Fig. 6.37, has been significantly low, as compared with other countries. This may be the result of companies' responses to excessive employment, but whether there were other factors causing decline in wages needs to be examined.

Figure 6.38 shows the annual rate of change in CPI (excluding food and energy) for the OECD average and Japan. The rate of change in CPI (excluding food and energy) in Japan has been lower than the OECD average by more than four percentage points, on average, since the latter half of the 1970s. To reiterate, Japan had a significantly lower inflation rate, as compared with other advanced countries, for the last few decades, and its inflation rate was declining almost consistently and approaching zero.

Background of the Predisposition to Low Inflation of the Japanese Economy—International Competition with Cost Restraint

What is the background of such a predisposition to low inflation of the Japanese economy? It may be due to the long-lasting yen appreciation (that reduces prices of imports) and the increase in low-priced imports from emerging market economies (import penetration). In addition to these factors, evolution of export price may have been relevant. Figure 6.39 shows

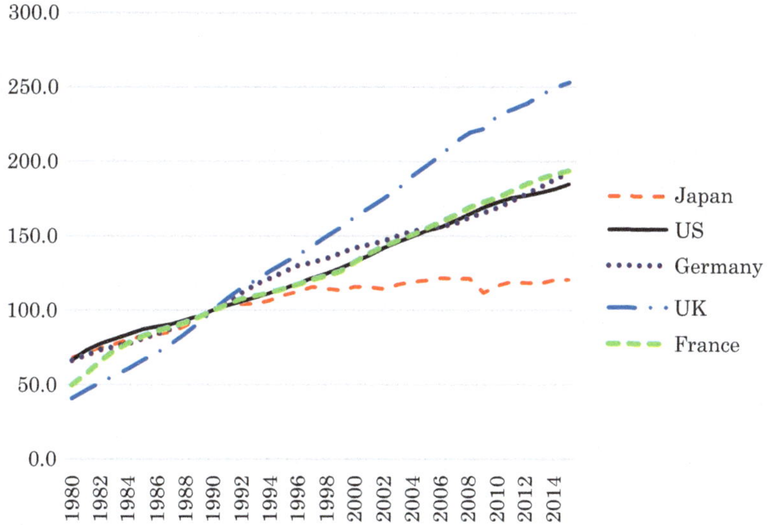

Fig. 6.37 Hourly earnings (manufacturing) (1990 = 100). Source: OECD

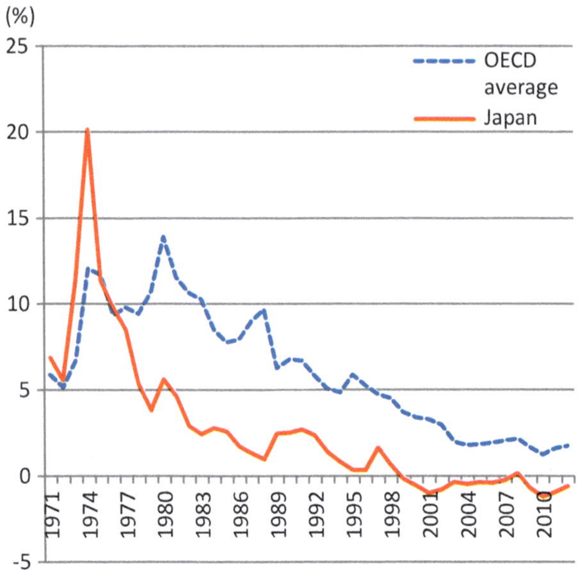

Fig. 6.38 Annual rate of increase in CPI (excluding food, energy). Source: OECD

Fig. 6.39 Export price index (yen base) (2015 = 100). Source: Bank of Japan

developments in the export price index (yen base, 2015 = 100). Export price has been largely on the decline since the 1980s.[14]

Such a continuous decline in export price (yen base) suggests that, in addition to the effects of technological progress, the pricing behavior of export industries focused on restraint of export prices in the situation of intensifying competitive pressure from emerging market economies and continuous yen appreciation. Restraint on export prices by export industries, which are leading industries in Japan, depressed prices of intermediate inputs and wages.

As we have seen, wage restraint has continued even after excess employment was eliminated by the mid-2000s. The continuing restraint may reflect the long-held company goal of maintaining international competitiveness through cost reduction, with labor cost reduction through wage restraint and replacement of regular with non-regular workers offering a very effective tool to accomplish this aim.

However, competition through such cost reduction seems to have placed Japanese economy in a more difficult position. The terms of trade on domestic production of manufacturers (output deflator / input deflator) has been deteriorating since the 2000s, and this development has made it more difficult to make profits, further depressing wages (Fig. 6.40).

Such a tendency is most articulated in electric machinery industries, which suffered significant decline in the output deflator. These developments in terms of trade were the outcome of companies' behavior in internationally competitive environments, but at the same time, worked as an impetus to expand low cost production abroad and to reduce domestic production. For the production of goods that can be easily standardized, international competition through cost restraint may have ceased to be an effective strategy, as Japan is a high-wage economy (Fig. 6.41).

Despite such efforts for exports price restraint, Japan's export share in world exports has declined significantly since the 1990s. This reflects decline in competitiveness and/or a shift of production bases abroad through foreign direct investment.

However, other industrial countries have also lost their share in world exports, with the rise of emerging market economies, particularly China,

[14] In terms of the rate of change, the average rate of change vis-à-vis previous year of Japan's export price index (yen base, monthly) over the period from January 1976 to December 2013 was −1.2%.

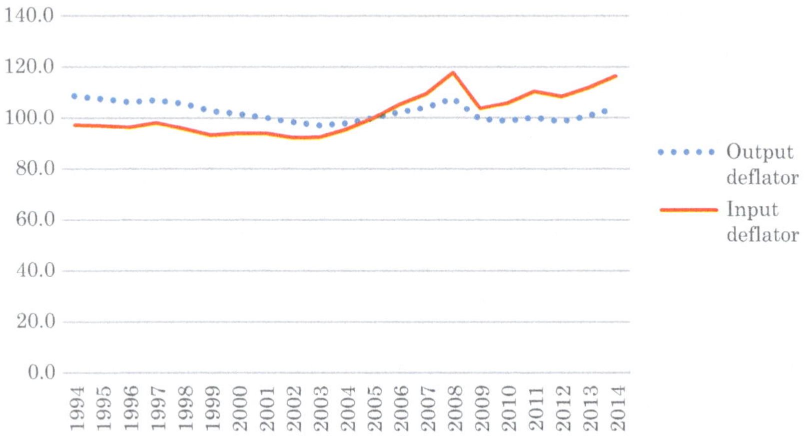

Fig. 6.40 Developments in terms of trade (output deflator and input deflator): manufacturing (2005 = 100). Source: Cabinet Office, GDP Statistics

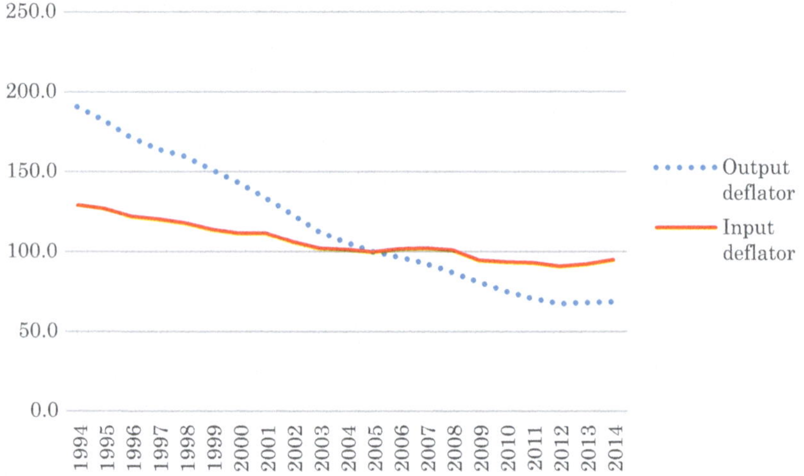

Fig. 6.41 Developments in terms of trade (output deflator and input deflator): electric machinery (2005 = 100). Source: Cabinet Office GDP Statistics

and therefore, the declining export share is not a phenomenon unique to Japan. Deterioration in Japan's export performance has been brought about partly by the rapid industrialization of the Chinese economy (Fig. 6.42).

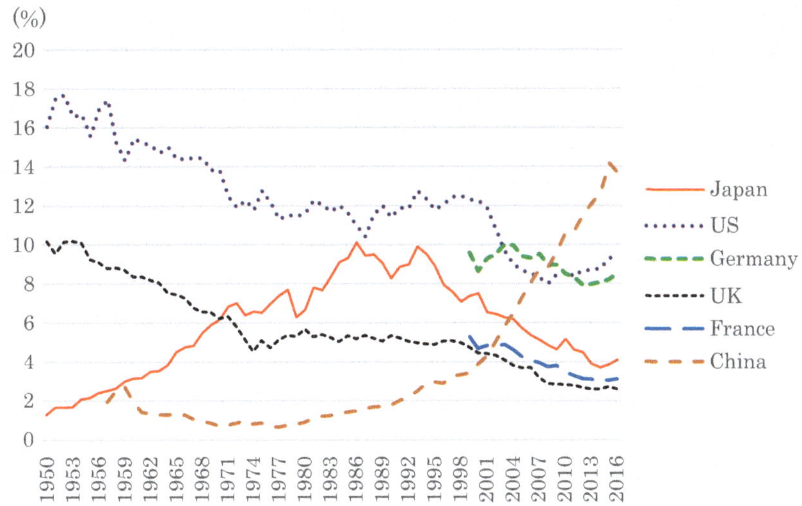

Fig. 6.42 Share of G5 and China in world exports. Source: IMF, "Direction of Trade"

Wage Restraint Coupled with Low Interest Rate and Consumption

In this subsection, we examine how wage restraints have affected consumption. Reduction in nominal wages, decline in the number of regular workers, and their replacement with non-regular workers have brought about a decline in employment income beginning in the 1990s. Although increasing in recent years, the total amount of employment income has declined by 13.1 trillion yen (equivalent to 4.9% of the total employment income in FY 1994 (i.e., the earliest year that GDP statistics with base year=2011 covers)) from FY 1994 to FY 2014. When compared to FY 1997, which was before the effects of the financial crisis had arisen, the reduction in the total employment income from FY 1997 to FY 2014 amounts to 26.5 trillion yen (equivalent to 4.7% of the total employment income in FY 1997) (Fig. 6.43).

Let us further look at interest income as an income source for households other than employment income. Due to the low-interest rate policy after the burst of the bubble, net interest received (interest received − interest paid) by households significantly declined. It declined by 12.9 trillion yen from 14.1 trillion yen in FY 1994 to 1.2 trillion yen in FY 2013, that is, a 91.4% decline from the level in FY 1994 (Fig. 6.44).

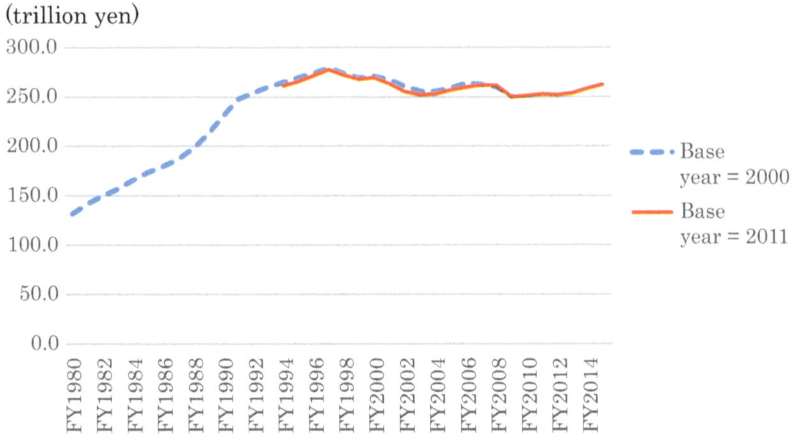

Fig. 6.43 Employment income. Source: Cabinet Office, GDP statistics

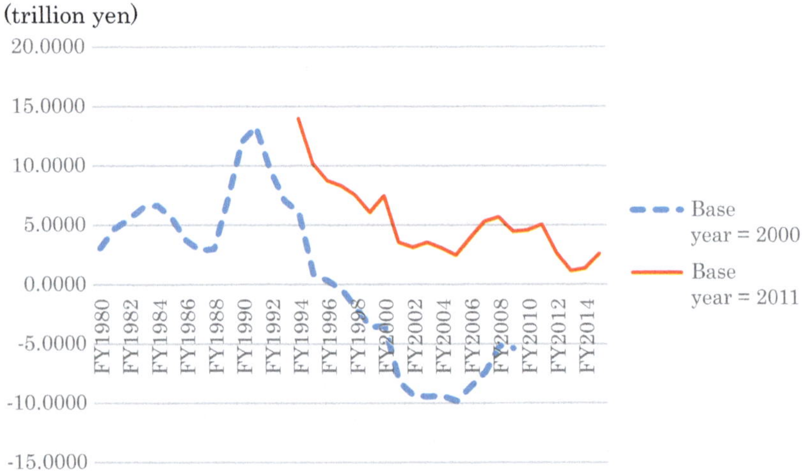

Fig. 6.44 Net interest received by households. Source: Cabinet Office, GDP statistics

The combined amount of employment income and net interest received by households declined by 31.1 trillion yen (25.4 trillion yen of employment income + 5.6 trillion yen of net interest received), or by 10.8% from the peak in FY 1997 to the bottom in FY 2012 (Fig. 6.45).

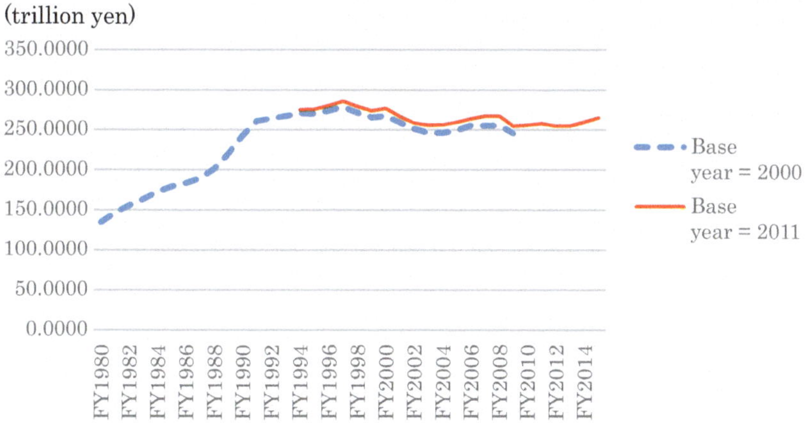

Fig. 6.45 Employment income + net interest received by household. Source: Cabinet Office, GDP

Let us look at developments in consumption. The ratio of household consumption to household income[15] was in the lower 70% range from the 1980s to the beginning of 1990s. It started to rise from the mid-1990s, exceeded 80% at the end of the 1990s, rose over 90% in the 2010s, and reached a peak of 91.5% in 2013 (Fig. 6.46).

At the same time, as we saw in Fig. 4.32, the household savings ratio, which was approximately 12–13% until mid-1990s, sharply declined thereafter, dropping below 10% at the end of the 1990s, and falling to −0.7% in 2013 (it has recovered somewhat since, but it is still at a low level, 5.1% in 2015).

Effects of Terms of Trade Deterioration

In this way, the decline in both employment income and interest received has made it difficult for consumption to increase. In addition to these factors, deterioration in terms of trade may have contributed to the erosion of real income. As shown in Fig. 6.47, Japan's export price index (yen base)

[15] The ratio of household consumption to household income is defined as the ratio of final consumption expenditure of households to the combined amount of nominal income of households, including employment income, property income such as net interest received, and operating surplus and mixed income (that is, personal business income).

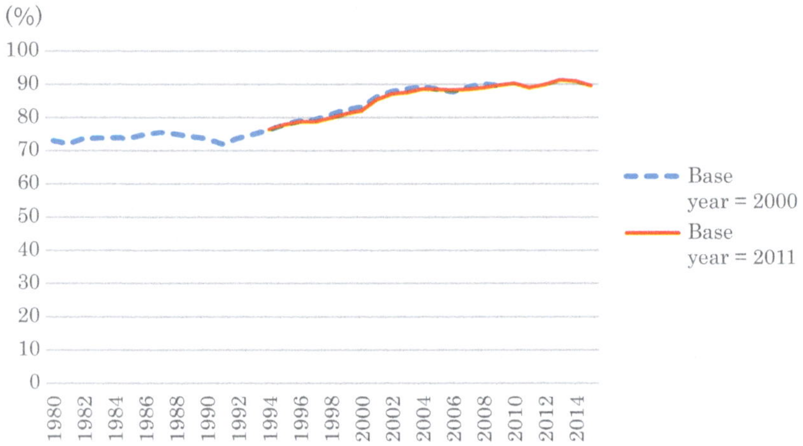

Fig. 6.46 Ratio of nominal household consumption to household income (including personal business income). Source: Cabinet Office, GDP statistics

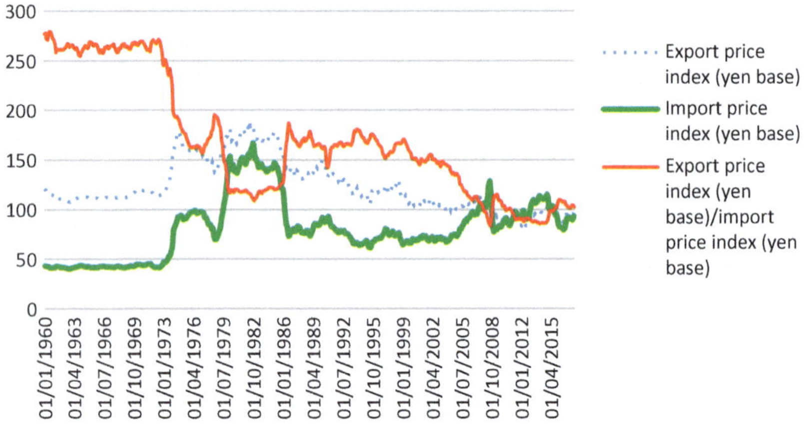

Fig. 6.47 Export price, import price, and terms of trade (2015 = 100). Source: Bank of Japan

has been declining since the mid-1980s. By contrast, Japan's import price index (yen base) had been stable from mid-1980s but increased substantially from the mid-2000s. Reflecting such developments in export and import prices, the terms of trade (export price index/import price index) followed a declining trend from the beginning of the 1970s. It tended to be stable from the 1980s but very rapidly deteriorated from the latter half of 1990s.

A deterioration of the terms of trade may bring about a decline in real wages, as indicated in the equation here, which is derived from the definition of the real wages:

$$W / CPI(\text{real wages}) = (WN / Y)(y / N)(d / CPI)$$
$$= (\text{labor share}) \times (\text{labor productivity}) \times (\text{the ratio of GDP deflator to CPI})$$

Where

W = nominal wage per worker
CPI = consumer price index
N = total number of workers
Y = nominal GDP
y = real GDP
d = GDP deflator

Even if the labor share (WN/Y) and the labor productivity (y/N) are kept unchanged, real wages decline if the GDP deflator declines more than the CPI. A deterioration in terms of trade (export price/import price) lowers the GDP deflator/CPI ratio, because a rise in import prices is reflected in the CPI but not in GDP deflator, and a decline in export prices is reflected not in the CPI but in the GDP deflator. A decline in the GDP deflator/CPI ratio makes an increase in nominal GDP (and, therefore, nominal wages) smaller than an increase in CPI, thereby reducing real wages. A stagnation in real wages in the 2000s could have been brought about by the deterioration in the terms of trade. We saw in Chap. 4 that the growth contribution of private consumption has been declining since the 2000s. The consistent decline in real wages due to factors including deterioration in the terms of trade seems to be among the causes of such decline.

3 Summary of the Causes of Deflation and Long Stagnation

This chapter tried to find a mechanism of long stagnation and deflation, drawing on corporate behaviors indicated in the examination of combined financial statements of the corporate sector as a whole. What we have found are as follows.

After the collapse of the bubble at the beginning of the 1990s, the total amount of the sales of the corporate sector stopped growing suddenly and subsequently started to decline. However, the amount of wages paid in total continued to increase for some time before flattening around the mid-1990s, which depressed the operating profits. The non-operational profits started to improve from the beginning of the 1990s, and reflecting this improvement, the current profits that include non-operational profits recovered into a rising trend at the end of the 1990s. However, different from the pattern up to the 1980s, improvements in current profits ceased to be reflected in an increase in wages. This new pattern has been maintained in and after the 2000s.

On the assets and liability side, the corporate sector expanded the size of its assets and liabilities from the mid-1980s at a pace far faster than the trend at that time indicated. Growth of assets and liabilities decelerated beginning in the 1990s, and the assets and liabilities started to shrink from the mid-1990s. Liabilities stopped declining at the beginning of the 2000s and stayed flat thereafter. By contrast, assets began a rising trend in the 2000s. However, physical assets, such as structures and machinery, consistently followed a declining trend from the latter half of the 1990s. The increase in assets was supported by an increase in securities held for investment purposes, and a substantial part of the increase of the latter was accounted for by outward FDI.

Developments in the net asset position indicate that the corporate sector started to rapidly strengthen its net asset position mainly through earned surplus from around the time of the financial crisis.

Drawing on these observations, this book contended that the stagnant period after the burst of the bubble may be divided into three stages: the first stage of stagnation preceding the financial crisis (called the "Period of passive response" based on corporate behavior), the second stage of stagnation after the financial crisis ("Period of crisis response"), and the third stage of stagnation since the mid-2000s ("Period of continued defensiveness"). The mechanism of stagnation in each of these three stages is explained here.[16]

In the first stage of stagnation after the burst of the bubble and before the financial crisis, stock adjustment conducted by the corporate sector that tried to address excessive investment in the bubble period brought about investment restraint. However, disposition of excessive assets did not progress in this period. On the contrary, as the period of low growth lengthened, the expected growth rate was adjusted downward, which further lowered the level of necessary (optimum) asset size. In other words, the size of excess assets increased, and this resulted in the lengthening of time of investment restraint.

Furthermore, in this period, even as sales stopped growing, the amount of wages continued to increase for some time, resulting in a rapid increase in the share of labor costs in value added. On both fronts—removal of excess assets and restraint on labor costs—response of the corporate sector was passive or inactive in this period.

In the second stage of stagnation (called the "Period of crisis response," based on corporate behavior) that started with the financial crisis, the corporate sector, faced with the outbreak of the crisis and the sharp tightening of lending by financial institutions, started to forcefully remove excessive assets and liabilities, reduce labor costs and other expenses such as interest payments, and strongly strengthen their financial positions through earned surplus. The corporate sector completed elimination of excess assets, excess liabilities, and excess employment by the mid-2000s. Through this process in the second stage, the economy continued to stagnate.

What is unique about Japan's long stagnation is the fact that, despite the corporate sector strengthening its balance sheets and proceeding with removal of excess employment after the financial crisis, as well as eliminating excess assets, excess liabilities, and excess employment, thereby removing the negative legacy of the bubble by the mid-2000s, the defensive attitude of companies to restrain investment and wages continued and led the economy to the third stage of stagnation ("Period of continued defensiveness"). Results of the examination in this chapter that sought to capture the mechanism of this third period are summarized here:

[16] Images of the stagnation mechanism in each of the first, second, and third stages are given in the supplement to this chapter.

There are two views on the motivation for the continuation of investment restraint. In one view, it is construed that the investment restraint was brought about by an irrationally defensive mindset of companies, which had been deeply ingrained as a result of the long-lasting low growth. From the other perspective, the investment restraint was viewed as the result of a rational choice made by companies to shift the production base to overseas, reflecting, one, low growth of the domestic economy over an extended period of time, and, two, a difference in profitability between domestic and foreign operations.

As for wages, the labor income share rose to an unprecedented high level in the first stage of stagnation. After the financial crisis, the corporate sector drastically changed its stance and rapidly proceeded with labor cost reduction through reduction of nominal wages of regular workers and their replacement with non-regular workers. As a result, excess employment was eliminated by the mid-2000s. However, wage restraint continued. This may have occurred because the labor cost reduction, through reduction of nominal wages of regular workers and their replacement with non-regular workers who were paid lower wages, could be utilized as an effective tool in competition through further cost reduction, even after the excess employment had been eliminated. This corporate behavior may have been influenced by pricing behavior that is, long-term restraint on export prices, which has been long employed by companies during the yen appreciation and faced with international competition.

With the continued wage restraint and the reduction in interest received by households under the low-interest policy, the ratio of household consumption to household income continued to rise and the savings ratio of households became negative. Due to deterioration in the terms of trade from the 2000s, the real wages further declined, making it difficult to expect a greater growth contribution from consumption.

The Japanese economy returned to a normal situation from the mid-2000s, after overcoming the negative legacy of the bubble and shocks of the financial crisis. Under these circumstances, the corporate sector still continued to restrain investment and wages. These defensive behaviors, together with the effects of the resultant decline in nominal wages and structuralized shortage of domestic demand, seem to have brought about continued deflation. Deflation itself in turn had depressing effects on the economy, by lowering sales expectations held by companies for the future and by rewarding defensive behavior of risk avoidance (for example, holding cash rather than investing). A vicious cycle might have been at work in which competition through cost reduction by companies could lead to restraint on wages, to stagnant consumption, and in turn to a stagnant domestic economy, depressing sales growth expectations, and then leading to restraint on domestic investment and further competition through cost reduction.

Cost reduction that is rational at a micro level may have been producing stagnation of the whole economy and imposing negative impacts on the companies.

No matter whether such continued restraint on investment and wages by companies is due to an excessively defensive mindset or the outcome of rational choice, it has been bringing about continuous shortage of domestic demand (with increase in trade dependence and rising external vulnerability) and restraint on domestic investment (with resultant decline in potential growth rate[17]). Structuralized domestic demand shortage and investment restraint may be the two most important problems that the Japanese economy developed after excesses were removed and impacts of the financial crisis were overcome.

Considering the current situation seems to be governed by the structuralized defensive attitude that has a certain degree of self-fulfilling nature, what should be done? In the next chapter, we will examine policies of the current administration (Abenomics) and assess what has been done and what needs to be done.

[17] Particularly due to restraint on investment in physical assets over an extended period of time, it is possible that supply capacity of companies may have been significantly reduced, leading to a decline of potential growth rate. The potential growth rate of Japanese economy estimated by the Cabinet Office declined from 4.4% in the 1980s, to 1.9% in the 1990s, and further, to 0.7% in the 2000s. Thereafter, it has risen somewhat, and it was estimated to be 1.0% as of second quarter of 2017.

Supplement

Mechanism of the Three Stages of Stagnation

(1) Mechanism of the first stage of stagnation (from the collapse of the bubble until just before the financial crisis: 1991–1997)

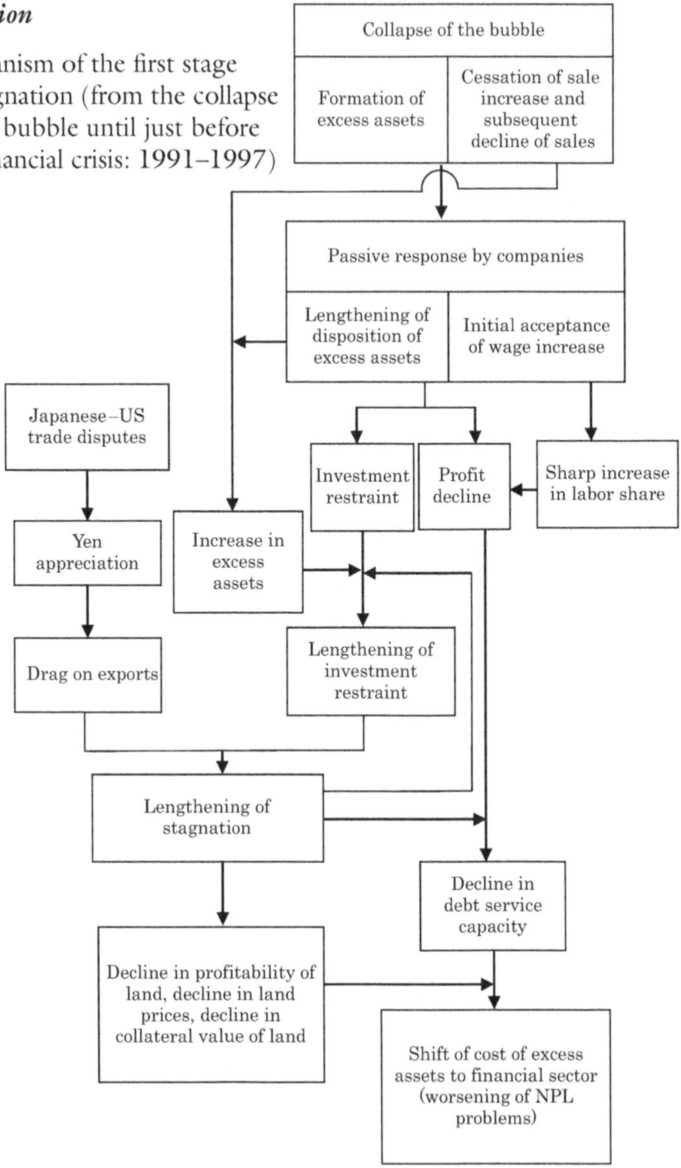

(2) Mechanism of the second stage of stagnation (from the financial crisis to the elimination of excess assets: 1998–first half of the 2000s)

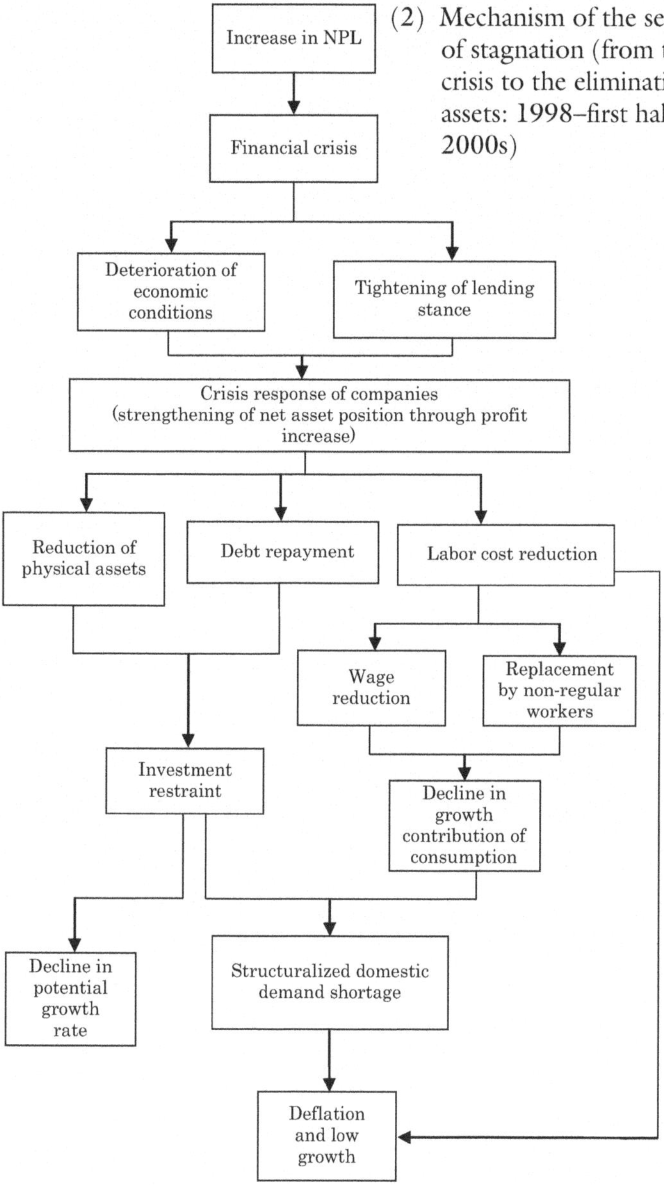

(3) Mechanism of the third stage of stagnation (from the elimination of excess assets to present: mid-2000s–present)

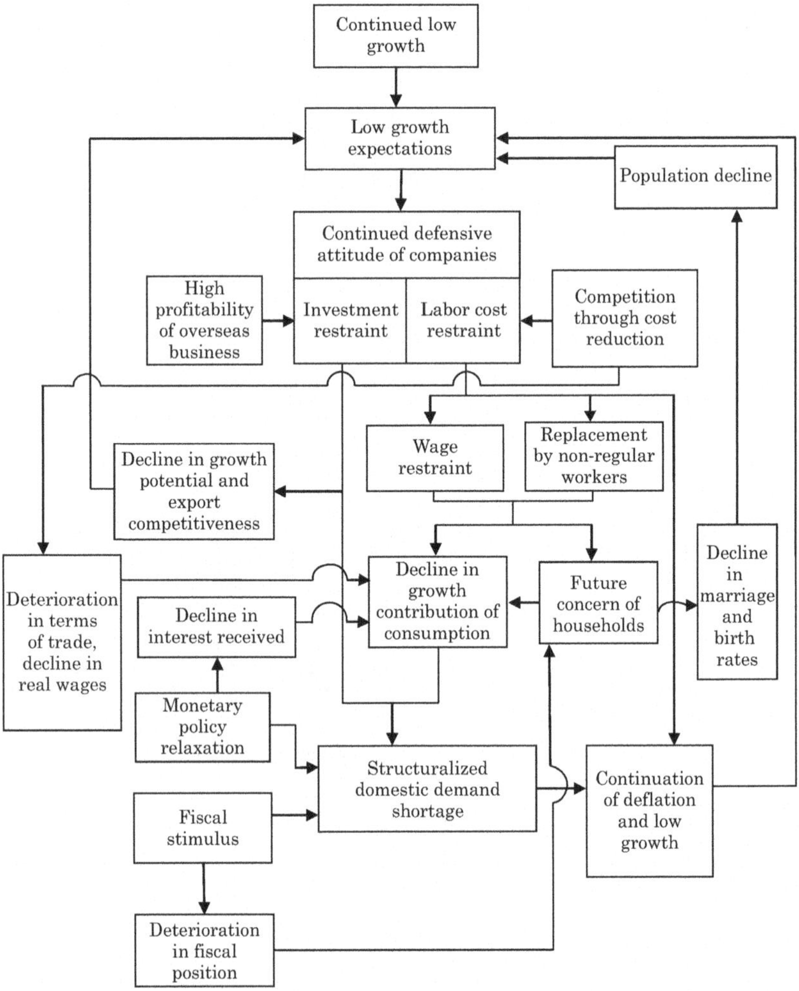

GDP Gap, Nominal Wages, and CPI

As shown in Fig. 6.48, nominal wages (year-on-year change) appear to move with the GDP gap (in percent of potential GDP). It seems most probable that efforts by companies to reduce cost under stagnant economic conditions have brought about decline in wages (Fig. 6.48).

Developments in nominal wages also appear to be correlated with developments in the CPI. It seems possible that economic stagnation has brought about reduction in nominal wages, which led to reduction in the CPI (Fig. 6.49).

Demographic Interpretation

Another interpretation of stagnation relates to demography. In 2010, a small book entitled *The True Origin of Deflation* (Motani 2010) became a bestseller. Motani's contention is that the demographic change, in particular, the absolute decrease in the working age population, which

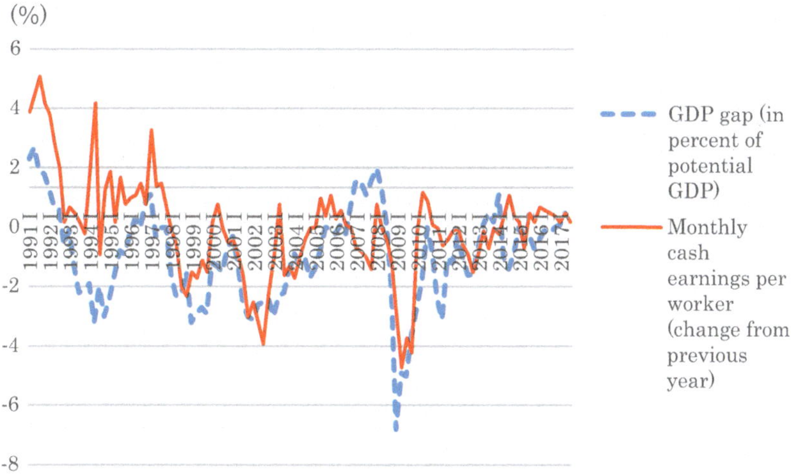

Fig. 6.48 GDP gap and changes of monthly cash earnings per worker from previous year. Source: Cabinet Office, Ministry of Health, Labor, and Welfare, "Monthly Employment Survey"

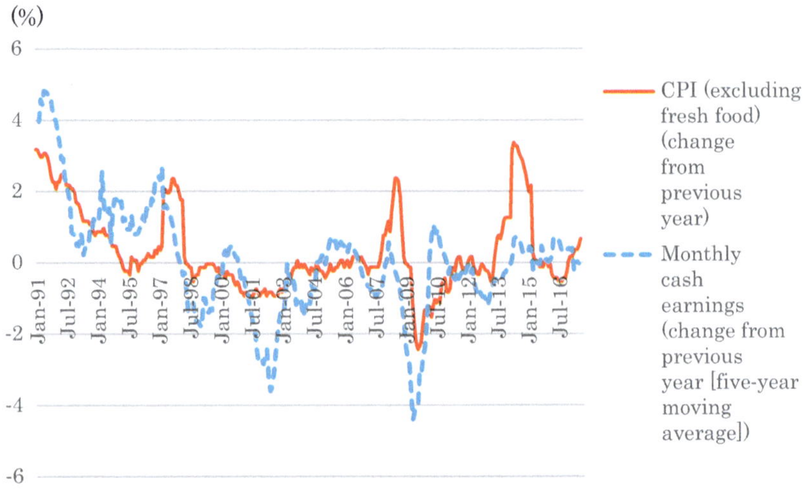

Fig. 6.49 Nominal wage and Consumer Price Index (excluding fresh food) (changes from previous year). Note: Nominal wage = total cash earning per employee (in the establishments with five or more employees). Source: Statistics Bureau of Japan, Ministry of Health, Labor, and Welfare, "Monthly labor survey"

began in 1996, reduces domestic demand, making business conditions for domestic demand-type industries more difficult.[18]

While Motani does not analyze deflation (fall in the general price levels), his simple message, "demography matters," seems to have had significant influence. For example, Bank of Japan (BOJ) Governor Shirakawa said, "Delayed responses to structural changes such as these [the declining birth

[18] Motani (2010, 140) wrote, "As the working age population continues to decline, the domestic demand-type industries, which account for a large part of employment, constantly suffer from excess supply and their business performance will never improve." Examples of demand stagnation in terms of quantity that Motani indicated include the following:

- The number of new cars sold domestically hit a peak in 2000, decreasing thereafter.
- The number of books and magazines sold domestically hit a peak in 1997.
- The quantity of goods transported domestically (weight × distance) hit a peak in fiscal year 2000.
- The quantity of alcoholic beverages sold domestically started to decrease from fiscal year 2002.
- The quantity of tap water used per one person hit a peak in 1997.

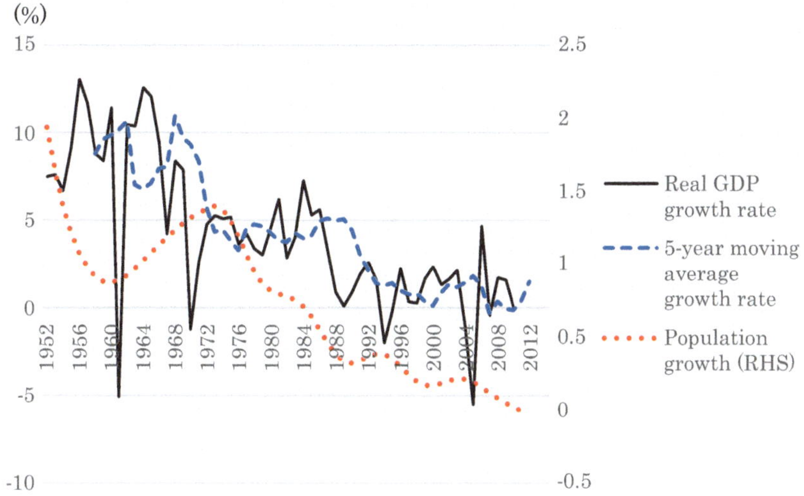

Fig. 6.50 Real GDP growth and population growth (Japan). Source: IMF, OECD

rate and the aging population] and to globalization ... are the fundamental causes of low growth and deflation" (Shirakawa 2012b).[19]

We look next at Fig. 6.50. The GDP growth rate may look like this, generally, following population developments in Japan. Does demography determine our future?

However, such a pattern does not seem to be universal. A similar but less clear pattern has been observed in France and the United States (Figs. 6.51 and 6.52), but not in the United Kingdom or in Germany (Figs. 6.53 and 6.54).

A fundamental rebuttal of Motani's argument, or any other arguments that relates demography to the two decade-long stagnation, is that demographic changes proceed only gradually and, therefore, would not be able to produce such an abrupt change as shown by the nominal GDP developments since 1990s in Fig. 6.55. Structural headwinds may be with us, but demographic changes do not wholly explain the long stagnation over two decades from the 1990s. Although it is an issue that warrants thorough examination—how long-term and structural factors such as demography were related to the long stagnation and the current condi-

[19] Shirakawa (2012a) further states, "In the 1990s, low growth was mainly brought about by the deleveraging associated with the unprecedented bursting of the bubble. In the 2000s and thereafter, the major causes of low growth in Japan have been rapid population aging and population decline."

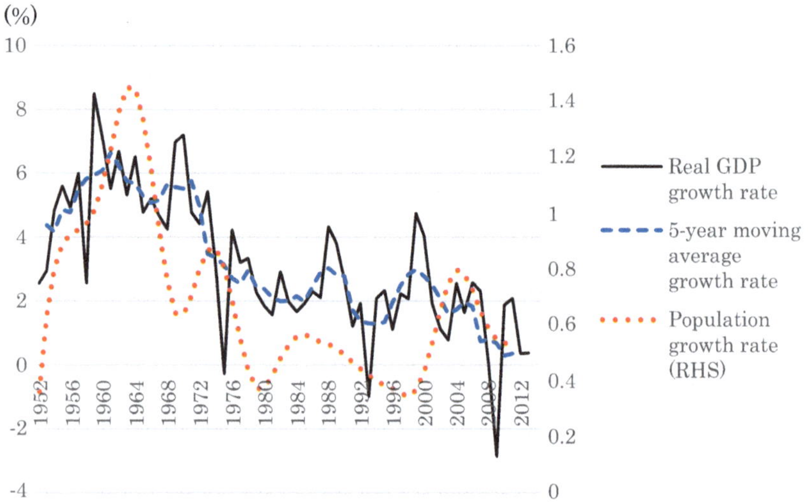

Fig. 6.51 Real GDP growth and population growth (France). Source: IMF, OECD

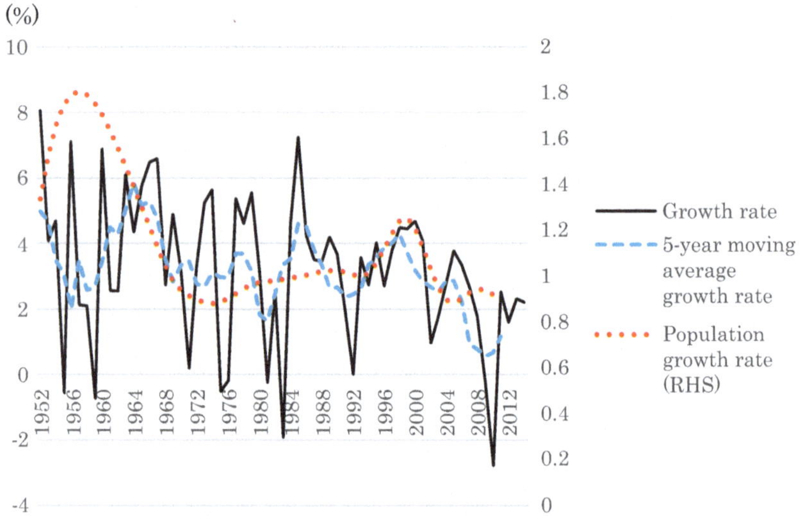

Fig. 6.52 Real GDP growth and population growth (US). Source: IMF, OECD

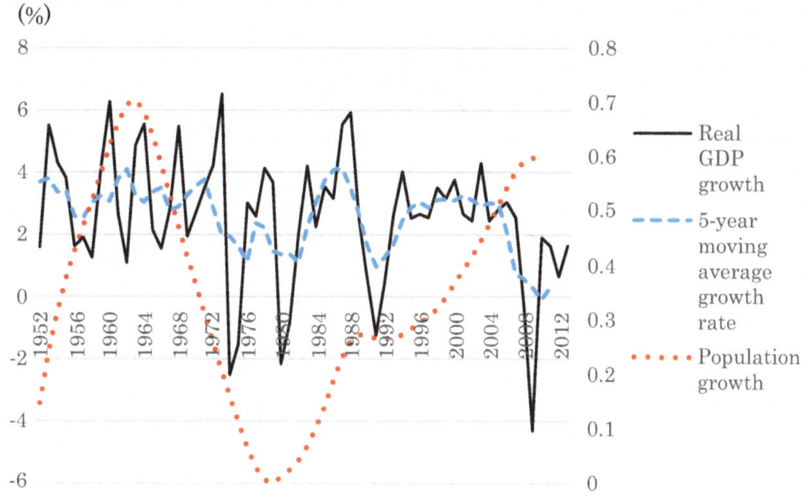

Fig. 6.53 Real GDP growth and population growth (United Kingdom). Source: IMF, OECD

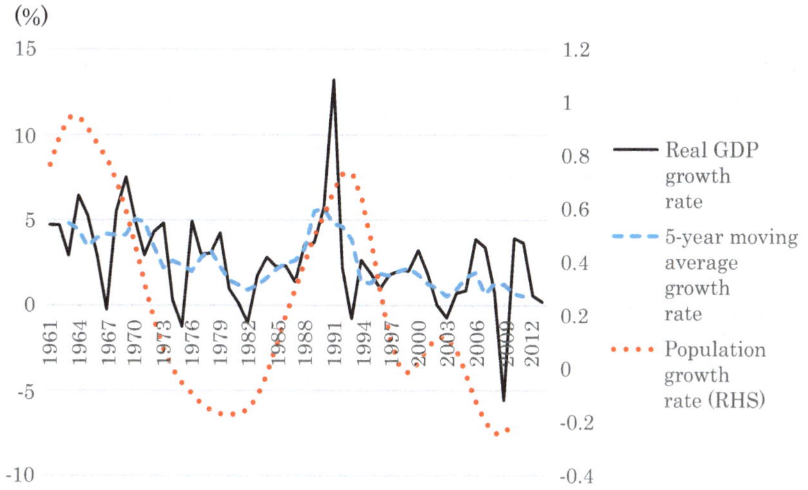

Fig. 6.54 Real GDP growth and population growth (Germany). Source: IMF, OECD

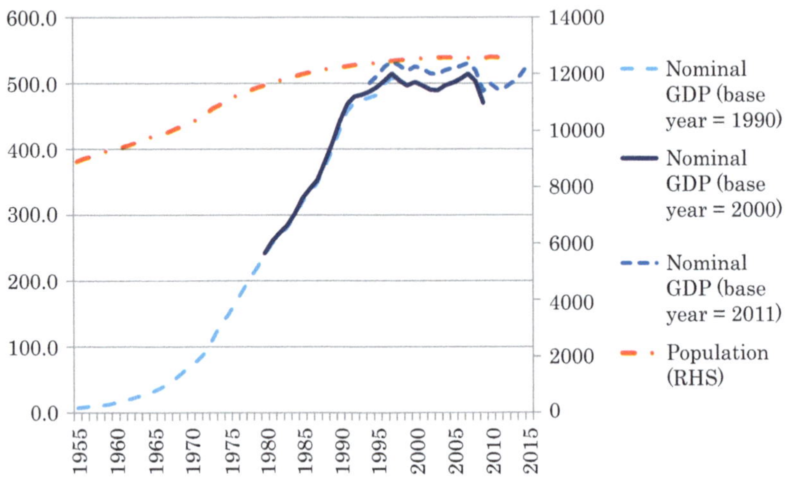

Fig. 6.55 Nominal GDP and population. Source: Ministry of Health, Labor, and Welfare, "Vital Statistics Report"; Cabinet Office, GDP statistics

tions of the economy—resorting to such factors does not seem to contribute to the understanding of the mechanism of the stagnation, which started abruptly and subsequently eternalized (Fig. 6.55).

Bibliography

English References

IMF (2014) "Japan 2014 Article IV Consultation- Staff Report; and Press Release," July.

Kang, Joong Shik (2014) "Balance Sheet Repair and Corporate Investment in Japan" *IMF Working Paper* WP/14/141, International Monetary Fund, Asian and Pacific Department.

Katz, Richard (1998) *Japan: The System that Soured: The Rise and Fall of the Japanese Economic Miracle.* Armonk, NY: M.E. Sharpe.

Shirai, Sayuri (2012) "Jinko Dotai no Henka ha Wagakuni no Makuro Keizai ni Eikyo wo Ataete Irunoka?" (Have Demographic Changes Affected Japan's Macroeconomic Performance?) September 7.

Shirakawa, Masaaki (2012a) "Deleveraging and Growth: Is the Developed World Following Japan's Long and Winding Road?" Lecture at the London School of Economics and Political Science, co-hosted by the Asia Research Center and STICERD, LSE, January 10.

Shirakawa, Masaaki (2012b) "Japan's economy and monetary policy," June 4, Bank of Japan.

Japanese References

Aoshima, Yaichi, Akira Takeishi, and Michael A. Cusumano (2010) *Meido in Japan ha Owaru noka* (Is Made in Japan to End?) Toyo Keizai Shimpo Sha.

Economic Planning Agency (1993) *Heisei 5 nen Nenji Keizai Hokoku* (1993 Annual Economic Report).

Bank of Japan (1994) "Heisei 5 nendo no Kinnyu oyobi Keizai no Doko" (Financial and Economic Developments in FY 1993). In *Chosa Geppo*, BOJ, June.

Bank of Japan (1998) "Change of the Guideline for Money Market Operations," September 9, Bank of Japan.

Bank of Japan (2001) "Saikin no Ginko Kashidashi Shijo no Doko nituite" (Recent Developments in Bank Credit Markets) October, *Market Review* 2001-J-10.

Bank of Japan (2003a) *Keizai Bukka no Shorai Tenbo to Risuku Hyoka* (Future Outlook of the Economy and Price and Risk Assessment) April.

Bank of Japan (2003b) *Keizai Bukka no Shorai Tenbo to Risuku Hyoka* (Future Outlook of the Economy and Price and Risk Assessment) October.

Bank of Japan (2004a) *Keizai Bukka no Shorai Tenbo to Risuku Hyoka* (Future Outlook of the Economy and Price and Risk Assessment) April.

Bank of Japan (2004b) *"Keizai Bukka no Shorai Tenbo to Risuku Hyoka"* (Future Outlook of the Economy and Price and Risk Assessment) October.

Bank of Japan (2005a) *Keizai Bukka no Shorai Tenbo to Risuku Hyoka* (Future Outlook of the Economy and Price and Risk Assessment) April.

Bank of Japan (2005b) "Wagakuni Kigyo niyoru Yurishi Fusai no Asshuku to Rieki Bunpai Saku" (Reduction of Interest-bearing Debt by Japanese Companies and Profit Distribution Policy) May, *Nichigin Review* 2005-J-7.

Bank of Japan (2005c) *Keizai Bukka no Shorai Tenbo to Risuku Hyoka* (Future Outlook of the Economy and Price and Risk Assessment) October.

Bank of Japan (2009a) *Kinnyu Keizai Geppo* (Monthly Financial and Economic Report) February.

Bank of Japan (2009b) "Kigyo Shueki no Kaizen to sono Nihon Keizai heno Ganni" (Improvements in Corporate Profits and Its Implications to Japanese Economy), September 20, Research and Statistics Department.

Bank of Japan (2012) "*Nihon no Jinko Dotai to Chuchoki tekina Seichoryoku: Jijitsu to Ronten no Seiri*" (Japan's Demography and Medium and Long-term Growth Potential: Facts and Issues), August, Research and Statistics Department.

Cabinet Office (2014) "Senzai Seichoritsu ni tuite (Chuchoki, Makuroteki Kanten karano Bunseki ①)" (On the potential growth rate (Analysis from mid- to long-term and macro economic viewpoints [1]), February 14, Heisei 26 http://www5.cao.go.jp/keizai-shimon/kaigi/special/future/0214/shiryou_02.pdf (viewed December 11, 2017).

Cabinet Office (2005) *Heisei 17 nendo Nenji Keizai Zaisei Hokoku* (Annual Report on the Japanese Economy and Public Finance FY 2005).

Cabinet Office (2008) *Heisei 20 nendo Nenji Keizai Zaisei Hokoku* (Annual Report on the Japanese Economy and Public Finance FY 2008).

Cabinet Office (2010) *Heisei 22 nendo Nenji Keizai Zaisei Hokoku* (Annual Report on the Japanese Economy and Public Finance FY 2010).

Cabinet Office (2012) *Heisei 24 nenban Kodomo Kosodate Hakusho* (White Paper on Children and Child-Rearing 2012).

Fukao, Kyoji (2012) *Usinawareta 20 nen' to Nihon Keizai – Kozoteki Yoin to Saisei heno Gendoryoku no Kaimei* ('Lost 20 years' and the Japanese economy - Identifying structural factors and the momentum for its revival). Nihon Keizai Shimbun Shuppan Sha.

Fukuda, Shin-ichi (2015) *"Ushinawareta 20 nen wo Koete"* (Beyond 'Lost Two Decades'). NTT Shuppan.

Itami, Takayuki (2006) *Nichi Bei Kigyo no Rieki Ritsu Kakusa* (Discrepancy in Profitability between Japanese and US Companies). Yuhi Kaku.

Kato, Hisakazu (2001) *Jinko Keizaigaku Nyumon* (Introduction to Demographic Economics). Nihon Keizai Hyoron Sha.

Kaufmann, Franz-Xaver (2011) *Shukugen suru Shakai – Jinko Gensho to sono Kiketsu* (Shrinking Society – Population Decline and Its Consequences). Hara Shobo.

Komine, Takao (2007) *Jinko Gen Shoshika Shakai no Mirai* (Future of the Society with Population Shrinkage and the Declining Birth Rate). Akashi Shobo.

Komine, Takao (2010) *Jinko Fuka Shakai* (Society with Demographic Burden). Nihon Keizai Shimbun Sha.

Koo, Richard (2007) *'In' to 'Yo' no Keizai Gaku* (Economics of 'The Sunny Side' and 'The Shadow Side'). Toyo Keizai Shimpo Sha.

Koo, Richard (2008) *Nihon Keizai wo Oou Futatsu no Nami* (Two Waves Hanging over the Japanese Economy). Tokuma Shoten.

Kumon, Takashi (2006) Jinko Defure ha Hajimatte iru (Demographic Deflation Has Already Set in). Toyo Keizai Shimpo Sha.

Matsutani, Akihiko (2004) *'Jinko Gensho Keizai' no Atarashii Koshiki* (A New Formula for 'the Economy with a Shrinking Population'). Nihon Keizai Shimbun Sha.

Ministry of Health, Labor and Welfare (2012) *Heisei 24 nenban Koreika Shakai Hakusho* (2012 White Paper on Ageing Society).

Motani, Kosuke (2010) *Defure no Shotai –Keizai ha Jinko no nami de Ugoku* (True Origin of Deflation: The Economy Moves by the Demographic Waves), Kadokawa One Tema 21.

Nukaga, Makoto (2005) "Juyo Shukusho no Kiki" (Crisis of Demand Shrinkage). NTT Shuppan.

Obuchi, Hiroshi (1997) *Shosika Jidai no Nihon Keizai* (Japanese Economy in the Era of Declining Birth Rate). Nihon Hoso Kyokai.

Obuchi, Hiroshi and Hitoshi Morioka (1981) *Keizai Jinko Gaku* (Economic Demography). Shin Hyoron.

Obuchi, Hiroshi and Hiroyuki Kanekiyo (2005) *Shoshika no Shakai Keizaigaku* (Socioeconomics of the Declining Birth Rate). Hara Shobo.

Obuchi, Hiroshi and Hitoshi Morioka (2006) *Jinko Gensho Jidai no Nihon Keizai* (Japanese Economy in the Era of the Shrinking Population). Hara Shobo.

Ogawa, Kazuo (2009) Baransu Shito no Kison to Jitsubutsu Keizai – 1990 nendai ikono Nihon Keizai no Jissho Bunseki (Damages to the Balance Sheet and the Real Economy – Empirical Analysis of the Japanese Economy since the 1990s). In *Furyo Saiken to Kinnyu Kiki*, (Non-Performing Loans and the Financial Crisis), edited by Kazuto Ikeo, (Cabinet Office "Baburu/defure kino Nihon Keizai to Keizai Seisaku 4" (Japanese Economy and Economic Policy in the Period of Bubble and Deflation 4)). Economic and Social Research Institute, Cabinet Office.

Shimizudani, Satoshi (2005) *Kitai to Fukakujitsu Sei no Keizai Gaku* (Economics of Expectation and Uncertainty). Nihon Keizai Shimbun Sha.

Shirakawa, Masaaki (2010a) "Nihon Keizai to Inobeshon" (Japan's Economy and Innovation) May 31.

Shirakawa, Masaaki (2010b) "Tokushu Sei ka Ruiji Sei ka? –Kinnyu Seisaku Kenkyu wo Meguru Nihon no Baburu Hokaigo no Keiken" (Uniqueness or Similarity?, Japan's Post-Bubble Experience in Monetary Policy Studies), September 16, Bank Of Japan.

Shirakawa, Masaaki (2011) "Kodo Seicho kara Antei Seicho he – Nihon no Keiken to Sinkokoku Keizai heno Ganni" (The Transition from High Growth to Stable Growth: Japan's Experience and Implications for Emerging Economies) May 5.

Shirakawa, Masaaki (2012a) "Derebarejji to Keizai Seicho – Senshinkoku ha Kakoni Nihon ga Ayunda 'Nagaku Magari Kunetta Michi' wo Tadotte Ikunoka" (Deleveraging and Growth: Is the Developed World Following Japan's Long and Winding Road?), January 10.

Shirakawa, Masaaki (2012b) "Saikin no Kinnyu Josei to Kinnyu Seisaku Unnei" (Recent Financial and Economic Developments and Monetary Policy Management) June 4, Bank of Japan.

Shirakawa, Masaaki (2012c) "Jinko Dotai no Henka to Makuro Keizai Pafomansu : Nihon no Keiken kara" (Demographic Changes and Macroeconomic Performance: Japanese Experience) May 30.

Sugihara, Shigeru, and Satoshi Ota (2002) "Shisan Kakaku no Geraku to Kigyo no Baransu Shito Chosei" (Decline in Asset prices and Balance Sheet Adjustments of Corporations). In *Defure no Jissho Bunseki*, (Empirical Analysis of Deflation), edited by Yutaka Harada and Kikuo Iwata, Toyo Keizai Shimpo Sha.

Takayama, Noriyuki, and Osamu Saito (2006) "Shoshika no Keizaigaku" (Economics of the Declining Birth Rate). Toyo Keizai Shimpo Sha.

Tsutani, Noriko, and Yoshio Higuchi (2009) "Jinko Gensho to Nihon Keizai" (Population Decline and the Japanese Economy). Nihon Keizai Shimbun Sha.
Yashiro, Naohiro (2004) *Shoshi Koreika no Keizaigaku* (Economics of the Declining Birth Rate and Aging). Toyo Keizai Shimpo Sha.
Yoshikawa, Hiroshi (2011) "Shoshi Koreika to Keizai Seicho" (The Declining Birth Rate and Aging and Economic Growth). In *Shoshi Koreika no moto deno Keizai Katsuryoku*, (Economic Vitality under the Declining Birth Rate and Aging), edited by Masahisa Fujita and Hiroshi Yoshikawa, Nihon Hyoron Sha.

CHAPTER 7

Abenomics and Challenges for the Japanese Economy

As we have seen in the preceding chapters, the corporate sector, which is the central player in the Japanese economy, assumed a very defensive attitude during the long stagnation and deflation. Such a defensive attitude started in the early 1990s under pressure from the persistence of unprofitable excess assets after the burst of the bubble, and it was drastically strengthened and structuralized in the shock of the financial crisis in the late 1990s. Such structuralized defensiveness has a self-reinforcing nature, whether due to an excessively defensive mindset or to rational choice. Restraint on investment tends to lower growth rate, and therefore, further restraint on investment may be justified. Restraint on labor costs tends to lower consumption, and therefore, resultant stagnation in sales and profits may well justify further restraint on wages. Furthermore, restraint on investment and labor costs could lead to deflation, rewarding risk avoidance (cash holding brings return). Repeated use of fiscal stimuli to support weak growth resulting from the defensive attitude of companies aggravated fiscal position, and may have raised anxiety for the future of households, thus strengthening defensive behavior of households. Expectation of population decline exists as an additional source of concern for both companies and households. Through all these channels, the Japanese economy has been led to an equilibrium governed by low-growth expectation and wariness about the future.

In late 2012, the Liberal Democratic Party (LDP) came back to the power, and Mr. Shinzo Abe, President of the LDP, started his second pre-

K. Aramaki, *Japan's Long Stagnation, Deflation, and Abenomics*,
https://doi.org/10.1007/978-981-13-2176-4_7

miership. He initiated a comprehensive package of economic policies, which was soon dubbed "Abenomics." Initial responses in the markets were quite significant.

We will see in this chapter, first, what the Abenomics is; second, what impacts it has brought about; and, third, whether the core problem of the Japanese economy has been addressed and improved.

1 Abenomics

Start of Abenomics

On November 14, 2012, then Prime Minister (PM) Noda of the Democratic Party (DP) declared in the Parliamentary discussion with Mr. Abe, president of the LDP, that he would dissolve the House of Representatives in two days, that is, on November 16. In the election on December 16, the LDP had won a landslide victory, gaining 294 seats from the pre-election level of 119, out of the total 480 seats, while the DP suffered a crushing defeat of reducing its seats by three-fourths from 230 to 57.

On December 26, 2012, the second Abe administration started and adopted its "Basic Policy" in the first cabinet meeting, in which it was stated about the economy:

A strong economy is the source of Japan's strength. Without its revival, there is no restoration of fiscal soundness nor Japan's future.

Through "three arrows" of bold monetary policy, flexible fiscal policy, and growth strategy that promote private investment, we overcome prolonged deflation, and aim to increase employment.

This is the declaration of the start of Abenomics.

Thoughts behind "three Arrows" are explained as follows:[1]

In order to eliminate a deflationary mindset, bold monetary policy is indispensable (bold monetary policy).

At the same time, the government needs to take a lead in creating demand and ignite the dampened economy (flexible fiscal policy).

However, as the government cannot continue to create demand for an indefinite time, therefore, it is necessary to restore the confidence of

[1] Refer to materials on Abenomics published on the home page of the Prime Minister's office including the manuscript of the press conference by Prime Minister Abe on January 11, 2013 (https://www.kantei.go.jp/).

companies and people for the future and raise private investment (growth strategy).

Following these thoughts, measures have been taken.

First Arrow: Bold Monetary Policy: Kuroda Bazooka (Initial QQE)

On March 20, 2013, Mr. Kuroda, former president of the Asian Development Bank (ADB), took the office of Bank of Japan (BOJ) governor.[2] On April 4, 2013, the BOJ introduced Quantitative and Qualitative Monetary Easing (QQE), which was composed of the following:

"Price Stability Target" of 2%

The BOJ introduced the price stability target of 2% in terms of the year-on-year rate of change in the Consumer Price Index (CPI) (excluding fresh food) and committed to achieve the target in the earliest possible time, with a time horizon of about two years.[3]

"Quantitative and Qualitative Monetary Easing"

To that end, BOJ introduced the QQE, consisting of the following:

The Adoption of the "Monetary Base Control"
Under the QQE, the main operating target for money market operations was changed from the uncollateralized overnight call rate to the monetary base. The BOJ would double the monetary base in two years. The BOJ would conduct money market operations, so that the monetary base will increase at an annual pace of about 60–70 trillion yen.

[2] Governor Kuroda is reported to have said in his inaugural speech to BOJ staff that the BOJ is the only central bank in the world that does not achieve its mission to realize price stability. Governor Kuroda is also reported to have said in his first meeting with BOJ executive staff, "First, you have to believe that you can do it."

[3] The BOJ under the former Governor Shirakawa had already introduced a price stability target of 2% in January 2013. The difference is that the QQE under Governor Kuroda set a time limit for its realization.

An Increase in Japanese Government Bonds Purchasing and Their Maturity Extension
With a view to encouraging a further decline in interest rates across the yield curve, the BOJ will purchase Japanese Government Bonds (JGBs), so that their outstanding amounts will increase at an annual pace of about 50 trillion yen. The BOJ will more than double the average remaining maturity of JGB purchases.

An Increase in Exchange Traded Funds and Japanese Real Estate Investment Trust Purchases
With a view to lowering the risk premium of asset prices, the BOJ will purchase exchange traded funds (ETFs) and Japanese real estate investment trusts (J-REITs), so that their outstanding amounts will increase at an annual pace of 1 trillion yen and 30 billion yen, respectively.

The Continuation of the QQE
The bank will continue with the QQE, as long as it is necessary to achieve the price stability target of 2% and maintain that target in a stable manner.

Strengthening of the QQE
The QQE has been strengthened as follows:

On October 31, 2014, the BOJ announced an expansion of the QQE, which included an increase of the targeted annual increase in base money from the previous amount of 60–70 trillion to 80 trillion yen.

Adoption of Supplementary Measures
On December 18, 2015, the BOJ introduced supplementary measures for the QQE, including lengthening of average remaining maturity of the Bank's JGB purchases (about 7–10 years in 2015 to about 7–12 years from 2016).

Introduction of a Negative Interest Rate
On January 29, 2016, the BOJ decided to introduce a negative interest rate of −0.1% to be applied to a part of the increase in the outstanding balance held by financial institutions in the current account with the BOJ ("QQE with a negative interest rate," effective on February 16, 2016).[4]

[4] The BOJ adopted a three-tier system: (1) an interest rate of +0.1% is applied to the average balance of the current account (less required reserves) during 2015, as before; (2) an

Introduction of Yield Curve Control

On September 21, 2016, the BOJ conducted a comprehensive assessment of the developments in economic activity and prices under "Quantitative and Qualitative Monetary Easing (QQE)" and "QQE with a Negative Interest Rate," as well as their policy effects, and based on the assessment, the BOJ decided to greatly change its policy and introduced "QQE with yield curve control." Under the new policy, the policy target was changed from a previous increase in base money to the short-term interest rate (a negative interest rate of −0.1% applied to a part of the outstanding balance held by financial institutions in the current account with the BOJ) and the long-term interest rate (the BOJ will purchase JGBs, so that ten-year JGB yields will remain more or less at the current level of around 0%).

Deletion of the Outlook on the Timing of Achievement of the 2% Price Stability Target

On April 27, 2018, the BOJ deleted, from its "Outlook for Economic Activity and Prices," submitted to the Monetary Policy Meeting held on the same day, the wording on the timing as to when the 2% price stability target was expected to be achieved, which the BOJ had maintained from the initiation of the QQE in April 2013.[5]

Second Arrow: Flexible Fiscal Policy

Adoption of Fiscal Stimulus

Over the five years since the start of Abenomics, the size of initial budget increased by 7.1 trillion yen or 7.9% from 90.3 trillion yen in fiscal 2012, before Abenomics, to 97.5 trillion yen in fiscal 2017. The rate of increase

interest rate of 0% is applied to the sum of the amount of reserves required and the outstanding amount of certain credit from the BOJ; and (3) a negative interest rate of −0.1% is applied to the outstanding balance in excess of the outstanding balance on (1) and (2) combined. The BOJ estimated that, as of the start of the new system, (1) would be about 210 trillion yen, (2) would be about 40 trillion yen, and if the outstanding balance of the current account increased to 260 trillion yen in February, then the negative interest rate of −0.1% would be applied to 10 trillion yen.

[5] At the start of the QQE, the BOJ stated in the "Outlook for Economic Activity and Prices" (April 26, 2013) that the 2% price stability target would be reached toward the latter half of the projection period (FY 2013–FY2015). Its outlook for the timing of the achievement of the target had been postponed six times before the wording itself was deleted in April 2018. In the monetary policy statement released on September 21, 2016, which introduced the yield curve control, objectives were stated as achieving the price stability target of 2% at the earliest possible time, with no mention of the specific timing of the achievement. The only occasion where the time limit for the achievement of 2% target was mentioned in the policy statement was when the original QQE was introduced on April 4, 2013.

vis-à-vis the previous year was 2.5% and 3.5% for fiscal years 2013 and 2014, respectively, but it has been contained to a level less than 1% for subsequent years. By contrast, during the period of less than five years, economic stimulus packages were compiled four times. Outlines of the packages are described here.[6]

On January 11, 2013, the government decided on "the Emergency Economic Measures for the Revival of Japan's Economy," with the central government expenditure amounting to 10.3 trillion yen and the expected impact on real GDP at about 2%. The focus is placed on the quickness of effects and demand creating impacts such as public work, including recovery from the Great Earthquake.

On December 5, 2013, the government decided on "The Economic Measures for Realization of Virtuous Cycles," with the central government expenditure amounting to 5.5 trillion yen and the expected impact on real GDP at around 1%.

On December 27, 2014, the government adopted "the Immediate Economic Measures for Extending Virtuous Cycles to Local Economies," with additional central government expenditure amounting to 3.5 trillion yen and expected contribution to real GDP growth at about 0.7%.

On August 2, 2016, the government adopted "Economic Measures for Realizing Investment for the Future," with additional central government expenditure of 13.5 trillion yen and expected short-term contribution to real GDP growth at about 1.3%.

Increase in Consumption Tax Rate and Treatment of Fiscal Consolidation

On January 22, 2013, the Cabinet Office, Ministry of Finance, and the Bank of Japan released the "Joint Statement of the Government and the Bank of Japan on Overcoming Deflation and Achieving Sustainable Economic Growth," to strengthen coordination between the government and the Bank of Japan. In the joint statement, it was clearly stated, "the Government will steadily promote measures aimed at establishing a sustainable fiscal structure with a view to ensuring the credibility of fiscal management."

On June 14, 2013, the government decided on "Basic Policy on Economic and Fiscal Management and Reform 2017—Overcoming Deflation and Revitalizing the Economy," which set it as a goal "to halve

[6] On the settlement basis, which includes supplementary budgets, after the size increased by 3.2% from 97.1 trillion yen in fiscal 2012 to 100.0 trillion yen in fiscal 2013, it declined somewhat. It was 97.5 trillion yen in fiscal 2016, slightly greater by 0.5% from fiscal 2012.

the size of primary balance[7] deficit (in GDP) of the central and local governments by fiscal 2015, as compared with fiscal 2010, to make the primary balance in surplus by fiscal 2020, and to aim at reducing steadily the size of outstanding debt (in GDP) thereafter." The primary balance deficit of central and local governments (in GDP) declined to −3.0%, achieving the target of halving the deficits from the level of fiscal 2010 (−6.6%).

Furthermore, Japan included the aforementioned fiscal consolidation goals in the "St. Petersburg Action Plan," adopted at the G20 summit meeting held in St. Petersburg, Russia, in September 2013.

On October 1, 2013, the government decided to raise the consumption tax rate from current 5% to 8% from April 1, 2014, as scheduled, which was the first increase of the rate in last 17 years. At the same time, the government decided to compile an economic package ("The Economic Measures for Realization of Virtuous Cycles") to cope with the risk of economic downturn caused by a reactionary fall in demand after the last minute surge before the rate increase.

On April 1, 2014, the consumption tax rate was increased from 5% to 8%. Then, the economy recorded negative growth in the second and third quarters consecutively, due to factors including reactionary demand fall after the last minute surge.

In November 2014, Prime Minister Abe announced that the consumption tax rate hike from 8% to 10% scheduled for October 2015 would be postponed by 18 months to April 2017, and that he would dissolve the lower house to ask for the people's judgment on Abenomics.

In "Basic Policy on Economic and Fiscal Management and Reform 2015" adopted by the Cabinet on June 30, 2015, previous goals were maintained that the government is to achieve surplus in the primary balance in fiscal 2020, and to this end, reduce the size of the primary balance deficit and that the government is to steadily reduce the level of outstanding debt (in GDP) in the medium and long term.

However, on June 1, 2016, Prime Minister Abe announced another postponement of the planned increase in consumption tax rate from 8% to 10% by 2 years and a half from April 1, 2017, to October 1, 2019.

[7] Primary balance is the balance between, on the one hand, revenues arising from taxes and other means of revenue, excluding assumption of debts through, for example, issuing government bonds, and; on the other hand, expenditures excluding interest and principal repayments for the debts such as government bonds that were issued in the past. Primary balance is a criterion to measure whether expenditures necessary to implement policies for the year are financed by taxes and other means of revenue, excluding debt assumption. We should note that, even if primary balance is in balance, the outstanding balance of government debt will increase by the amount of interest payable to the debts assumed in the past.

Furthermore, Prime Minister Abe announced that the use of additional revenue, to be obtained by the rate increase from 8% to 10% for the consumption tax, would be changed. Previously, it was decided that one-fifth of the additional revenue, amounting in total to more than 5 trillion yen from the tax increase, would be used for improving social security and the remaining four-fifths (that is, more than 4 trillion yen), for repayment of debt. Prime Minister Abe made it clear that the remaining four-fifths would be used in order to transform the social security system to the one for all generations by, for example, making early childhood education free of charge. Prime Minister Abe also declared that, because he was changing previous policy, he would dissolve the lower house to ask for the people's judgment. In the election conducted on October 22, 2017, the ruling LDP had an overwhelming victory, by gaining 284 seats, far exceeding the majority of total 465 seats.

Third Arrow: Growth Strategy

As part of its growth strategy, the administration has placed into force a wide range of measures; the major ones are described here:

2013

June The government decided on the "Japan Revitalization Strategy—Japan is Back" and for "A New Decade of Revival," after the 20 years of stagnation; the strategy set as its goal to aim at achieving around 3% nominal and 2% real GDP growth, on average, over the coming 10 years (thereafter, the growth strategy is revised in June of each year up to 2016).[8]

September "The Trilateral Forum for Realization of Virtuous Cycles among the Government, Companies, and Employees" was established, so as to form a common understanding on such issues as wage increases and to pass through the increase in cost of inputs onto the prices paid to subcontractors through participation by relevant ministers and representatives from business and labor.

[8] The growth strategy, revised in June 2014, included the following reforms: ① Aiming to reduce the effective corporate tax rate to a level below 30% (the effective corporate tax rate was reduced to a level below 30% beginning April 2016); ② Revising the basic asset allocation policy of the Government Pension Investment Fund (GPIF), the world largest pension fund (the basic asset allocation policy was revised on October 2014, as described in the text, and the share of risk assets has been increased); ③ Strengthening corporate governance (as described in the text, the amendment to the Company Act placed into force on May 1, 2015, held accountable certain companies, including listed companies, if they did not hire directors of their boards from the outside); ④ Other reforms including deregulation in vital areas such as agriculture, healthcare, energy, and the introduction of national strategic zone, where further deregulation will be applied in such areas as medical care, employment, education, redevelopment of cities, agriculture, and utilization of historic buildings.

2013

June	Japan revitalization strategy—Japan is back and a new decade of revival: aim of 2% GDP growth over coming 10 years.
September	"Trilateral forum for realization of virtuous cycles among the government, companies, and employees" formed.

2014

February	The Financial Services Agency formulated a stewardship code, under which institutional investors are required, on a "comply or explain" basis, for example, to have clear guidelines on such issues as execution of the voting rights they have and publication of their voting decisions.
June	The Company Act was amended (implemented in May 2015) to make certain companies, including listed companies, accountable for non-hiring of directors on their board from the outside, on a "comply or explain" basis.
October	The basic asset allocation policy of GPIF (the world largest pension fund) was changed as below: Domestic bond 60%→35% Domestic equity 12%→25% Foreign bond 11%→15% Foreign equity 12%→25%

2015

June	The Tokyo Stock Exchange formulated and put into force a corporate governance code by revising listing rules, under which listed companies are required to hire more than one independent director on their board on a "comply or explain" basis.
September	Prime Minister Abe proposed "Three new arrows," composed of "Robust economy (nominal GDP to be 600 trillion yen in 2020)," "Childcare supports (desirable birth rate of 1.8 targeted)," and "Social care that provides reassurance (no one forced to leave their job for nursing care of elderlies)," and also set a policy goal to maintain population of 100 million even 50 years later.
October	Basic agreement reached for the Trans-Pacific Partnership (TPP) A forum between government and the private sector for investment for the future was established (meetings were held for five times from October 2015 to April 2016 with participation by the Prime Minister, relevant ministers, chairman of Keidanren (Japan Business Federation), and others to discuss challenges to address in order for the expansion of private investment)
November	Outline of comprehensive TPP-related policy measures adopted
December	Outline of tax reform approved by cabinet (effective corporate tax rate to be reduced to a level below 30% (29.27%) from fiscal 2016)

2016

June	Plan for dynamic engagement of all citizens adopted, incorporating work-style reform (a principle of "equal pay for equal work," correcting long working hours, promotion of employment of the aged) and provision of favorable environments for child care and nursing
September	The implementation meeting for work-style reform established to discuss an implementation plan for work-style reform, with participation by Prime Minister, relevant ministers, representatives from business and labor, and experts

2017

March	The implementation meeting for work-style reform adopted an implementation plan for work-style reform (incorporating guidelines for "equal pay for equal work" prepared by the government, and the introduction of a regulation with a penalty for violation to impose an upper limit on overtime work)
July	A framework agreement reached for Japan–European Union economic partnership agreement
November	Basic agreement reached for TPP 11[9]

2 Reactions of Foreign Exchange and Stock Markets Under Abenomics

Dramatic Initial Reactions and Subsequent Changes

Initial reactions to Abenomics in foreign exchange and stock markets from late 2012 to 2013 were dramatic. The Nikkei stock index (Nikkei 225) rose by 88.0% from November 14, 2012 (when then Prime Minister Noda declared the dissolution of the House) to end 2013. The yen–dollar rate

[9] In addition to these measures, the administration has been continuing its efforts to reform and strengthen the economy through such actions as below:

Adoption of an enforcement plan of regulation reform (June 2014, June 2015, June 2016, and June 2017)

Adoption of an enforcement plan for the strengthening of industrial competitiveness (February 2013 and February 2016)

Adoption of five commitments for the encouragement of inward foreign direct investment (March 2015)

started to depreciate sharply from the end of 2012 and fell by 20.6% from 79.91 yen to the dollar on November 14, 2012, to 100.63 yen at the end of May 2013. However, subsequent developments were not one-sided or dramatic as in the initial period, but mixed, consisting of positive developments and stagnation.

While it is a very rough grouping, we may be able to classify developments in stock and foreign exchange markets under the Abenomics into five periods: ① dramatic change, ② deceleration, ③ re-acceleration, ④ adverse developments, and ⑤ stabilization.

To explain Fig. 7.1, making use of Table 7.1, in about half a year from November 2012 when dissolution of the House was declared to May 2013, the most dramatic changes occurred; the yen rate (monthly average) depreciated by 19.2%, and the stock price index (end of month) rose by 45.8%. In the following year and a half, while depreciation of the yen and stock price increase continued, the pace significantly decelerated and became somewhat stagnant. After the BOJ introduced the QQE expansion measures at the end of October 2014, the yen rate depreciated fur-

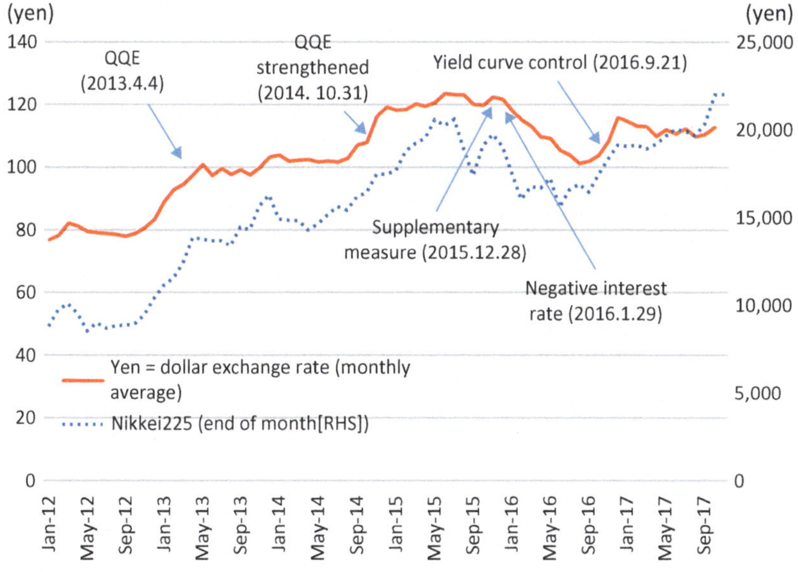

Fig. 7.1 Developments in the stock and foreign exchange market: Five subperiods under Abenomics. Source: Bank of Japan, Yahoo Finance. https://stocks.finance.yahoo.co.jp/stocks/history/?code=998407.O DL accessed on November 18, 2017

Table 7.1 Five periods in relation to developments in stock price and the yen rate under Abenomics

Periods	*Events*	*Changes in foreign exchange rate*	*Changes in stock price*
November 2012~May 2013 (6 months) [Period of dramatic change]	House dissolved (November 2012) Introduction of QQE (April 2013)	−19.2% (80.9 yen/ dollar→101.0 yen/dollar)	45.8% (9,446 yen→13,775 yen)
May 2013~October 2014 (17 months) [Period of deceleration]	Sharp drop of crude oil price (from August 2014)	−8.5% (101.0 yen/ dollar→108.0 yen/dollar)	19.2% (13,775 yen→16,414 yen)
October 2014~December 2015 (14 months) [Period of re-acceleration]	Expansion of QQE (October 2014)	−11.3% (108.0 yen/ dollar→121.8 yen/dollar)	16.0% (16,414 yen→19,034 yen)
December 2015~September 2016 (9 months) [Period of adverse developments]	Supplementary measures (December 2015) Another sharp drop in crude oil prices (from end-2015) Introduction of a negative interest rate (January 2016)	19.4% (121.8 yen/ dollar→102.0 yen/dollar)	−13.6% (19,034 yen→16,450 yen)
September 2016~October 2017 (13 months) [Period of stabilization]	Introduction of yield curve control (September 2016) Victory by Mr. Trump in US presidential election (November 2016)	−9.7% (102.0 yen/ dollar→112.9 yen/dollar)	33.9% (16,450 yen→22,012 yen)

Note: Yen/dollar rate is the monthly average of the rate at 5 p.m. in the Tokyo market, and the stock price is end-month Nikkei 225

Source: BOJ, Yahoo Finance

ther to around 120 yen to the dollar. The stock price, which had been on a rising trend from around the summer of that year, continued to rise further. However, from end-2015, together with a recurrence of the sharp fall in crude oil prices, the yen rate substantially appreciated close to 100 yen to the dollar and the stock price also fell. Subsequently, after the BOJ changed its policy from the base money targeting to the yield curve control, based on the comprehensive assessment of the QQE, the yen depreciated and the stock price rose, partly helped by the US stock price surge and dollar appreciation after the victory of Mr. Trump in the US presidential election.

Background of the Dramatic Initial Change

It appears that the dramatic initial change was brought about mainly by foreign investors in financial markets.

Figure 7.2 shows trading amounts by investor type in the Tokyo Stock Exchange, 1st section. Investors that recorded a substantial amount of net purchases in 2013 were foreign investors, and domestic investors were net sellers in that year.

Fukuda (2015) examined daily price changes in stock and foreign exchange markets for different time zones (the article divided a day into two time zones, that is, Japan daytime and Japan nighttime) from January 2012 to October 2014. He found that both the rise in stock price and the exchange rate depreciation took place in the Japan nighttime.

For example, Nikkei 225 futures are traded not only in Osaka but in other places including Chicago. Figure 7.3 shows accumulated price changes of Nikkei 225 futures for Japan daytime (9:00–15:15) and for Japan night time (15:15–6:15) from October 30, 2012 (= 0). Nikkei 225 futures significantly rose during the Japan nighttime, particularly, through May 2013, but declined during the Japan daytime. Fukuda (2015) con-

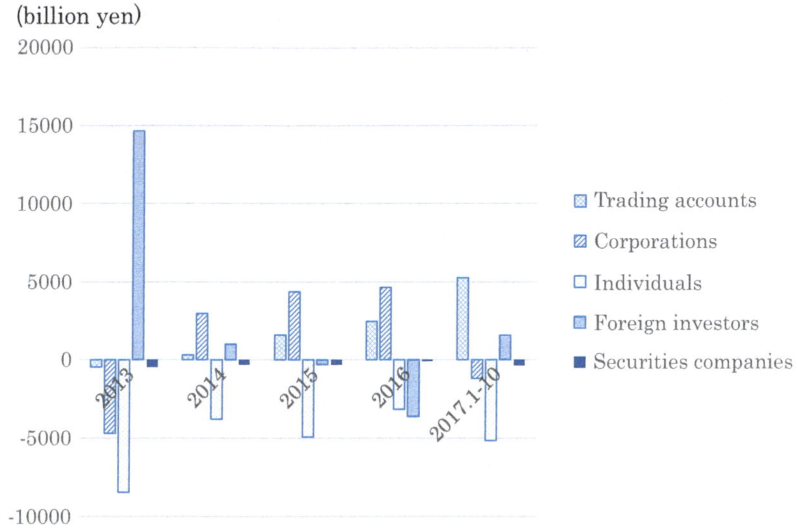

Fig. 7.2 Trading amounts by investor type in Tokyo, 1st section. Source: Japan Exchange Group, "Trading amounts by investor type in Tokyo Stock Exchange, 1st section"

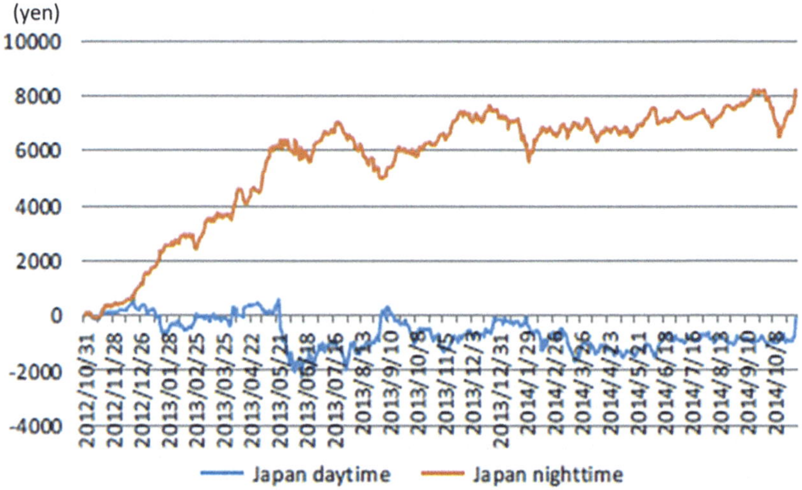

Fig. 7.3 Accumulated change of Nikkei 225 (October 31, 2012 = 100). Source: Fukuda (2015)

tended that the dramatic stock market boom under Abenomics happened only in time zones when foreign investors were active and concluded that foreign investors' responses to the new regime played a leading role in improving the market sentiments.

Figure 7.4 shows, as in the previous figure, accumulated yen–dollar exchange rate changes for Japan daytime (9:00–17:00) and Japan nighttime (I = 17:00–9:00, II = 17:00–7:00) from October 31, 2018 (= 0).[10] In the same way as the stock price, yen depreciation took place in the Japan nighttime when foreign investors were active.[11]

Abenomics and the Real Economy

Yen Depreciation and Stock Price Rise and the Real Economy

Let us look at how real GDP developed under yen depreciation and the rise in stock prices. Figure 7.5 shows evolution of the yen–dollar exchange

[10] Depreciation of the yen rate is indicated by a vertical upward movement.

[11] Japan nighttime II excludes Japan's morning hours when the Sydney market starts trading from the definition of Japan nighttime. While, under this alternative nighttime definition (from 5 p.m. in Tokyo to 7 a.m. in Tokyo in the following business day), the yen's depreciation in nighttime was less dramatic, the basic feature is maintained.

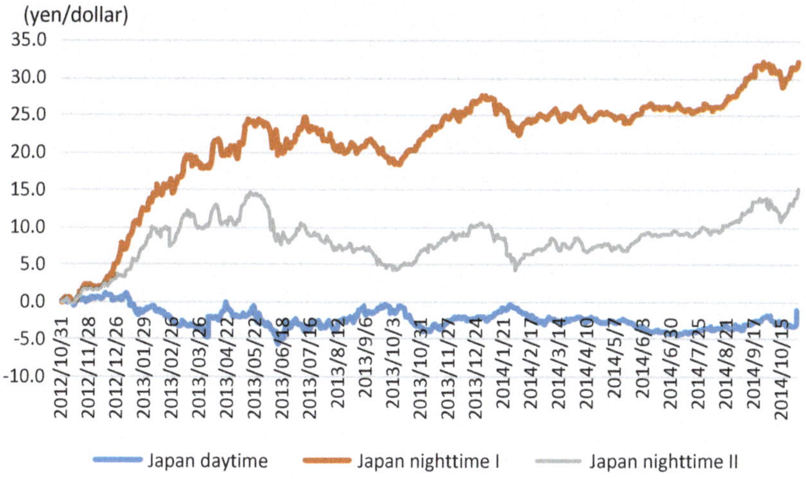

Fig. 7.4 Accumulated change of yen = dollar exchange rate (October 31, 2012 = 0). Source: Fukuda (2015)

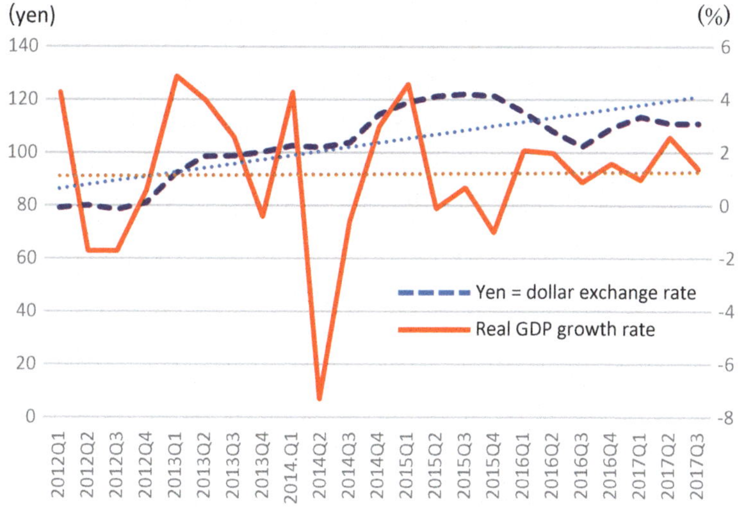

Fig. 7.5 Yen = dollar exchange rate and real GDP growth rate. Source: Bank of Japan, Cabinet Office, GDP statistics

rate (period average) and the development in real GDP growth rate (quarter-to-quarter rate of change, annualized). While the yen–dollar exchange rate substantially changed, there has not been a significant change in real GDP growth rate.

Figure 7.6 shows developments in stock prices and the real GDP. Here, again, the rise in stock prices has not been accompanied by any significant changes in the real GDP growth rate.

Contributions to Real GDP Growth by Demand Components
Figure 7.7 shows the real growth rate and growth contribution by demand components in two periods, that is, the three-year period preceding the Abenomics in the 2010s (2010Q1–2012Q4) and about a five-year period of Abenomics (2013Q1–2018Q1).[12]

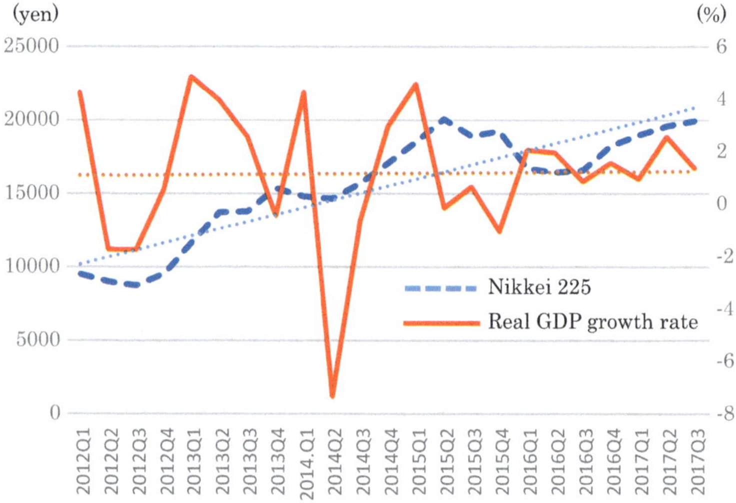

Fig. 7.6 Nikkei 225 and real GDP growth rate. Source: Yahoo Finance, Cabinet Office GDP statistics

[12] As the outcome of the two-period comparison significantly changes depending on how we define the preceding period, we need to cautiously assess analysis in this part. In the text, we excluded the year of 2009 that includes the period of sharp contraction of the economy immediately after the Lehman shock (−18.2% annualized quarter-to-quarter rate of change in 2009Q1) and subsequent substantial recovery (8.7% annualized quarter-to-quarter rate of change in 2009Q3) and accordingly, defined the preceding period as starting from 2010Q1.

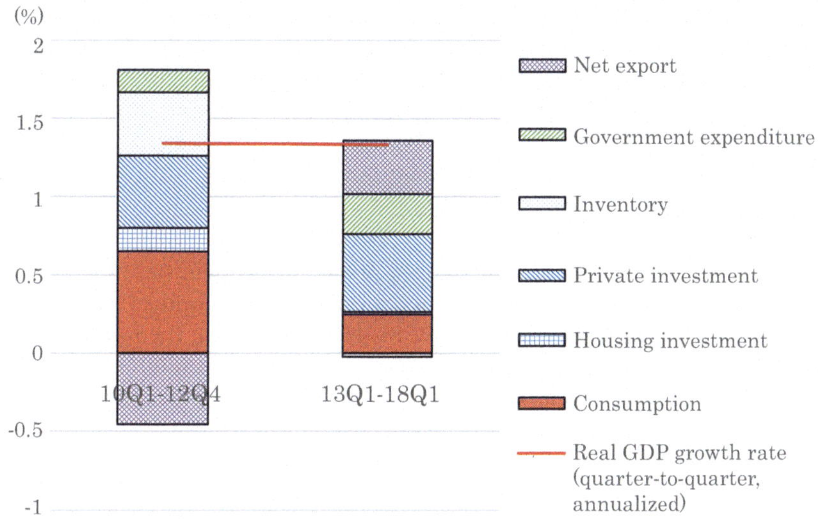

Fig. 7.7 Real growth rate and growth contribution by demand components: Preceding period (2010Q1–2012Q4) and Abenomics period (2013Q1–2018Q1). Note: The figures show a simple average of quarter-to-quarter growth rates (annualized) and the average growth contribution by each demand component, and the line shows real GDP growth rate. Source: Cabinet Office, GDP statistics, Bank of Japan

The average real GDP growth rate stayed the same from 1.3% in the preceding period to 1.3% in the Abenomics period. If we define the preceding period as covering 2009Q2 or 2009Q3 to 2012Q4, the average growth rate in the Abenomics period was marginally lower than that in the preceding period. Therefore, it may be duly said that there has not been a significant change in GDP growth under Abenomics.

By contrast, there has been a significant change in the composition of growth contribution by demand components. Growth contribution of net exports increased by 0.8 point from −0.5 point to 0.3 point. Government expenditure nearly doubled its growth contribution from 0.1 point (more precisely, 0.14 point) to 0.3 point (more precisely, 0.25 point), but consumption reduced its growth contribution to a level smaller than half of the level in the preceding period from 0.7 point to 0.2 point. There has not been a big change in growth contribution of private investment.

What is characteristic of the Abenomics period is that, as the impediments to exports, arising from sharp appreciation of the yen in the preceding period, were removed, net export recovered its growth contribution and government expenditure supported growth, while private investment did not increase significantly and consumption substantially reduced its growth contribution.

Developments in Major Demand Components

Investment

As we saw in the preceding subsection, private investment has not shown a large increase. Is it that the very eased monetary policy under Abenomics has not been effective? Figure 7.8 shows developments in the interest rate on Japanese government bonds by maturity. The interest rate on the government bonds has declined since Abenomics started across the maturities. Bold monetary policy has been effective in this respect.[13]

Both the interest rate on government bonds and the lending rate were on a declining trend from 2006 and from 2008, respectively. As Figs. 7.8

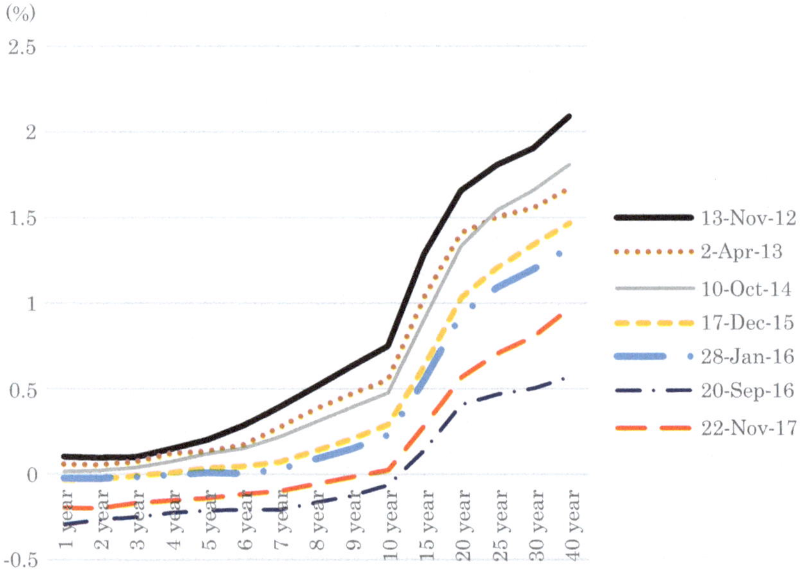

Fig. 7.8 Interest rate on government bonds by maturity. Source: Ministry of Finance HP

[13] Fig. 7.8 shows interest rates across maturity one day before the day when major policy action was taken mainly in the field of monetary policy.

and 7.9 show, the rates continued to decline further from 2013, and bank lending continued to increase after bottoming out in 2010.

The amount of real private investment dropped with the Lehman shock, hit the bottom of 65.4 trillion yen in 2009Q4, then started to increase and became 85.2 trillion yen in 2017Q4, exceeding the peak that had been reached before the Lehman shock. However, the pace of increase has not shown a big difference between before and after Abenomics started. Furthermore, as we saw previously, private investment has not increased much relative to the amount of cash flow (see Fig. 6.20 in Chap. 6). While companies are in possession of a large amount of cash and deposits, as we see in the next subsection (Fig. 7.21), private investment by companies has not shown a large increase and its growth contribution has not significantly increased either (Figs. 7.7 and 7.10).

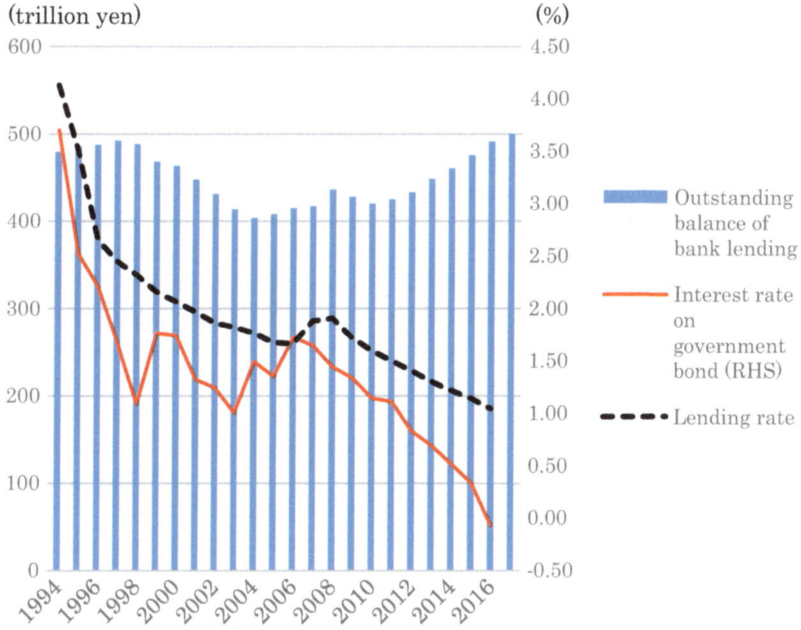

Fig. 7.9 Interest rate on government bonds, lending rate, and outstanding balance of bank lending. Source: Bank of Japan; IMF, IFS

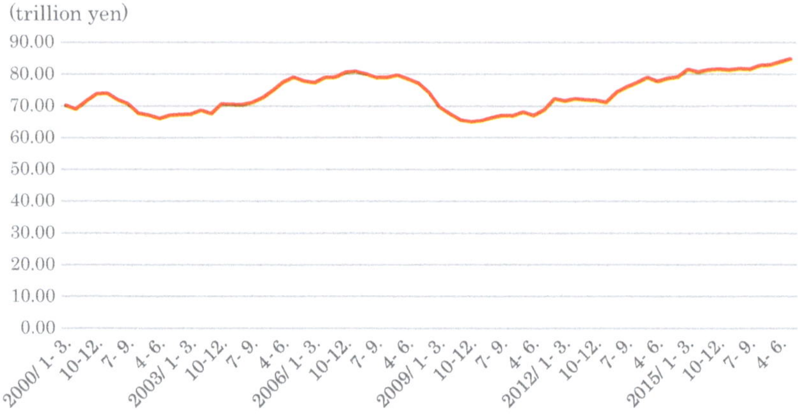

Fig. 7.10 Real private investment. Source: Cabinet Office, GDP statistics

Consumption

Consumption has reduced its growth contribution, as we have seen. Developments in the amount of real private consumption since 2007, that is, the peak year before the Lehman shock, shows that, after it dropped with the Lehman shock, it began a recovery. Then, due to factors including a reactionary fall, after a last minute surge in demand preceding the increase in consumption tax rate in April 2014, private consumption significantly declined. Thereafter, it started to recover, but the pace of recovery is slow.

This is what the figure may indicate. However, if we look at the developments in real consumption more closely, we can see that the amount of real consumption became almost flat from 2013Q2, two quarters before 2014Q1, when the last minute surge in demand before the consumption tax increase was observed (Fig. 7.11). Behind this stagnation of consumption lies a fact that, as we saw in the preceding chapter, consumer prices started to increase from mid-2013 and the pace of the decline in real wages accelerated (for example, real wage index [2015 = 100] declined by 2.9% in half a year from 105.2 in June 2013 to 102.2 in December 2013) (Fig. 6.28).

Exports

Exports were flat after recovering from the fall following the Lehman shock, and even under Abenomics, the recovery was relatively slow and stagnant on a real-term basis, despite sharp depreciation of the yen–dollar exchange rate. From around the latter half of 2016, exports started to show a mild increase. By contrast, imports have been stagnant (Fig. 7.12).

Fig. 7.11 Real private consumption. Source: Cabinet Office, GDP statistics

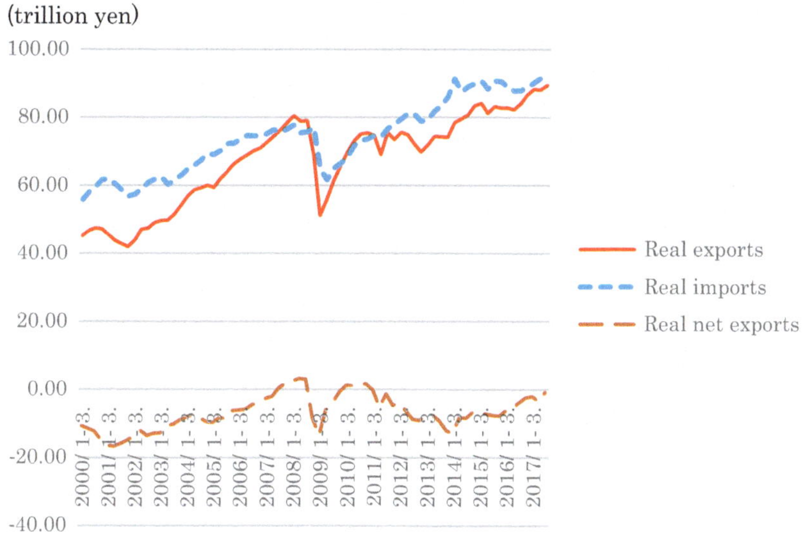

Fig. 7.12 Real exports, real imports, and real net exports. Source: Cabinet Office, GDP statistics

Government Expenditure

Real government expenditure mostly declined in the 2000s. However, due to the fiscal stimulus adopted after the Lehman shock, it turned to follow a rising trend. Thereafter, real government expenditure continued rising, even after the real GDP became 508.4 trillion yen in 2013Q2, exceeding the peak of 507.3 trillion yen in 2008Q1 before the Lehman shock. Injection of public demand seems to have become a normal aspect of the economy (Fig. 7.13).

Developments in Prices

In January 2013, the government and the BOJ issued a joint statement, in which the BOJ stated that it set a price stability target of 2% and aimed to achieve the target at the earliest possible time. Under the QQE in April 2013, the BOJ committed to achieve 2% price stability target at the earliest time, with a time horizon of about two years (inflation targeting with time limit). The price stability target of 2% was defined in terms of the year-on-year rate of change in the CPI (excluding fresh food). While this indicator tended to become negative from 2012 to the beginning of 2013, it started to show a clear positive trend from May 2013. However, it then fell into a negative territory again from August 2015. It became positive from January 2017. While the pace of increase is constantly positive, it stays at 0.8% year-on-year, that is, less than 1%, as of July 2018 (Fig. 7.14). Meantime, while the BOJ stated in the initial period after the introduction

Fig. 7.13 Real government expenditure. Source: Cabinet Office, GDP statistics

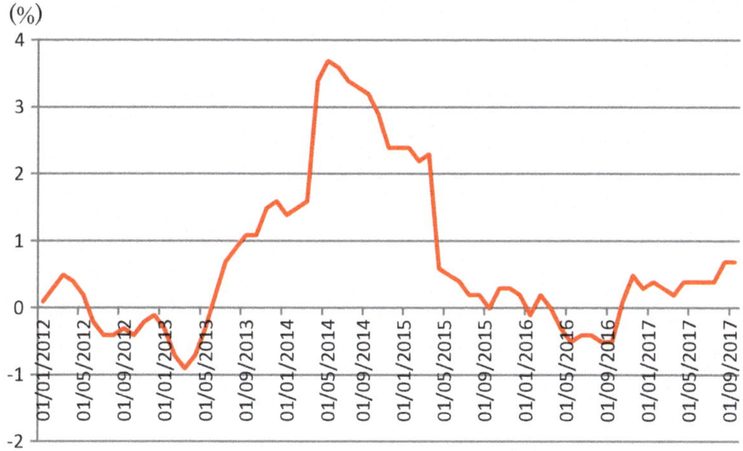

Fig. 7.14 Consumer Price Index (excluding fresh food) (year-on-year change). Source: Statistics Bureau, Ministry of Internal Affairs and Communications

of the QQE that the price stability target of 2% would likely be reached toward the latter half of the three-year period from FY 2013 to FY 2015, that their projection covered. However, the projected timing of achieving the price target has been postponed six times. In the Monetary Policy Meeting held on April 27, 2018, the Bank of Japan deleted the wording on the timing when the 2% target is reached from "The outlook of economic activities and price (April 2018)."

Under the initial QQE, it was considered an important policy transmission channel to raise inflation expectation through measures, including expansion of base money, reducing the real interest rate (nominal interest rate – expected rate of inflation), and thereby, stimulating real economy.[14] The expected inflation rate (average) held by private sector economists substantially rose from 2012 to 2013, became flat in mid-2014, started to decline from the end of 2015, and recently, has stayed around 1%. Expected inflation rate held by companies, which the Tankan survey of the BOJ began to collect in April 2014, also started to decline from mid-2014 and became flat at around 1% since the latter half of 2016 (Figs. 7.15 and 7.16).

[14] See Iwata (2013).

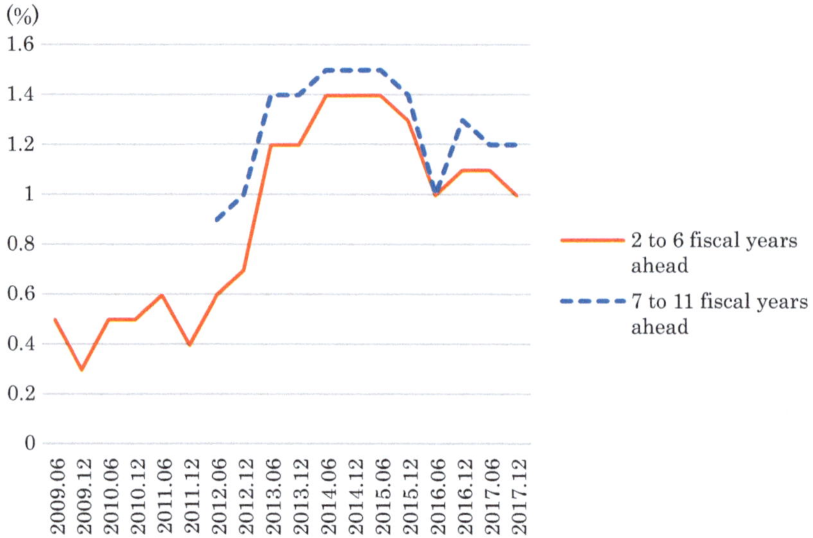

Fig. 7.15 Expected inflation rate held by private sector economists (average). Source: Tabulated drawing on data provided on website of the Japan Center for Economic Research

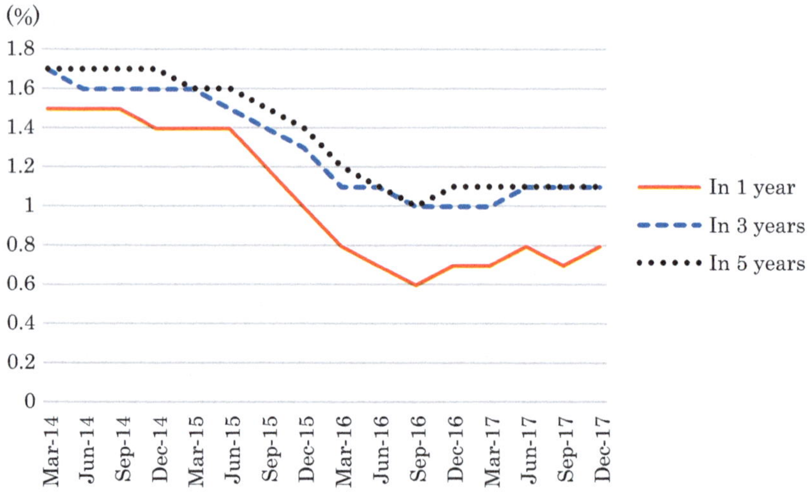

Fig. 7.16 Expected inflation rate held by companies (all industries). Source: Bank of Japan, "Tankan survey"

Figure 7.17 shows the year-on-year rate of change in CPI (excluding fresh food, excluding effects of increase in consumption tax rate), the yen–dollar exchange rate, and the crude oil price since 2012. The rate of change in CPI (excluding fresh food, excluding effects of increase in consumption tax rate) was continuously positive for longer than two years, from May 2013. Behind this development was the fact that, as we saw previously, the yen rate depreciated vis-à-vis the dollar by 19.2% from November 2012 to May 2013, and this pushed the CPI upward through higher import prices. Then, as the crude oil price fell sharply to a level below 100 US dollars per barrel beginning in September 2014, the rate of increase of the CPI (excluding fresh food) from the previous year fell sharply close to zero. After that, as the crude oil price became flat in the range of 50 to 60 dollars per barrel and the yen rate further depreciated to 120 yen to the dollar, the rate of increase in the CPI (excluding fresh food) from the previous year also became flat. Then, as the crude oil price further dropped below 30 dollars from the end of 2015, and the yen rate appreciated to around 100 yen to the dollar, the rate of increase in CPI (excluding fresh food) fell into the negative range again.

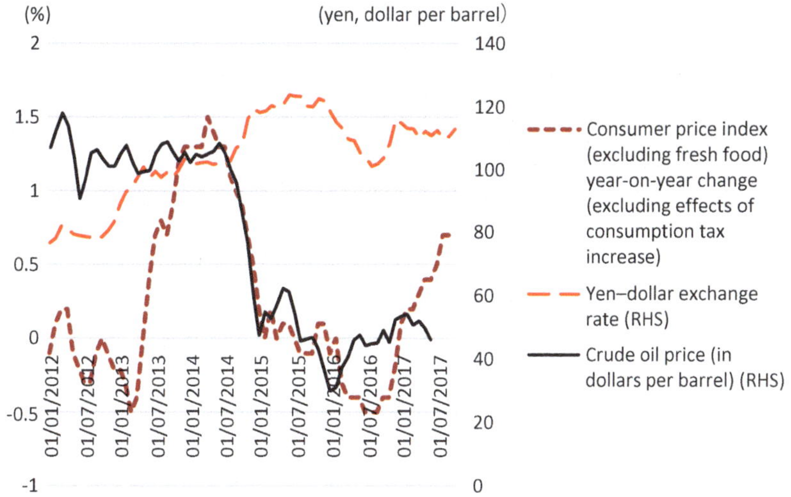

Fig. 7.17 Consumer Price Index (excluding fresh food) (year-on-year change, excluding effects of consumption tax increase), yen–dollar rate, and crude oil price. Source: Cabinet Office, Bank of Japan, IMF

Figure 7.18 shows developments in the rate of change in the CPI, which excludes, in addition to fresh food, oil products, and other special factors (also excluding effects of increase in consumption tax rate). Different from the previous figure, the rate of change in the CPI (excluding fresh food, oil products, and other special factors) continued to be positive even after the crude oil price fell sharply from autumn 2014. When the appreciation of the yen rate proceeded in 2016, the CPI turned steeply downward. As the CPI excludes oil products, effects of the sharp fall of crude oil price do not seem to be reflected in the CPI. We can see that developments in the CPI are significantly influenced by the changes in yen–dollar rate.

On the whole, the CPI (excluding fresh food) seems to have been strongly influenced by the yen rate and crude oil price, and the increase in the CPI (excluding fresh food) for more than two years from mid-2013 does not seem to be the outcome of tightening of demand-supply conditions under economic recovery. From around the end of 2016, the rate of increase in the CPI (excluding fresh food) is almost constantly positive.

Company Profits and Investment

We have looked thus far at reactions in the financial markets and developments in the real economy and prices. Now, let us look at what sort of changes are observed in the corporate sector.

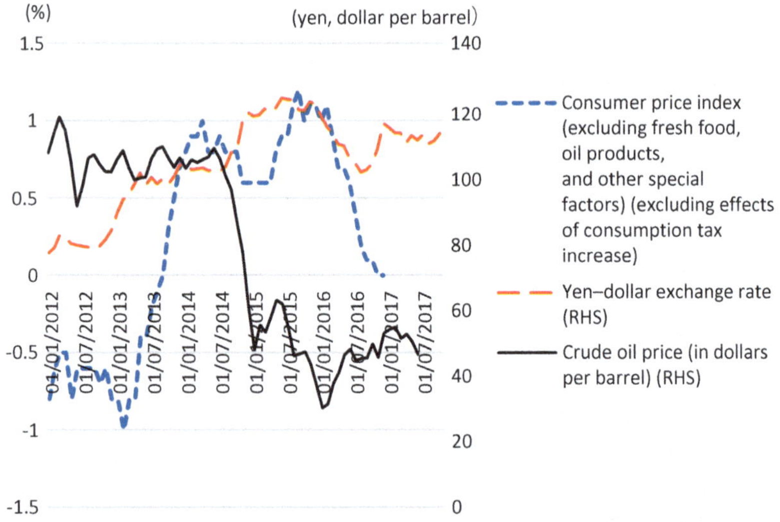

Fig. 7.18 Consumer Price Index (excluding fresh food, oil products and other special factors), yen–dollar exchange rate, and crude oil price. Source: Cabinet Office, Bank of Japan, IMF

Figures 7.19 and 7.20 indicate that combined current profits of all the profit-making companies have been increasing as the yen rate depreciated and the stock prices rose.

Figure 7.21 shows developments in current profits, investment, and cash and deposit holding. Current profits have been recording a historic high. Under these circumstances, while investment has increased, cash and deposits that companies hold has increased more sharply. Although companies are making large amounts of profits, they have not increased investment significantly, but have substantially increased cash and deposit holdings.

Continued Restraint on Labor Cost and Difference Observed in Labor Markets of Regular and Non-regular Workers

Not only with investment, but also restraint continues with labor cost. Figure 7.22 shows developments in the labor share that is the share of labor income in the national income. The labor share, after a sharp increase under the Global Financial Crisis (GFC), has been declining consistently since 2010.

Looking at the current labor market conditions, the unemployment rate has been declining, and it is 2.5% as of July 2018, which is the lowest

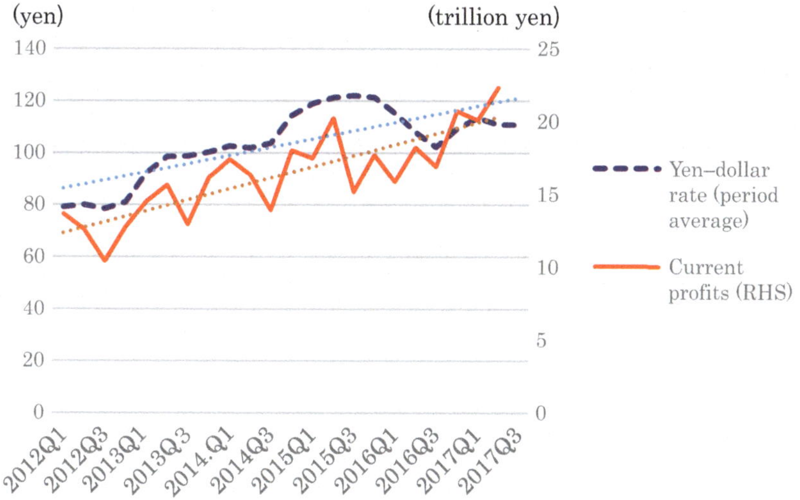

Fig. 7.19 Yen–dollar exchange rate, and current profits. Source: Ministry of Finance, "Statistics of financial statement of companies," Bank of Japan

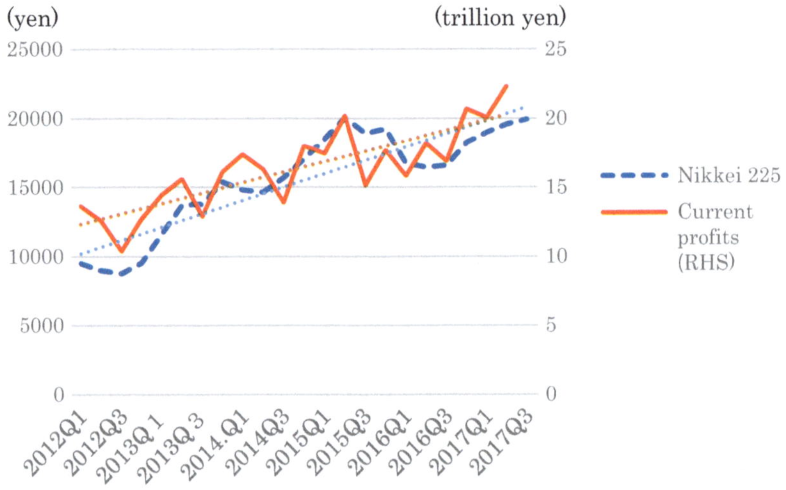

Fig. 7.20 Nikkei 225 and current profits. Source: Ministry of Finance, "Statistics of financial statement of companies," Yahoo Finance

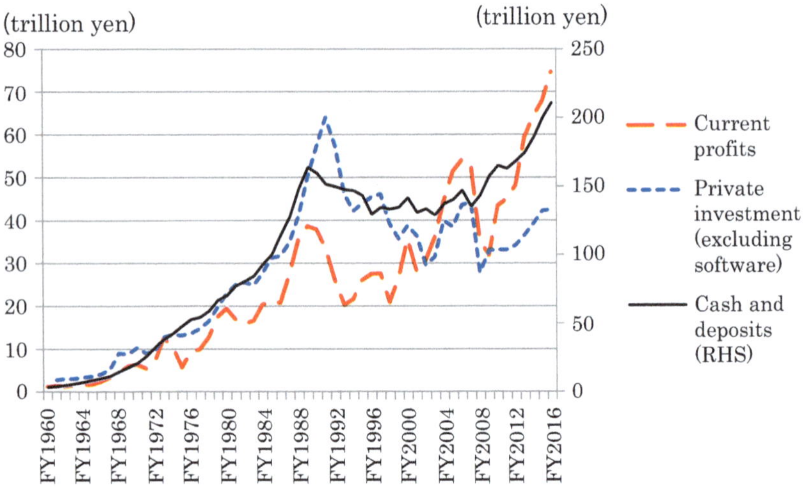

Fig. 7.21 Current profits, investment, cash, and deposits. Source: Ministry of Finance, "Statistics of financial statement of companies"

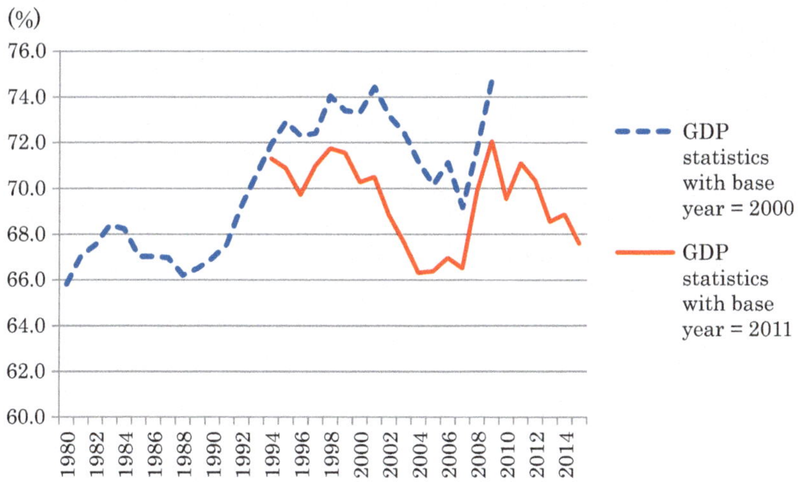

Fig. 7.22 Labor income share. Note: Labor income share = compensation for employee/national income (factor price base). Source: Cabinet Office, GDP statistics

in the last 25 years since August 1993. However, as Fig. 7.23 shows, the improvement started in 2010, and the improvement in the Abenomics period is the continuation of this trend.

Despite such a tightening in the labor markets, the rate of increase in wages per worker has been low, as we have seen before. This partly reflects the fact that the tightening of labor market is not so strong for regular workers who have by far higher wages, compared with non-regular workers.

The effective ratio of job offers to job seekers indicates that improvements in labor market conditions are more substantial for part-timers, particularly, those part-time workers who are not permanent, as compared with regular workers. While the effective ratio of job offers to job seekers for regular workers has been improving, the ratio is around 1, recording 1.02 in April 2018 (it was 1.70 for part-timers at that time) (Fig. 7.24).

Reflecting difference in the degree of tightening of labor market conditions, the rate of increase in hourly wage of non-regular workers is higher than that for regular workers in recent years (Fig. 7.25). The labor market tightening has been influencing non-regular workers more favorably than regular workers.

Fig. 7.23 Unemployment rate. Source: Statistics Bureau of Japan, "Labor force survey"

Fig. 7.24 Ratio of jobs offers to job seekers. Source: Ministry of Health, Labor, and Welfare, "Employment stabilization operation statistics"

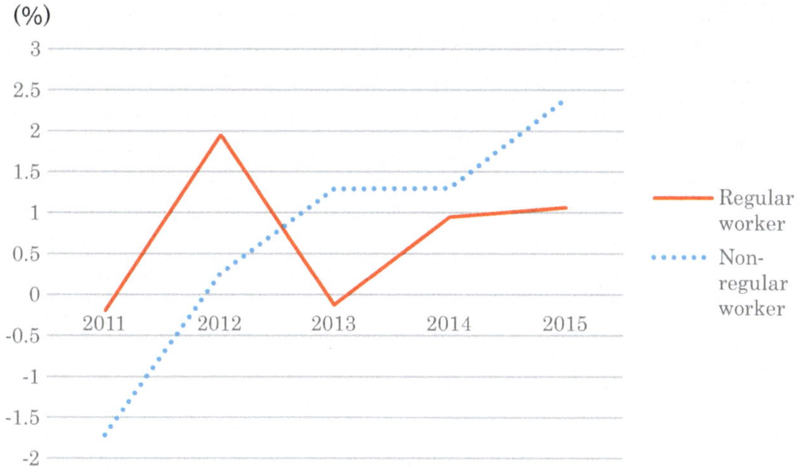

Fig. 7.25 Hourly wages for regular and non-regular workers (year-on-year change). Note: Hourly wage = contractual wage (i.e., excluding overtime payment and bonuses) paid in June of each surveyed year, divided by the total contractual hours worked in June of that year. Source: Ministry of Health, Labor, and Welfare, "Basic wage structure survey"

Assessment of the Abenomics and Challenges for the Japanese Economy

Assessment of the Abenomics

Let us make an assessment of Abenomics, drawing on the examination we have made so far.

First, Abenomics has brought about a substantial depreciation of the yen rate and a surge in stock prices, particularly, in its initial period. It seems most probable that the bold monetary easing changed expectations held by foreign investors about the Japanese economy or stock prices and exchange rate, and these changes in expectation substantially influenced stock prices and exchange rate.

Second, neither the substantial depreciation of the yen rate nor the stock price surge has affected very much real GDP growth trend yet. However, the interest rate has declined across maturity, and bank lending has maintained an increasing trend that started in the recovery period after the Lehman shock. So, recovery momentum has been maintained.

Third, the breakdown of the growth rate by demand component in the Abenomics period shows that, compared with the period preceding the Abenomics period, growth contribution of net exports significantly expanded and government expenditure almost doubled its growth contribution, but, in contrast, consumption halved its growth contribution and the growth contribution of private investment has not changed much.

Fourth, the rate of change in the CPI (excluding fresh food) was kept positive for more than two years from May 2013. This seems to have been due to the influence of the effects of exchange rate depreciation.

Fifth, company profits have been recording historic highs in recent years. However, investment, while increasing, has not shown a substantial increase, and restraint on labor costs continues, with cash and deposit holdings by companies reaching record highs.

Sixth, while the unemployment rate is the lowest since the mid-1990s, tightening of labor market conditions is stronger for non-regular workers than for regular workers, and the rate of increase in wages is higher for non-regular workers than for regular workers. Companies have not basically altered their attitude toward restraint of labor costs.

Challenges for the Japanese Economy

Abenomics is a comprehensive policy package that encompasses not only macroeconomic policy but also extensive micro policy, such as governance reform, TPP promotion, and labor market (work style) reform. It is also a remarkable undertaking in that the policy package has been strongly implemented for more than six years under the same administration. Furthermore, it is a rare policy formation, and evolution in that policy focus has continuously shifted from monetary and fiscal policy to micro and social structural policies, such as wage increase, promotion of investment, governance reform, and work-style reform, the birth rate and population target, and productivity enhancement.

However, the current growth structure of the Japanese economy has important problems. The defensive attitude of the corporate sector has brought about a stagnant increase in growth contribution of investment, declining growth contribution of consumption under wage restraint, and the continued growth dependence on government expenditure. Why has the behavior of companies not changed? In what follows, we examine three issues, that is, that investment does not expand fully, that consumption has been losing its growth contribution, and that government expenditure continues to hold a substantial share in growth contribution, and consider what challenges the Japanese economy faces.

Investment Restraint by Companies

As we have seen, companies have not significantly expanded investment in spite of very favorable environments, including low interest rates and increasing profits. Why is this? As we examined in Chap. 6, the fundamental reason is the low-growth expectation of the domestic economy held by companies.

Figure 7.26 shows developments in expected growth rate of the domestic economy held by companies for the next three years and actual real economic growth rate (three-year-moving average). Expected growth rate, which once was around 3% at the beginning of the 1990s, consistently declined to a level below 1% beginning in the 2000s, and beyond that has stayed around 1%. Decline in expected growth rate proceeded together with the decline in the actual growth rate, and it became deeply rooted as the economic stagnation was extended. In other words, the fact of prolonged low growth strongly constrains future expectations. Most troublesome is the possibility that low growth expectation works as a restraining factor on investment and wages (consumption), limiting growth of domestic demand, and therefore, economic growth in a self-

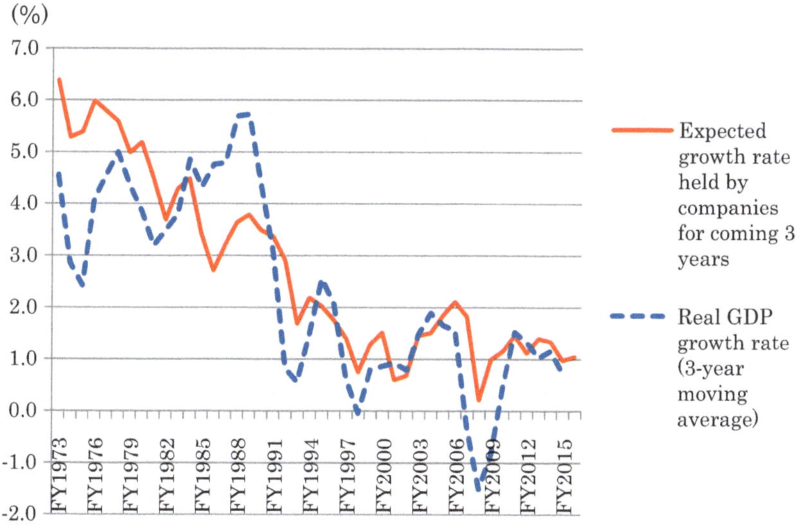

Fig. 7.26 Real GDP growth rate and expected growth rate held by companies. Source: Cabinet Office, "Survey on company behavior"

fulfilling way. Furthermore, due to the need to make up for lack of self-sustained high growth, the economy cannot lower its dependence on government expenditure. High dependence on government expenditure, together with wage restraint, may raise concerns for the future for households, thus strengthening the mechanism of low growth through its dampening effects on consumption. The Japanese economy does not seem to have exited from such a vicious circle yet. Stimulating demand through the promotion of lending with low interest rates is a policy that focuses on the cost side of investment activity. It has become clear by the implementation of bold monetary easing under Abenomics that unless a sales increase is expected, the effects of cost lowering on investment activity are limited.

What seems to have started to impose significant effects on growth expectation of domestic economy, particularly, from around 2010, is population decline. The total fertility rate, which dropped lower than the population replacement level of 2.07 in 1974, has been at the 1% level for more than 40 years. However, it is only recently that population decline was recognized as a serious problem by the general public. It is probably since the 2010 publication by Hiroshi Motani of "Defure no Shotai: Keizai ha jinko no nami de ugoku" (True origin of deflation—The economy moves by the demographic waves).[15,16] To be sure, as Fig. 7.27 shows, the magnitude of expected population decline in Japan is very

[15] The Bank of Japan has conducted very extensive research on the effects of the population on the economy since the publication of Motani's book. The executive members of the BOJ, including then Governor Shirakawa, started to frequently mention effects of population decline in their public communication.

[16] Motani's (2010) book is important, as it directed the attention of the public to the issue of population decline, particularly to its impacts on the demand side of the economy. Although there are many books on population decline, there are only a handful of books focusing on the demand side, to the author's knowledge, examples of which include Nukaga, Makoto (2005) "Juyo Shukusho no Kiki-Jinko Gensho Shaki no Keizaigaku" (Demand shrinkage crisis—Economics of population decline) NTT Publication; and Adachi, Makiko "Shoshi Koreika ga Kakei Bumon ni Ataeru Eikyo" (Impacts of declining birth rate and aging population on household sector) (Mizuho Soken Ronshu (2004 I), pp. 1–35. Mizuho Sogo Kenkyujo). Although there were very few reactions from researchers and scholars to Motani's arguments, very limited exceptions include Yoshikawa, Hiroshi (2011) "Shoshi Koreika to Keizai Seicho" (The declining birth rate and aging population and economic growth), RIETI Discussion Paper Series 11-P-006 January 2011; and Yoshikawa, Hiroshi (2016) "Jinko to Nihon Keizai" (Population and the Japanese economy), Chu Ko Shinsho.

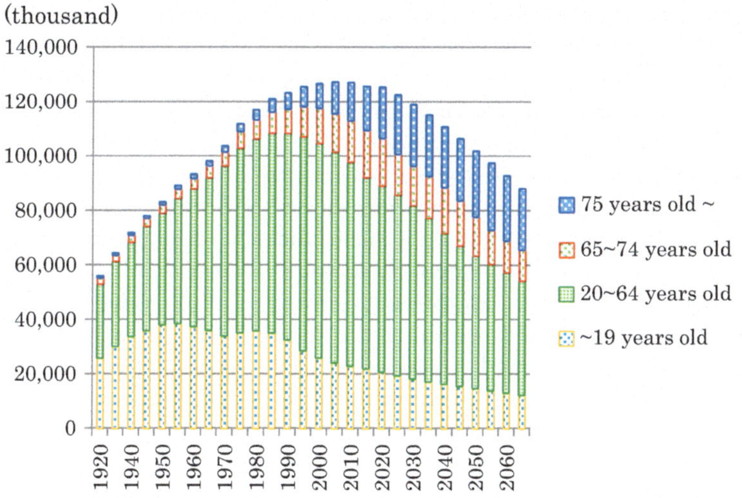

Fig. 7.27 Population of Japan and its future estimates. Source: National Institute of Population and Social Security Research, "Population statistics [2017 revision]"

large, and it is considered to act as a strong restraining factor on future growth expectation.[17]

Keeping in mind that while population decline may have worked to depress growth expectation since the 2010s and would continue to function as a negative factor on the formation of growth expectation in the future, too, it probably was not significantly relevant to the decline in growth expectation in the period up to the 2000s. The reason for the decline in growth expectation and also the reason for the underlying decline in actual growth performance up to the 2000s were, as we examined in Chap. 6, to be found in the corporate behavior after the collapse of the bubble. Persistence of defensive attitudes by companies, even after the excesses of companies had been finally removed by mid-2000s, seems to have been brought about by low-growth expectations for the domestic economy held

[17] "Population statistics data (2017, revised version)" (Medium fertility assumption [medium mortality assumption]) by the National Institute of Population and Social Security Research indicates that Japan's population is projected to decline by 39.018 million (30.7%) in 50 years from 127.095 million in 2015 to 88.077 million in 2065. This corresponds to a decline of 0.780 million per year. It means that one prefectural capital city, such as Niigata (0.81 million population), Hamamatsu (0.8 million population), or Kumamoto (0.74 million population) is projected to disappear each year.

by companies that had been deeply embedded during the prolonged low-growth performance. It is difficult to judge whether the low-growth expectation of companies at this time is due to an irrational defensive mindset, or due to rational consideration of factors such as population decline and relatively high profitability of overseas operation. Still, companies seem to be at least partly constrained by the negative legacy of the 15-year-long low-growth performance that the corporate sector had brought about.

If the low-growth expectation is due to the defensive mindset, it should be effective, although seemingly paradoxical, to realize a higher growth performance than in the past through promotion of economic activities in such areas where activities were not constrained by low growth in the past (for example, exports and alteration of foreign demand into domestic demand through tourism, including medical tourism, promotion of inward foreign direct investment, and utilization of special economic zones). Furthermore, it is necessary to encourage more positive behaviors by companies through, for example, governance reform to promote participation of outside people in their management. At the same time, however, it is necessary to cope with substantive issues for the future. In particular, it is critically important to mitigate the population decline, which poses the biggest restraint on growth expectation for the future. Most importantly to that end is introducing such measures that will enable women to have and raise children without having their careers interrupted and negatively affected.

In relation to impacts of population decline on growth, there is a view that contends that, while Japan's economy has been behind other advanced countries in terms of GDP growth, it has not been so in terms of the rate of growth of GDP per capita or the rate of growth of GDP per working-age population.[18] Figure 7.28 shows the rate of GDP growth of five advanced countries, including Japan, in every five years. Japan's growth performance has been low as compared with other countries since the 1990s.

Figure 7.29 shows the rate of growth of GDP per capita for every five years. The figure indicates Japan's performance stagnated in the 1990s, but it has been neither on the high side nor on the very low side since the 2000s.

[18] For example, see Masaaki Shirakawa (2012a) "Deleveraging and growth: Is the developed world following Japan's long and winding road?", a lecture by the then governor of the London School of Economics and Political Science on January 10, 2012.

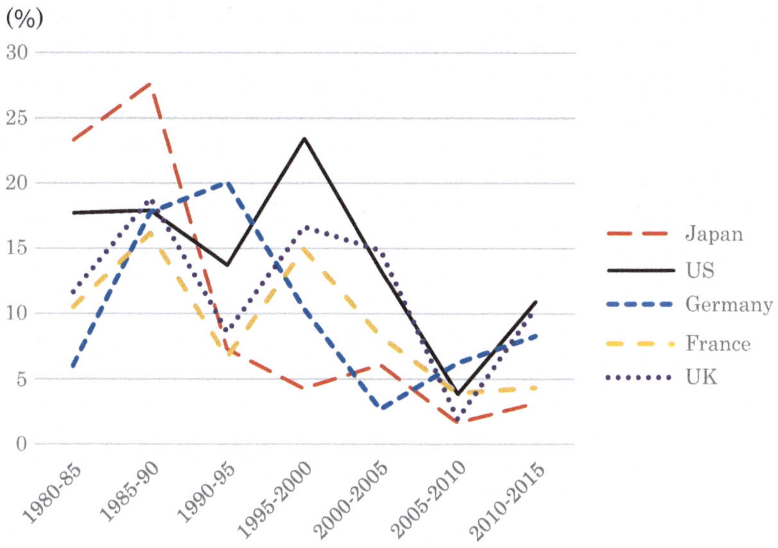

Fig. 7.28 Five-year real GDP growth rate. Source: United Nations, IMF

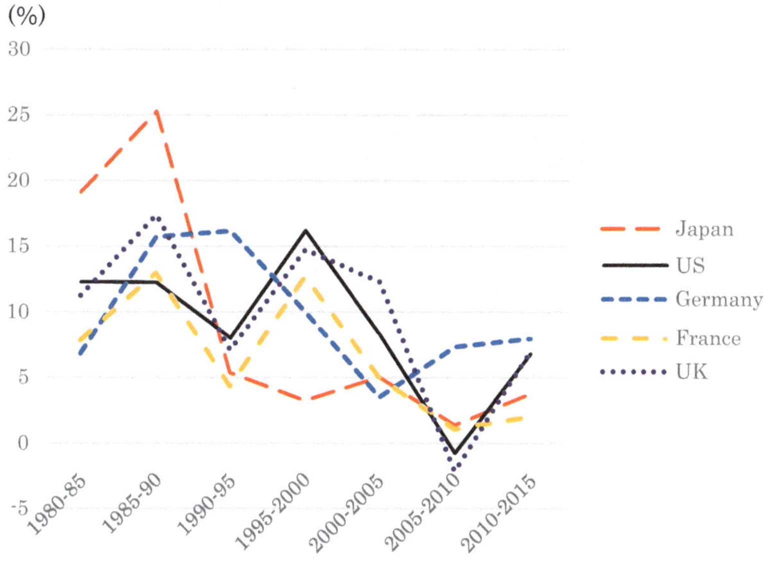

Fig. 7.29 Five-year growth rate of real GDP per capita. Source: United Nations, IMF

Furthermore, Fig. 7.30 shows the rate of growth of GDP per working-age population for every five years. Japan's performance has been low but close to the average level of four advanced countries since the 2000s. However, we note that, in Japan, the rate of increase of the number of persons actually employed has been consistently higher than that of the working-age population (or in the case of decline, the rate of decline is smaller for the number of persons actually employed than for the working-age population), and, therefore, the rate of growth in GDP per persons actually employed will be lower than the figure shows.[19]

These figures show that, viewed from the supply capacity side, the growth rate of GDP per working-age population has been on the low side, as compared with other countries, even after incorporating the positive effects of a rising labor participation rate. So, in order to raise performance, it is essential to enhance productivity through technological progress or education and training. Furthermore, costs to keep and maintain the society include such expenses as defense and security or maintenance

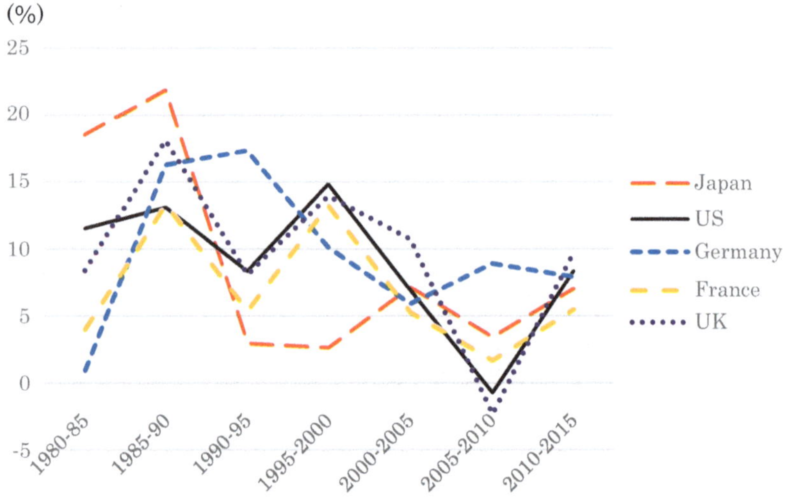

Fig. 7.30 Five-year growth rate of real GDP per working-age population (15–64). Source: United Nations, IMF

[19] For example, while the rate of increase in the working-age population from 2010 to 2015 is −5.2%, the number of actual employment increased over the same five-year period by 1.6%, indicating that an increase in the labor force participation ratio has been making up for the decline in the working-age population.

costs for economic infrastructure that accrue regardless of the size of population. Therefore, it is difficult to maintain the stable management of a society if the economy grows only in terms of per capita GDP or per working-age population GDP and not in terms of total GDP. So, it is necessary to aim for a certain growth of total GDP while attempting to transform the society into a compact one, which can economize on overhead common costs in line with population decline.

However, the working-age population is expected to decline further, and it is not possible to indefinitely raise the labor force participation rate. So, given future demographic change that is expected, it is difficult to expect the growth rate of total GDP to substantially increase in the future, without technological progress or other factors significantly raising the growth rate of GDP per working-age population beyond the level experienced in recent years.

Figure 7.31 shows the GDP gap ([actual GDP – potential GDP]/ potential GDP), which was frequently negative after the collapse of the bubble, narrowed in the Abenomics period, and has been positive recently. Demand shortages that the Japanese economy has long suffered from the collapse of the bubble may have been finally resolved.

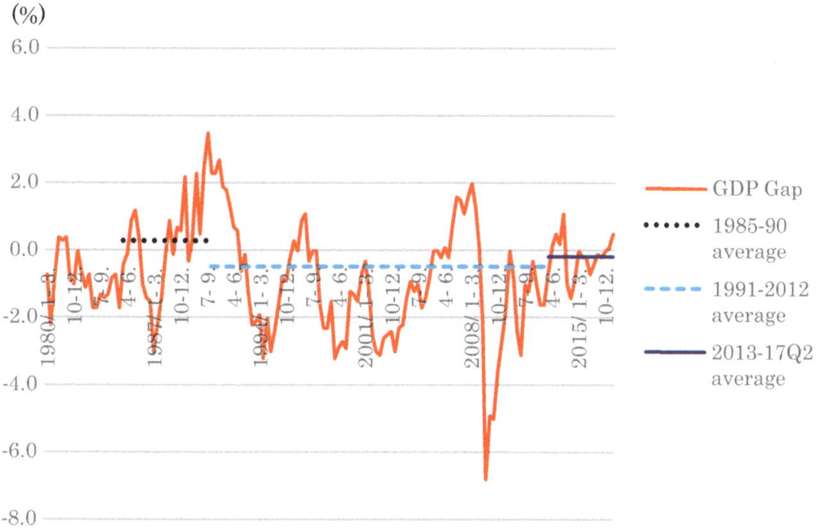

Fig. 7.31 GDP gap. Source: Cabinet Office, GDP statistics

However, there is a cautious view that the elimination of a negative GDP gap may not be necessarily a positive development. Figure 7.32 shows developments in potential growth rate estimated by the Cabinet Office. Japan's potential growth rate, which was at the 4% level at the beginning of the 1990s, continued to decline after the burst of the bubble, falling to a level just below 1% after the financial crisis in the late 1990s. It fell further to near 0% around the GFC, and subsequently, recovered somewhat but stayed flat at the 1% level up to the present. It is possible that such a decline in growth potential might have contributed to the elimination of the negative GDP gap under the expansion of demand.[20]

Wage Restraint and Consumption Stagnation

As we have seen, restraint on wages and labor costs seems to have brought about a decline in the growth contribution of consumption. Figure 7.33 shows the growth contribution (period average) of demand components for

Fig. 7.32 Potential growth rate. Source: Tabulated using data provided from the Cabinet Office website. (http://www5.cao.go.jp/keizai3/getsurei/getsurei-index.html)

[20] The "2017 White paper on small and medium enterprise in Japan" (pp. 12) notes the average age of equipment and machinery as of 2016 was 1.5 times older for large companies and about 2.0 times older for small and medium companies, as compared with 1990, indicating increased aging of equipment and machinery. Prolonged investment restraint has imposed negative impacts on competitiveness and growth potential of companies.

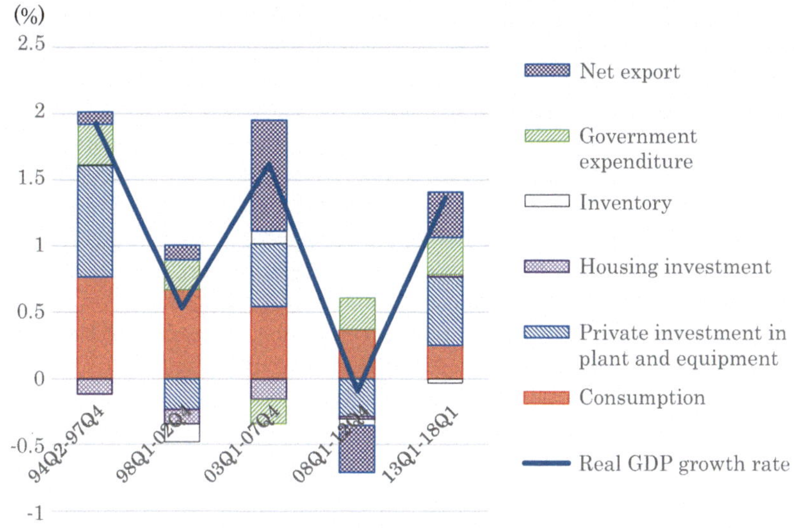

Fig. 7.33 Growth contribution by demand components. Source: Cabinet Office, GDP statistics

each of the five subperiods, covering about 24 years since 1994.[21] Growth contribution of consumption has consistently declined from 0.8 point in 1994–1997 to 0.3 point in the Abenomics period. In the background is the decline in real wages, as we saw previously. There has not been a big change in the corporate attitudes toward restraining labor costs. Although labor market conditions has been tightening, it is tighter in the market for non-regular workers. Duality in the labor market between regular and non-regular workers, and the existence of differences in wages and other working conditions between them, provide companies with an opportunity to contain labor costs through increased use of non-regular workers. In other words, duality in the labor market offers an effective tool for international competition through cost reduction. However, there is a limit for high-wage countries in how far they can compete internationally through cost-cutting. Restraint on wages contains consumption, and contributes to low growth, creating a vicious cycle of low growth. Also, duality of the labor market without rational basis seems to have produced external diseconomies to the society, by, for example, contributing to the falling marriage rate,

[21] Twenty-four years are divided into five subperiods, that is, four subperiods that broadly correspond to subdivision of the period of stagnation described in Chap. 3 plus the Abenomics period.

accompanied by the decline in birth rate.[22] In addition to trying to raise wages, in order to exit from the vicious cycle of low growth that seems to be self-fulfilling, it is also important to correct the disparity of treatments between regular and non-regular workers or that based on age or gender with no rational basis and to encourage changes in the way companies utilize human resources. However, we cannot entirely deny the possibility that the defensive attitude of companies is not just due to the mindset but is the outcome of rational response based upon expected shrinkage of the domestic economy and intensifying international competitive pressure. If there is rational basis, an increase in wages in excess of productivity growth will jeopardize international competition, promoting further shift of the production base overseas, and increase in domestic investment can result in accumulation of low-profitability assets. As stated before, in order to respond to the shrinking population and to have international competitiveness that is sustainable with high wages, it is necessary to increase wages and enhance productivity growth at the same time. A fundamental review and improvement of the way our human resources are used and also, how investment in human resources is conducted is critically important to raising of productivity.[23] We should note that trying to enhance competitiveness by regarding labor just as costs and simply curtailing it is self-defeating in the longer term.

[22] According to The Japan Institute for Labor Policy and Training, "Jakunensha no shugyo jokyo kyaria shokugyo noryoku kaihatu no genjo ② heisei 24 nen ban 'shugyou kozo kihon chosa' yori ('Current status of employment, career and work capacity development of young people ② based on 'basic survey of employment structure 2012')," JILP document series No. 144 September 2014, the share of those having a spouse at ages 30 to 34 is 57.8% for regular workers, and 23.3% for non-regular workers, such as part-timers. The share at the ages 35 to 39 is 68.6% for regular workers and 28.1% for non-regular workers. In short, the share of those having a spouse for non-regular workers is lower than half of that for regular workers.

[23] The Japanese government is currently pressing forward with "work style reform." This reform effort has positive elements such as regulation of long work hours and realization of the principle of "equal pay for equal work." However, how to achieve productivity increase that this reform aims at by labor market reform is an issue that needs cautious examination and thought through formulation of appropriate framework based on scientific and objective evidence. The most important premise when considering labor market reform is the fact that workers and companies do not stand on an even ground. Workers enter, and work under, an employment contract in an overwhelmingly disadvantageous (weak) position. As an individual, a worker is normally not in a position to choose the work style. In this sense, what is needed is not the "work style reform" but a reform of "humane resource development and utilization" under which the way companies or our society in general develop and utilize our human resources is examined and reformed where necessary and appropriate.

Continued Dependence of Growth on Government Expenditure

As we have seen, the degree of dependence of growth on government expenditure has been significantly higher in the Abenomics period, compared to the preceding period. It is worrisome that, when the corporate sector has been making historically high profits, dependence of growth on government expenditure is rising.

Figure 7.34 shows developments in the amount of annual issuance of government bonds. It is not that the amount has increased significantly in the Abenomics period, but government bonds amounting to 150–170 trillion yen, which is equivalent to close to one-third of GDP, are issued each year.

The structure of government bond holding is another matter of concern. Figure 7.35 shows shares by holder in the outstanding balance of government bonds and FILP bonds.[24] The deposit-taking financial institutions held 299.7 trillion yen, accounting for the largest share, 37.9% as

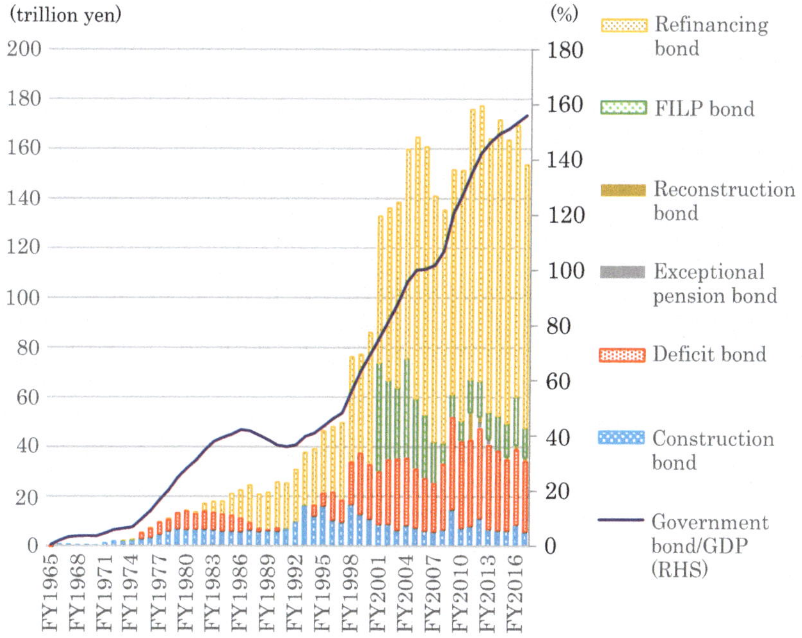

Fig. 7.34 Annual issuance of government bonds: FY 1965–2017. Source: Tabulated using data provided on the website of the Ministry of Finance

[24] FILP (Fiscal Investment and Loan Program) represents investment and lending operations by the government. The FILP bond is a type of government bond that the government issues as a low-interest fundraising tool based on sovereign credit for the operation of the program.

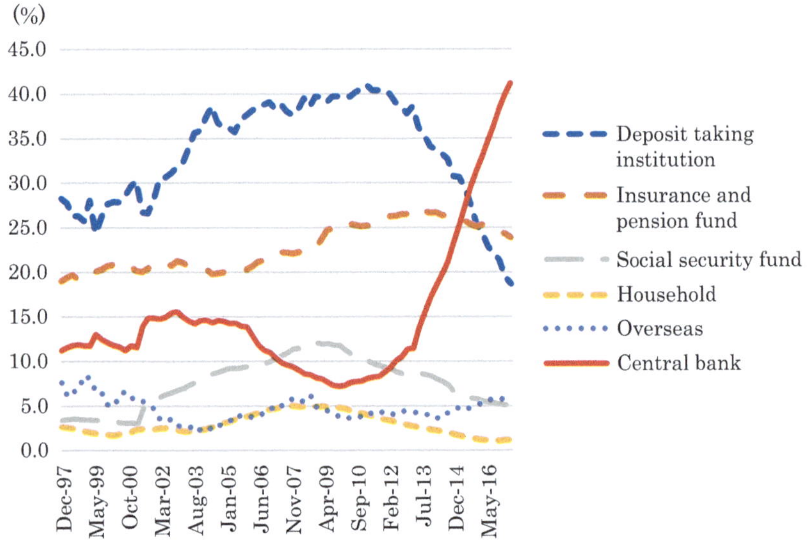

Fig. 7.35 Share in outstanding government bonds and FILP bonds held by major holders. Note: FILP bond is a government bond issued by the government on account of, and registered with, the FILP account of the government. As a financial product, it is the same as an ordinary government bond (see Footnote 24). Source: Tabulated data provided on the website of the Bank of Japan.

of December 2012. However, the amount of holdings and their share declined to 182.2 trillion yen and 18.7%, respectively, as of June 2017. By contrast, the amount and share held by the Bank of Japan increased from 90.9 trillion yen and 11.5% as of December 2012, to 401.9 trillion yen and 41.3% as of June 2017, respectively. Under the yield curve control, that is, control by the BOJ of both short-term and long-term interest rates, the government bond yields stay at a very low levels. Because of the large amount of purchase by the BOJ, government bond holding has shifted from banks to the BOJ on a large scale, and current account deposits with the BOJ held by banks have been sharply increasing in return. The huge amount of current account deposits with the BOJ bears basically a positive interest of 0.1%. As other profit-making opportunities for banks are limited, we cannot expect that the rapid increase in deposits in the current account (in other words, increase in the base money) could have large impacts on the real economy. Replacement of government bonds held by banks with deposits in the current account with the BOJ indicates that the financial position of banks will significantly depend on the financial soundness not of the government but of the BOJ. Therefore, in the process of exiting from the current condition of extremely eased monetary policy, it will become important for the stability of the financial system to maintain soundness of the BOJ. In other words, in order for the continued dependence of economic growth on government expenditure, coupled with eased monetary policy, not to raise risk to the financial system, it is becoming increasingly important to accomplish as soon as possible a private sector-led economic growth structure.

Under the declining strength of consumption, it is sometimes argued that we need to further strengthen the social security system because consumption has been contained by concern about the future among young people under the wage restraint and replacement of regular by non-regular workers. However, judging from the projections of population decline and further aging in the years to come, it is inevitable for social security expenditure, which currently accounts for one-third of expenditures in the government budget, to further increase. Therefore, what is necessary for maintaining fiscal capability to respond to such policy needs as national defense and security or maintenance of minimum infrastructure is to raise taxes and to reduce social security expenditure. In order to alleviate concerns for the future held by young people, it is important to raise the share of expenditures targeted at young people in such expenditures as social security. However, if such a shift in focus is accompanied by further deterioration of fiscal position, then it could have negative impacts on the concerns for the future of young people. Figure 7.36 shows, for each age group of respondents, the share, among all respondents with concern for the future, of those who listed deterioration in fiscal, employment, or economic conditions as a factor causing their concern. The share of respondents who listed any of these three factors is larger for the younger age groups.

Considering the need to alleviate concern for the future, while pressing forward with restraint on total social security expenditure and also with a shift of focus toward the younger generation and strengthening education and job training, it is important to implement such reforms of the social system that would not raise the fiscal burden. In other words, it is necessary not only for individuals but also for companies and local communities to move to a society that is based on a principle of "self-help and self-reliance." We need individuals who do not depend on public support, companies that do not depend on economic stimulus or subsidies from the government, and local communities that do not depend on fiscal support

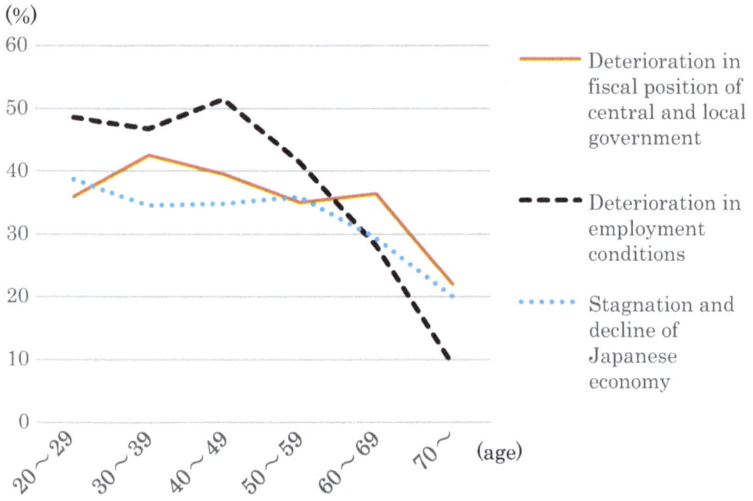

Fig. 7.36 Share of respondents for each age group who listed deterioration in fiscal, employment, or economic conditions as the cause of their concern for the future. Note: The figure shows the share of respondents for each age group who listed deterioration in fiscal conditions, employment conditions, or economic stagnation as a cause of their concern for the future. Respondents are those who had previously answered that they had concern for the future. Source: Cabinet Office, "Opinion survey on future image of Japan related to population, economy, and society," 2012

from the central government such as local distribution tax and subsidies. It will be inevitable for policies under Abenomics and subsequent policy developments to shift to the ones that encourage self-reliance of economic agents and promote their self-help.

Present Status of the Japanese Economy and the Challenges Ahead

The Japanese economy has turned into an economy governed by low-growth expectations and concerns for the future, after the anomaly and difficulties extending over more than 30 years. In particular, low-growth expectations held by companies has brought about restraint on domestic investment and wages with negative impacts on consumption, and also has produced such by-products as increasing potential financial risks arising from the policy of extremely low interest rates and the inability to reduce dependence on government expenditure and concerns for the future of the younger generation. The low-growth expectation is partly due to the outcome of a mindset in the sense that it is constrained by actual growth performance in the past, but at the same time, we cannot deny that it has a rational basis such as expectation of quantitative shrinkage of the domestic markets due to population decline.

In order to exit from this vicious cycle, companies need an expectation of sales increase, and households need an expectation of stable increase in income. As we have already touched on the immediately needed measures such as transformation of foreign demand to domestic demand and governance reform, we will briefly list medium- and long-term measures in concluding this book.

First, in order to achieve sales increase, while it may appear to be a roundabout way, it seems most important to reform the way companies utilize human resources. Presently, an option is open to companies to conduct a price-cut competition through reduction of labor costs by long work hours by regular workers and a shift to non-regular workers. However, effectiveness of such price-cut competition is limited for advanced countries that have relatively higher wages. Also, competition through labor cost reduction by shifting to non-regular workers has brought about social costs, including significantly lower marriage rates among non-regular workers. Therefore, it is necessary to encourage companies to move away from a competition through labor cost-cutting toward a competition through sales increase, by appropriately regulating long work hours and correcting irrationally differentiated treatments between regular and non-regular workers. Together with removing irrationally differentiated treatments between regular and non-regular workers, it seems necessary to separate stability of employment and stability of wages. No matter whether the worker is regular or non-regular, it is important to provide stable employment where possible, based on a principle of "equal pay for equal work."[25] At the same time, it is necessary to link wages to performance of the company and also introduce competition among workers for higher wages. If employment security for regular workers is combined with wage security, it is difficult to expect productivity increase. A system is in order where both regular and non-regular workers compete for higher productivity on a level paying field. Although cautious

[25] With a view to reducing duality between regular and non-regular workers in the Japanese labor market, Aoyagi and Ganelli (2013) proposed to introduce a Single Open Ended Contract (SOEC) for all new hires, in which employment protection, including severance pay, will increase with tenure. The SOEC would imply lower job security compared to current regular employment, but higher job security compared to current non-regular employment. In this regard, the paper refers to the Danish flexicurity model, which is composed of

analysis is necessary when institutionalizing such system, what is needed is a system to expose regular workers to external competition.[26]

Population is the biggest challenge for the Japanese economy and society, in light of its negative impacts (its effects on the expectation formation of sales and growth decline, decline of actual growth rate, and decline of national power). The biggest barrier to arresting population decline (raising the birth rate) is the costs accruing to women from career interruption arising from having and raising children. It is most important to help provide accommodating working environments where companies accept such work styles that careers are not interrupted by having and raising children (e.g., supporting establishment of an intracompany nursery school, and promoting work styles in harmony with respective stages of life in the form of working at home or part-time or flexible work hours). For the moment, until the birth rate is sufficiently raised, it is important to make maximum use of existing human resources including the aged, women, and non-regular workers. It is necessary to establish a society where any person can work and gain stable income based on a principle of self-help and self-reliance, without irrationally differentiated treatments, so long as the individual is healthy and willing to work.[27]

Utilization of foreign labor has to be examined with a long-term perspective, taking into account the impacts of settlement of foreign people that will inevitably arise (if foreign people settle, then they are immigrants). Regarding foreign labor solely as labor force and making use of them with short-sighted objectives will inevitably create problems for the future. Bearing in mind that what is at issue is not an economic matter but

(1) flexibility in the labor market (including reduction of protection of regular workers), combined with (2) social security protection through unemployment benefits, and (3) an active labor market policy. The main idea of flexicurity is that of protecting workers rather than jobs. However, the authors pointed out that the most difficult part for Japan is the high fiscal cost of the flexicurity model.

[26]As stated before, how to enhance labor productivity under any given framework is an issue that needs cautious examination based on scientific evidence.

[27]The mandatory age-limit retirement system, while a logical consequence of lifetime long employment coupled with a seniority-based wage system, is a system that can bring about enormous waste of human resources that is beyond imagination under a productivity-based employment and wage system. When we hear anecdotally about retired highly skilled workers being employed by foreign competitor companies and contributing to the strengthening of their competitiveness, we feel deeply how insensitive our society has been to the social losses that arise from a system of strong job security coupled with a seniority-based wage system. Intrinsic to current age-based system are, one, objectives to encourage employees to stay longer with the

a choice to alter the composition of a nation's people, it is indispensable to form a national consensus and wholly review and adjust current social institutions and systems that do not presume a large inflow of foreign people.

Influences of deterioration of fiscal position have already started to surface. For example, deterioration of the financial position of national and public universities and prolonged non-regular working conditions for post-doctoral researchers are bound to drive talented human resources away from research jobs and negatively affect, without fail, Japan's research level and technological advancements in the future. Furthermore, aging of economic infrastructure, such as roads and tunnels, is becoming an immediate problem. In light of population decline, a shift to a geographically concentrated inhabitation is a must, and restraint on social welfare expenditure is inevitable. Individuals, companies, and local communities all need to act on a principle of self-help and self-reliance, without relying on fiscal support from the government or short-sighted resort to the use of foreign laborers.

In particular, the way local government finance is operated poses a serious problem. Presently, local government finance is managed under a very centralized system, which incorporates very strong intervention by the central government, such as its annual formulation of local governments' fiscal programs and legal provision of standard tax rates for local taxes. The basis of fiscal democracy at the local level is in the approval by local residents of public expenditure by the local government and collection of local taxes to finance them. However, we do not often hear about cases where the assemblies of local government with relatively abundant revenues cut local taxes and those with insufficient revenue raise local taxes. Many local taxes have the nature of national taxes earmarked for local expenditure, in other words, taxes for specific purposes. Detrimental impacts of earmarked taxes are significant, with no need to refer to the case of road-related earmarked revenues. Local governments do not have to raise tax by obtaining approval of their residents in order to finance public services. They seem to stand in a

company, and, two, difficulty to introduce and operate a wage system that is based on company performance and assessment of productivity of each employee. As a result, companies continue to pay wages that may be higher than the productivity of the employees up to the retirement age and dismiss those employees who can produce more than their wages because they have reached the retirement age, together with those who cannot. We need to wholly review the current employment system including the mandatory age-limit retirement system.

position of using revenues that are distributed by the central government.[28] In 2018, a new forest environment tax was approved to be introduced as a national tax, which is predetermined to be transferred to local governments. This new tax symbolizes the essential nature of the current system of local government finance, that is, the central government prepares the revenue and the local government uses it.

Japan's social system, including its social welfare and economic infrastructure, seems to have been based on the assumption that the population and the economy would continue to expand. It is becoming difficult for such a basic system of society to operate smoothly with the decline of the population and low growth of the economy. It is good and appropriate to aim to mitigate population decline and increase economic growth. However, policy needs to be prepared for the case when neither population nor the economy expands. Now is the time when we have to fundamentally review our social system with a presumption that the economy will not expand and population will decline. The key concept for the review seems to be, as stated before, "self-help and self-reliance." We need to reestablish our society based on a principle of "self-help and self-reliance" that applies to companies, individuals, and local authorities.

[28] This is easily seen by looking at the gigantic and stately building of the Tokyo metropolitan government and the lavish, high-rise local government offices of central wards in Tokyo. The problem with current local government finance is exemplified by the fact that local assemblies of these local governments do not examine the balance between such expenditures and tax burden borne by local residents, and do not consider tax cuts.

Supplement

Chronology of Abenomics

2012

November 14 Then Prime Minister Noda of the Democratic Party (DP) declared in the Parliamentary discussion with Mr. Abe, president of LDP that he would dissolve the House of Representatives in two days, that is, on November 16.

November 15 Mr. Abe publicly stated that, once the LDP returned to the power, the government and the BOJ would set an inflation target of 2~3%, and implement limitless monetary easing.

December 16 In the election on December 16, the LDP had a landslide victory, gaining 294 seats from the pre-election level of 119, out of the total 480 seats, while the DP suffered a crushing defeat, reducing its seats by three-fourths from 230 to 57.

December 18 Governor Shirakawa of BOJ visited President Abe in the LDP headquarters.

December 26 The second Abe administration started and adopted its "Basic Policy" in the first cabinet meeting, which listed four focused areas (economy, foreign and security policy, education, and people's living) in addition to the recovery from the Great Earthquake and nuclear plant accident, and, in the area of the economy, stated:

A strong economy is the source of Japan's strength. Without its revival, there is no restoration of fiscal soundness nor of Japan's future. Through the "three arrows" of bold monetary policy, flexible fiscal policy, and growth strategy that promote private investment, we overcome prolonged deflation, and aim to increase employment.

2013

January 11 The government decided on "the Emergency Economic Measures for the Revival of Japan's Economy," with the central government expenditure amounting to 10.3 trillion yen and the expected impact on real GDP of about 2%,

January 22 The Cabinet Office, Ministry of Finance, and the Bank of Japan issued a joint statement on policy coordination between the government and the BOJ to get out of deflation and achieve sustainable economic growth, in which the BOJ committed to the establishment of a price stability target of 2%, in terms of year-on-year change of the CPI and aimed to achieve this target as soon as possible.

On the same day, the BOJ made public the changes in monetary policy.

March 20 Mr. Haruhiko Kuroda, former president of ADB, became governor of the BOJ.

April 4	The BOJ introduced the QQE in its first Monetary Policy Committee meeting after the change of the governor (from Shirakawa to Kuroda) and deputy governors (new deputies included Professor Iwata of Gakushuin University, a long-time outspoken critic of the BOJ).
June 14	The government decided on the "Basic Principles for Economic and Fiscal Management and Reform," which presents the directions of economic and fiscal policy management and the basic strategy for achieving Japan's revival, including the promotion of the "three arrows" in an integrated manner.
June 14	The government decided on the "Japan Revitalization Strategy," which is composed of three action plans, that is, plans for the revitalization of Japanese industry, strategic market creation, and a strategy of global outreach.
August 8	The government approved the medium-term fiscal program, which includes the following three goals: To halve the primary balance deficit of central and local governments combined from the level in FY 2010 (6.6% of GDP) by FY2015; To change the combined primary balance of central and local governments into surplus by FY 2020; and To reduce steadily the debt-to-GDP ratio thereafter.
September 1	The government decided to set up a forum between relevant ministers and representatives from both companies and employees, so that they could exchange views and form common understanding necessary to cope with challenges for achieving virtuous economic cycles.
October 1	The government decided to raise the consumption tax rate from the current 5% to 8% from April 1, 2014, which is the first increase of the rate in the last 17 years. At the same time, the government decided to compile an economic package to cope with the risk of economic downturn caused by reactionary fall in demand after the last minute surge before the rate increase.
December 5	The government decided on "The Economic Measures for Realization of Virtuous Cycles," with the central government expenditure amounting to 5.5 trillion yen and the expected impact on real GDP around 1%.
December 20	The forum of ministers and representatives from companies and employees issued a statement that, under the policy efforts for the virtuous cycles by the government, companies and employees will, based on performances of respective companies, let an increase in profits lead to an increase in wages.
2014	
April 1	Consumption tax rate was raised for the first time in 17 years from 5% to 8%.
April 1	Effective corporate tax rate was reduced by 2.4%.
June 24	The revised "Japan Revitalization Strategy" was released (aimed at reducing effective corporate tax rate to below 30% in a few years, enhancing corporate governance, enhancing women's participation, enabling flexible working practices, attracting foreign talent, reforming agricultural policy, etc.).

August 13	Real GDP was estimated to have declined from the previous quarter at an annualized rate of 6.8% in Q2 2014.
October 31	The BOJ announced an expansion of QQE (increase of the targeted annual increase in base money from the previous 60–70 to 80 trillion yen, etc.).
November 17	Real GDP was estimated to have declined from the previous quarter at an annualized rate of 1.6% in Q3 2014.
November 18	Prime Minister Abe announced that the increase in consumption tax rate, from 8% to 10% scheduled for October 2015, would be postponed by 18 months to April 2017, and that he would dissolve the lower house to ask for the people's judgment on Abenomics.
November 21	The Lower House dissolved (election on December 14, 2014).
December 14	In the general election on December 14, 2014, the LDP won 291 seats, just 2 seat less than before the election, and the coalition government with the Komeito, which obtained 35 seats, maintained the overwhelming majority of 326, which accounts for more than two-thirds of the total 475 seats.
December 24	The third Abe cabinet was formed.
December 27	The government decided on "The economic package for the spread of virtuous cycles to local areas" with additional budget expenditure of 3.5 trillion yen and expected contribution to real GDP growth of about 0.7%.
2015	
September 24	Prime Minister Abe declared the Abenomics shift to the second stage and announced new three arrows (targets), that is, strong economy (GDP of 600 trillion yen targeted), support for child-rearing (desirable birth rate of 1.8 targeted), and sound social security (no job departure due to nursing care of elderlies), and a target of maintaining a population of 100 million half a century into the future.
December 18	The BOJ adopted supplementary measures for the QQE, including some lengthening of average remaining maturities of JGB purchased.
2016	
January 29	The BOJ decided to introduce a negative interest rate of −0.1% to be applied to part of the outstanding balance of financial institutions' current account at BOJ (implemented from February 16) and declared that it would cut the interest rate further if necessary.
June 1	Prime Minister Abe announced that the increase in consumption tax rate scheduled for April 1, 2017 would be postponed again by 2 years and a half to October 1, 2019.
August 2	The government adopted "Economic measures for realizing investment for the future" with additional central government expenditure of 13.5 trillion yen and expected contribution to real GDP growth of about 1.3%.

September 21	The BOJ released the results of the comprehensive assessment of the developments under "Quantitative and Qualitative Monetary Easing (QQE)" and "QQE with a Negative Interest Rate," and a new policy called "yield curve control" was announced, in which the policy target was changed from the previous increase in base money to the control of both short-term and long-term interest rates (as for the short-term interest rate, a negative interest rate of −0.1% is applied to a part of the outstanding balance held by financial institutions in the current account with the BOJ, and as for the long-term interest rate, the BOJ will purchase JGBs so that 10-year JGB yields will remain more or less at the current level around 0%).
October 22	In the election of the Lower House, which was called by Prime Minister Abe on the grounds that he had changed his policy as to how to use additional revenue arising from the consumption tax increase, the LDP had a sweeping victory gaining 284 seats, which is well over half of the total 465 seats.

Bibliography

English References

Aoyagi, Chie, and Giovanni Ganelli (2013) "The Path to Higher Growth: Does Revamping Japan's Dual Labor Market Matter?" IMF Working Paper No. 13/202, International Monetary Fund, Washington, DC.

Fukuda, Shin-ichi (2015) "Abenomics: Why was it so successful in changing market expectations?" *Journal of the Japanese and International Economies* vol 37, 1–20.

IMF (International Monetary Fund) (2014) "Japan 2014 Article IV Consultation—Staff Report; and Press Release." July, IMF Country Report 14/236, IMF, Washington, DC.

Iwata, Kikuo (2013) "Quantitative and qualitative monetary easing and its transmission mechanism: Logic behind the first arrow." August 28, 2013, Bank of Japan.

Kuroda, Haruhiko (2013) "Public policy study and monetary policy management." December 7, 2013, Bank of Japan.

Shirakawa, Masaaki (2012a) "Deleveraging and Growth: Is the Developed World Following Japan's Long and Winding Road?" A Lecture by the Then Governor at the London School of Economics and Political Science on January 10.

Small and Medium Enterprise Agency (2017) *2017 White paper on small and medium enterprise in Japan.*

Japanese References

Adachi, Makiko (2014) "Shoshi Koreika ga Kakei Bumon ni Ataeru Eikyo (Impacts of Declining Birth Rate and Aging Population on Household Sector)" (Mizuho Soken Ronshu (2004 I), pp. 1–35. Mizuho Sogo Kenkyujo.

Bank of Japan (1997) "Kozo Chosei ka no Setsubi Toshi Kaifuku ni tsuite" (On the Recovery of Plant and Equipment Investment under Structural Adjustments) February 26, Research and Statistics Department.

Bank of Japan (1999) "90 nendai niokeru Hi-seizogyo no Shueki Teimei no Haikeinitsite" (On the Background of Profit Stagnation of Non-manufacturing Industry in the 1990s) February 2, Research and Statistics Department.

Bank of Japan (2006) "Kinnen no Seizogyo no Setsubi Toshi Zoka nitsuite" (On the Recent Increase in Plant and Equipment Investment of Manufacturing Industry) *Bank of Japan Review* 2006-J-17.

Dai-Ichi Seimei Keizai Kenkyu Jo (2003) *Shisan Defure de Yomitoku Nihon Keizai* (Understanding Japanese Economy Through Asset Price Deflation) 2003. Nihon Keizai Shimbun Sha.

Hayakawa, Hideo (2016) *Kinnyu Seisaku no 'Gokai' – 'Sodai na Jikken' no Seika* ("Misunderstanding" of monetary policy—Outcome of a "spectacular experiment"). Keio Gijuku Daigaku Shuppan Kai.

Japan Institute for Labor Policy and Training (Rodo Seisaku Kenkyu Kenshu Kiko) (2014) "Jakunensha no shugyo jokyo, kyaria, shokugyo noryoku kaihatu no genjo ② heisei 24 nen ban 'shugyo kozo kihon chosa' yori" (Current status of employment, career and work capacity development of young people ② based on 'basic survey of employment structure' 2012), JILP Document Series No. 144, September 2014.

Kaizuka, Keimei (2006) *Keizai Kakusa no Kenkyu* (A Study of Economic Inequality). Chuo Keizai Sha.

Nakao, Takehiko (2008) "Amerika no Keizai Seisaku : Tsuyosa ha Jizoku Dekiru noka" (Economic Policy in the United States: Can the Strength be Sustained?).

Nukaga, Makoto (2005) "Juyo Shukusho no Kiki-Jinko Gensho Shaki no Keizaigaku- (Demand shrinkage crisis-Economics of population decline)" NTT Publication.

Ogawa, Kazuo (2009) "Baransu Shito no Kison to Jitsubutsu Keizai – 1990 nendai ikono Nihon Keizai no Jissho Bunseki" (Damages to the Balance Sheet and the Real Economy – Empirical Analysis of the Japanese Economy since the 1990s). In *Furyo Saiken to Kinnyu Kiki* (Non-performing loans and the financial crisis), edited by Kazuto Ikeo, Cabinet Office, "Baburu/defure kino Nihon Keizai to Keizai Seisaku 4" (Japanese Economy and Economic Policy in the Period of the Bubble and Deflation 4), Economic and Social Research Institute, Cabinet Office.

Oshio, Takashi (2005) *Jinko Gensho Jidai no Shakai Hosho Kaikaku* (Social Security System Reform in the Era of Declining Population). Nihon Keizai Shimbun Sha.
Ota, Kiyoshi (2005) "Furita no Zoka to Rodo Shotoku Kakusa no Kakudai" (Increase in "Freeter" and Expanding Inequality of Earned Income). ESRI Discussion Paper Series No.140, May.
Otake Fumio (2005) *Nihon no Fubyodo* (Inequality in Japan). Nihon Keizai Shimbun Sha.
Sato, Toshiki (2000) *Fubyodo Shakai Nippon : Sayonara So Churyu* (Japan An Unequal Society: Goodbye All Middle Class Society). Chuko Shinsho.
Shimizudani, Satoshi (2005) *Kitai to Fukakujitu Sei no Keizai Gaku* (Economics of Expectation and Uncertainty). Nihon Keizai Shimbun Sha.
Sugihara, Shigeru, and Satoshi Ota (2002) "Shisan Kakaku no Geraku to Kigyo no Baransu Shito Chosei" (Decline in Asset Prices and Balance Sheet Adjustments of Corporations). In *Defure no Jissho Bunseki* (Empirical Analysis of Deflation)., edited by Yutaka Harada and Kikuo Iwata, Toyo Keizai Shimpo Sha.
Tachibanaki, Toshiaki (1998) *Nihon no Keizai Kakusa* (Economic Inequality in Japan). Iwanami Shinsho.
Tachibanaki, Toshiaki (2006) *Kakusa Shakai: Nani ga Mondai Nanoka* (Unequal Society: What is the Problem?). Iwanami Shinsho.
Yamada, Masahiro (2004) *Kibo Kakusa Shakai: 'Makegumi' no Zetsubo Kan ga Nihon wo Hikisaku* (Society of Unequal Hope: Despair of "the Failed" will divide Japan). Chikuma Shobo.
Yoshikawa, Hiroshi (2011) "Shoshi Koreika to Keizai Seicho" (The declining birth rate and aging population and economic growth) RIETI Discussion Paper Series 11-P-006 January.
Yoshikawa, Hiroshi (2016) "Jinko to Nihon Keizai" (Population and the Japanese economy). Chu Ko Shinsho.
Yugami, Kazufumi (2003) "Nihon no Shotoku Kakusa wo Do Miruka" (How to Assess Income Disparity in Japan?) *JIL Rodo Seisaku Report* 2003.3.

Bibliography

Reference in English

Ahearne, Alan, J. Gagnon, J. Haltmaier, and S. Kamin (2002) "Preventing deflation: Lessons from Japan's experience in the 1990s." International Finance Discussion Paper Number 729, Board of Governors of the Federal Reserve System, Washington, DC.

Aoyagi, Chie, and Giovanni Ganelli (2013) "The Path to Higher Growth: Does Revamping Japan's Dual Labor Market Matter?" IMF Working Paper No. 13/202, International Monetary Fund, Washington, DC.

BOJ (Bank of Japan) (1998) "Change of the Guideline for Money Market Operations," September 9, Bank of Japan.

Bernanke, Ben (2000) "Japanese monetary policy: A case of self-induced paralysis?" In *Japan's Financial Crisis and Its Parallels to U.S. Experience*, edited by Ryoichi Mikitani and Adam. S. Posen. 149–66. Washington, DC: Institute for International Economy.

Cabinet Office, Government of Japan (2001) Annual Report on the Japanese Economy and Public Finance 2000—No Gains Without Reform, December.

Flath, David (2005) *The Japanese Economy*, 2nd edn., Chapter 8. Oxford: Oxford University Press.

Fujiki, Hiroshi, Kunio Okina, and Shigenori Shiratsuka (2001) "Monetary Policy under Zero Interest Rate: Viewpoints of Central Bank Economists" *Monetary and Economic Studies*/February 2001, Bank of Japan.

Fukuda, Shin-ichi (2015) "Abenomics: Why Was It So Successful in Changing Market Expectations?" *Journal of the Japanese and International Economies* 37: 1–20.

K. Aramaki, *Japan's Long Stagnation, Deflation, and Abenomics*,
https://doi.org/10.1007/978-981-13-2176-4

Hayashi, Fumio, and Edward C. Prescott (2002) "The 1990s in Japan: A Lost Decade." *Review of Economic Dynamics* 5 (1): 206–35.

IMF (International Monetary Fund) (1995) "The Nordic Banking Crises: Pitfalls in Financial Liberalization?" IMF Working Paper WP/95/61, IMF, Washington, DC.

IMF (International Monetary Fund) (2003) *World Economic Outlook,* April , IMF, Washington, DC.

IMF (International Monetary Fund) (2014) "Japan 2014 Article IV Consultation—Staff Report and Press Release," July 2014.

Iwata, Kikuo (2013) "Quantitative and qualitative monetary easing and its transmission mechanism: Logic behind the first arrow," August 28, Bank of Japan.

Jinushi, Toshiki, Yoshihiro Kuroki, and Ryuzo Miyao (2000) "Monetary policy in Japan since the late 1980s: Delayed policy actions and some explanations." In *Japan's Financial Crisis and Its Parallels to U.S. Experience,* edited by Mikitani Ryoichi, and A. S. Posen, 115–48. Washington, DC: Institute for International Economy.

Kang, Joong Shik (2014) "Balance Sheet Repair and Corporate Investment in Japan." IMF Working Paper WP/14/141, International Monetary Fund, Asian and Pacific Department.

Katz, Richard (1998) *Japan: The System that Soured: The Rise and Fall of the Japanese Economic Miracle.* Armonk, NY: M. E. Sharpe.

Kosai, Yutaka (1986) The Era of High-Speed Growth – Notes on the Postwar Japanese Economy. Tokyo: University of Tokyo Press.

Krugman, Paul (1998) "It's baaack: Japan's Slump and the Return of the Liquidity Trap." *Brookings Papers on Economic Activity,* 2: 137–205.

Krugman, Paul (2000) "Thinking about the liquidity trap" *Journal of the Japanese and International Economies* 14: 221–37(2000).

Kuroda, Haruhiko (2013) "Public policy study and monetary policy management," December 7, Bank of Japan.

Mori, Naruki, Shiratsuka Shigenori, and Hiroo Taguchi (2001) "Policy Responses to the Post-bubble Adjustments in Japan: A Tentative Review." *Monetary and Economic Studies* 19 (S1): 53–112, Institute for Monetary and Economic Studies, Bank of Japan.

Motonishi, Taizo, and Hiroshi Yoshikawa (1999) "Causes of the Long Stagnation of Japan During the 1990s: Financial or Real?" NBER Working Paper No. 7351, National Bureau of Economic Research, Cambridge, MA.

Nakao, Takehiko (2002) "Japan's experience with fiscal policy in the 1990s in the aftermath of the bubble economy." Presentation at the 4th Banca d'Italia Workshops on Public Finances, "The Impact of Fiscal Policy," March 21–23.

Nakaso, Hiroshi (2001) "The financial crisis in Japan during the 1990s: How the Bank of Japan responded and the lessons learnt." BIS Papers No. 6, BIS, Basel.

Nakaso, Hiroshi (2014) "What the lost decades left for the future." Keynote speech, 2014 International Conference of the International Association of Deposit Insurers, Asia–Pacific Regional Committee, Bank of Japan, April 23.

Nishizaki, Kenji, Toshitake Sekine, and Yuichi Ueno (2012) "Chronic deflation in Japan." Bank of Japan Working Paper Series, No. 12-E-6, Bank of Japan.
Okina, Kunio and Nobuyuki Oda (2000) "Additional Monetary Easing Options under the Non-negative Constraint of Interest Rate: Issues Drawing on Japan's experience." *Kinnyu Kenkyu* 2000.12, Institute for Monetary and Economic Studies, Bank of Japan.
Okina, Kunio, Masaaki Shirakawa, and Shigenori Shiratsuka (2001) "Asset price bubbles and monetary policy: Japan's experience in the late 1980s and the lessons: Background Paper." *Monetary and Economic Studies* 19 (S1): 395–450.
Okina, Kunio, and Shigenori Shiratsuka (2002) "Asset Price Bubbles, Price Stability, and Monetary Policy: Japan's Experience" *Monetary and Economic Studies* Vol.20, No3/October 2002, Bank of Japan.
Sakakibara, Eisuke (2000) "US-Japanese economic policy conflicts and coordination during the 1990s)." In *Japan's Financial Crisis and Its Parallels to U.S. Experience*, edited by Ryoichi Mikitani and Adam S. Posen. Washington, DC: Institute for International Economy.
Shirakawa, Masaaki (2010) "Japan's economy and monetary policy," January 29, Bank of Japan.
Shirakawa, Masaaki (2012a) "Deleveraging and Growth: Is the World Following Japan's Long and Winding Road?" Lecture at the London School of Economics (LSE) and Political Science (Co, co-hosted by the Asia Research Center and Suntory and Toyota International Centres for Economics and Related Disciplines (STICARD), LSE), January 10, 2012, Bank of Japan.
Shirakawa, Masaaki (2012b) "Japan's economy and monetary policy." June 4, Bank of Japan.
Small and Medium Enterprise Agency (2017) *2017 White paper on small and medium enterprise in Japan.*
Swenson, Lars E. (2003) "Escaping from a Liquidity Trap and Deflation: Foolproof Way and Others." NBER Working Paper 10195, National Bureau of Economic Research, Cambridge, MA.
Ugai, Hiroshi (2007) "Effects of the Quantitative Easing Policy: A Survey of Empirical Analysis." *Monetary and Economic Studies*/March 2007, BOJ.
Yamaguchi, Yutaka (1999) "Monetary Policy and Structural Policy: A Japanese Perspective." Remarks by Yutaka Yamaguchi, Deputy Governor of the Bank of Japan, before Colloque Montaire International at Banque de France, October 8–9.

Reference in Japanese

Adachi, Makiko (2014) "Shoshi Koreika ga Kakei Bumon ni Ataeru Eikyo (Impacts of Declining Birth Rate and Aging Population on Household Sector)" (Mizuho Soken Ronshu (2004 I), pp. 1–35. Mizuho Sogo Kenkyujo.
Adachi, Seiji, (2013) "Kinnyu seisaku kettei purosesu to kinnyu seisaku ronso no keifu" (Process of Monetary Policy Determination and Developments in

Monetary Policy Debates). In *Mazu defure wo tomeyo* (Stop Deflation, First), edited by Kikuo Iwata, Nihon Keizai Shimbun Sha.
Asahi Shimbun (2009) *Henten Keizai* (Economy in Transition), News Crew on Ushinawareta '20 nen' (Lost "20 Years"). Iwanami Shoten.
Aoshima, Yaichi, Akira Takeishi, and Cusumano, Michael A. (2010) *Meido in Japan ha Owaru noka* (Is "Made in Japan" to End?). Toyo Keizai Shimpo Sha.
Bank of Japan (1990) *Chosa Geppo* (Monthly Research Report), April.
Bank of Japan (1993) "Heisei 5 nendo no Kinnyu oyobi Keizai no Doko" (States of Finance and Economy in FY 1993), in BOJ *Chosa Geppo*, June.
Bank of Japan (1997) "Kozo Chosei ka no Setsubi Toshi Kaifuku ni tsuite" (On the Recovery of Plant and Equipment Investment under Structural Adjustments) February 26, Research and Statistics Department.
Bank of Japan (1998a) "Hayami Sosai Kisha Kaiken Yoshi" (Manuscript of press conference by Governor Hayami), July 21.
Bank of Japan (1998b) "Hayami Sosai Kisha Kaiken Yoshi" (Manuscript of press conference by Governor Hayami), August 13.
Bank of Japan (1999a) "90 nendai niokeru Hi-seizogyo no Shueki Teimei no Haikei nitsite" (On the Background of Profit Stagnation of Non-manufacturing Industry in the 1990s), February 2.
Bank of Japan (1999b) "Hayami Sosai Kisha Kaiken Yoshi" (Manuscript of press conference by Governor Hayami), May 20.
Bank of Japan (1999c) "Hayami Sosai Kisha Kaiken Yoshi" (Manuscript of press conference by Governor Hayami), August 17.
Bank of Japan (1999d) "Hayami Sosai Kisha Kaiken Yoshi" (Manuscript of press conference by Governor Hayami), September 21.
Bank of Japan (2000a) "Hayami Sosai Kisha Kaiken Yoshi" (Manuscript of press conference by governor Hayami), February 15.
Bank of Japan (2000b) "Hayami Sosai Kisha Kaiken Yoshi" (Manuscript of press conference by Governor Hayami), March 10
Bank of Japan (2000c) "Hayami Sosai Kisha Kaiken Yoshi" (Manuscript of press conference by Governor Hayami), April 12.
Bank of Japan (2000d) "Hayami Sosai Kisha Kaiken Yoshi" (Manuscript of press conference by Governor Hayami), June 14.
Bank of Japan (2000e) "Hayami Sosai Kisha Kaiken Yoshi" (Manuscript of press conference by Governor Hayami), July 19.
Bank of Japan (2000f) "Wagakuni no Bukka Doko—90 nendai no Keiken wo Chushin ni" (Developments in Prices in Japan—Centering on the Experience in the 1990s), October, Department of Research and Statistics.
Bank of Japan (2001) "Saikin no Ginko Kashidashi Shijo no Doko nituite" (Recent Developments in Bank Credit Markets), October, *Market Review* 2001-J-10.
Bank of Japan (2003a) *Keizai Bukka no Shorai Tenbo to Risuku Hyoka* (Future Outlook of the Economy and Prices and Risk Assessment), April.

Bank of Japan (2003b) *Keizai Bukka no Shorai Tenbo to Risuku Hyoka* (Future Outlook of the Economy and Prices and Risk Assessment), October.

Bank of Japan (2004a) *Keizai Bukka no Shorai Tenbo to Risuku Hyoka* (Future Outlook of the Economy and Prices and Risk Assessment), April.

Bank of Japan (2004b) *Keizai Bukka no Shorai Tenbo to Risuku Hyoka* (Future Outlook of the Economy and Prices and Risk Assessment), October.

Bank of Japan (2005a) *Keizai Bukka no Shorai Tenbo to Risuku Hyoka* (Future Outlook of the Economy and Prices and Risk Assessment), April.

Bank of Japan (2005b) "Wagakuni Kigyo niyoru Yurishi Fusai no Asshuku to Rieki Bunpai Saku" (Reduction of Interest-bearing Debt by Japanese Companies and Profit Distribution Policy), May, *Nichigin Review* 2005-J-7.

Bank of Japan (2005c) *Keizai Bukka no Shorai Tenbo to Risuku Hyoka* (Future Outlook of the Economy and Prices and Risk Assessment), October.

Bank of Japan (2006) "Kinnen no Seizogyo no Setsubi Toshi Zoka nitsuite" (On the Recent Increase in Plant and Equipment Investment of Manufacturing Industry).

Bank of Japan (2009a) *Kinnyu Keizai Geppo* (Monthly Financial and Economic Report) February.

Bank of Japan (2009b) "Kigyo Shueki no Kaizen to sono Nihon Keizai heno Ganni" (Improvements in Corporate Profits and Its Implications to Japanese Economy), September 20, Research and Statistics Department.

Bank of Japan (2012) "Nihon no Jinko Dotai to Chuchoki tekina Seichoryoku: Jijitsu to Ronten no Seiri" (Japan's Demography and Medium and Long-term Growth Potential: Facts and Issues), August, Research and Statistics Department.

Bernanke, Ben (2001) "Mizukara Kino Mahi ni Ochitta Nihon no Kinnyu Seisaku" (Japanese Monetary Policy—A Case of Self-induced Paralysis?). In *Nihon no Kinyu Kiki—Beikoku no Keiken to Nihon heno Kyokun* (Monetary Policy in Japan—US Experiences and Their Lessons for Japan), edited by Ryoichi Mikitani and Adam A. Posen, Toyo Keizai Shimpo Sha.

Cabinet Office (2001) *Heisei 13 nendo Nenji Keizai Zaisei Hokoku—Kaikaku Nakushite Seicho Nashi* (Annual Report on the Japanese Economy and Public Finance FY 2001—No Gains without Reforms), December.

Cabinet Office (2005) *Heisei 17 nendo Nenji Keizai Zaisei Hokoku* (Annual Report on the Japanese Economy and Public Finance FY 2005), July.

Cabinet Office (2008a) *Heisei 20 nendo Nenji Keizai Zaisei Hokoku* (Annual Report on the Japanese Economy and Public Finance FY 2008).

Cabinet Office (2008b) Nihon Keizai 2008–2009 (Japanese Economy 2008–2009), December.

Cabinet Office (2010) *Heisei 22 nendo Nenji Keizai Zaisei Hokoku* (Annual Report on the Japanese Economy and Public Finance FY 2010).

Cabinet Office (2012a) *Heisei 24 nenban Kodomo Kosodate Hakusho* (White Paper on Children and Child-rearing 2012).

Cabinet Office (2012b) "Choki Keizai Tokei Heisei 24 Nendo" (Long-term economic statistics FY 2012), http://www5.cao.go.jp/j-j/wp/wp-je12/h10_data00.html (accessed on October 7, 2018).

Cabinet Office. (2014) "Senzai Seichoritsu ni tuite" (Chuchoki, Makuroteki Kanten karano Bunseki ①) (On the potential growth rate (Analysis from mid- to long-term and macro economic view points(1)) February 14, Heisei 26) (http://www5.cao.go.jp/keizai-shimon/kaigi/special/future/0214/shiryou_02.pdf (accessed on December 11, 2017).

Dai-Ichi Seimei Keizai Kenkyu Jo (2003) *Shisan Defure de Yomitoku Nihon Keizai* (Understanding the Japanese Economy through Asset Price Deflation). Nihon Keizai Shimbun Sha.

Deposit Insurance Corporation of Japan (2005) "Kinnyu Kikan Hatan ni kansuru Teiryo Bunseki" (Quantitative Analysis of Failures of Financial Institutions), *Yokin Hoken Kenkyu*, September.

Economic Planning Agency (1984) *Nenji Keizai Hokoku* (Annual Economic Report) 1984.

Economic Planning Agency (1991) *Nenji Keizai Hokoku* (Annual Economic Report) 1991.

Economic Planning Agency (1993) *Heisei 5 nen Nenji Keizai Hokoku* (1993 Annual Economic Report).

Fujii, Mariko (2009) *Kinnyu Kakushin to Shijo Kiki* (Financial Breakthrough and Market Crisis). Nihon Keizai Shimbun Sha.

Fujii, Yoshihiro (2001) *Kinnyu Saisei no Gosan* (Miscalculations of Financial Recovery). Nihon Keizai Shimbun Sha.

Fukao, Kyoji (2002) "Nihon no Chochiku Choka to 'Baburu' no Hassei" (Japan's Excess Savings and the Emergence of the 'Bubble'). In *Heisei Baburu no Kenkyu I* (Study of the Heisei Bubble I), edited by Michio Muramatsu and Masahiro Okuno, Tokyo: Toyo Keizai Shimpo Sha.

Fukao, Kyoji (2012) *'Usinawareta 20 nen' to Nihon Keizai—Kozoteki Yoin to Saisei heno Gendoryoku no Kaimei* ("Lost Two Decades" and the Japanese Economy—Identifying Structural Factors and Momentum for Revival), Nihon Keizai Shimbun Shuppan Sha.

Fukao, Mitsuhiro (2002) "1980 nendai Kohan no Shisan Kakaku Baburu Hassei to 90 nendai no Fukyo no Gennin" (Causes of Asset Price Bubble in the Late 1980s and Recession in the 1990s). In *Heisei Baburu no Kenkyu I* (Study of the Heisei Bubble I), edited by Michio Muramatsu and Masahiro Okuno,, Toyo Keizai Shimpo Sha.

Fukao, Mitsuhiro (2009a) "Choki Fukyo to Kinnyu Seisaku Kawase Reto Ginko Shinnyo" (The Long Stagnation and Monetary Policy, Foreign Exchange Rate and Bank Credit). In *Furyo Saiken to Kinnyu Kiki* (Non-performing Loans and Monetary Policy), edited by Kazuto Ikeo, ("Baburu/defure kino Nihon Keizai to Keizai Seisaku 4" (Japanese Economy and Economic Policy in the Period of Bubble and Deflation 4)), Economic and Social Research Institute, Cabinet Office.

Fukao, Mitsuhiro (2009b) "Ginko no Keiei Akka to Hatan Shori" (Deterioration of Performance of Banks and Their Resolution). In "*Furyo Saiken to Kinnyu Kiki*," (Non-Performing Loans and Financial Crisis), edited by Kazuto Ikeo, ("Baburu/Defure ki no Nihon Keizai to Keizai Seisaku 4" (Japanese Economy and Economic Policies in the Period of Bubble and Deflation, 4)), Economic and Social Research Institute, Cabinet Office.

Fukuda, Shin-ichi (2009) "Baburu Hokai gono Kinnyu Shijo no Doyo to Kinnyu Seisaku" (Instability of Financial Markets after the Collapse of the Bubble and Monetary Policy). In *Defure Keizai to Kinnyu Seisaku* (Deflationary Economy and Monetary Policy), edited by Hiroshi Yoshikawa ("Baburu/defure kino Nihon Keizai to Keizai Seisaku 7" (Japanese Economy and Economic Policy in the Period of Bubble and Deflation 7)), Economic and Social Research Institute, Cabinet Office.

Fukuda Shin-ichi (2015) *'Ushinawareta 20 nen' wo Koete* (Beyond "The Lost 20 Years"), NTT Shuppan.

Funabashi, Yoichi (1998) *Tsuka Retsu Retsu.* Asahi Shimbun Sha. English translation: *Managing the Dollar – From the Plaza to the Louvre.* Institute for International Economics.

Hamada, Koichi, and Akiyoshi Horiuchi (2004) *Ronso: Nihon no Keizai Kiki—Choki Teitai no Shin-in wo Kaimei suru* (Debates: Japan's Economic Crisis—Examining Real Cause of the Long Stagnation), Nihon Keizai Shimbun Sha.

Harashima, Motomu (2005) *Nihon Keizai Shippai Gaku* (Failure Theory of the Japanese Economy), V2 Solution.

Hattori, Shigeyuki (2008) *Kinnyu Seisaku no Gosan* (Miscalculations of Monetary Policy). NTT Shuppan.

Hayakawa, Hideo (2016) *Kinnyu Seisaku no 'Gokai'—'Sodai na Jikken' no Seika* ("Misunderstanding" of Monetary Policy—Outcome of a "spectacular experiment"). Keio Gijuku Daigaku Shuppan Kai.

Hayami, Masaru (1998) "Azia Keizai to Nihon no Yakuwari" (The Asian Economy and Japan's Role"), Keynote speech at the 24th business conference for Japan and ASEAN countries, Bank of Japan, October 29.

Hayashi, Fumio (2003) "Kozo Kaikaku Nakushite Seicho Nashi" (No Growth without Structural Reform). In "*Usinawareta 10 nen no Shin-in ha Nanika*" (What Is the Real Cause of the Lost Decade?), edited by Kikuo Iwata and Tsutomu Miyagawa,. Toyo Keizai Shimpo Sha.

Heisei Kinnyu Kiki heno Taio Kenkyu Kai (2005) "Hatan Shori Shuho no Shinka to Kanren Ho no Seibi (Kinnyu Saisei Ho Igo)" (Progress in Tools for Resolution of Failed Institutions and Provisions of Relevant Laws since the Financial Recovery Act) *Yokin Hoken Kenkyu* Vol. 4, September.

Himino, Ryozo (2005) "Kensho BIS Kisei to Nihon" (Examining BIS Regulations and Japan). Kinnyu Zaisei Jijo.

Hori, Masahiro (2009) "Ajia no Hatten to Nihon Keizai—Gaiju Doko Kawase Reto to Nihon no Kyoso Ryoku" (Growth of Asia and Japan's Economy—Evolution of Foreign Demand, Foreign Exchange Rate, and Japan's

Competitiveness). In *Makuro Keizai to Sangyo Kozo,* (Macroeconomy and Industrial Structure), edited by Kyoji Fukao ("Baburu/defure kino Nihon Keizai to Keizai Seisaku 1"(Japanese Economy and Economic Policy in the Period of Bubble and Deflation 1)), Economic and Social Research Institute, Cabinet Office.

Hori, Mashiro, and Hideaki Kitaki (2004) "Ginko Kino Teika Genkyo Setsu ha Settoku Ryoku wo Mochiuruka" (Is the Argument to Blame Declining Bank Function Convincing?). In *Ronso: Nihon no Keizai Kiki—Choki Teitai no Shin in wo Kaimei suru* (Debates: Japan's Economic Crisis—Examining Real Cause of the Long Stagnation), edited by Koichi Hamada and Akiyoshi Horiuchi, Nihon Keizai Shimbun Sha.

Horioka, Charles Yuji (2007) "Nihon no 'Ushinawareta 10 nen' no Gen-in" (Cause of Japan's "Lost Decade"). In *Keizai Teitai no Gen-in to Seido* (Causes of Economic Stagnation and Institutions), edited by Fumio Hayashi, Keiso Shobo.

Hoshi, Takeo, and Hugh Patrick, eds. *Nihon Kinnyu Shisutemu no Kiki to Henbo* (Crisis in Japan's Financial System and Its Transition). Nihon Keizai Shimbun Sha.

Ikeo, Kazuto, ed. (2009) *Furyo Saiken to Kinnyu Kiki* (Non-Performing Loans and the Japanese Economy) ("Baburu/defure kino Nihon Keizai to Keizai Seisaku 4 " (Japanese Economy and Economic Policy in the Period of Bubble and Deflation 4),) Economic and Social Research Institute, Cabinet Office.

Ishii, Shigeru (1998) *Ketsudan naki Keiei* (Management without Decision). Nihon Keizai Shimbun Sha.

Itami, Takayuki (2006) *Nichi Bei Kigyo no Rieki Ritsu Kakusa* (Discrepancy in Profitability between Japanese and US Companies). Yuhi Kaku.

Ito, Mitsutoshi (2002) "Choki Teikinri Seisaku no Seiji Keizai Gaku" (Political Economy of the Prolonged Low Interest Rate Policy). In *Heisei Baburu no Kenkyu II* (Study of the *Heisei* Bubble II), edited by Michio Muramatsu and Masahiro Okuno, Toyo Keizai Shimpo Sha.

Ito, Motoshige, ed. (2009) *Kokusai Kankyo no Henka to Nihon Keizai* (Changes in International Environments and the Japanese Economy), (Cabinet Office "Baburu/defure kino Nihon Keizai to Keizai Seisaku 3" (Japanese Economy and Economic Policy in the Period of Bubble and Deflation 3)), Economic and Social Research Institute, Cabinet Office.

Iwata, Kazumasa (2010) *Defure tono Tatakai* (Battle against Deflation). Nihon Keizai Shimbun Sha.

Iwata, Kazumasa, and Economic and Social Research Institute, Cabinet Office, eds. (2011) *Baburu/Defure ki no Nihon Keizai to Keizai Seisaku—Ware Ware ha Nani wo Mananda noka* (Japanese Economy and Economic Policy in the Period of Bubble and Deflation—What Have We Learned?), Economic and Social Research Institute, Cabinet Office.

Iwata, Kikuo (1992) Nichigin Riron wo Hoki seyo (Give up the BOJ Theory). *Shukan Toyo Keizai*, September 12.

Iwata, Kikuo (1993) *Kinnyu Seisaku no Keizai Gaku —'Nichigin Riron' no Kensho* (Economics of Monetary Policy—Examination of the "BOJ Theory"). Nihon Keizai Shimbun Sha.

Iwata, Kikuo, ed. (2000) *Kinnyu Seisaku no Ronten* (Issues on Monetary Policy). Toyo Keizai Shinpo Sha.

Iwata, Kikuo (2001) *Defure no Keizaigaku* (Economics of Deflation). Toyo Keizai Shimpo Sha.

Iwata, Kikuo (2009) *Nihon Ginko ha Shinnyo Dekiruka* (Is the Bank of Japan Trustworthy?). Kodansha Gendai Shinsho.

Iwata, Kikuo (2011) *Defure to Cho Endaka* (Deflation and Super High Yen). Kodansha Shinsho.

Iwata, Kikuo, ed. (2013a) *Mazu defure wo tomeyo* (Stop Deflation, First). Nihon Keizai Shimbun Sha.

Iwata, Kikuo (2013b) *Refure ha Tadasii* (Reflation is Right). PHP Kenkyu Jo.

Iwata, Kikuo, and Miyagawa Tsutomu, eds. (2003) *Ushinawareta 10 nen no Shin-in ha Nanika* (What is the Real Cause of the Lost Decade?), Economics Series. Toyo Keizai Shimpo Sha.

Japan Institute for Labor Policy and Training (Rodo Seisaku Kenkyu Kenshu Kiko) (2014) "Jakunensha no shugyo jokyo, kyaria, shokugyo noryoku kaihatu no genjo ② heisei 24 nen ban 'shugyo kozo kihon chosa' yori" (Current status of employment, career and work capacity development of young people ② based on 'basic survey of employment structure' 2012), JILP Document Series No. 144, September 2014.

Japan–US Joint Working Group of Special Meeting on Yen–Dollar Exchange Rate and Financial and Capital Markets (1984) "Nichi Bei Kyodo En-doru Reto Kinnyu Shihon Shijo Tokubetsu Kaigo Sagyo Bukai Hokoku Sho." (Report of the Japan–US Joint Working Group of Special Meeting on Yen–Dollar Exchange Rate and Financial and Capital Markets) (Report of the Yen–Dollar Committee), May.

Jinushi, Toshiki, Yoshihiro Kuroki, and Ryuzo Miyao (2001) "1980 nendai Kohan iko no Nihon no Kinnyu Seisaku- Seisaku Taio no Okure to sono Riyu" (Monetary Policy in Japan from the Latter Half of the 1980s—Delay in Policy Response and its Background). In *Nihon no Kinnyu Kiki – Beikoku no Keiken to Nihon heno Kyokun* (Monetary Policy in Japan—US Experience and Their Lessons for Japan), edited by Ryoichi Mikitani and Adam A. Posen, . Tokyo: Toyo Keizai Shimpo Sha.

Kaizuka, Keimei (2006) *Keizai Kakusa no Kenkyu* (A Study of Economic Inequality). Chuo Keizai Sha.

Kanagawa, Toru (1987) *Boeki Masatsu to Kokusai Keizai no Shomondai-Nihon to Amerika no Boeki Masatsu wo Chusin ni* (Trade Frictions and Issues in International Economy—Centering on Trade Frictions between Japan and the US). Keibun Sha.

Kanagawa, Toru (1989) *Nichi Bei Boeki Masatsu-Tairitsu to Kyocho no Kozu* (Japan–U.S. Trade Frictions—Structure of Confrontation and Cooperation). Keibun Sha.

Kano, Tadashi (2006) *Doru En Soba no Seiji Keizaigaku—Kawase Hendo nimiru Nichibei Kankei* (Political Economy of the Yen=Dollar Exchange Rate—Japan–US Relationship Observed in the Foreign Exchange Movements). Nihon Keizai Shimbun Sha.

Karube, Kensuke (2004) *Dokyumento Zero Kinri—Nichigin vs Seifu Naze Tairitsu Surunoka* (Documentary Zero Interest Rate—BOJ vs. the Government: Why Do They come into collision?). Iwanami Shoten.

Karube, Kensuke, and Nishino Tomohiko (1999) *Kensho Keizai Shissei—Dare ga Nani wo Naze Machigaetaka* (Examining Economic Policy Mistakes—Who Made What Mistakes and Why?). Iwanami Shoten.

Kataoka, Goshi (2010a) *Nihon no 'Ushinawareta 20 nen'—Defure wo Koeru Keizai Seisaku ni Mukete* (Japan's "Lost Two Decades"—For the Economic Policy Beyond Deflation). Fujiwara Shoten.

Kataoka, Goshi (2010b) *Nihon no 'Ushinawareta 20 nen'* (Japan's "Lost Two Decades"). Fujiwara Shoten.

Kato, Hisakazu (2001) *Jinko Keizaigaku Nyumon* (Introduction to Demographic Economics). Nihon Keizai Hyoron Sha.

Katz, Richard (1999) *Kusariyuku Nihon toiu Sisutemu* (Japan, the System that Soured). Tokyo: Toyo Keizai Shimpo Sha.

Kaufmann, Franz-Xaver (2011) *Shukugen suru Shakai—Jinko Gensho to sono Kiketsu* (Shrinking Society—Population Decline and Its Consequences). Hara Shobo.

Kawai, Masahiro, and Shinji Takagi (2009) "Kawase Reto to Kokusai Shushi—Puraza Goi kara Heisei Fukyo no Makuro Keizai Gaku" (Foreign Exchange Rate and Balance of Payments—Macroeconomics of the Plaza Accord to Heisei Stagnation). In *Kokusai Kankyo no Henka to Nihon Keizai* (Changes in International Environments and the Japanese Economy), edited by Motoshige Ito (Cabinet Office, "Baburu/defure kino Nihon Keizai to Keizai Seisaku 3"(Japanese Economy and Economic Policy in the Period of Bubble and Deflation 3)), Economic and Social Research Institute, Cabinet Office.

Kimura, Takeshi, Tsuyoshi Shimatani, Ken-ichi Sakura, and Hiroaki Nishida (2001) "Mane to Seicho Kitai: Bukka Hendo no Mekanizumu wo Megutte" (Money and Growth Expectation: on the Mechanism of Price Movements), August, Institute for Monetary and Economic Studies, BOJ *Kinnyu Kenkyu*.

Kojo, Yoshiko (2009) "Kokusai Seiji to Nihon no Kisei Kanwa, Kozo Kaikaku" (International Politics and Deregulation and Structural Reform in Japan). In *Kozo Mondai to Kisei Kanwa* (Structural Problems and Deregulation), edited by Juro Teranishi ("Baburu/defure kino Nihon Keizai to Keizai Seisaku 7"(Japanese Economy and Economic Policy in the Period of Bubble and Deflation 7)), Economic and Social Research Institute, Cabinet Office.

Komine, Takao (2005) *Nihon Keizai no Shin Kyokumen* (New Phase of the Japanese Economy). Chuo Koron Sha.

Komine, Takao (2007) *Jinko Gen Shoshika Shakai no Mirai* (Future of the Society with Population Shrinkage and the Declining Birth Rate). Akashi Shobo.

Komine, Takao (2010) *Jinko Fuka Shakai* (Society with Demographic Burden). Nihon Keizai Shimbun Sha.

Komine, Takeo, ed.(2011a) *Nihon Keizai no Kiroku—Dai Niji Sekiyu Kiki heno Taio kara Baburu Hokai made (1970 nendai~1996 nen)* (Record of Japanese Economy from Responses to the 2nd Oil Shock and the Collapse of the Bubble, 1970s to 1996), ("Baburu/defure kino Nihon Keizai to Keizai Seisaku Rekisi hen dai 1 kan"), (Japanese Economy and Economic Policy in the Period of Bubble and Deflation—History, Vol. 1)), Economic and Social Research Institute, Cabinet Office, Japanese Government.

Komine, Takao, ed. (2011b) *Nihon Keizai no Kiroku—Kinnyu Kiki, Defure to Kaifuku Katei (1997 nen~2006 nen)* (Record of Japanese Economy—Financial crisis, Deflation and Recovery Process [1997 to 2006]), ("Baburu/defure kino Nihon Keizai to Keizai Seisaku Rekisi hen dai 2 kan" (Japanese Economy and Economic Policy in the Period of Bubble and Deflation — History, Vol. 2)), Economic and Social Research Institute, Cabinet Office, Japanese Government.

Komiya, Ryutaro, ed. (2002) "*Kinnyu Seisaku no Soten—Nichign Hihan to Sono Hanron*" (Issues in Monetary Policy Debates—Criticism of BOJ and Counterarguments). Nihon Keizai Shimpo Sha.

Kondo, Takehiko (1999) *Puraza Goi no Kenkyu* (A Study of the Plaza Accord). Toyo Keizai Shimpo Sha.

Koo, Richard (2007) *'In' to 'Yo' no Keizai Gaku* (Economics of "The Sunny Side" and "The Shadow Side."). Toyo Keizai Shimpo Sha.

Koo, Richard (2008) *Nihon Keizai wo Oou Futatsu no Nami* (Two Waves Hanging over the Japanese Economy). Tokuma Shoten.

Kosai, Yutaka, Osamu Ito, and Ritsuko Arioka (2001) "Baburuki no Kinnyu Seisaku to sono Hansei" (Monetary Policy in the Bubble Era and Its Reconsideration). In *Baburu to Kinnyu Seisaku—Nihon no Keiken to Kyokun,* (Bubble and Monetary Policy—Japan's Experience and Lessons), edited by Yutaka Kosai, Masaaki Shirakawa, and Kunio Okina, . Nihon Keizai Shimbun Sha.

Kubota, Isao (2008) *Shogen: Miyazawa Daiichiji [1986–1988] Tsuka Gaiko* (Testimony—First Currency Diplomacy [1986–1988] by Miyazawa). Nishi Nihon Shimbun Sha.

Kumon, Takashi (2006) *Jinko Defure ha Hajimatte iru* (Demographic Deflation Has Already Set In). Toyo Keizai Shimpo Sha.

Kuroda, Haruhiko (2005) *Zaisei Kinnyu Seisaku no Seiko to Shippai* (Success and Failure of Fiscal and Monetary Policy). Nihon Hyoron Sha.

Kusano, Atsushi (1998) *Yamaichi Shoken Hatan to Kiki Kanri—1965 and 1998* (Failure of Yamaichi Securities and Crisis Management: Years of 1965 and 1997. Asahi Shimbun Sha.

Kusu, Toshiharu (2005) "Baburu no Gennin Saiko (jo)" (Re-examining Causes of the Bubble [1]). In Yokin Hoken Kiko (Deposit Insurance Corporation) *Yokin Hoken Kenkyu,* October.

Kusu, Toshiharu (2006) "Baburu no Gennin Saiko (ge)" (Re-examining Causes of the Bubble [2]). In Yokin Hoken Kiko (Deposit Insurance Corporation) *Yokin Hoken Kenkyu,* November.

Land Economy and Construction Industries Bureau, Ministry of Land, Infrastructure, Transport and Tourism (2012) "Fudosan Shijo niokeru Shisan Kakaku Hendo ni kansuru Kenkyu Kai Hokoku Sho" (Report of the Study Group on Asset Price Developments in Real Estate Markets).

Matsushima, Shigeru, and Harukata Takenaka, eds. (2011) *Nihon Keizai no Kiroku—Jidai Shogen Shu (oraru Hisutori)* (Record of Japanese Economy—Collection of Testimonies of the Period [Oral History]), "(Baburu/Defure ki no Nihon Keizai to Keizai Seisaku—Rekishi Hen dai 3 kan" (Japanese Economy and Economic Policies in the Period of Bubble and Deflation, History, Vol. 3)), Economic and Social Research Institute, Cabinet Office. Japanese Government.

Matsutani, Akihiko (2004) *'Jinko Gensho Keizai' no Atarasii Koshiki* (A New Formula for "the Economy with a Shrinking Population"). Nihon Keizai Shimbun Sha.

Matsuzaki, Masahiro (1988) *Nichi Bei Masatsu no Seiji Keizai Gaku* (Political Economy of Japan–US Frictions). Yachiyo Shuppan.

Mieno, Yasushi (2000) *Ri wo Mite Gi wo Omou* (When Seeing Profits, Thinking about Justice). Chuo Koron Sha.

Mikitani, Ryoichi, and Adam A. Posen, eds. *Nihon no Kinyu Kiki—Beikoku no Keiken to Nihon heno Kyokun* (Monetary Policy in Japan—US Experiences and Their Lessons for Japan). Toyo Keizai Shimpo Sha.

Ministry of Finance (1984) "Kinnyu no Jiyuka oyobi En no Kokusaika nitsuiteno Genjo to Tenbo" (Current Conditions and Future Prospects of Financial Liberalization and Internationalization of the Yen), May.

Ministry of Finance (1992) "Kinnyu Gyosei no Tomen no Unnyo Hoshin" (Current Policy of Financial Administration), August 18, 1992. In Banking Bureau, Ministry of Finance, "*dai 42 kai Ginko kyoku Kinnyu Nenpo Heisei 5 nen ban*" (42nd Annual Report of Banking Bureau Heisei 5).

Ministry of Finance (1993) "Shisan kakaku hendo no mekanizumu to sono keizai koka" (The Mechanism of Asset Price Movements and its Economic Impacts), November, *Finansharu Rebyu,* Fiscal and Monetary Research Institute, Ministry of Finance, Japan.

Ministry of Health, Labor and Welfare (2012) *Heisei 24 nenban Koreika Shakai Hakusho* (2012 White Paper on Ageing Society).

Miyagawa, Tsutomu (2003) "'Ushinawareta 10 nen' to Sangyo Kozo no Tenkan" ("Lost Decade" and Changes in Industrial Structure). In *Ushinawareta 10 nen no Shinn-in ha Nanika,* (What is the Real Cause of the Lost Decade?), edited by Kikuo Iwata and Tsutomu Miyagawa, Economics Series. Toyo Keizai Shimpo Sha.

Miyao, Ryuzo (2004) "Ginko Kino no Teika to 90 nendai Iko no Defure Teitai—'Kashi Shiiburi' Setsu to 'Oigashi' Setsu no Kento" (Deterioration of Banks' Function and Deflationary Stagnation since the 1990s— "Credit Crunch" Theory and "Rescue Loans" Theory). In *Ronso nihon no keizai kiki* (Debate on Japan's Economic Crisis), edited by Koichi Hamada and Akiyoshi Horiuchi. Nihon keizai Shimbun Sha.

Miyazaki, Giichi (1992) *Fukugo Fukyo—Posuto Baburu no Shohosen wo Motomete* (Complex Recession—Seeking Prescriptions in the Post-Bubble Era). Chuo Koron Sha.

Motani, Kosuke (2010) *Defure no Shotai—Keizai ha Jinko no nami de Ugoku* (The True Origin of Deflation: The Economy Moves by the Demographic Waves). Kadokawa One Tema 21.

Nakagawa, Satoshi (1996) "Wagakuni Kinnyu Kikan no Furyo Saiken no Genjo nituite" (On the Current Status of Non-Performing Loans of Japanese Financial Institutions), Ministry of Finance, *Fainansu* October.

Nakahara, Nobuyuki (2006) *Nichigin ha Dareno Monoka* (Who is the BOJ for?). Chuo Koron Sha.

Nakao, Takehiko (2008) "*Amerika no Keizai Seisaku: Tsuyosa ha Jizoku Dekiru noka*" (Economic Policy in the United States: Can the Strength be Sustained?).

Nihon Keizai Shimbun Sha (2000) *Kensho Baburu—Han-i Naki Ayamachi* (Examining the Bubble—Fault without Intention). Nihon Keizai Shimbun Sha.

Nishimura, Kiyohiko (2005) *Nihon Keizai Miezaru Kozo Tenkan* (Japanese Economy—Invisible Structural Transition). Kansai Shakai Keizai Kenkyujo.

Nishimura, Kiyohiko, and Yoshiro Miwa (1990) *Nihon no Kabuka Chika Keisei no Mekanizumu* (Mechanism of Stock and Land Price Formation in Japan). Tokyo: Tokyo University Press.

Nishimura, Yoshimasa (1999) *Kinnyu Gyosei no Hai-in* (Cause of Defeat in Financial Administration). Bunshun Bunko.

Nishimura, Yoshimasa (2009) "Furyo Saiken Shori no Keii to Ronten" (Process and Issues of Disposition of Non-Performing Loans). In *Furyo Saiken to Kinnyu Kiki* (Non-Performing Loans and the Financial Crisis), edited by Kazuto Ikeo, (Cabinet Office, "Baburu/defure kino Nihon Keizai to Keizai Seisaku 4" (Japanese Economy and Economic Policy in the Period of Bubble and Deflation 4)), Economic and Social Research Institute, Cabinet Office.

Nishimura, Yoshimasa (2011) *Kinnyu Shisutemu Kaikaku 50 nen no Kiseki* (50-Year History of Financial System Reform). Kinnyu Zaisei Jijo Kenkyu Kai.

Nishino, Tomohiko (2001) *Kensho Keizai Meiso—Naze Kiki ga Tsuzuku noka* (Examining the Economy Straying off Course: Why Does the Crisis Continue?). Iwanami Shoten.

Nishino, Tomohiko (2003) *Kensho Keizai An-un—Naze Sakiokuri Surunoka* (Examining the Economy under Clouds—Why Is It Put Off?). Iwanami Shoten.

Nishizaki, Kenji, Yoichi Ueno, and Tanaka Masahiro (2011) "Nihon no Bukka Hendo no Haikei: Jijitsu to Ronten Seiri" (Background of Price Developments in Japan: Facts and Issues) December, Bank of Japan, Working Paper Series No. 11-I-9.

Noguchi, Asahi (2002) "*Keizaigaku wo Shiranai Ekonomisuto Tachi*" (Those Economists Who Do Not Know Economics), Nihon Hyoron Sha.

Noguchi, Asahi (2005, 2006) "Heisei Keizai Seisaku Ronso" (Heisei Economic Policy Debates). In Nihon Hyoron Sha, *Keizai Seminar*, April 2005—March 2006.

Noguchi, Asahi (2006) "*Ekonomisuto Tachi no Yuganda Suishodama*" (Distorted Crystal Balls of Economists). Tokyo Keizai Sjimpo Sha.

Noguchi, Asahi (2013) "Kozo mondai to defureshon" "(Structural Problems and Deflation)." In *Mazu defure wo tomeyo* (Stop Deflation, First), edited by Kikuo Iwata. Nihon Keizai Shimbun Sha.

Noguchi, Asahi, and Yasushi Okada (2003) "Kinnyu Seisaku no Kino Teishi ha Naze Shojita noka" (How Was the Dysfunction of Monetary Policy Brought About?). In *Ushinawareta 10 nen no Shinn-in ha Nanika* (What is the Real Cause of the Lost Decade?), edited by Kikuo Iwata and Tsutomu Miyagawa, , Economics Series, Toyo Keizai Shimpo Sha.

Noguchi, Yukio (1992) *Baburu no Keizaigaku—Nihon Keizai ni Nani ga Okotta noka* (Economics of the Bubble: What Happened to the Japanese Economy?). Nihon Keizai Shimbun Sha.

Noguchi, Yukio (2005) *Nihon Keizai Kaizo Ron* (Arguments for Fundamental Reform of Japan's Economy). Toyo Keizai Shimpo Sha.

Noguchi, Yukio (2010) *Nihon wo Hametsu kara Sukuu Tameno Keizaigaku* (Economics to Save Japan from Catastrophe). Diamond Sha.

Nukaga, Makoto (2005) "Juyo Shukusho no Kiki-Jinko Gensho Shaki no Keizaigaku- (Demand shrinkage crisis-Economics of population decline)" NTT Publication.

Obuchi, Hiroshi (1997) *Shosika Jidai no Nihon Keizai* (Japanese Economy in the Era of Declining Birth Rate). Nihon Hoso Kyokai.

Obuchi, Hiroshi, and Hitoshi Morioka (1981) *Keizai Jinko Gaku* (Economic Demography). Shin Hyoron.

Obuchi, Hiroshi, and Hiroyuki Kanekiyo (2005) *Shoshika no Shakai Keizaigaku* (Socioeconomics of the Declining Birth Rate). Hara Shobo.

Obuchi, Hiroshi, and Hitoshi Morioka (2006) *Jinko Gensho Jidai no Nihon Keizai* (The Japanese Economy in the Era of a Shrinking Population). Hara Shobo.

Ogawa, Kazuo (2009a) '*Ushinawareta 10 nen'no Shinjitsu—Jittai Keizai to Kinnyu Shisutemu no Sokoku* (Truth of the "Lost Decade"—Conflict between Real Economy and Financial System). Tokyo: Toyo Keizai Shimpo Sha.

Ogawa, Kazuo (2009b) "Baransu Shito no Kison to Jitsubutsu Keizai—1990 nendai ikono Nihon Keizai no Jissho Bunseki" (Damages to the Balance Sheet and the Real Economy—Empirical Analysis of the Japanese Economy since the 1990s). In *Furyo Saiken to Kinnyu Kiki* (Non-Performing Loans and Financial Crisis), edited by Kazuto Ikeo, ("Baburu/defure kino Nihon Keizai to Keizai Seisaku 4," (Japanese Economy and Economic Policy in the Period of Bubble and Deflation 4)), Economic and Social Research Institute, Cabinet Office.

Ogawa, Kazuo, and Heizo Takenaka (2001) *Seisaku Kiki to Nihon Keizai* (Policy Crisis and the Japanese Economy). Nihon Hyoron Sha.

Okada, Yasushi, and Hamada Koichi (2009) "Baburu Defure ki no Nihon no Kinnyu Seisaku" (Monetary Policy in Japan during the Period of Bubble and Deflation). In *Defure Keizai to Kinnyu Seisaku* (Deflationary Economy and Monetary Policy), edited by Hiroshi Yoshikawa, ("Baburu/defure kino Nihon Keizai to Keizai Seisaku 2"(Japanese Economy and Economic Policy in the Period of Bubble and Deflation 2)), Economic and Social Research Institute, Cabinet Office.

Okamoto, Naoki (2001) "Defure ni Chokumen suru Wagauni Keizai—Defure no Teigi no Saiseiri wo Fukumete," (Japanese Economy Facing Deflation—Including Redefining Deflation) Cabinet Office, Business Condition Judgment and Policy Analysis Discussion Paper DP/01-1.

Okina, Kunio (1992) "Nichigin Riron ha Machigatte inai" (BOJ Theory Is Not Wrong). In *Shukan Toyo Keizai,* October 10.

Okina, Kunio. (2009) "Baburu no Seisei Hokai no Keiken ni Terashita Kinnyu Seisaku no Ayumi—FED View to BIS View wo Fumaete" (Evolution of Monetary Policy in Light of Experience of the Formation and Collapse of the Bubble—Drawing on FED Views and BIS Views). In *Defure Keizai to Kinnyu Seisaku* (Deflationary Economy and Monetary Policy), edited by Hiroshi Yoshikawa, ("Baburu/defure kino Nihon Keizai to Keizai Seisaku 2"(Japanese Economy and Economic Policy in the Period of Bubble and Deflation 2)), Economic and Social Research Institute, Cabinet Office.

Okita, Yoichi (2010) *Sengo Nihon Keizai Ron—Seicho Keizai kara Seijuku Keizai heno Tenkan* (Post-War Japanese Economy—Transition from a Growing to a Matured Economy). Tokyo: Toyo Keizai Shimpo Sha.

Oshio, Takashi (2005) *Jinko Gensho Jidai no Shakai Hosho Kaikaku* (Social Security System Reform in the Era of Declining Population). Nihon Keizai Shimbun Sha.

Ota, Kiyoshi (2005) "Furita no Zoka to Rodo Shotoku Kakusa no Kakudai" (Increase in "Freeter" and Expanding Inequality of Earned Income) ESRI Discussion Paper No.140, May.

Otake, Fumio (2005) *Nihon no Fubyodo* (Inequality in Japan). Nihon Keizai Shimbun Sha.

Otake, Fumio, and Noriyuki Yanagawa (2004) *Heisei Fukyo no Ronten* (Issues in Heisei Recession). Toyo Keizai Shimpo Sha.

Otsuka, Satoshi, Shigenori Shiratsuka, and Masayuki Nakakuki (2004) "Seisansei Shijo no Yugami to Kokunai Keizai Chosei" (Distortions in Production Factor Markets and Domestic Economic Adjustments), IMES Discussion Paper No. 20040J-1.

Sakuragawa, Masaya (2003) "Furyo Saiken Mondai ga Nihon Keizai ni Ataeta Dageki" (Damage to Japanese Economy by Non-Performing Loan Problems). In *Ushinawareta 10 nen no Shinn-in ha Nanika* (What is the Real Cause of the Lost Decade?), edited by Kikuo Iwata and Tsutomu Miyagawa, Economics Series. Toyo Keizai Shimpo Sha.

Sakurai, Ryoji (1993) *Baburu Keizai no Hokai to Nihon Keizai no Honshitsu* (Collapse of the Bubble Economy and the Real Nature of the Japanese Economy). Hokei Ronshu Dai 71 Go.

Sato, Takafumi (2003) *Sinnyo Chitsujo Seisaku no Saihen—Wakugumi Ikoki toshiteno 1990 nendai* (Reorganization of Policies for the Maintenance of Stable Financial System—1990s as a Period of Framework Transition). Nihon Tosho Center.

Sato, Takafumi (2010) *Kinnyu Gyosei no Zahyo Jiku—Heiji to Yuji wo Koete* (Coordinate Axis for Financial Administration—Beyond Times of Peace and Crisis). Toyo Keizai Shimpo Sha.

Sato, Toshiki (2000) *Fubyodo Shakai Nippon: Sayonara So Churyu* (Japan, An Unequal Society: Goodbye to All Middle Class Society). Chuko Shinsho.

Shimizu, Hironori (2001) "Goso Sendan Kisei, Ginko Keiei to Nihon no Kinnyu Kiki" (Convoy-based Regulations, Management of Banks, and Financial Crisis in Japan). In *Nihon no Kinnyu Kiki—Beikoku no Keiken to Nihon heno Kyokun* (Monetary Policy in Japan—US Experiences and Their Lessons for Japan), edited by Ryoichi Mikitani and Adam A. Posen, Toyo Keizai Shimpo Sha.

Shimizudani, Satoshi (2005) *Kitai to Fukakujitsu Sei no Keizai Gaku* (Economics of Expectation and Uncertainty). Nihon Keizai Shimbun Sha.

Shimpo, Seiji (2002) "Defure wo Motarashita noha Kozo Yoin ka Kinnyu Seisaku ka" (Is It a Structural Factor or Monetary Policy That Has Brought about Deflation?). In *Kinnyu seisaku ronso no soten—nichigin hihan to sono hanron*, (Issues in Monetary Policy Debates—Criticism of the Bank of Japan and Counterarguments) edited by Ryutaro Komiya. Nihon Keizai Shimbun Sha.

Shirai, Sayuri (2012) "Jinko Dotai no Henka ha Wagakuni no Makuro Keizai ni Eikyo wo Ataete Irunoka?" (Have Demographic Changes Affected Japan's Macroeconomic Performance?) September 7.

Shirakawa, Masaaki (2002) "Ryoteki Kanwa Saiyo go 1 nenkan no Keiken" (1-Year Experience since the Introduction of Quantitative Easing). In *Kinnyu seisaku ronso no soten—nichigin hihan to sono hanron* (Issues in Monetary Policy Debates—Criticism of the Bank of Japan and Counterarguments), edited by Ryutaro Komiya. Nihon Keizai Shimbun Sha.

Shirakawa, Masaaki (2008) "Gendai no Kinnyu Seisaku" (Current Monetary Policy). Nihon Keizai Shimbun Sha.

Shirakawa, Masaaki (2010a) "Nihon Keizai to Inobeshon (Japan's Economy and Innovation)", May 31, Bank of Japan.

Shirakawa, Masaaki (2010b) "Tokushu Sei ka Ruiji Sei ka?—Kinnyu Seisaku Kenkyu wo Meguru Nihon no Baburu Hokaigo no Keiken" (Uniqueness or Similarity? Japan's Post-Bubble Experience in Monetary Policy Studies), September 16, Bank of Japan.

Shirakawa, Masaaki (2011a) "Kodo Seicho kara Antei Seicho he—Nihon no Keiken to Sinkokoku Keizai heno Ganni" (The Transition from High Growth to Stable Growth: Japan's Experience and Implications for Emerging Economies), May 5, Bank of Japan.

Shirakawa, Masaaki (2011b) "Baburu, Jinko Dotai, Shizen Saigai" (Bubbles, Demographic Change, and Natural Disasters) June 1, Bank of Japan.

Shirakawa, Masaaki (2012a) "Derebarejji to Keizai Seicho—Senshinkoku ha Kakoni Nihon ga Ayunda 'Nagaku Magari Kunetta Michi'wo Tadotte Ikunoka" (Deleveraging and Growth: Is the Developed World Following Japan's Long and Winding Road? Lecture at the London School of Economics and Political Science (co-hosted by the Asia Research Center and STICERD, LSE), January 10, Bank of Japan.

Shirakawa, Masaaki (2012b) "Saikin no Kinnyu Josei to Kinnyu Seisaku Unnei" (Recent Financial and Economic Developments and Monetary Policy Management), June 4, Bank of Japan.

Shirakawa, Masaaki (2012c) "Jinko Dotai no Henka to Makuro Keizai Pafomansu: Nihon no Keiken kara" (Demographic Changes and Macroeconomic Performance: Japanese Experience), May 30, Bank of Japan.

Study Group on Structural Economic Adjustments for International Coordination (1986) "Kokusai Kyocho no tameno Keizai Kozo Chosei Kenkyu Kai Hokoku Sho" (Report of the Study Group on Structural Economic Adjustments for International Coordination) (Maekawa Report) April 7, (http://worldjpn.grips.ac.jp/documents/texts/JPUS/19860407.O1J.html (accessed August 17, 2018).

Sugihara, Shigeru, and Satoshi Ota (2002) "Shisan Kakaku no Geraku to Kigyo no Baransu Shito Chosei" (Decline in Asset prices and Balance Sheet Adjustments of Corporations). In *Defure no Jissho Bunseki*, (Empirical Analysis of Deflation), edited by Yutaka Harada and Kikuo Iwata. Toyo Keizai Shimpo Sha.

Tachibanaki, Toshiaki (1998) *Nihon no Keizai Kakusa* (Economic Inequality in Japan). Iwanami Shinsho.

Tachibanaki, Toshiaki (2006) *Kakusa Shakai: Nani ga Mondai Nanoka* (Unequal Society: What is the Problem?). Iwanami Shinsho.

Takayama, Noriyuki, and Osamu Saito (2006) *Shoshika no Keizaigaku* (Economics of the Declining Birth Rate). Toyo Keizai Shimpo Sha.

Takenaka, Harukata (2005) "Chika Baburu heno Taio ha Naze Okureta ka—Tokyo no Mondai ga Nihon no Mondai ni Naru made" (Why Was the Response to the Land Price Bubble Delayed?—When the Problem in Tokyo Became the Problem of Japan). In *Heisei Baburu—Saki Okuri no Kenkyu*, (Heisei Bubble—A Study of Forbearance), edited by Michio Muramatsu. Toyo Keizai Shimpo Sha.

Takita, Yoichi (2002) *Nihon Keizai Fusakui no Tsumi* (Japanese Economy: A Crime of Omission). Nihon Keizai Shimbun Sha.

Takita, Yoichi (2006) *Nichibei Tsuka Kosho —20 nenme no Shinjitsu* (Japan–US Currency Negotiations—Real Story after 20 Years) Nihon Keizai Shimubun Sha.

Tanaka, Hideomi, and Seiji Adachi (2003) *Heisei Dai Fukyo to Showa Kyoko —Purakutyikaru Keizaigaku Nyumon* (Heisei Great Stagnation and Showa Depression—Introduction to Practical Economics). Nihon Hoso Shuppan Kai.

Tanaka, Takayuki (2002) *Gendai Nihon Keizai—Baburu to Posuto Baburu no Kiseki* (Current Japanese Economy—Trajectory of the Bubble and Post-Bubble). Nihon Hyoron Sha.

Tanaka, Takayuki (2008) *Ushinawareta 15 nen to Kinnyu Seisaku—Nichigin ha Naniwo Okonai Naniwo Okonawa nakatta noka* ("Lost 15 Years" and Monetary Policy—What Did BOJ Do and Not Do?). Nihon Keizai Shimbun Sha.

Tanaka, Takayuki (2009) *Kinnyu Kiki ni Do Tachi Mukau ka —Ushinawareta 15 nen' no Kyokun* (How to Cope with Financial Crises? Lessons from "the Lost 15 Years"). Chikuma Shobo.

Tatebe, Masayoshi (2010) "*Kinnyu Kikika no Nichigin no Kinnyu Seisaku*" (BOJ's Monetary Policy under the Financial Crisis). Chuo Daigaku Shuppan Bu.

Tsutani, Noriko, and Yoshio Higuchi (2009) *Jinko Gensho to Nihon Keizai* (Population Decline and the Japanese Economy). Nihon Keizai Shimbun Sha.

Ueda, Kazuo (2001) "1990 nendai niokeru Nihon no Furyo Saiken Mondai no Gennin" (Cause of Non-Performing Loan Problems in the 1990s in Japan). In "*Nihon Kinnyu Shisutemu no Kiki to Henbo,*" (Crisis in Japan's Financial System and Its Transition), edited by Takeo Hoshi and Hugh Patrick,. Nihon Keizai Shimbun Sha.

Ueda, Kazuo (2005) *Zero Kinri tono Tatakai* (Battle against Zero Interest Rate). Nihon Keizai Shimbun Sha.

Umeda, Masanobu (2011) *Nichigin no Seisaku Keisei 'Gijiroku' nado ni Miru Seisaku Handan no Doki to Seigosei* (Policy Formation of the BOJ—Motives of Policy Determination and Their Coherence in Light of Committee Minutes). Toyo Keizai Shimbun Sha.

Uemura Shuichi, and Sato Yoshiko (2000) "Saikin no Chika Keisei no Tokucho nituite" (On the Characteristics of Recent Land Price Formation), October, BOJ, *Chosa Geppo*.

Volker, Paul, and Toyoo Gyoten (1992) "*Tomi no Kobo—En to Doru no Rekishi*" (Rise and Fall of Wealth—History of the Yen and the Dollar). Toyo Keizai Shimpo Sha.

Wakatabe, Masazumi (2013) *Keizai Gakusha Tachino Tatakai—Datsu Defure wo Meguru Ronso no Rekishi* (Battle of the Economists—History of Debates over Exit from Deflation). Toyo Keizai Shimpo Sha.

Watanabe, Takashi (2001) *Furyo Saiken ha Naze Kienai* (Why Have Non-Performing Loans not Disappeared?). Nikkei BP Sha.

Watanabe, Tsutomu (2009) "Shihan Seiki no Bukka Hendo" (Price Developments over a Quarter of a Century). In *Defure Keizai to Kinnyu Seisaku*, (Deflationary Economy and Monetary Policy), edited by Hiroshi Yoshikawa, ("Baburu/defure kino Nihon Keizai to Keizai Seisaku 7" (Japanese Economy and Economic Policy in the Period of Bubble and Deflation 7)), Economic and Social Research Institute, Cabinet Office.

Watanabe, Tsutomu (2012) "Zero Kinri kano Choki Defure" (Chronic Deflation under the Zero Interest Rate), BOJ Working Paper Series No.12 ~J~3, March.

Watanabe, Tsutomu (2013) "Defure Dakkyaku no Joken" (Conditions for Exit from Deflation) March 26, Canon Institute for Global Studies, http://www.canon-igs.org/research_papers/macroeconomics/20130326_1816.html (accessed August 17, 2018).

Yamada, Masahiro (2004) *Kibo Kakusa Shakai: 'Makegumi' no Zetsubo Kan ga Nihon wo Hikisaku'* (Society of Unequal Hope: Despair of "the Failed" Will Divide Japan). Chikuma Shobo.

Yashiro, Naohiro (2004) *Shoshi Koreika no Keizaigaku* (Economics of the Declining Birth Rate and Aging). Toyo Keizai Shimpo Sha.

Yoshikawa, Hiroshi (1992) *Nihon Keizai to Makuro Keizai Gaku* (Japanese Economy and Macroeconomics). Toyo Keizai Shimpo Sha.

Yoshikawa, Hiroshi (1997) *Kodo Seicho—Nihon wo Kaeta 6000 Nichi* (High Speed Growth—6000 days that Changed Japan). Yomiuri Shimbun Sha.

Yoshikawa, Hiroshi(1999)*Tenkanki no Nihon Keizai* (The Japanese Economy at a Turning Point). Iwanami Shoten.

Yoshikawa, Hiroshi (2009a) "Defureshon to Kinnyu Seisaku" (Deflation and Monetary Policy). In *Defure Keizai to Kinnyu Seisaku* (Deflationary Economy and Monetary Policy), edited by Hiroshi Yoshikawa, ("Baburu/defure kino Nihon Keizai to Keizai Seisaku 7"(Japanese Economy and Economic Policy in the Period of Bubble and Deflation 7)), Economic and Social Research Institute, Cabinet Office.

Yoshikawa, Hiroshi, ed. (2009b) *Defure Keizai to Kinnyu Seisaku* (Deflationary Economy and Monetary Policy), ("Baburu/defure kino Nihon Keizai to Keizai Seisaku 7"(Japanese Economy and Economic Policy in the Period of Bubble and Deflation 7)), Economic and Social Research Institute, Cabinet Office.

Yoshikawa, Hiroshi (2011) "Shoshi Koreika to Keizai Seicho" (The declining birth rate and aging population and economic growth) RIETI Discussion Paper Series 11-P-006 January.

Yoshikawa, Hiroshi (2016) "Jinko to Nihon Keizai" (Population and the Japanese economy). Chu Ko Shinsho.

Yoshikawa, Mototada (1998) *Mane Haisen* (Defeat in Monetary War). Bunshun Bunko.

Yoshitomi, Masaru (1998) *Nihon Keizai no Shinjitsu* (The Truth of the Japanese Economy). Toyo Keizai.

Yuasa, Shoyo, and Masahiro Tsujihiro (1996) *Dokyumento Jusen Hokai* (Documentary Collapse of Jusen). Diamond Sha.

Yugami, Kazufumi (2003) "Nihon no Shotoku Kakusa wo Do Miruka" (How to Assess Income Disparity in Japan?), *JIL Rodo Seisaku Report* 2003.3.

Index[1]

[1] Note: Page numbers followed by 'n' refer to notes.

K. Aramaki, *Japan's Long Stagnation, Deflation, and Abenomics*,
https://doi.org/10.1007/978-981-13-2176-4

The manufacturer's authorised representative in the EU is Springer Nature Customer Service Centre GmbH, Europaplatz 3, 69115 Heidelberg, Germany. If you have any concerns regarding our products, please contact ProductSafety@springernature.com

Printed and bound by CPI Group (UK) Ltd, Croydon, CR0 4YY
30/09/2026
02225443-0010